Memorial Book of
Nowy Zmigrod - Galicia, Poland

Compiled by William Leibner

Edited by Jane Waldman Aronson

Published by JewishGen

An Affiliate of the Museum of Jewish Heritage - A Living Memorial to the Holocaust
New York

Memorial Book of Nowy Zmigrod - Galicia, Poland

Copyright © 2015 by JewishGen, Inc.
All rights reserved.
First Printing: November 2015, Kislev 5776
Second Printing: March 2019, Adar II 5779

Compiled by William Leibner
Editor: Jane Waldman Aronson
Layout: Alan Roth
Image Editor: Larry Gaum
Cover Design: Rachel Kolokoff Hopper
Indexing: Jonathan Wind

Published by JewishGen, Inc.
An Affiliate of the Museum of Jewish Heritage
A Living Memorial to the Holocaust
36 Battery Place, New York, NY 10280

Printed in the United States of America by Lightning Source, Inc. Library of Congress Control Number (LCCN): 2015956818

ISBN: 978-1-939561-37-4 (hard cover: 338 pages, alk. paper)

Cover photographs: Interior of Nowy Zmigrod Synagogue Courtesy of the Jewish Historical Institute, Warsaw, Poland

JewishGen and the Yizkor-Books-in-Print Project

This book has been published by the **Yizkor-Books-in-Print Project,** as part of the **Yizkor Book Project** of **JewishGen, Inc.**

JewishGen, Inc. is a non-profit organization founded in 1987 as a resource for Jewish genealogy. Its website [www.jewishgen.org] serves as an international clearinghouse and resource center to assist individuals who are researching the history of their Jewish families and the places where they lived. JewishGen provides databases, facilitates discussion groups, and coordinates projects relating to Jewish genealogy and the history of the Jewish people. In 2003, JewishGen became an affiliate of the **Museum of Jewish Heritage - A Living Memorial to the Holocaust** in New York.

The **JewishGen Yizkor Book Project** was organized to make more widely known the existence of Yizkor (Memorial) Books written by survivors and former residents of various Jewish communities throughout the world. Later, volunteers connected to the different destroyed communities began cooperating to have these books translated from the original language—usually Hebrew or Yiddish—into English, thus enabling a wider audience to have access to the valuable information contained within them. As each chapter of these books was translated, it was posted on the JewishGen website and made available to the general public.

The **Yizkor-Books-in-Print Project** began in 2011 as an initiative to print and publish Yizkor Books that had been fully translated, so that hard copies would be available for purchase by the descendants of these communities and also by scholars, universities, synagogues, libraries, and museums.

These Yizkor books have been produced almost entirely through the volunteer effort of researchers from around the world, assisted by donations from private individuals. The books are printed and sold at near cost, so as to make them as affordable as possible. Our goal is to make this important genre of Jewish literature and history available in English in book form, so that people can have the personal histories of their ancestral towns on their bookshelves for themselves and for their children and grandchildren.

A list of all published translated Yizkor Books in the project with prices and ordering information can be found at:

http://www.jewishgen.org/Yizkor/ybip.html

Lance Ackerfeld, Yizkor Book Project Manager

Joel Alpert, Yizkor-Book-in-Print Project Coordinator

JewishGen
Yizkor Book Project

This book is presented by the
Yizkor Books in Print Project
Project Coordinator: Joel Alpert

Part of the
Yizkor Books Project of JewishGen, Inc.
Project Manager: Lance Ackerfeld

These books have been produced solely through volunteer effort
of individuals from around the world. The books are printed and
sold at near cost, so as to make them as affordable as possible.

Our goal is to make this history and important genre of Jewish
literature available in English in book form so that people can have
the near-personal histories of their ancestral towns on their bookshelves for themselves and for their children and grandchildren.

Any donations to the Yizkor Books Project are appreciated.

Please send donations to:
Yizkor Book Project
JewishGen
36 Battery Place
New York, NY 10280

JewishGen, Inc. is an affiliate of the
Museum of Jewish Heritage
A Living Memorial to the Holocaust

Foreword

A visitor to Nowy Zmigrod today would never believe that a Jewish community existed here for centuries and that one day the Jews were killed, the synagogues torched and the Jewish institutions destroyed. We hope that the Yizkor Book will provide the visitor with the documentary evidence that a Jewish community existed here for many centuries.

Nowy Zmigrod Yizkor Book Summary

This is the Yizkor or Memorial Book for the Jewish Community of Nowy Zmigrod in Galicia, Poland.

This written edition of the Nowy Zmigrod Yizkor Book is over 300 pages long. It contains information on the town's institutions, organizations, buildings, and families as recounted by survivors and prewar emigrants in addition to first-hand reports of survivors of the massacre and of Jews who joined the partisans, family histories of extended families of the town and all the photographs and illustrations from the Shoah survivors of the hamlet.

Records of the earliest history show Jews living in Nowy Zmigrod as early as 1410. Local tradition had it that the Jews came because of commercial opportunities. The Jewish population numbered 1330 in 1880 (53% of the total), 1,240 in 1900 (54%) and 940 in 1921 (48%). This vibrant small Jewish community was best known for producing wines from grapes that came from Hungary and for the Moorish style synagogue that was recognized by the Polish government as a historic building. A sizable number it the town's Jews emigrated to the USA settling primarily in New York City. By the late 1930s there were a sizable number of Jews living in New Jersey. The Jews were primarily in the peddling, retail, garment occupations. When the Nazi forces occupied _Nowy Zmigrod in 1939, the Jews were shot in the woods of Halbow near Zmigrod. Approximately 1250 Jews were murdered at Halbow, mostly Jews of Nowy Zmigrod, Osiek Jasielski and other places. Most of the Jews of Nowy Zmigrod were murdered in the Holocaust. A few survivors escaped or survived the camps, or managed to hide or survived in the Soviet Union. Their stories are presented in this volume as well as the dynamic story of Nowy Zmigrod when it was a living part of world Jewry prior to 1939 as recalled by prewar emigrants who contributed to the Yizkor project. Today there are a few descendants of Nowy Zmigrod living around the world today, especially in the USA Read the details in the survivor's own words as they remember and bring to life the once vibrant Jewish community of Nowy Zmigrod. Today there are no Jews living in Nowy Zmigrod, Galicia. Poland.

Geopolitical Information:

Alternate names for the town are: Nowy Żmigród [Polish], Żmigród Nowy [Polish], Zhmigrod [Yiddish], Schmiedeburg [German], Żmigród, Zhmigrod Novy

Nowy Żmigród, Poland: 49°37' N, 21°32' E

Time Period	Town	District	Province	Country
Before WWI (c. 1900):	Żmigród Nowy	Jasło	Galicia	Austrian Empire
Between the wars (c. 1930):	Żmigród Nowy	Jasło	Kraków	Poland
After WWII (c. 1950):	Nowy Żmigród			Poland
Today (c. 2000):	Nowy Żmigród			Poland

Jewish Population in 1900:	1,330 (in 1880), 940 (in 1921)
Notes:	37 miles SE of Tarnów, 36 miles SW of Rzeszów, 9 miles SSE of Jasło. [Not to be confused with Żmigród (former Trachenberg) in Lower Silesia].

Nearby Jewish Communities:

Osiek Jasielski 3 miles WNW
Dukla 8 miles ESE
Jedlicze 9 miles NE
Jasło 10 miles NNW
Krosno 12 miles ENE
Korczyna 14 miles ENE
Kołaczyce 15 miles NNW
Biecz 15 miles WNW
Rymanów 15 miles E
Frysztak 15 miles NNE
Jaśliska 17 miles SE
Gorlice 17 miles WNW
Nižný Komárnik, Slovakia 18 miles SSE
Brzostek 19 miles NNW
Ladomirová, Slovakia 20 miles SSE
Jodłowa 20 miles NNW
Zborov, Slovakia 20 miles SSW
Jasienica Rosielna 21 miles ENE
Strzyżów 21 miles NE
Zarszyn 22 miles E
Domaradz 22 miles ENE
Svidník, Slovakia 22 miles S
Brzozów 22 miles ENE

Čertižné, Slovakia 23 miles SE
Wielopole Skrzyńskie 23 miles N
Vislava, Slovakia 24 miles SSE
Niebylec 24 miles NE
Habura, Slovakia 25 miles SE
Rzepiennik Strzyżewski 25 miles WNW
Wisłok Wielki 25 miles SE
Bukowsko 26 miles ESE
Bardejov, Slovakia 26 miles SSW
Ryglice 26 miles NW
Grybów 26 miles W
Pilzno 26 miles NNW
Czudec 27 miles NNE
Kurima, Slovakia 27 miles S
Bobowa 27 miles WNW
Ciężkowice 28 miles WNW
Tisinec, Slovakia 28 miles S
Krynica-Zdrój 28 miles WSW
Tuchów 29 miles NW
Stropkov, Slovakia 29 miles S
Medzilaborce, Slovakia 30 miles SE
Lukov, Slovakia 30 miles SW
Gromnik 30 miles WNW

Map of Poland with Nowy Zmigrod

A Shorty History of Nowy Zmigrod

By William Leibner

The little hamlet is tucked away in the foothills of the Carpathian mountains. We know very little of the early Jewish history of Zmigrod. The fact remains that the hamlet accepted Jews throughout history. The Jews were not limited to particular sections of the hamlet. Eventually, the center of the hamlet or the *rynek* was surrounded by Jewish homes and stores. Very few Poles lived in the center of the hamlet. Most Poles lived on the edges of Zmigrod. The surrounding villages were predominantly Christian and tilled the soil. Very few Jews owned farms. Most of the Jews dealt in commerce or provided services namely repairing clothing, tools, shoes. The Jews also provided a large number of peddlers that would sell their wares amongst the farming population. Monday was market day in Zmigrod and all farmers or merchants would attend the fair where agricultural and poultry products were sold and tools and clothing purchased. The Jewish community built a magnificent synagogue in the Moorish style. The place looked like a Middle Age fortress and seemed to have been built to defend the Jews in need of protection. The walls were massive and huge columns supported the roof. With time the synagogue required repairs and slight changes. The entire interior of the synagogue was hand painted by a Viennese painter.

Zmigrod was a wine center that provided wines to Jewish and non-Jewish religious services. The grapes arrived from Hungary and were converted into wines in Zmigrod. This provided a great deal of employment to the local Jews.

The Jewish population reached its peak with the beginning of the industrialization and massive transportation development. The railroads bypassed Zmigrod and brought goods from the area to large areas. The Austro-Hungarian Empire also introduced radical changes namely Jews could live where they wanted. Jews of Zmigrod began to move to other cities like Krosno, Jaslo and Rzeszow. Of course some even went further namely to the big cities of Vienna and Berlin and some even ventured to the USA. World War One forced many Jews of Zmigrod to leave the hamlet and some of them did not return to the city. The economic situation of Zmigrod kept declining and the number of Jews that left the hamlet increased. It is estimated that in September 1, 1939, Zmigrod's Jewish population reached about 800 souls. The Germans soon occupied the hamlet and torched the synagogue that burned for three days. Some sections of the walls remained standing for a long time. Then on July 7,1942, the Germans killed most of the Jews of Zmigrod, Osiek Jasielski and other places at a place called Halbow near Zmigrod.

An old Jewish community was decimated within a day. Amongst the victims were my paternal and maternal families who lived for generations in Zmigrod.

May they rest in eternal peace.

Note to the Reader:

A list of this book and all books available in the Yizkor-Book-In-Print Project along with prices is available at:

http://www.jewishgen.org/Yizkor/ybip.html

Interior of Nowy Zmigrod Synagogue
Courtesy of the Jewish Historical Institute, Warsaw, Poland

Notes

Nowy Zmigrod, Poland
49°37' / 21°47'

Compiled by William Leibner

Acknowledgments

Project Coordinator: William Leibner

Edited by Jane Waldman Aronson

Acknowledgements

We would like to acknowledge and expterss our sincere thanks to the following people and organizations without whom the book could not have been written: Avner Shalev, Chairman of the Yad Vashem Directorate; Rachel Barkai, Director of Commemoration and Public Relations, Yad Vashem; Dr. Robert Rozette, Director of Yad Vashem library; Rachel Cohen, Secretary of Yad Vashem library; Mimi Ash at the Yad Vashem Media Center in Jerusalem; Yad Vashem staff at the various research stations in Jerusalem; the National Library of Israel, Shachar Beer of the JDC (Joint Distribution Committee) archives in Jerusalem; Misha Mistel of the New York JDC's media center; We'd also like to thank Rochelle Rubinstein of the Central Zionist Archives; Itka at The Central Archives for the History of the Jewish People, and as a JDC volunteer in DP camps in Germany; To Dora Weisman for her recollections of the British entry into the Bergen Belsen concentration camp.

To Emil Leibner for his technical and computer assistance in getting the Yizkor book on paper.

To Claudette Leibner for endless patience and assistance while the project stretched on from month to month.

We thank all the people that contributed materials, pictures and information to enrich the Yizkor book of Zmigrod and Osiek.

And apologizes to anyone unintentionally overlooked.

Halbów

Near

Nowy Zmigrod

Community of Nowy Zmigrod near Jaslo

Galicia, Poland

by William Leibner

Edited by Jane Waldman Aronson

HALBÓW

THE ETERNAL RESTING PLACE OF THE JEWS OF

NOWY ZMIGROD, OSIEK JASIELSKI and

Other Places in Poland

The total expulsion of Jews from Osiek Jasielski to Nowy Zmigrod

and

The total destruction of the Jewish community of Nowy Zmigrod

as told by William Leibner

Jacob Leibner, son of Ephraim Leibner and Shprince nee Findling Leibner was a native of Zmigrod and survived the Shoah

Seril nee Lang, was the daughter of Chaim Lang and Feige Reisel Findling, a native of Zmigrod who survived the Shoah. She was married to Jacob Leibner

Table of Contents

CHAPTER I
The Jews of Zmigrod

Nowy Zmigrod in blue. This is presently the Krosno district, Galicia, Poland

The meaning of the name Zmigrod: Gro'd refers to "town" while "Z'mi" refers to the Polish word "z'mija," which means snake. Thus Zmigrod means Snaketown or Vipertown. The symbol of the hamlet is indeed an imaginary looking snake. Zmigrod, near Jaslo, Galicia, is already mentioned in 1305 and in 1332, was granted the status of a city, according to Andzej Potocki, author of the book "Zydzi w Podkarpackie," or Jews in the Sub-Carpathian region of Poland. Zmigrod is situated along the trading routes leading to the Ukraine in the east and Hungary in the south. Zmigrod received the status of a city in the 14th century. The entire region including the city belonged to a local feudal family. The city developed rapidly during the century due to the growing import of Hungarian wines. Zmigrod was destroyed during the Hungarian invasion of 1474 and burned down in 1522 and in 1577. In spite of these disasters, the hamlet kept growing physically and economically until the end of the 18th century. Then, the new roads and railroads bypassed the area and relegated the area to stagnation. The economic stagnation continued without interruption until World War II.

Jews appeared in Zmigrod in the second half of the 16th century. With the end of the century, there was already a full-fledged Jewish community. The community built a synagogue in the year 1606 and established a cemetery. In 1676 there were already 33 Jewish families in Zmigrod. The Jewish population steadily grew and by 1765 reached a population of 683 people. The table below shows the growth of the Jewish population of Zmigrod through the ages.

Year	Jews	Non-Jews
1765	683	?
1880	1300	2508
1900	1240	2280
1921	940	1959

The statistics clearly indicate Jewish growth in Zmigrod until 1880, and then a decline set in that continued until World War II. The general population also declined, indicating the economic stagnation of the place.

Most of the Christian population worked in agricultural, lumbering and spinning activities. They inhabited the fringes of Zmigrod and the surrounding areas. Due to the declining population and economic stagnation, the city lost its town status in 1919. Things did not improve during the wars. More and more Jews left Zmigrod and the area for bigger cities in Poland, or other cities in Europe and many left for the USA. Following World War II, Nowy (New) was added to the hamlet of Zmigrod. Of course, the population of the hamlet changed entirely. Most of the Jews were killed and the survivors did not return to the hamlet except to participate in memorial services for their lost ones.

The Jewish community of Zmigrod is a very old Jewish community that goes back to the Middle Ages when it had independent judicial powers that governed Jewish life in the community. The front of the synagogue still had a wooden hold where condemned Jews were tied up at the neck and feet to a wooden post for his transgressions. The judges were the rabbis of the community. The Jewish population expanded since the wine trade between Hungary and Poland expanded and provided Jewish merchants with nice incomes.

The Jews were never limited to a particular section of the hamlet but they concentrated in the center of the hamlet while the non-Jewish population concentrated on the outskirts of the hamlet. The Jews were drawn to Zmigrod since it had no religious limitations and offered commercial opportunities, something very rare for Jews at the time. Hence, the Jewish community grew and became the largest in the area.

The Moorish-style building was the synagogue of Zmigrod. The small building is the beit hamidrash, or study center, that was also used as a synagogue. Entire complex torched by the Germans during World War Two

It built a massive synagogue in the 16th century that was later remodeled. According to Leo Rosner, son of Moses David Rosner and Ester Findling-Rosner, a native of Zmigrod, the massive entrance door led you to "the inside of the synagogue [that] was very impressive and reminded one of an old style feudal ball room. The high dome was painted with a variety of animals and fish. The stained glass windows permitted the sun's rays to enter the synagogue in various colors. The "bima," or stage, where the Torah is read was elevated and one had to ascend a few steps to reach it. A huge and massive chandelier provided light.

The upper walls had large scriptural quotes inscribed at specific intervals. The massive pillars upholding the synagogue inspired confidence amongst the worshippers. According to Jacob Leibner, the son of Ephraim and Shprince Leibner, an eagle representing the Polish kings was inserted in the wall of the synagogue. Nobody knew who inserted it or when it was inserted, nor do we know the reason or cause for its being granted to this synagogue. The fact remains that the royal Polish eagle was plastered into the wall not a very common item in Jewish synagogues in Poland. The synagogue also owned several antique items, amongst them the washbasin and the ark curtain. The synagogue was declared a Polish national historical monument by the Polish government following World War One.

Massive metal entrance doors to the Zmigrod synagogue

The small building was the "beit hamidrash," or study center, that was also used as a synagogue Zmigrod did not have a yeshiva in modern times but some bright Talmudic students that graduated from the various advanced cheders, or parochial schools, continued their daily studies in the study center. They started their studies at the crack of dawn and studied until morning services began and then resumed their intensive studies. The famous Hebrew poet Chaim Nachman Bialik dedicated a famous poem entitled "Matmid" or dedicated to these Yeshiva students.

Very few local yeshiva students managed to reach the sleep away yeshivas, notably the famous yeshivas like Ponevezh or Slobodka. These yeshivas were very expensive and highly competitive. According to Shimon Lang, the nearest sleep-away yeshiva from Zmigrod was in the city of Sosnowiec. He obtained all the letters of recommendation but the family could not afford the yeshiva and Shimon could not obtain a scholarship, so he continued to study at the study center with other students. The study center was also a place where retired people or those with time on their hands would come and continue their religious studies or listen to lectures. The place was heated in the winter and cool in the summer due to the thick walls. Few people read newspapers and the study center was also the place where information was passed about between the men.

From left standing: **Jacob Leibner and Moshe Berger**
From left sitting: **Wolf Gross, Yossef Nebentzahl and Ben Zion Nebe**

Another very important Jewish institution in Zmigrod was the mikvah that was an essential part of orthodox Jewish life. The ritual bath was open daily, winter and summer, and provided hot or cold baths. The bath was maintained by the community and the attendant was salaried by the kehilla.

The community also maintained a cemetery. The Zmigroder cemetery was very old and was used not only the Jewish residents of Zmigrod but also the neighboring Jewish communities like Gorlice and Jaslo. These Jewish communities, such as Gorlice and Jaslo, were attached to the Jewish community of Zmigrod and used the Jewish burial facilities of the hamlet. Jaslo used the Zmigrod cemetery until about 1872.

The inside of the Zmigroder synagogue

The antique oil lamp in the Zmigroder synagogue with an engraving dated 1606

A parochet, or holy ark curtain, dated1670 (or Tal) at the synagogue

Cemetery plots had to be bought from the community, and sometimes negotiations lasted too long. The cemetery was very old and extensive. Some restoration is being done by a Polish volunteer from the area named Jerzy Debiec. He has already restored some burial stones. The cemetery was maintained by the community. In the winter there was a serious problem, for the ground was frozen and had to be thawed by building a fire to soften the ground so that the hevra kadisha, or burial society, could dig out the grave and bury the deceased. The hevra kadisha consisted of religious Jewish volunteers who considered burial activities a religious commandment.

The main square of the hamlet of Zmigrod. The picture is recent. Prior to World War II, the Catholic church in the center of the picture was surrounded by Jewish homes and stores

The "Pochenia," or shopping passage, of Zmigrod facing the market place of Zmigrod. The shopping passage was destroyed during the war. Most of the storekeepers in the shopping passage were Jews

The Wisloka River flowing near Zmigrod provided the mikvah, or ritual bath, with a constant supply of fresh waters

The Zmigroder mikvah, or bathhouse, next to the river marked by the tall trees. The building survived the war

The Zmigroder cemetery after World War Two

Jerzy Debiec, a Polish volunteer, is clearing the old Jewish cemetery in Zmigrod. Below are some of the old tombstones that were restored and cleared

Zmigrod steadily lost Jews. As a matter of fact, the first Jewish settlers of Jaslo were two Jews from Zmigrod, Chaim Steinhaus and Leibish Widenfeld. Their example was followed by other Jews of Zmigrod, namely the Zimets, the Citronenboims, the Engels, Rabbi Sinai Halbershtam and others. Jaslo grew at a rapid pace and so did the Jewish community of Jaslo.

Economic opportunities presented themselves and the Jews of Jaslo took advantage of them. Jaslo's gain was Zmigrod's loss. As these communities grew, developed and even surpassed Zmigrod, they gained their religious and communal independence. The great fire of 1577 and the war between the Cossacks and the Swedes further weakened the economic base of the city, especially the Jewish base, for the Jewish mainstay was commerce. The Jewish community took heavy loans to rebuild the economy of the town. It repaid these loans and was forced to take another loan in 1694 from the church in Krosno that was repaid in 1785.

In 1765, the Jewish community of Zmigrod consisted of 683 Jews and another 1,263 Jews in the nearby villages. These figures included 159 head-households, which included 41 self employed, such as 1 tax collector, 2 shopkeepers, 8 tailors, 7 hat makers, 2 glove makers, 2 jewelers, 1 butcher, 1 rabbi, 1 cantor, 7 religious teachers and 1 musician. Jews owned 67 homes that were very overcrowded. Some homes had as many as 5 families living on top of each other.

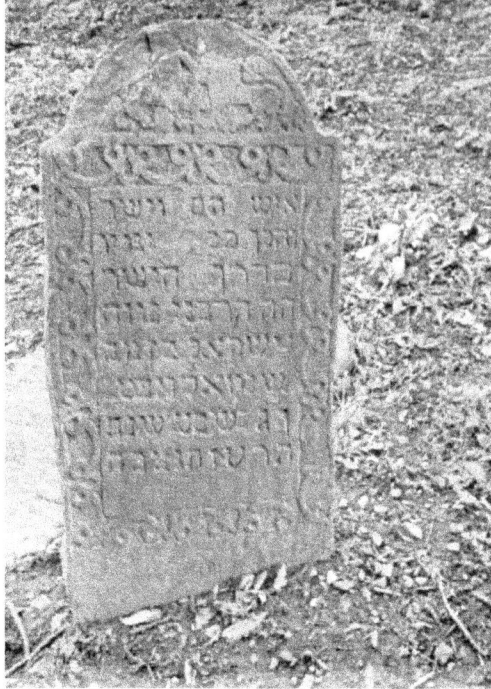

The inscription reads: "He was an honest man and always followed the right path. Israel son of Shmuel. Passed away 12 days in Shvat 1856. May his soul rest eternally." Zmigrod Jewish cemetery

The inscription reads: "Here is buried an important and modest lady. She was. Mrs. Miriam daughter of Sahar Itzhak. She passed away on the second day of Passover in the year 1839. May her soul rest eternally." Zmigrod cemetery

In 1781, under Austrian rule, most taxpayers in the city were poor people. Zmigrod had 350 taxpaying Jews of whom 181 paid less than 25 guilden [Austrian imperial currency], 160 paid between 25-100 guilden, 6 paid between 100-300 guilden and one person paid more than 300 guilden. The authorities forced the Jews of Zmigrod to pay all the arrears, which amounted to 34 guilden. Under the edict of spreading the Jews out to the country, the Zmigrod community undertook to resettle 17 families in the surrounding villages. Each family was to receive 250 florins. Only 4 families left the city by 1805.

The golden age of Jewish Zmigrod lasted from the 16th century until the end of the 18th century. The rabbi of the community was very influential. The town had a yeshiva and some famous rabbis such as Rabbi Abraham in 1680 followed by his son Rabbi Yaacov, then Rabbi Menahem Mendel, followed by Rabbi Zeev Wolf Rimner [1698], Rabbi Abraham Heshel Blomfeld [1770]. With the economic decline of the city, the kehilla could no longer afford to attract influential rabbis. Most of the Jews of Zmigrod were pious and Hasidic Jews. The most influential group of Hassidim in Zmigrod was the followers of the rabbi of Sandz, the well-known tzadik Chaim Halbershtam who lived and passed away in Nowy Sacz or Sandz. His Hassidim played an important role in the selection of the town rabbi.

The first Sandzer rabbi in Zmigrod was Rabbi Benyamin Zeev, a student of Rabbi Chaim of Sandz who founded the Sandzer Hasidic court. Rabbi Mordecai David Unger and Rabbi Asher Yeshayahu Rubin followed. Then in 1907, the town selected Rabbi Sinai Halbershtam as rabbi. He was a scion of the famous Halbershtam rabbinical family in Nowy Sacz, Galicia. He left Zmigrod prior to World War II and his son, Aaron Halbershtam, became the last rabbi of Zmigrod and Oshick (or Osiek Jasielski in Polish), a village next to Zmigrod.

With the dismemberment of Poland, the Austrian Empire took control of most of Galicia. The Austrian Empire removed some of the travel restrictions and residence requirements for Jews. Many Jews began to leave Zmigrod. Their example was followed by other Jews of Zmigrod.

The cities of Jaslo, Krosno and Tarnow grew at a rapid pace and so did their Jewish communities. All of these cities were interconnected with new highways and railways. Cheap and massive transportation brought brought many industrialized products to Galicia including Zmigrod. Many tailors, shoemakers and coachmen lost their source of income. The Jewish economic sector was hardly hit by the massive importation of industrial products. Many Jews of Zmigrod lost all hope of making a living and decided to head to America to start anew.

The reconstructed tomb of Rabbi Chaim Halbershtam in Nowy Sacz. Most of the rabbi's sons were also rabbis and were buried near their father

As things became harsher in the small isolated hamlets like Zmigrod, the number of Jews leaving the place increased by the day. Usually, the men left first to Hamburg, Germany where they embarked aboard ships heading to the USA. They then send money and tickets for their families to follow them to the new country. Occasionally, men broke all contacts with their family back home and left their families stranded. However, most families managed to join their husbands in America. Nathan Leibner also joined the wave of immigrants to the United States. He arrived and settled on the Lower East side of New York.

Nute Nathan Leibner in New York City about 1919

Nowy Zmigrod PSA Births 1866-89 Lwow Wojewodztwa / Rzeszow Province
(records in Fond 573 in Skolyszyn Archive)

Surname	Given	Event	Sig	Year	Sex
LEIBNER	Nute Natan				
LEIBNER	Perel				
LEIBNER	Efroim	B	24	1868	M
LEIBNER	Saul Mendel	B		1876	M
LEIBNER	Rachel Witte	B		1877	
LEIBNER	Burech Leib	B	9	1879	
LEIBNER	Moses Józef	B		1881	

The record is from the office of the birth registrar in Nowy Zmigrod. The daughter, Sheindel Leibner born in 1874 to Nathan-Perel Leibner, is not listed. Also not recorded is the death of Burech Leib Leibner, who died shortly after his birth

Nathan Leibner sent tickets for the entire family to come to the USA. Nathan's sister, Ester Leibner, refused to leave Zmigrod and insisted that Nathan's oldest son Efroim Leibner remain with her since she had no family.

Efroim Leibner remained in Zmigrod, grew up and married Shprince Ruchel Findling.

The Leibners were joined by the Krills, the Langs, the Findlings, the Kohens, the Stechers and many other families. They traveled by families or individuals and headed to the United States, primarily to New York City. Nathan moved to the Lower East side where there were many people from Zmigrod. There was even a "shtibel," or small synagogue, of Zmigroder Jews. They organized and incorporated a Zmigroder Jewish society named "Hebrah Benjamin Ze'ev-Anshei Zmigrod," or people of Zmigrod. The president of the society was Louis Stern. The society was a mutual benefit society to help recent Zmigroder arrivals, to assist Jews in Zmigrod and to acquire a burial site for Zmigroder Jews in New York. The stream of Jews continued. Nathan Leibner brought his entire family to the United States except for one son, Ephraim Leibner. Dozens of Zmigroder Jews did likewise.

The late Ephraim Leibner was left in Zmigrod, where the Germans killed him and his family at Halbow on July 7, 1942. The late Ephraim Leibner was left in Zmigrod, where the Germans killed him and his family at Halbow on July 7, 1942

The Leibner house in Zmigrod

Zmigrod had its first blood libel case in March 1905. A Pole accused a Jewish family of planning to murder his daughter for ritual purposes. Five Jews, among them Yossef Zimet, his wife, his son and two daughters, were arrested and held in prison during the lengthy investigation. Interventions from Vienna finally led to the release of the accused. The girl of 14 was subsequently found guilty of lying and sentenced to a three-month prison term at the courthouse of Jaslo, district city of the area. Feeling was very tense in town, and villagers kept coming to see the "holy maiden," which caused quite a commotion in the area. Many years passed before Zmigrod returned to a superficial calm.

The Jewish migration out of Zmigrod continued unabated and even increased prior to and during World War I, when Jews left Zmigrod before the advancing Russian army that eventually occupied and pauperized the Jewish population of the hamlet. The Russian army was known for its systematic looting of Jewish stores and homes. Despite the hardships, the Jews of Zmigrod tried to help the Jaslo Jews during World War I by sending them a cart loaded with bread; but the Russian soldiers detected the merchandise and viciously attacked the driver, Henech Berger, with their whips and batons. The loaves of bread were tossed into the mud and trampled. Henech Berger, brother-in-law of Leibish Zimet from Zmigrod, was lucky to escape alive and returned to Zmigrod. The Austrians recaptured Zmigrod but then the Austro-Hungarian Empire collapsed and Poland received its independence.

The independence was celebrated by staging an anti-Jewish pogrom. The pogrom began in Zmigrod in November 1918. The pogrom started when a local mob with the help of outside villagers came to shop for "bargains." The mob broke into Jewish homes and stores and looted and destroyed everything of value. Some Jews were beaten and injured. The Polish population stood by or helped the mob. The local police disappeared and frantic calls were made to Jaslo [district police office] for help. Police units arrived and restored order. They then reported that things were peaceful in Zmigrod except for some Jewish troublemakers who had disturbed the peace.

World War I pauperized the Jewish community. A mutual aid society that was established in 1894 under the leadership of Chaskel Erdheim was reactivated in Zmigrod to help the poor Jews and by 1929 it had distributed 30 loans. The society was assisted by the American Joint Organization, former Jews of Zmigrod in the United States, and the American Zmigroder society in New York.

In contrast to the pervasive Jewish poverty, a magnificent synagogue stood, a remainder of the glorious past of Jewish Zmigrod. The synagogue was declared a historical monument by the Polish government. The Jewish community, or "kehilla," was represented by 12 and then by eight members who were elected by the members of the Jewish community. The rabbi was always a member of the kehilla council. The latter assessed and collected taxes that provided money for the cheder teachers, ritual slaughterers, mikvah attendants, synagogue and mikvah maintenance, the salary for the rabbi and cantor and the hevra kadisha, or burial society.

CERTIFICATE OF INCOPORATION

O F T H E

CHEBRAH BENJAMIN ZEV

ANSCHEI ZMIGROD.

I, the undersigned, Justice
of the Supreme Court, City and
County of New York, residing in
the First Judicial District in
the City of New York, do hereby
approve of the form and
sufficiency of the within
Certificate of Incorporation,
and hereby consent that the same
be filed in the proper pffice.
Dated N. Y. May 5th 1893.

Justice.

Adolph Cohen,
Attorney at Law,
#319 Broadway,
N. Y. City.

FILED AND RECORDED

*Zmigroder society in New York City
incorporated on April 18, 893*

According to the late Max (Mordechai) Findling, son of Chaim and Sisel Findling, a native of Zmigrod who survived the Shoah, Zmigrod had a "cheder," or religious school, for poor children behind the synagogue and smaller cheders for the well-to-do children. There were also cheders of higher learning.

The late Max (Mordechai) Findling

Max studied German with Rabbi Eller Inkberg. The official language was Polish, but the Jews spoke and wrote Yiddish. He attended the local public school that was mandatory. The elementary school reached seven grades. The environment at school was very anti-Semitic because the Jewish students were the best students; there were always fights. Max studied history, spelling, language, geography and arithmetic. Jewish boys wore "peyot," or side curls, and hats or skullcaps. The Polish boys tried to rip off headgear from the Jewish boys. Sometimes the Polish students would bring pork sandwiches to school and tempt the Jews with their food. Public school was until 1:00 P.M.; then Max walked to cheder, where he stayed until after the "minha," late afternoon prayer service in the evening. It was dark on the way home but he had a candle stuck in a potato that lit the way home.

Leo Rosner, also born in Zmigrod on April 4, 1922, to Esther (Findling) and Moses David Rosner, also natives of Zmigrod, wrote a book entitled "The Holocaust Remembered" in which he described very affectionately his experiences in his native hamlet. "In the winter Zmigrod would be buried under what we called 'mountains of snow,' snow so high that it sometimes reached the tops of the houses. The townspeople would dig tunnels from one house to another, or would be unable to leave their homes for days at a time. Frost would cover the windows in tiny crystals, splashing sunlight against the walls." There were other occasions, Rosner wrote, "when we would go ice-skating on a nearby frozen lake. As children, my friends and I would spend hours playing in the deep, fluffy snow. Sledding down the hillside was the main form of winter entertainment for the shtetl's, or town's, children. My parents had bought me a real sled, but there were times I didn't have my sled, and I would join the other children, sliding down the mountain on overturned tables."

"Zmigrod was a beautiful little mountain town located near Jaslo, about 150 kilometers east of Krakow and about 30 kilometers from the present day Slovak border. Zmigrod was part of the Austrian-Hungarian Empire. In Zmigrod, horse and wagon was the primary means of transportation. Jews sold supplies and housewares to the farmers, and the latter would sell agricultural products to the Jews of Zmigrod. Most of the summer was spent buying and storing food for the winter season.

According to Rosner, "Zmigrod was a Jewish community of approximately 1,200 Jewish families. It had numerous Jewish organizations, such as *Agudath Israel, Mizrachi, Bnei Akiva,* and *Betaar.* There was one Jewish doctor, a Jewish lawyer, and a Jewish dentist. There was only one telephone, located at the post office, and one radio for the whole community. The Jewish community kept very close together. A neighbor's wedding was everyone's holiday, and a stranger's funeral, everyone's sorrow.

"In the spring the sparkling white landscape would explode in color. The mountainsides would be covered with flowing green pastures; cows would roam the fields outside our town. The summer air was clean and fresh, perfectly accommodating to the joys of youth. We spent the warm days hiking through hills around our hometown or picking blackberries from the bushes. We enjoyed the sport of shooting plums and apples off trees with slingshots, along with games of soccer we would play with our young Polish neighbors.

"The town, too, would burst into life. The streets would become busy and fill up with people hustling to and fro. Mothers would go about their business pushing their babies in carriages, and children would sit around in the sun, singing songs. The town center would be transformed into a marketplace. Every morning the gentile farmers would bring their produce to sell to the local people."

Most homes in Zmigrod had dirt floors. There was no electricity or running water; gas lamps or kerosene lanterns or candles provided light. Some streets were not paved. There were no stoves as we know them; ovens and ceramic devices were used for heat and cooking. Most of the food was cooked and baked at home. There were stores of basic needs such as groceries, food, grains, fabrics, ironware, pots, hardware, and clothing. There was also a pharmacy and a Jewish restaurant. Most of the stores were located along a partially enclosed arcade. Most of the shopping was done at the market that took place one day a week. Here the nearby farmers sold their merchandise and bought many of their products.

The marketplace was also the place where the Polish population met the Jewish population. There were no social inter-relations between the two populations. Around Zmigrod also lived a large Greek Orthodox population that the Jews called "Yevonim" or Greeks. Most of the Jews were merchants, peddlers and artisans. There were few Jewish workers. Zmigrod had no industry to speak of. Most of Jewish life revolved around the synagogue or synagogue-related activities. There were a host of social or charitable societies that helped the poor, the sick, the orphans and the poor couples. There was a mutual financial fund to grant cheap loans to merchants and artisans.

In spite of the difficult economic situation, the Jews of Zmigrod did not forget other Jews in need. Below is a sheet with names of the Jews who contributed to the maintenance of the Jewish community in Palestine.

The first sign of Zionism came to Zmigrod with the opening, in 1919, of the first lecture hall named "Hatehiya" or reawakening. Some years later, the youth division of the General Zionist party opened the first Zionist youth branch in 1933; the Akiva religious Zionist group followed suit. The most active group was the Akiva Zionist Youth group. There was also the Mizrahi or moderate religious group and the Aguda, or very orthodox group.

| 20/02/06 list of Jews | from | Zmigrod | Galicia | |
that gave	charity to	Kollel	Galicia	prior WWII
ALTER	Aaron			
ALTZTER	Aaron			
ARBELES	Hersh			
BECK	Mendel Yeh			
BEER	Dawid Lipa			
BERGER	Chaim			
BERGER	Henoch			
BESZANER	Baruch			
BESZANER	Chaim			
BINDER	Yehezkel			
BIRENBACH	Moshe Chaim			
BLAUGROUND	Hersh			
BOBKER	Itzhak			
BOBKER	Arieh			
BRAND	Matityahu			
BRAUNFELD	Yaakow			
BROCHE	Moshe Yeh			
BUKSBAUM	Riva			
BUKSBAUM	Yehuda			
CESZANOWER	Tzipora			
CITRONENBAUM	Zishe			
DANTZIGER	Benjamin			
DENNEN	Shmuel			
DOBRES	Shmuel Cha			
EICHNER	Yosef			
EINHORN	Eliezer			
EISENBERG	Itzhak			
EISENBERG	Chaim			
EISENBERG	Reuven	Rabbi		
ENGEL	Mordechai			
ENGELHARD	Moshe			
ENGELHARD	Shia			
ENGELHARD	Mendel			
ENGELHARD	Hersh			
ERREICH	Lleibish			
ERRENREICH	Aaron			
FASSER	Noah			
FEDER	Shimshon			
FEFERBERG	Miriam			
FELDSTEIN	Awraham			
FENIG	Bersh			

Partial list of Zmigroder Jews contributing money to Meir Baal Hanes organization to help poor Jews in Palestine

The Zionist parties had to fight their way into the Jewish community since the majority of the Jews were orthodox or Hasidic Jews. The Zionist parties attracted the youth, who saw no outlet for themselves in Zmigrod. So they went to the Zionist youth clubs, listened to lectures, music and spoke about Palestine. The clubhouses were frequently attacked by the very religious elements but this did not stop the growth of the Zionist movements in Zmigrod. There was even a "hachshara," or training farm, to teach young Zionist pioneers to be farmers in Palestine.

For the Zionist Congress selection in 1931, there were 25 dues-paying members in Zmigrod and they voted for the center Zionist party. Most Zionist parties gained many adherents, since the Polish anti-Semitic laws drove the Jews to despair, notably the ban on Jewish slaughter of animals in 1937. All Jewish slaughterers in Zmigrod were thus unemployed except for one butcher who could only slaughter chickens. Kosher meat had to be brought from the city of Jaslo. The economic decline of Jewish commerce continued, although the Jewish population remained static since the gates to the United States were almost closed due to the quota system that practically eliminated Jews from entering the United States. With the rise of Hitler, Germany was not only closed to Jewish migration but Jews were forced to leave Germany.

Some Jews came back to Poland, and even Zmigrod received some former Jewish residents. Western European countries slowly closed their borders to Jewish migrants. The Jews of Poland were thus landlocked and the escape valve for emigration was almost closed. Of course, the Polish government knew how many Jews lived in Poland, as shown by the above residence notes, but it never published official statistics after the last official census in 1921. Everybody estimated the Jewish population. Zmigrod was estimated to have about 800 Jews in September 1939, according to the Polish researcher of the area, Andzej Potocki. The Jews had no place to go, except to move inside Poland if the opportunity presented itself. The Polish authorities kept a close watch over the movement of people, especially Jews, and recorded every change.

Top registration note states that Jakob Leibner left his Zmigrod residence and moved to Krosno to the Lang residence in the marketplace.

Bottom note states that he left Zmigrod. The Polish government maintained a close watch over the movement of people. The documents were those of my father, Jakob Leibner, who left Zmigrod where he lived to go to Krosno to marry my mother, Seril Lang

A Zionist meeting in Zmigrod.

Zmigrod, 1935. The above photograph was taken around 1935 in Nowy Zmigrod. We are not sure of the occasion. However, many of the folks have been identified.

Men standing, top row, left to right: Chaskel Bobker, Yankel Czeszanover, Peisseh Kratzer, Mina Getz, Moshe Einhorn, Nachman Wrubel (Nachmu Kiszku), Lisze Shtein.
Second row, left to right: Sima Leibner, Chaim Kaufman, Seril Leibner, Tema Haber, Mina ?, Haya Blauground, ? Zimet and David Lang (man with the large hat).

Third Row, standing, left to right: Haim Leib's daughter, Shapse Haber, Leah Shamir, Haya Findling, David Weinberg, Dolish Blauground, woman-unknown, woman-unknown, Suniv Stein.

Sitting: Hersh Stecher (with his child), Frumit (Yankel Sziszter'sdaughter), Suniv Kreiss, Szmeil Getz, Scheindel Stecher Getz (Mrs. Oszer Getz), Jakiv Itche Getz, Sheindel Krebs, Baruch Krebs. Children: first three belong to Hersch Stecher, youngest Getz boy, boy-unknown.

Israel has assisted with the identification of those pictured left to right:

Back Row, Standing: ? Krischer, ?, ? Kranz, ?, Schabson Haber, Meir Gross, ? Rosenman, girl in white?, Ester Laks, Tova Krischer, girl?, Manya Laks, Mojsze Holihock Weinsztein, Berta Kreps (white collar), Dawid Haber, Chaja Ester Findling, man behind ?, Berish Berger, Jacob Findling, Lajzer Beer (hat), ?, Mojsze Beer (dark suit)

Kneeling: ?, Chaja Hirszel (white collar), Raizl Leibner, Mendl Wimiszner, Barish Berger (tie), Jacobitze (Itzak) Zanger, Schprinca Ingber (girl in front), Berta Lachs, Mojsze Leibner, Berish Krebs (white shirt & tie), Henoch Rotenberg (behind), Schlomo Gross (white shirt & tie), ? Findling (in Hat)

Girls Sitting, front row: ? Kranz, ?, ? Rosenman, Szlomo Kranz, Sara Wimiszner, plaque, Golda Laks, Laibisz Szperling, ? Rosenman, Golda Bobker.

CHAPTER II
World War II in Zmigrod

With the outbreak of World War II, some Jews left town for Eastern Galicia, which was soon occupied by the Soviet army. Many Jews returned to Zmigrod with the end of the hostilities. Those who remained in the Soviet–controlled areas were soon shipped to Siberian camps in Russia where many died of starvation, notably Rabbi Sinai Halbershtam, former rabbi of Zmigrod.

The Germans soon imposed travel restrictions and the wearing of armbands. Searches were conducted frequently under any pretext. Once, the Germans searched for weapons and ordered all Jewish males to report to the market. While the men were standing in the square, their homes were being looted and ransacked by the soldiers. The search finished, the young Jews were forced to board trucks that took them away. The old people were sent home. Of course, no weapons were found.

According to Shimon Lang, son of Pinkas and Raizl Lang, a native of Zmigrod who survived the Shoah, he was at the synagogue on the first day of Rosh Hashanah, September 14, 1939, when German soldiers burst in through the doors and mercilessly beat the congregants who barely managed to escape with their lives. They continued to search for Jews and assigned them to all kinds of work details. No one dared to appear for prayers the next day of Rosh Hashanah. The synagogue was empty as though in mourning, and so it would remain until torched by the Germans at the end of the Sukkot holiday. Some Jews were hiding while other Jews worked for the Germans. No young Jew was safe and patrols constantly looked for Jews. Military order was established and even the Poles felt it.

A few days after the Germans entered the hamlet, the Poles thought of staging a small pogrom to display their feelings toward their Jewish neighbors. The Poles, however, forgot to notify the Germans of their intentions and when the German soldiers saw masses of Poles with sticks and pitchforks marching to Zmigrod, they thought it was an uprising and opened fire. A few Poles were killed and others were wounded. The crowd immediately dispersed. The dead were loaded on a horse–driven cart and buried. The town crier was told to announce that the uprising was over.

The policy of terror and intimidation of the Jewish population continued unabated. According to Potocki, about 150 Jews were caught hiding and were killed at the Jewish cemetery in Zmigrod in 1940. Then Germans created a Judenrat headed by Hersh Eisenberg. The other members were Yekel Bronfeld, Moshe Haim Birenbaum, Shia Wahl, Hersh Duvid Zilber, Shia Bobker, Shia Zilber, Shmiel Weinstein, Yekel Diamant and Nute Parness.

The influential Jewish families in Zmigrod were the Wymishler, Eisenberg, Sheinwetter and Fisher families. Hersh Eisenberg was ordered to conduct a census of the Jewish population in the city. The report was handed to the Gestapo in Jaslo. According to Rywka Klein, a native of Zmigrod, the Germans never had a permanent office in Zmigrod. They never remained in the hamlet beyond the day and returned to Jaslo, the administrative city of the region.

Based on the census, the Germans were constantly demanding more workers. The latter were hardly fed, mistreated and overworked. Some sustained serious injuries since they lacked the skills, tools or motivation. They worked on roads, bridges and even on farms. The Judenrat paid them meager salaries that were collected from the Jews of Zmigrod. The taxes also paid for the absorption of Jewish refugees from nearby Krosno and from the distant cities of Krakow and Lodz.

A ghetto was created in Zmigrod to absorb all the refugees who were deprived of everything. A free soup kitchen was organized that provided lunches for the needy regardless of their length of residence in Zmigrod. But the stream of refugees kept coming and taxed the community beyond its means. The local Jewish community was already pauperized by the harsh German economic extortion policies.

Aid arrived in the form of financial assistance from the J.S.S., or Jewish Self–help Service, in Krakow. The J.S.S. organization, under the leadership of Dr. Weihart, borrowed money from various Jewish organizations, notably the Joint Distribution Committee, and distributed the funds throughout the Jewish communities.

Each community established a J.S.S. to help the Jewish community. Zmigrod was no exception and the local chapter was headed by Hersh Rab, who would pay dearly for running the office. Hersh Rab was the president of the local J.S.S., which also included Hersh Sheinwetter, Shia Zimmet, Getzil Shiff, Haim Shia Birnhan, Miriam Fessler, Idesen's son–in–law and David Leizer. They provided for the social, nutritional and sanitary needs of the poor Jews in town regardless of their length of residence. They established a public kitchen that distributed each day 350 breakfasts and lunches. Money was obtained from various sources including weekly contributions from the well– established families in town. The latter also maintained the Judenrat. The office worked as well as conditions enabled it to function. Cases that refused to cooperate with J.S.S. were referred to the office of the Judenrat that handled these situations

In the spring of 1942, the Germans transferred all the Jews from the village of Osiek Jasielski to Zmigrod. Presently, the entire area was clear of Jews except for Zmigrod, which now had a population of about 2,800 Jews. The conditions were appalling; people lived on top of each other with limited sanitary facilities. Hunger was everywhere.

The Judenrat and the local chapter of the J.S.S. did their best to create jobs, especially outside the ghetto. This provided contact with the outside world and enabled food to come in to the ghetto. These workers reported that terrible things were happening to nearby Jewish communities. Eyewitnesses said they saw heavy earth digging equipment on the road outside Zmigrod. Soon, orders were posted throughout Zmigrod that all the Jews must report to the marketplace on Tuesday, July 7, 1942, at 7 A.M. Anyone disobeying the order would be shot.

Monday, July 6, 1942, was declared a day of fasting and prayer. Tuesday July 7, 1942, was a beautiful summer day. The 22nd day in Tamuz, Tashab or 5702, presented no hope for the Jewish community. Jews began to congregate in the marketplace until most of the Jewish population was present. Some Jews hid in prepared shelters. Then, the heads of the Judenrat came out of their office and led the community to Bal's meadow as ordered by the Germans. The area was already surrounded by German, Polish and Ukrainian police units.

According to Shimon Lang, "The Gestapo chief ordered the Jews to line up in several rows. He then ordered all Jews of age 40 and above to move to another section of the park. Many Jews assumed that this group would be sent home and decided to join the group. A line was drawn between the two groups. You could always join the so–called elderly group but you could not leave it to return to the original group." According to the German charge sheet of 1972 against Dr. Walter Gentz, "kreishauptman" or district leader of Jaslo district that included Zmigrod during World War II, "He personally selected Jews of Zmigrod to be sent to Halbow and killed."

Gentz then ordered the head of the Judenrat, Hersh Eisenberg, to appear and beat him mercilessly with his big stick. Eisenberg was bleeding profusely and Gentz told him, "You will watch the entire proceedings." A table was then placed in front of the original group. The Gestapo chief sat himself down at the table and began to call each person to approach the table. Those who failed the test were ordered to join the elderly group. The young and strong he sent to another section of the place and stamped their paper identity cards. This selection process went on most of the day. At the end of the day, Shimon Lang and the other young people were forced to leave the area and return home.

The pleas of the women, children, old and sick people were hopeless. Most of the Gestapo and policeman were highly intoxicated, having consumed large amounts of alcohol during the day. The various police units surrounded the Jews and kept them in place. Trucks soon began to appear and were loaded with the Jews who remained in the park. The latter were pushed, shoved or thrown into trucks that transported them to a place called Halbow, a wooded area near Zmigrod, where large pits had been dug by forced Polish workers the previous days. On arrival at Halbow, the Jews were lined up, ordered to undress and led to the lip of the pit and bullets hit them from the back. Their bodies then fell into the pit. Some of the people were still alive or lightly wounded but more and more bodies fell and crushed the bodies under them. Since there were few trucks, the condemned had to wait their turn.

The head of the Judenrat, Hersh Eisenberg, who was mercilessly beaten, had to observe the entire selection. He was sent to Halbow with the last truck, as was the head of the local J.S.S. chapter, Rab and his family. According to the Polish researcher of the area Andzej Potocki, it is estimated that about 1,257 Jews were killed that day at Halbow, including Rabbi Aaron Halbershtam and his family, but nobody knows the exact number. During the next few days, the Germans had Polish workers spread lime, sand and gravel over the pit.

The Halbow forest where the Zmigroder Jews were shot.
The fence was erected after the war by Pincas Wohlmuth in Zmigrod

Forest vegetation soon reclaimed the entire area. The same day of the action, about 40 Jews were caught hiding; they were led to the Jewish cemetery in Zmigrod and shot.

The Jews who returned home from the meadow were traumatized beyond belief; most of them had just lost most of their relatives. They looked at the walls and searched for the familiar faces but there were none. Some took inventory of the situation and began to think of escaping or hiding. Some tried to contact Poles they knew and asked them for hiding places; others began to plan hiding places and some even decided to leave for the forest.

On Sunday July 12, 1942, most of the surviving Jews were led back to the selection site and about 500 able–bodied Jews were ordered to immediately mount awaiting trucks that left Zmigrod. The rest of the Jewish population in Zmigrod was ordered to return home. The transport went to Jaslo and then to Plaszow, near Krakow. Plaszow was then a work camp; later it would become a concentration camp, but conditions were appalling.

The Polish inscription reads: "Here are buried 1,250 Jews, murdered on July 7, 942, by the henchmen of Hitler." The monument was erected by the Polish authorities and is located in the forest of Halbow, near Zmigrod

A partial list of Jews of Zmigrod that were sent to the labor camp in Plaszow

Last name	First name	Birth date	Birth place
BARACHAN	Moses		Brzezyni
BARACHAN	Mendel		
BLEDER	Saul		
BLEDER	Henri		
BLAUGRUND	Leib		
BRZEGOWSKI	Elias		
CZIESZANOWER	Naftali		
CZIESZANOWER	Jakob		
DERDZEWIC	Mozes		
EINHORN	Josef		
EISENBERG	Moses		
ERREICH	Aaron		
ERREICH	Noam		
ERREICH	Mordech		
ERREICH	Salomon		Zmigrod
FEDER	Chaim		
FEIER	Isak		Osiek
FELD	Salomon		
FINDLING	Jakub		
FINDLING	Yehuda	06/12/1919	
GELB	Alter		Halbo
GELB	Hersz		

GETTENBERG	Eisik		
GETZLET	Itzhak		
GLASSER	Roman		Krakow
GOLDBERG	Ita		
GOLDFARB	Sz.		
GRUBER	Leib		
GRUBER	Nuchem		
GRUBER	Leib		
GRUNIS	Henryk		Kalisz
GUTWEIN	Isak	10/06/1924	
HEREN	Izydor		
HIRSCHBERG	Adolph		
HIRSCHBERG	Natan	22/06/1934	Zmigrod
HIRSCHBERG	Leon		
JUST	Josef		
KALB	Jozef		
KALINSKI	Mozes		
KAMPF	Chaskel		
KANNER	Naftatali		
KELLER	Jozef		

KESERLAUF	Salomon		
KOHN	Abraham		
KOHN	Hersch		

KOLBER	Jakob		
KOLBER	Jdel		
KOLBER	Josef		Zmigrod
KOLLBAUER	Leiser		
KREBS	Pinkas		
KAMER	Salomon		Zmigrod
KRIEGER	Jakob		
KURSCHNER	Mendel		
LANG	Michael		
LANG	Szymon		Zmigrod
LANG	Pinkas		
LEIBNER	Szymon		Zmigrod
LEIBNER	Moses		
LEISER	Necha		
LEIZER	David		
LERMAN	Chaim		
LERMAN	Markus		
LERMAN	Mendel		
LERMAN	Szymon		
LERMAN	Cila		
LESLAU	Jakub		Lodz
LIBERMAN	Benjamin		
LIBERMAN	Moses		

LIBERMAN	Leon		
LIEDERBAUM	Dawid		
MARGULES	Leib		
NAUMAN	Natan		
NEUGER	Nutek		
NEUMAN			
ORGLER	Dawid		
PEILLER	Josef		
PELLER	Chaim		
PELLER	Izak		
PELLER	Nuchem		
POSTRENK	Lezer		
RAB	Chaskel		
REGLICH	Schulem		Lodz
RETFELD	Szulem		
RICHMAN	Naftali		
ROSENHAN	Chaim Leiser		
ROSENHAN	Hersh Leib		
ROSENHAN	Markus Dawid		
ROSENHAN	Szymon		
ROSNER	Moses Dawid		
SCHMIER	Leiser		

SCHMIER	Jakub		Zmigrod
SCHMIER	Natan		
SCHREINER	Elias		
SEIDLINGER	Naftali		
SEIDLINGER	Izak		
SCHUMAN	Mozes		
SILBER	Hersz		
SILBER	Salomon		
SMETANA	Izak	18/03/1898	Lodz
SMIETANA	Israel		
SOMMER	Isak	10/12/1898	Osiek
STRYCHARZ	Elias		
STADTFELD	Pinkas		
WASSERLAUF	Noe		
WASSERLAUF	Jacob		
WEINSTEIN	Isak		Zmigrod
WEINSTEIN	Zygmunt		
WEINSTEIN	Isak		
WEINTRAUB	Bernard		Zmigrod
WEINTRAUB	Leib		
WIELICZKER	Berl		
WISTREICH	Hersz		
WOHLMUT	Dawud		
WOHLMUT	Pinkas		

WOHLMUT	Jakub		
WROBEL	Moses		Lodz
ZAKON	Abraham		
ZAKON	Moses		
ZIMET	Osias		
ZIMET	Shia		
ZIMET	Leib		
ZWASS	Hersz		
ZWASS	Moses		
ZWASS	Samuel		
ZWASS	Abraham		

The list contains 128 names that we were able to collect from the existing documents. These were the people who were sent to Plaszow from Zmigrod on July 12, 1942

In Plaszow, people worked long hours with little food. Shimon Lang was building railroad tracks and barely received food. The attrition rate was enormous but the Germans did not care; the Jews were expendable. The Jews of Zmigrod in Plaszow sent letters back home pleading for help. The newly established Judenrat (the members of the old Judenrat had been killed at Halbow) decided to revive the J.S.S. chapter in Zmigrod. This office collected food and clothing among the survivors of the first selection and began to send packages to the Zmigroder inmates in Plaszow.

Below is a letter dated August 7, 1942, from the J.S.S. office in Zmigrod to the office in Plaszow where the inmates of Zmigrod are informed that 700 kilograms of packages were sent to the camp to be distributed among them. The letter also informs the inmates that they did not manage to obtain bread from the Judenrat due to the lack of time. The J.S.S. office promised to send bread in the next shipment.

Below is the Polish letter from the J.S.S. in Zmigrod to the Plaszow office in Krakow concerning the packages for the Zmigroder Jews

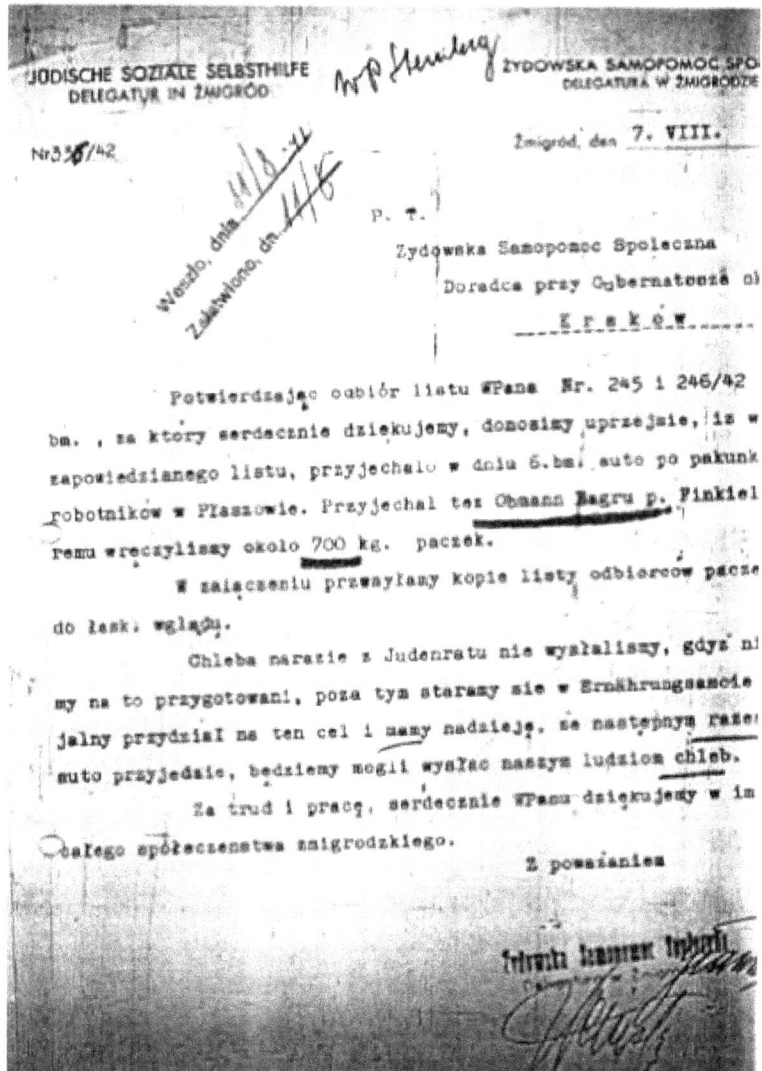

On August 15, 1942, the Germans sent skilled Jewish workers to the Zaslav labor camp. Nobody survived. According to Leo Rosner, most of the Jews of Zmigrod became very apprehensive and expected the appearance of the Gestapo any day to round up the remaining Jews. The latter began to build hiding places, contact Polish friends to seek help or left home for the forest. Rosner and his family decided to use the attic of the house as a shelter. It was a good hiding place and nobody could detect it from outside or inside the house. Preparations were made and some food stored. They expected the action every day and then the new Judenrat announced that all Jews of Zmigrod were to assemble in the square with their luggage on September 3, 1942. A warning was added that anyone hiding would be shot on discovery.

Rosner, his family and some relatives went to the attic on the particular day as did some other Jews of Zmigrod. Some Jews left the hamlet and went to the forest or to pre–arranged hiding places. Most of the hopeless and hapless Jews went to the meeting place. The Germans realized that many Jews were hiding and began to search homes. On discovery, some Jews were led to the meeting place while others were shot on the spot. Finally, all Jews mounted trucks and headed to the nearest railway station. The transport headed to Przemysl, Galicia, where some young able–bodied Jews were removed from the train. The remainder, including Mina Zimet, the wife of Shia Zimet, and her family continued to the death camp of Belzec where they all perished.

The Rosners' hiding place was not discovered but they could not stay in the tiny attic forever. Food and water were needed and had to be provided in spite of the constant lurking dangers of being spotted by Poles and reported to the police. Days passed and the food situation was getting more difficult. The Polish police also checked the area for hidden Jews and eventually the residents of the Rosner attic were discovered, arrested and taken to prison in Zmigrod. The prison consisted of a cellar in a building. The Polish police brutalized and tortured them, looking for hidden cash or valuables. Finally the Gestapo came and took the Jews to the Jaslo prison. Similar instances occurred throughout Zmigrod and vicinity. The hidden Jews were starving, isolated and helplessly exposed to unfriendly eyes. Slowly but steadily, the Jews of Zmigrod were caught and shot or sent to Jaslo prison where they were shot or sent to the death camps.

Prior, during and after the big selection, several dozen young Jews escaped to the forest. The group soon reached 60–70 people, according to Shmuel Rosenhan from Osiek. The group was constantly on the move. They lacked

weapons and were hunted by the Germans, local Polish police and villagers. Shmuel Rosenhan describes in his testimony how he joined a partisan group of Zmigroder Jews, as well as his capture by the Polish police. During the battles between the partisan group and the German and Polish police units, Jews were killed; others were captured, tortured and then sent to the Jaslo prison.

Most of the Jewish prisoners were then taken to the outskirts of Jaslo, in the forest of Warzyce, and shot. Slowly the partisan group was eliminated. The Germans and Polish police units continued to hunt Jews in Zmigrod and vicinity. As late as March 1944, six Jews were caught in Faliszowica near Zmigrod and killed together with the Polish woman, Wladyslawa Krysztiniaka, who hid them. Thus, Zmigrod became free of Jews; a span of hundreds of years of Jewish existence was erased. Zmigrod became "Judenfrei," or free of Jews.

The Jews who found hiding places among the local population were in constant danger of being kicked out of their hiding place, being discovered by informers, or both. Some of the Poles kicked out the Jews that they were hiding once the money payments ended. Such expulsion meant a death sentence for the lonely Jew in a hostile environment.

This is a case of hidden Jews as told by the late Jakob Leibner. Following the war, Jakob Leibner visited Zmigrod and Halbow, where he recited Kadish for his parents, sisters and their families as well as for the entire Jewish community that was murdered here. On leaving Halbow, he returned to Zmigrod to visit Pinkas Wohlmut, a native of Zmigrod who had survived the

Shoah but lost his entire family. Pinkas was the only Jew who lived in the entire area. He refused to abandon his ancestors and decided to live a lonely, isolated life in Zmigrod. This is what Pinkas told Jakob Leibner regarding Jakob's father Ephraim and his mother Shprince Leibner and his sister Sara Leibner–Gross. They were all killed at Halbow. Jakob's brothers, Moshe and Shimon, and sister Reisel Leibner survived the selection and were sent home. Moshe and Shimon Leibner were sent to Plaszow with the other surviving able–bodied Jews. The late Shimon Lang confirmed their presence in Plaszow. Both brothers managed to bribe the guards at the camp and disappeared. Slowly they made their way back home to Zmigrod. They avoided Zmigrod and headed directly to a farmer who they knew in Brezew, near Zmigrod. He provided them with shelter and food for payment. They paid American dollars that they had from home and also told the farmer that they had clothing buried in a cave.

Nr	Empfänger	Absender	Verpackung	Brutto Kg
1	SAM. ZWAS	BARUCH ZWAS	1 SACK	8.0 Kg
2	JONAS ZANGER	JOSEF WEINBERGER	1 SACK	15.0
3	SZYMON LANG	PINKAS LANG	1 KISTE	29.0
4	HENRIK GRUNIS	EVA LEISER	1 PACKET	4.0
5	JSAK EICHNER	SALA EICHNER	1 SACK	6.0
6	CHASKIEL KAMPF	JTA KAMPF	1 SACK	7.5
8	JSAK SMETANA	L. SMETANA	1 SACK	2.8
9	JOSEF KOLBER	TEMA KOLBER	1 SACK	2.8
10	SALOMON FELD	JOSEF STRENGER	1 SACK	7.5
11	NACHMAN HROBEL	FRYMETA HRUBL	1 KISTE	3.5
12	NATAN SCHMIER	ZLATA SCHMIER	1 KISTE	8.0
13	CHAIM L. ROSENHAN	MARIA ROSENHAN	1 SACK	6.5
14	LAZAR FENIG	HERSCH FENIG	1 KISTE	17.0
15	LEON GRÜNBAUM	LEA GRÜNBAUM	1 SACK	2.0
16	JSAK WEINSTEIN	MANIA WEINSTEIN	1 SACK	6.0
17	TOBIAS SZCEGELSKI	SCHENKELE JSKi	1 KISTE	13.0
18	CHASKIEL KRISCHER	NECHA KRISCHER	1 SACK	22.5
19	SALOM. WASSERLAUF	NOE WASSERLAUF	1 KISTE	22.5
20	LEIB BLAUGRUND	NATAN BLAUGRUND	1 SACK	5.5
21	JSAK ROTH	HELA ROTH	1 KISTE	7.5
22	ISRAEL ROSNER	SABINE ROSNER	1 SACK	5.0
23	MECHEL KELLER	HENA KELLER	1 SACK	8.0
24	ABRAHAM ZWAS	HERMAN ZWAS	1 SACK	12.5
25	MONEK BARACHAN	E. BARACHAN	1 PACKET	6.5
26	JAKOB LESLAV	GENIA LESLAV	1 PACKET	3.0
27	PINKAS STADTFELD	STADTFELD	1 SACK	8.0
28	BENJAM. LIBERMAN	LEA LIBERMAN	1 KOFFER	13.0
29	ELIAS STRYCHARZ	ROSA STRYCHARZ	1 PACKET	4.0
30	HENOCH SCHILDWACH	SALA SCHILDWACH	1 PACKET	5.0
31	JOSEF JUST	ERNA JUST	1 SACK	2.5
32	JOSEF SEILER	S. KOHN	1 SACK	8.0
33	M. ZAKON	B. ZAKON	1 SACK	7.0
34	LEISER KOLBAUER	KOLBAUER	1 SACK	10.5
37	DAVID LEISER	NECHA LEISEN	1 SACK	5.5
38	ROMAN GLASER	A. ROCHMAN	1 SACK	28.0
39	HERSCH SCHUMAN	DORA SCHUMAN	1 SACK	14.0
40	CHAIM FEDER	PEPKA FEDER	1 SACK	13.0
41	MOSES DAVID ROSKER	ESTER ROSNER	1 SACK	8.0
42	LEO HIRSCHBERG	LULI HIRSCHBERG	1 PACKET	8.0
43	NAFTALI CZESZANOWER	SARA MEISNER	1 PACKET	6.0
44	JAKOB CZESZANOWER	HENRYK SCHÖNWETTER	1 PACKET	2.5
45	MOSES EISENBERG	SZ. GOLDFARB	1 PACKET	2.5
46	EISIG GETTENBERG	BEILA GETTENBERG	1 KORB	7.5
47	NATAN HIRSCHBERG	LEIB HIRSCHBERG	1 SACK	19.0
48	HERSCH HIELICZKER	SALA STEIN	1 SACK	2.5
49	NUCHEM PELLER	JSRAEL PELLER	1 SACK	13.0
50	PINKAS HOHLMUT	NIEDER HOHLMUT	1 SACK	12.0
51	NYTEK HANTASCH	HERSCH ORGLER	1 SACK	11.0
52	NAFTALI KANNER	GOLDA KANNER	1 PACKET	4.5
53	HERSCH ZIMET	MINA ZIMET	1 KOFFER	13.5
54	HERSCH GELB	RACHELN GELB	1 KOFFER	20.0
55	HERSCH KOHN	SYMCHE KOHN	1 KISTE	12.5
56	ADOLF HIRSCHBERG	NATAN HIRSCHBERG	1 SACK	22.0
57	MOSES LIBERMAN	NKHE LIBERMAN	1 SACK	5.5
58	DAVID NEUMAN	TEMA NEVMAN	1 KISTE	14.0
59	JSRAEL GOLDBERG	JTA GOLDBERG	1 SACK	21.0
60	JSAK PELLER	GIMPEL PELLER	1 KISTE	17.5
61	CHAIM ROSENHAN	ANA ROSENHAN	1 SACK	23.0
62	JOSEF EINHORN	LAZAR KAPPEL	1 SACK	6.0
63	ARON ERREICH	RYFKE ERREICH	1 SACK	32.0
64	ZYGMUNT WEINSTEIN	JOSEF WEINSTEIN	1 PACKET	6.5
65	DAVID NISTREICH	JSRAEL SOMMER	1 PACKET	5.0
66	HENDL LEHRMAN	CILA LEHRMAN	1 PACKET	3.0
67	LEISER PFEFFER	LEISER BEER	1 SACK	16.5
68	SALOMON BLEDER	JUDENRAT	1 PACKET	4.0
69	ABRAH. KOHN	JUDENRAT	1 SACK	10.5
70	JOEL KOLBER	NATAN BLAUGRUND	1 BECK	4.5
71	PINKAS KREBS	JUDENRAT	1 SACK	10.0
72	OSIAS ZIMET	MINA ZIMET	1 KOFFER	4.5

List of Zmigroder Jews in Plaszow who received packages. Middle column are the senders and the right column is the weight of each package

The family had a clothing store and hid most of the clothing with the outbreak of the war. The farmer kept his deal and kept the brothers hidden for a short period of time and then apparently discovered their hidden treasure. He decided to kill both brothers by using the pretext that they had to be moved individually to another safe hiding place. During the transfer he managed to kill each brother separately by hacking them to death. He then took possession of their hidden belongings.

Sometime later the farmer attended a party, drank too much and began to brag a bit. Someone called the Gestapo office in Jaslo and reported the conversation. The Gestapo arrived in Zmigrod, took an interpreter and headed to the farm in Brezew. They arrested the farmer and beat him mercilessly until he revealed the entire story, including the whereabouts of the clothing that he removed from the hiding place. The Germans removed all the hidden clothing and anything extra that looked good and placed it in their cars. They took the farmer into the woods and shot him and dumped his body in a pit. To this day, his body has not been found. The Germans were furious at the farmer, not for killing a Jew, but for doing it without their permission. Furthermore he had violated the order that called for reporting Jews to the police.

Zmigrod prison where hidden Jews were kept in the cellar following their discovery after all the Jews were killed at Halbow or deported from Zmigrod from the hamlet. Leo Rosner visits the prison where the Poles kept him following the war

The Germans left the farm, dropped off the interpreter in Zmigrod and headed to Jaslo. The interpreter slowly revealed the story among his neighbors. Of course, no one knows the whereabouts of the grave of Moshe and Shimon Leibner. The fate of Reisel Leibner is totally unknown.

Nobody saw or heard of her following the first selection, which she had survived. Jakob Leibner said good–bye to Pinkas Wohlmut and left Zmigrod for Krosno, where he took the train to Walbrzych or Waldenburg, Silesia, Poland. He returned home a changed person. Jacob Leibner saw no hope for Jewish life in Poland and decided to leave the country by any means. He was joined by thousands of other Polish Jews who streamed to the borders of Czechoslovakia and onward to the D.P. (Displaced Persons) camps of Germany, Austria and Italy.

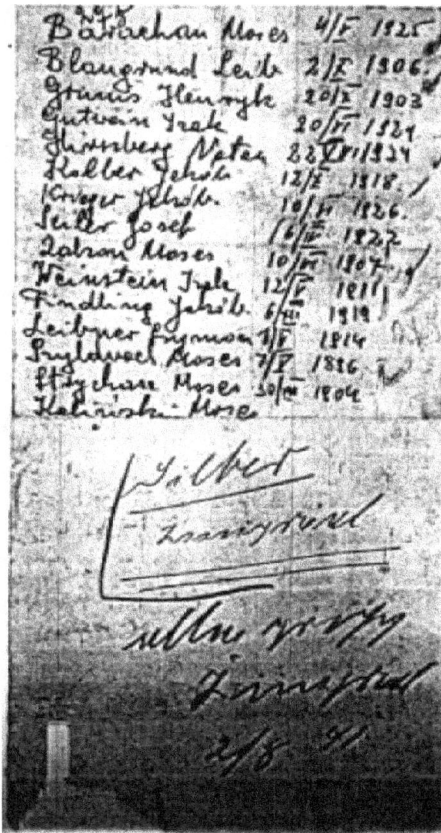

Szymon (Shimon) Leibner is listed on the scrap sheet of a labor gang in Plaszow headed by S. Silber

Reisel Leibner as group leader of the Zionist Akiva youth group in Zmigrod

CHAPTER III
Zmigrod Following the War

With the end of the war, some Zmigroder Jewish survivors returned, visited the shtetl and Halbow and left the area. One of these was Leo Rozner who went on to visit Mathausen concentration camp where he spent the war years.

Leo Rozner visits the Mathausen concentration camp where he spent some of the war years

Only one Jewish family returned to Zmigrod and resumed a lonely Jewish life, Pinkas Wohlmut and his wife. Pinkas survived all actions and concentration camps but lost his entire family. He remarried and insisted on living in Zmigrod near his ancestors in spite of the dangers facing Jews in these areas. Jews who visited Zmigrod always stopped to visit and chat with Pinkas. He kept in contact with many survivors and asked for donations to restore the overgrown Halbow burial plot. Slowly the area was cleared and fenced in.

A small monument was erected inside the fenced area describing the event that took place. On the fourth yahrtzeit, or memorial day, of the killings at Halbow, July 7, 1946, Shia (Yehoshua) Zimet, a native of Zmigrod and a survivor of the Shoah, son of Sender (Alexander) and Mirele Zimet, organized a memorial ceremony at Halbow that was attended by a few survivors from Zmigrod.

Memorial tombstones were erected by survivors for their families murdered at Halbow

Jews of Zmigrod Memorialized

Bluma (Zimet) Engelhardt, a relative of Shia Zimet, kindly sent us a copy of the memorial poem and eulogy that Shia Zimet composed in memory of the Jews of Zmigrod who were murdered and buried in the mass grave of Halbow near Zmigrod, close to Jaslo, Galicia, Poland. The murderous event took place on July 7, 1942, when about 1,257 Jews were murdered.

Shia Zimet delivered the memorial poem, written in classical Yiddish, at the mass gravesite in 1946. With him were a few of the Zmigroder survivors who were still in Poland at the time.

The poem is barely legible and I (William Leibner) took the liberty of restoring the text and I then loosely translated it to English.

Here is the poem.

צום 4טן יארצייט פון די
זמיגראדער קדושים

כ'ב תמוז תש'ב

'הנאהבים והנעימים בחייהם
ובמותם לא נפרדו'

מיט א צעבראכן הארץ און א
פארוווּנדיקטער נשומה;
מיט א געבויגענעם קאָפ
דערמאן איך היינט;
די 1200 קדושים פון אונזער
שטעטל;
וועלעכע זענען אויף אן
אכזריוודיקען אויפן
אומגעקומען;
דורך די רוצחישע הענט

פאר מיינע אויגן שטייט דאס
בילד
פון מיין שטעטעלע,
די שול, דאס בית המדרש,
די כשרע קינדערלעך מיט
שוואַרצע חיינעוודיקע אייגלעך
און שוואַרצע געלאקטע
פּאָהלעך
אין מיינע אוירען קלינגען.
זייערע זיסע שטימעלעך
פון דער מזרח וואַנט אמן,...
יהא שמה רבא

פון דעם אלעם איז היינט נישט
מער
געבליבן ווי א בארג ערד
אויף דעם גרויסען פאמיליע
גרוב
אויפן האַלבעוווער בארג
דארט וווּ עס געפינט זיך דער
ספר פון זמיגראדער ייִדן

יהושע צימעט

Translation:
To the 4th memorial day (yahrzeit) of the slaughter of the Jews of Zmigrod

Tuesday, July 7, 1942

"In life and death the Jews of Zmigrod were never separated"
(Biblical quotation referring to the friendship of Jonathan and David)

With a broken heart and an injured soul,
head bowed,
I memorialize today the 1,200
Saintly Jews from our township
who were so cruelly murdered by the killers.

Before my eyes appears the picture
of my little hamlet;
the synagogue, the study center,
the precious children with their shining black eyes,
their curled side curls.

In my ears ring the sweet little voices
And from the Eastern wall (in the synagogue, we hear)
"Amen, May his Great Name…"
(A line from the Kaddish repeated by the congregation)

From all this nothing remains but a heap of earth
on top of the big family grave
on the hill of Halbow
Where the book (of History) of Zmigroder Jews is located.

Shia Tzimet then recited the Kaddish, followed by the reciting of several psalms. He then continued with his eulogy.

I bow my head before you 1,200 saints of my city Zmigrod, who were so brutally murdered by beastly hands. My heart is torn apart when I read these few lines. What can I, as a survivor of the holy community of Zmigrod, say on behalf of the massacred people? I, merely a human being, an earthly creature, what can I do for you? Presently, I am not able to pay the full respect and honor that you saintly murdered Jews deserve. With the lighting of a candle, reciting the Kaddish and reading a section of mishnayot, I think that these acts will please you murdered people who suffered so much until your souls left you. My conscience is not satisfied with these deeds. I am hopeless, I stand here with my arms crossed and I do not know what else I can do for you.

As the Jewish presence in Poland declined, Zmigrod received fewer and fewer Jewish visitors. Pinkas Wohlmut continued to live in total Jewish isolation in Zmigrod. He tended to Halbow and the Jewish cemetery in Zmigrod. The survivors of the camps and the repatriated Jews of Zmigrod left Poland and headed to the German and Austrian D.P. camps.

The Jews remained in the D.P. camps several years and then most of them left for Israel when the State of Israel was proclaimed and it opened the doors to all Jews wanting to come to the country. Other Jews went to the USA, Canada, Australia, South America and Western Europe. Many of them did not forget their little town of Zmigrod and formed societies of former Zmigroder residents. Below is a partial list of members of the Zmigroder society in Israel. The society was active for a number of years. It held annual memorial meetings on July 7, or 22 Tamuz, according to the Jewish calendar. The society continued to memorialize yearly the tragedy of the Jewish community of Zmigrod and Osiek.

The society helped the needy Jews of Zmigrod in Israel. The society also sent money to Pinkas Wohlmut in Zmigrod to repair and maintain the cemetery of Zmigrod and the Halbow burial ground. The former Zmigroder in New York established a new society called "Ahavat Achim" or brotherly love society under the leadership of Jakob Leibner. The old Zmigroder society had ceased to exist. The new Zmigroder society established a cemetery for the members, and assisted needy Zmigroder in the USA and Israel. The society also helped Pinkas Wohlmut to maintain the Halbow burial ground. The society also memorialized the Zmigroder Jews that perished in the Shoa.

Below is a partial list of the members of the Zmigroder association in Israel. The names follow the Hebrew order of names below.

Partial list in Hebrew of the members of the Zmigroder society in Israel

Edelstein, Hannah
Leshkowitz, Zahava
Weinberg, David
Findling, Mark

Feller, Israel
Engel, Yehoshua
Kinderman, Sara
Leizer, Yehiel
Westreich, Mina
Findling, Chaim

ארגון יוצאי ז'מיגרוד

ב"ה

לכבוד

ה ז מ נ ה

כב' מוזמן בזה להשתתף באזכרת אבל

לזכר קדושי עירנו וסביבתה

ש ת ת ק י י ם

ביום _____ כ"ב חמז. _____ ש.ז. בשעה 6.00 בערב

בבית הכנסת ע"ש .חבד' רחוב הרב קוק 16. תל-אביב.

נא לדייק!

בכבוד רב
בשם הועד הזמני
של יוצאי ז'מיגרוד והסביבה
ז א ב ג ר ו ס
תל-אביב, אריסטובול 4

Rare blank of the invitation letter to the members of the Zmigroder society in Israel to memorialize the martyred Jews of Zmigrod and vicinity. The society has ceased to exist for lack of living members.

Ze'ev Gross was the temporary head of the committee located at 4 Aristobul Street in Tel Aviv

Entrance gate to the Zmigroder section of the cemetery in New Jersey

The Zmigroder society "Ahavat Achim."
The columns are inscribed with the names of Zmigroder Jews who perished in the
Shoah. Behind the columns we see burial tombs of former Zmigroder Jews who died in
the USA

The intention was to represent the continuation of Jewish life that the Nazis and their helpers tried to erase from memory. My late father, Jakob Leibner, the son of Ephraim and Shprince Reisel Findling–Leibner, a native son of Zmigrod, devoted a great deal of time and energy to this society.

Pinkas Wohlmut's "matzevah," or gravestone, in Zmigrod

Pinkas Wohlmut continued to live a lonely Jewish life in Zmigrod. He tended to the Jewish cemetery and to the Halbow burial ground. He died on June 22, 1956.

His wife buried him at the old Jewish cemetery next to his ancestors as he wished. She left Zmigod for Israel. Pinkas's grave indeed closed Jewish history in Zmigrod. Jews continue to visit Zmigrod and reminisce of past days when Jews were an integral part of Zmigrod.

The late Jacob Leibner

Since the Jews could not be in Zmigrod any longer, they formed various groups or "landesmanshaften" wherever there were Zmigroder in the world. Jakob Leibner was very active on behalf of the Zmigroder society in New York and kept in touch with many of the Zmigroder survivors.

Second from left, Max (Mordechai) Findling, Leo Rosner and Shimshon Findling, son of Yechiel Hersh and Sima Findling. The Findlings were first cousins, natives of Zmigrod and survived the Shoah. They met in Zmigrod wth a former Polish acquaintance in the square of Nowy Zmigrod

Max Findling and Leo Rosner devoted a great deal of time, energy and money to maintain and preserve the Halbow monument and the Jewish cemetery at Zmigrod.

Max Findling and his wife visited Zmigrod on several occasions and supervised repairs and maintenance of the Halbow burial ground and the Jewish cemetery of Zmigrod. Max was very attached to Zmigrod and did everything in his power to memorialize the shtetl.

Below is a German record of Mordechai's work record during WWII.

Mordechai Findling's war record card maintained by the German authorities

The document was obtained from the Arolson files at Yad Vashem in Jerusalem. It is in poor condition but it describes the various horrible places where he was detained by the Germans.

Findling Mordechai (Markus), son of Eisk and
Rachel Findling. Stateless Jew.
Born in Nowy Zmigrod on July 23, 1923.
1940–1942 Arrested in Nowy Zmigrod and sent to
Dukla as a forced laborer.
12/7/1942 Returned to Zmigrod. Sent to Plaszow
labor camp.
1/5/1943– 1/1945. He was transferred to
Czenstochowa labor camp from Plaszow.
1/1945. Marched out of Czestochowa to another
camp but was freed along the way.
The card also indicates that he left Germany for Italy
and was on his way to Israel.

Simon (Shimon) Findling at the entrance to the Zmigrod courthouse.

Simon Findling is a native of Zmigrod, the son of Chiel Hersh and Sima Findling. The family left for France following WWI. Simon was in the French Arny.

With the defeat of France, he was interned in Switzerland but escaped to France where he joined the French resistance.

Max Findling surveying the restored Jewish tombs at the Zmigrod Jewish cemetery

The little hamlet of Zmigrod lost its entire Jewish population during WWII. There are no traces of the Jewish presence in Zmigrod except on some doorposts at the entrance of the house where the "mezuzah," or quotations of the bible, used to be inserted in the door frame. We also find a Jewish presence at the Jewish cemetery. But Zmigrod has no Jews. As a matter of fact, the entire Jaslo–Krosno region has no Jews. We find a few Jews in Krakow. It is indeed a sad story of an entire region that had a dense vibrant Jewish population and within a few years was converted into the biggest Jewish cemetery.

The Jewish cemetery of Zmigrod proper as seen recently by Jean Krieser, a descendant of Zmigrod.
(Photo courtesy of Jean Krieser)

CHAPTER IV
A Survivor's Story

Destruction of the Jewish Community of Zmigrod
Eyewitness account by Yehoshua Zimet

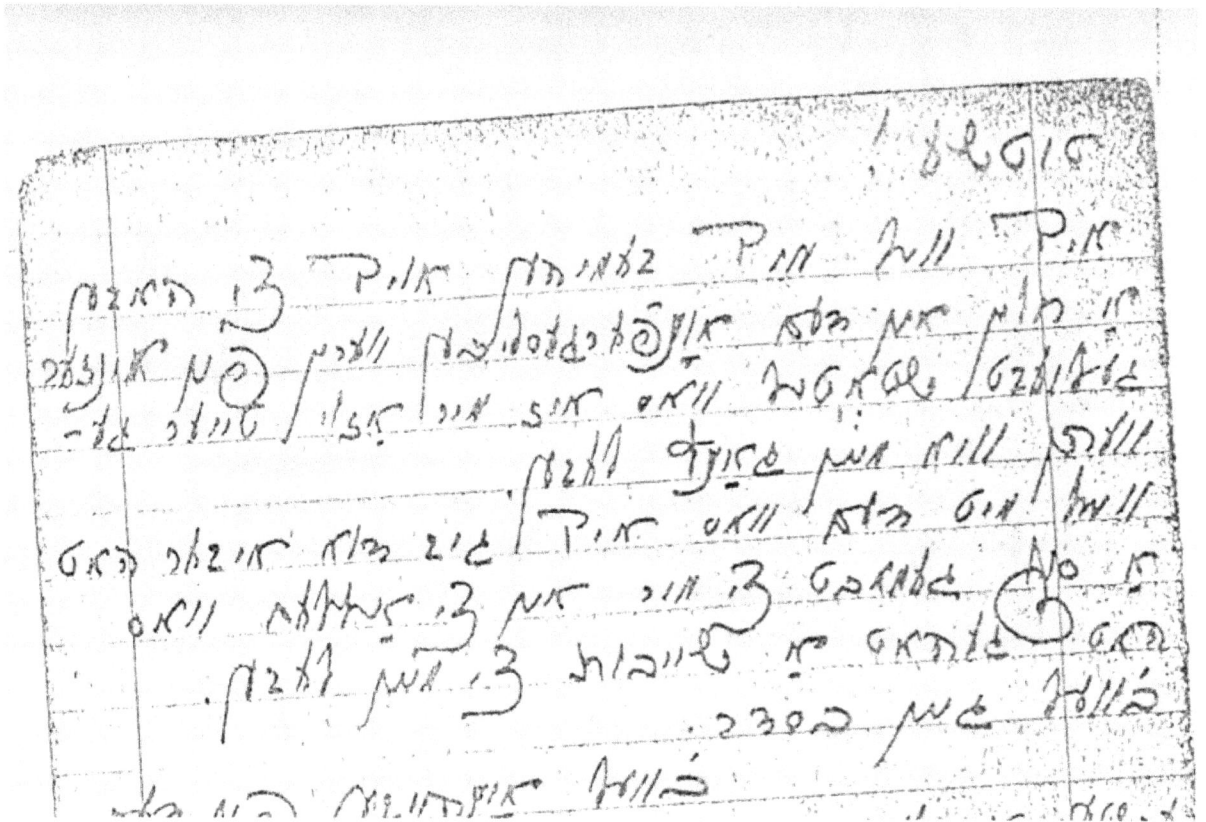

The document was written in Yiddish following the war by Shoah survivor Shia (Yehoshua) Zimet

The shtetl of Nowy Zmigrod is located south of Jaslo and Krosno, Galicia, Poland. The hamlet had a sizable Jewish population from the middle ages to the Shoah.

A survivor's testimony about the destruction of the Jewish community of Zmigrod [the name was officially changed after World War II to Nowy Zmigrod], in Galicia, Poland. The date of this written testimony in Yiddish is unknown, although we can safely assume that the document was written sometime after the war. The author did not sign the document but we can easily infer his name from the written pages as Shia [Yehoshua] Zimet. He was a member of a well–known family in Zmigrod and was well–versed in Jewish religious studies. He wrote the document to his friend, Naphtali Bromfeld, who spent the war years in Russia and wound up in New York City, where he remarried after his first family was killed in Zmigrod. Naphtali Bromfeld was supposed to have written a book dedicated to the Jews of Zmigrod and asked Shia Zimet to write the chapter dealing with the destruction of Jewish Zmigrod during the war, since he was a refugee at the time in Russia. We don't know whether the book was written or published, for none of the libraries has such a volume.

Hence the need to know what happened to the Jews of the city during the war.

Tutshe, [Term of endearment for Naphtali Bromfeld who was a dear friend of Yehoshua Zimet]

I will try to participate in your work dedicated to our lovely little town that was so dear to me. The material that I am providing drained me emotionally and all those that affected my life.

I will try to tell the story in a chronological time sequence as far as my memory permits.

The German Army entered Zmigrod shortly after the war started on September 1, 1939. Their arrival was uneventful. As a former Austrian Imperial soldier [Zmigrod was part of the Austro–Hungarian Empire] who had participated in the war under the command of the German General von Mackensen in World War I, I took the initiative and crossed the market place. I was going from my father's house to the place where I lived. My house was a tall country home which I feared might be shelled by rifle or artillery fire since it was prominently situated and was visible in the distance. To the south one could see the Slovakian border, to the east the cities of Dukla and Sanok, to the west the Jaslo–Tarnow–Krakow highway from one side and to Gorlce and Nowy–Sacz from the other side

I crossed the market, still wearing my beard but somewhat trimmed in a modern fashion. I must also mention that a group of about twenty young Jews had been working for the last few days cleaning the market place under the supervision of an Austrian soldier. As a matter of fact, most of the German troops that entered Zmigrod were Austrian and their behavior was much milder than their replacements, who were primarily German. Still, the Austrian supervisor decided to have some fun with the beards of these Jews and did not expect to hear a complaint from them, certainly not in German. I took the opportunity to present myself as a former Austrian Imperial soldier who was a candidate for the military chaplaincy and explained the meaning of the beards. I must have made an impression on him because he paid me an indirect compliment by pulling the beard of a young Jew and pointing to my beard, and saying that he should tend to his beard as I tend to mine.

I continued to cross in the direction of the house. The place was full of cannons and heavy field guns stretched out in all directions, ready to swallow everything in their midst under God's creation. On the rooftops were anti– aircraft cannons ready to fire at the skies. One such anti–aircraft cannon could be seen distinctly on the roof of the pharmacy and the other one on Shprincza the hunchback's roof [nickname by which people were frequently referred to without having anything to do with the particular noun or disability]. I walked and my heart raced, fearful of everything. I noticed the way in which the soldiers exchanged glances amongst each other as if thinking about me. As soon as I had crossed the market, suddenly a commotion began. The soldiers blocked all the exits of the market and rounded everybody up, Jew and Gentile. All the arrested were led to the courthouse and kept there for about two days. Then all of them, about 150 people, were released except for one Gentile who was shot for having part of a bullet in his possession. So ended one of the first Fridays of occupation.

On Sunday, the first day of Selichot [days prior to the Jewish New Year when special services are held and the shofar is blown in anticipation of the High Holidays], the Germans began to impose their rule. Indeed they were the masters in town. Searches began all over town under the pretext that weapons were being concealed. The soldiers zealously carried out their activities and turned everything upside down. Things began to disappear as though they never existed. Items were trampled and kicked about as if they were pieces of garbage. Finally, the search for weapons ended and ordinances began to appear. Each day new orders were posted on the walls.

Slowly the Germans were tying a rope around our neck and we were not even aware of it. Slowly the knot began to tighten and we began to experience breathing difficulties. A few days later, an order was posted on the walls ordering all Jews, young and old, to assemble within 15 minutes in the marketplace or face death. Simultaneously, as if on cue, German soldiers began to force their way into Jewish homes and forced all males into the street. Jews were driven like cattle to the market. Before the pharmacy were placed three small tables and behind each of them sat an official who issued everybody a piece of paper that would serve as an identity card. On it were written the name, the date, and the stamp of the military commander. The elder people were sent home immediately. The younger ones were placed on trucks, hands above their heads, and taken away. Moshe Kalman, Shia [Yehoshua] Buksbaum's grandson, who was on one of these trucks, returned by miracle six months later and told us the horrors that they experienced, but this somewhat later.

The troubles of the day and the fears of the night became a regular feature of our life. We already knew that we couldn't undress for the night since we might have to seek shelter in the cellar or in the attic. Sometimes we had to leave the house and run alongside the marketplace down the mountain towards the villages of Samokleski, Brezew and others. On other occasions, we ran in the opposite direction, which led us straight into the fields where the running water covered our tracks. Even in the distance we could hear the rifle fire directed at shadows trying to find shelter. A few days later, these nightly escapes were no longer possible since no one was permitted to leave town. Anyone caught beyond the town signs delineating Zmigrod could be and was shot on the spot, as was David (who is this referring to?), the dumb, or the few refugees from the village of Podzer who wanted to get some potatoes from the farmers in order to subsist. Food presented a serious problem and would get worse with time, but I shall return to the food situation in the following pages.

Rosh Hashanah [the Jewish New Year] was on September 14 and 15, 1939. On the first day of the holiday the Jews assembled at the synagogue and services began. My father, may he rest in peace, in his customary traditional New Year intonation [each holiday has a traditional intonation that is used by cantors in conducting services], led the congregation in reciting the opening prayer of Adon Olam [Master of the World], with great fervor. He barely finished the first lines when a band of German soldiers burst into the place and began to beat mercilessly anyone in their way. The congregants dispersed in every direction and considered themselves lucky that the incident had ended in such a manner, since in other places such as Dynow, a small hamlet near Zmigrod, the Germans shot all the congregants at the Rosh Hashanah service. Amongst those shot were a few Jews from Zmigrod who sought refuge there and were never permitted to leave the place after the Germans arrived. They were Moshe Shia Tzanger and his son from the village of Fristig and Israel Gross's son, Hozek. Thus we spent the first day of Rosh Hashanah in Zmigrod.

Yom Kippur was on the 23rd of September, 1939. On the eve of the holiday, some neighbors came and begged me to hold services in my place. I had ample space and a main gate which could be closed and watched. However the danger was there and I knew what to expect in case of trouble. But it was the eve of Yom Kippur, the holiest night in the Jewish year and Jews everywhere would be reciting the Kol Nidrei prayers [special prayers for the eve of Yom Kippur]. I was still debating the question when my wife, may she rest in peace, entered the discussion and said that perhaps the recitation of these prayers under these circumstances would have the desired effect and all evil decrees against the Jews will be overturned. I was swayed by the argument since I, too, wanted to pray and open my heart to the Almighty and relieve the heavy pressure that had built up inside me. I gave my consent and we prepared ourselves to pray and open our hearts to the Almighty, especially at the Kol Nidrei service.

Towards evening the worshippers began to filter in. Some women and children also came and entered a separate room. The doors were closed, the curtains were shut and the gate was bolted. My wife lit the candles [candles are lit on the eve of Sabbath and all the holidays]. As I recall this moment it burns my heart, the tears swell my throat and I feel that I could cry at any moment. I will never be able to forget these moments in my life. The congregation began to recite the Tefilah Zake [individual prayer recited before the Kol Nidrei service]. Now we needed a cantor to lead the congregation in prayer. We looked around; unfortunately, no experienced or professional cantor was available. The congregation demanded that I conduct the service and despite all my protestations, I had to accept the job. I approached the task with trepidation since I had to pray not only for myself and my family, but for an entire congregation, and at a critical time. Still I began to intone quietly the traditional Kol Nidrei chant, intermingled with the tears and sobs that I could barely control. At any moment, the entire congregation would begin to cry and as we continued our prayers; indeed we heard the crying of the women and children for our suffering had exceeded all imagination.

Thus the service continued, each person pleading with the Almighty to alleviate our pain and suffering, and I began to recite the prayer Yaale Tachnouneinou, accept our begging, our lamentations, our prayers for forgiveness, please accept them, if not for our sake then for the sake of the small children. So we prayed and cried and eventually finished the service. We all considered ourselves lucky that the service had ended without incident and all the congregants left.

Yom Kippur morning services couldn't be held, as the Germans were grabbing Jews for work so everyone was trying to hide. Thus we spent the holiest day of the year in Zmigrod.

Succoth [the holiday of booths in memory of the Jews wandering through the desert on their way to Israel] soon arrived. Most Jewish homes used to have a sukkah in which they would partake of their meals, study and even sleep during the 8 days of the holiday. Now, one could only see them hidden in courtyards or behind walls since no one wanted to attract attention. People who did not have a sukkah did not think of going to a neighbor for fear of attracting attention or overstepping the evening curfew, which began at 7 p.m. Any Jew found in the street beyond this hour was shot. Jews tried to make themselves disappear.

On the last days of Succoth or to be exact, the night of the Simhat Beit Hashoeva [the ancient festival of drawing water for the Temple], the synagogue of Zmigrod began to burn. Since the incident of Rosh Hashanah, services had not been held in the big synagogue and it was completely empty. Nevertheless the fire started and then spread to the study center. Both buildings were huge places [the synagogue was an old historical building with a circular dome and thick walls that gave it the appearance of a Moorish structure. It also had encrusted the Polish eagle, a rare event in Polish synagogues, and nobody knew the reason. The structure was declared a national historical building by the Polish government after World War I.]. The study center was built of metal and cement and was a more recent building. It had huge 12–meter running beams of steel to support the roof. The study center was also used for services since the synagogue was unable to accommodate all the congregants. Both buildings burned throughout the night. Apparently, special squads placed dynamite and other inflammable materials into these edifices in order to create infernos of this nature. These units seemed to specialize in the destruction of synagogues and Jewish study centers. Of course, no one could approach the fire since it was after curfew. Nevertheless, the only buildings to burn were these two buildings. The surrounding buildings were not affected although they were close by. On one side of the synagogue was the house of Tuvia Ginsberg and on the other side was the one of Yudel Tzanger. Amazingly, the huge flames didn't affect anything but these holy places.

The fire having raged for some time, the Germans then ordered the neighboring Jews to start extinguishing the fires. The Jews were told to use buckets and to put out the fire which was by now raging beyond control. The Germans pushed the Jews to run with their buckets into the synagogue and some of them caught fire, as in the case with Shalom Pepper, who barely escaped being burned alive. Since I did not live close by, I did not have a front–row seat but I saw the sky and it was like a sheet of flames. The crying and shouting could be heard throughout the township, but we couldn't help as the curfew was in force and we lived a distance from the fire. We spent the night in fear, panic and terror. In the morning we all filtered our way to the synagogue and the study center and saw for ourselves the destruction of our third temple. The Germans, of course, acted dumb and asked everybody questions about the fire in the hope that a Jew would point the finger at them and this would give them an excuse to stage a riot directed at the Jews.

The physical destruction of Jewish books, a common practice in the dark ages, made its reappearance. Jewish books and texts were burned in the middle of the market square. All good things in Zmigrod seemed to start on Tuesday, the day that G–d saw only beauty in His creation and continued with His celestial endeavors. The day began as a beautiful morning appeared on the horizon. I do not remember the date [probably, November 20th, 1939]. The sun was already spreading its rays in all directions and awakening the earthly creatures from their nightly slumber. Nobody anticipated a thing.

Suddenly a unit of about 80 Germans appeared out of nowhere and claimed that they had been sent as a punishment detail for an infraction that the city committed against the occupants. They surrounded the town, dressed in battle gear and ready for action, but nobody knew what form it would take. The Jewish population was resigned. The puzzle was soon solved as they began to seize Jews in the street and from their homes to do their dirty work for them. The Germans now had a work detail of about 50–60 Jews to carry out their orders. They distributed these people amongst the various search parties that began to search individual Jewish homes. The search meant turning each household upside down and inside out, so to speak. Everything from food to furniture was confiscated and had to be carried out into the street. One Jew, Zalman Tzanger, omitted an old bedspread. He was badly beaten–up and only several hours later managed to be carried to his house. Reuven Eisenberg was amongst these workers. The people from Zmigrod knew him well, for he was a Talmudic scholar and well versed in its literature. He continued his studies and was very observant. The search continued until Friday. People aged before their time due to fear and panic. Some developed heart conditions and others had seizures. The scenes were beyond description and yet continued until everything had been taken from the Jews.

As soon as the searches stopped, the Germans began their assault on the Jewish spirit. The most priceless possessions of the Jewish home were now destined to be burned. Every Jew had to bring all Jewish books, regardless of language, to the pharmacy in the marketplace. They also had to bring the religious articles in their possession. Tefilin [phylacteries used in daily morning payers by religious Jews], talit [prayer shawl worn by married men during the morning service], Jewish religious artifacts and of course all Jewish religious books had to be carried to the marketplace. All these items were collected into a huge pile, doused with gasoline and ignited with a match. All this work had to be done by the Jews themselves.

At this point, I would like a few moments to describe my father's library which was also dear to me. Who in Zmigrod did not know my father's library where we spent so much time studying the books of Sender Zimet. You [Bromfeld] were certainly familiar with the library where you spent so much time. The books were indeed beautiful both in appearance and content. It is not easy to describe their significance, especially the Talmud set that was printed in Wilno [one of the printing centers of religious books in Eastern Europe]. Each volume had its own name, and stories abounded about them, especially about the Talmud set. Many legends were spun about the manner in which these volumes had been acquired, and hand written comments were added in some of the margins.

My father loved these books and cared for them so that they were in good condition. The bindings displayed a variety of colors ranging from copper to gold, which could be seen through the glass windows, for the books were all enclosed in six huge library bookcases. It was a rich Jewish library that contained: the Talmud Bavli [Babylonian Talmud, named after the country where the complex religious–judicial work was developed and codified], the Talmud Yerushalmi [complex religious–judicial work developed and codified in Palestine but much smaller in scope than the previous one], the volumes of the Shulhan Aruch [book that codifies the behavior of religious Jews in their daily life], the work of the Baal Haturim [commentaries on various religious books], the works of Rambam [Maimonides, referred to as the eagle], Midrashim [religious commentary books explaining certain passages or concepts],

Mishnayot with running commentaries and without, books of Jewish philosophers, original manuscripts as well as literary works, such as the first edition of "Love of Zion" by Abraham Mapu [one of the early Hebrew writers in Eastern Europe].

You are probably curious to know what happened to the library. The search party did not miss my father's house; but the Germans planned it so that it would be last house to be searched. Indeed, 10 Germans soon burst into the house followed by about 30 Jews. Books were found in the attic, the cellar and the pantry. The Germans were very happy with the booty and ordered the Jews to carry out the books to the front of the house. The work lasted two hours. They then lined up the Jewish workers and any other Jew found in the area into a single line. Now they insisted that the owner of the books present himself to the chief of the search party or they would look for him throughout Zmigrod. My father was hidden but overheard the German demand and feared the forthcoming search. He surrendered and presented himself to the Germans.

Their leader signaled for the show to begin. They took my father to the head of the column and put his large Turkish Sabbath talit [many religious Jews prayed on Sabbath and holidays in a special talit and had another one for regular weekly services. The material for these talitot came originally from the Orient, hence the name] with its large silver embroidery and placed it on his head as though as he was about to pray. They then called two of his granddaughters, one aged 20 and the other one 22, and told them to support his arms. They stretched out his arms as far as they could reach and placed the heaviest volumes on them. The two young ladies supported the arms since the books were heavy. Now the order was given to all the Jews to pick up as many books as they could carry and to line up in an orderly fashion behind the old man. One is reminded of the old traditional procession in Zmigrod, which was called Green Thursday when the local priest was led under a canopy to the services in the church. So they led my father to burn his books.

The people took another three trips to carry all the books while my father stood and watched as his library was being turned into a pile of rubble. Then the order was given to toss all these books into the burning fire and my father was told to place his volumes on top and cover them with his talit. The flames soon devoured the beautiful library as well as all the Jewish books in Zmigrod. The Jews were then ordered to go home. Imagine the joy of some of our hateful neighbors on seeing the destruction of our spiritual and cultural heritage in Zmigrod.

Sometime later, I became the head of the social services of the Jewish Community, the old established organizational framework within the kehilla [Jews in Eastern Europe were always organized into a communal framework which provided essential services such as education, charity, health, mutual support and burial facilities] had ceased to exist. Each person tried to distance himself from responsibility and from the community. People tried to be invisible; this was much healthier and safer. But some people had no choice, and one nasty Wednesday in Heshvan [Jewish month], or November, the mayor of our town, Mr. Radweinski, entered the store. He was never known to be friendly to Jews; on the contrary, he was quite anti–Semitic. But he seemed a bit sentimental, and I inquired as to the nature of his visit. He then informed me in Polish that he just received a call from the German district official in Jaslo [main administrative center in the area] who told him that Zmigrod would be receiving about 40 Jewish destitute families. The Polish secretary also informed him that a large transport of Jews just arrived in Jaslo. These Jews came from Lodz and would be dispersed throughout the area. They were stripped of everything of value and faced starvation. He then walked out of the store.

The information left me speechless and I relayed the story to my wife, who had just entered the store. She insisted that I tackle the situation, and my wife can be very demanding at times. After all, she is the daughter of Pinkas and Lea Dworah Lang, who were great benefactors of charity and saw to it that poor people were assisted in town. The news awakened in her the call to action. She already imagined seeing the poor, naked and hungry children standing about in this cold weather at the Jaslo railway station. She began to plead and to cry. The tears did it, for I loved my wife and had to take action in order to avoid more tears and sermons. I, too, was aware of the cruel times when entire Jewish families were uprooted from their homes, fathers were sent to Krosno [small town in the area], mothers perished, some of the children were sent to Gorlice [small town in the area] and others were sent to Zmigrod. They were robbed of their belongings and would be arriving like paupers to the new places and would depend for everything on the poor local Jews. Yesterday's manufacturer from Lodz is today's street cleaner or sewer worker. Yesterday's affluent woman is today's potato peeler. The student from last week is today's street cleaner or coach cleaner.

I was carried away with this notion of help and left the store. I went to the market and entered Heinech Berger's store and told him the story. He was an old activist and a well–known community figure. I also spoke to Moshe Shtrenger, who was also well known in the community. The three of us met and set in motion a plan to receive the Jews of Lodz. We also enlisted the aid of some women to organize a welcoming committee. It was headed by Mrs. Baile Krebs and Mrs. Golda Kanner. Our group was soon joined by other young men and women who helped us assemble clothing and blankets which we sent to Jaslo for the refugees so that they didn't freeze on their way to our township.

Simultaneously, preparations were made to receive the destitute families. Food, clothing and bedding items were donated without second thoughts. Indeed, these were the first Jewish families to be so brutally uprooted from their homes and sent to Zmigrod.

About 200 people arrived in town. The transport contained young, old, children and families. Each brought with them their problems and needs. A hot meal was prepared for them, which consisted of potato soup and hot tea. I would summarize their reception by saying that all the people were lodged as best as possible, given the little time and the few resources that we had at our disposal. Our activities were soon overtaken by the official Jewish Social Self– Help Organization, known as the J.S.S., which had branches in many Jewish communities in Poland [all Jewish social and welfare organizations were ordered to work within the framework of the J.S.S. or the Judische Sociale Selbsthilfe. This organization was placed under the leadership of Dr. Michael Weichert with headquarters in Krakow]. The branch in Zmigrod was founded by a former native son who returned to Zmigrod, namely Hersh Rab. He and his family would pay dearly for his activities, but this somewhat later.

It seemed that the Germans wanted to make their job easier and decided to let the Jews do their dirty work, such as rounding up workers, assembling furniture, clothing, coffee, soles for shoes and anything that was not bolted down. They gave an order that a Judenrat be established consisting of 12 men which would carry out

German orders. Hence no need to involve oneself in executing orders [the actual order came from the office of Heidrich in his famous Schnelbrief dated 21/9/1939 affecting all recent occupied areas as a general policy and had nothing to do with the individual Gestapo or police chief in the local township].

Negotiations and dealings started amongst the Jews of Zmigrod as to who should be a member of this Judenrat until it was finally selected. None of the members of this office lived long enough to make it to the concentration camps [which would be the next stop for some of the Jews of Zmigrod]. People such as Hersh Eisenberg, young and strong, could have possibly survived the camps, yet he was beaten mercilessly by the German district chief. He did not even want to use a bullet and kill him. Instead, he just beat him, struck his head repeatedly with his riding whip. He was the head of the Judenrat. The others members were Yekel Bronfeld, Moshe Haim Birenbaum, Shia Wahl, Hersh Duvid Zilber, Shia Bobker, Shia Zilber, Shmiel Weinstein, Yekel Diamant and Nute Parness [I am not certain about his membership] and still other members whose names I do not recall.

The Judenrat was given offices and began to function under the direct orders of the Gestapo office in Jaslo. The latter office would send officials to Zmigrod several times a week as the need arose. These officers would present their orders to the Judenrat. This body would then have to implement the orders or face the consequences. Life began to flow under this arrangement. Occasionally, 15–20 trucks would pull into town and search parties would begin. Everything of value was confiscated. Many items disappeared into the pockets of the searching soldiers and the rest was loaded onto the trucks. When the pickings began to decline, they would compensate themselves by grabbing young Jews and pushing them into the trucks. These people would be sent to heavy construction sites and after a few months would be released. Most of them returned as ghosts, since they were never fed or equipped for these heavy jobs.

Another popular sport was to seize a Jew and to shoot him in front of people as in the case of Haim Itzik Freund. He was killed as a joke; supposedly his son Kalman Mendel Freund sold some cigarettes. Such events occurred frequently and when they ended with one victim the township considered itself lucky. When there were no victims, we were all very happy. We were condemned people and above our heads hung the death sentence. We got accustomed to the searches and the German shows, for we had nothing more to give. Life, however, continued in spite of the daily horrors, miseries and fears.

I have to shorten the story since it is affecting me. I will concentrate on the activities of the local J.S.S., where Hersh Rab and his family ended their lives in tragedy. He received his death sentence the same day that the rest of the Jewish community was killed in Yosh. Hersh Rab was the president of the local J.S.S., which also included Hersh Sheinwetter, myself [Shia Zimet], Getzil Shiff, Haim Shia Birnhan, Miriam Fessler, Idesen's son-in-law and David Leizer. We provided the social, nutritional and sanitary needs of the poor Jews in town regardless of length of residence. We established a public kitchen that distributed, each day, 350 breakfasts and lunches. Money was obtained from various sources, including weekly contributions from the well established families in town. The latter also maintained the Judenrat. Our office worked, as well as conditions enabled us to function, and we tried to be helpful. Cases that refused to cooperate with us were referred to the office of the Judenrat and they handled these situations.

One day, 5 truckloads of Jews from Krakow arrived in town. The police escort informed us that more Jews were on their way to Zmigrod. We were stunned, for we were incapable of receiving more refugees since our resources, financial and physical, were already stretched to the limit. We decided to appeal for help to Jaslo. Hersh Rab turned officially to the J.S.S. district office in Jaslo and asked for material and financial help. He also asked the office to use their connections to stop sending refugees to Zmigrod since the town had no more facilities. Jaslo did not reply, so Hersh Rab decided to send a telegram to one of the main offices of J.S.S. in Krakow, where he explained the town's situation. The presiding officer, Dr. Titham Gleich [there seems to be an error here, the head of the organization was Dr. Michael Weichert] received the cable and intervened in Jaslo. The complaint was recorded and the German district official in Jaslo took it as a personal act against him. The next day, Hersh Rab received an order to appear in his office and to bring with him his correspondence with the J.S.S. office in Krakow. We, the members of the local committee, were unaware of the telegram. Finally, we were shown the document and became aware of the gravity of the situation. We decided to intervene on his behalf by offering a heavy bribe to the food commissioner who extricated Rab from the district henchmen. The latter, however, never forgave him for the telegram; he merely postponed his vengeance for a later day.

That day indeed soon arrived when all the Jews were assembled in Bals place and waited. The district chief arrived in a cab, and on leaving it, called for Rab. The latter stepped forth, whereupon the German slapped him across the face and told him: "Now you will also impose on me Mr. Gleich? Where is your family?" Fearfully, his wife, Fridka, and children, Yumek and Shmerek, took a few steps in the direction of the German. I do not have to describe the painful scene and to say that every Jew of Zmigrod wanted to be as far away as possible from this place. As soon as the family reached the German, they were told to climb onto one of the standing trucks that came to take away the crowd of Jews to the forest of Halbow.

Here I will describe the day that ended Jewish life in Zmigrod. For on this day, our dearest and nearest ceased to exist, killed in the most brutal manner yet invented by the human mind. This day is chiseled in my mind and inscribed in my heart with bloody letters. This is the bloody Tuesday in Zmigrod, July 7th, 1942 [22 Tammuz, Tasha`b].

A few days before this tragic date, we discovered what happened to the Jews in the nearby hamlet of Fristig [Frysztak], to be exact five days earlier. The Germans assembled about 800 Jews: young and old, men and women, boys and girls. They were taken to the woods and there they were killed. Having traveled a great deal with Hersh Rab, since we worked in the J.S.S. office together and were familiar with the surroundings, enabled us to carry out our job to the best of our ability.

We didn't think that we could let things go as far as they did in Fristig. We thought that we could avoid the destruction of the Jewish community by reaching an agreement with the German district chief, Dr. Genz. He was tall, had a lanky body and limped as he walked. He looked at you with two steel– blue German eyes, always had a riding whip in his hand and an angelic smile. He received us and we talked to him while he paced the room. We were convinced that we had an agreement when he assured us not to worry and insisted that the matter was settled. Also the chief of the Gestapo, Mr. Rashwitz, gave the same assurances.

We had to put up a 24–hour collateral of 100,000 zlotys [Polish currency] to show good bargaining faith. This sum was huge, given the financial situation of the Jewish community in Zmigrod and the limited time available to collect the sum. Help was asked from some of the Gentile neighbors such as the local notary and a few others. The sum was at last raised and presented to the district chief. It was accepted with the usual smile but it soon transpired that all the plans were implemented as though there was no agreement. Heavy trucks loaded with digging material soon passed the town. Rumors had it that huge pits were being dug along the Hungarian road, outside Zmigrod. Others rumors also began to circulate. The readers can imagine our thoughts at these moments.

People began to assemble in small groups in the marketplace, at homes, in well–hidden places; tragedy was everywhere. We resorted to the usual Jewish weapons: fasting, reciting psalms and candle lighting. The fast was announced for one day. An entire day was spent in fasting and praying in makeshift praying places and what was left of the study center. At the cemetery, candles were lit everywhere. We hoped that G–d would revoke the impending edict and save us for the sake of the small children.

Monday passed and the order was already posted that on Tuesday, at 7 a.m., all living Jewish souls will assemble in the square under the bridge. The whole night, no one slept a wink, the darkest thoughts crossed our minds and somehow the night passed.

My dear readers you, too, will overcome reading these pages, just as you managed to overcome the reading of the painful pages of Spain [reference to the exile of the Jews of Spain and the Inquisition], Chmielnitzky [large–scale massacres of Jews throughout the Pale of settlements], etc. However, those who did not witness it in person cannot conceive of it happening unless they are gifted with creative artistic skills. Tuesday morning began to appear, a beautiful sun in a blue sky. The majestic rays warmed every free heart but not our Jewish hearts. The birds were chirping their morning tunes and down below the Jewish mothers were awakening their little children from their nightly slumber not knowing what fate awaited them.

Soon, Jewish policemen burst into the homes and rushed us to our appointment with death. An order from the Germans was holy to them and had to be carried out to the letter. The crowd in the market grew by the minute. Nobody seemed missing, thanks to the effective job done by the Jewish police. Besides, people did not believe in disobeying orders or in hiding, not that it would have helped, and most answered the call.

The leaders of the Judenrat came out of their office and led the procession towards the square under the bridge. People embraced each other, kissed each other, cried and bemoaned their fate, especially mothers who were supposed to lead their children to the wedding canopy were presently leading them to their death. The people threw their last glances at the town so familiar to them. Never did they imagine that these were their last glimpses of their ancestral homes. The column moved, we passed the destroyed synagogue, the study center, each of us involved in himself, still everybody glanced at these places. Here we used to sit and spin far–fetched dreams. We entered the square with our dark thoughts.

Various police formations, Polish, Ukrainian and German units surrounded the square. All exits were sealed. Everybody stood in fear and faced a dark unknown fate but terror was everywhere. Each person was wrapped up in his innermost thoughts, young mothers were breast–feeding their infants, everybody waited.

Soon, some empty trucks appeared and they formed a special line which revealed to some people their intention. Now, they were certain that the rumors they heard about the pits were correct. The huge ditch, 20 meters long, 30 meters wide and 3 meters deep was ready. Several private cars arrived, the district chief and the chief of the Gestapo stepped out. The former immediately called for the chief of the Judenrat, Mr. Hersh Eisenberg. The latter handsome, tall as a tree in blossom, was a bit crestfallen due to the beating he received from the German. He took a few steps in the direction of the officials and was ordered to produce tables and benches as well as food and beverages. He was also told that all the gold and jewelry in the possession of the Jews must be handed over instantly. Naturally a collection began on the spot and everything of value was taken. Watches, gold chains, rings, pearls, valuables and cash were seized and placed in a pile on the ground. These items were to be supposedly returned after the assembly. It turned out to be wishful thinking and soon proved fatal.

The tables and benches were set up as was the buffet. The tables were loaded with food and drinks which consisted of fine liquors, wines and a large assortment of bottles of beer. Hersh Sheinwetter was sent especially home to keep sending beer and cases kept coming. The party finished, the show started. No other word could describe the action that followed. Indeed, it was a regular show for these murderers and it wasn't their first or last act of entertainment.

First call, Rab stepped out, then the next call, all those 60 years of age and over stepped forth. There were about 1,600 Jews presently in Zmigrod: natives, villagers from nearby places such as Osiek and refugees who came since the war from Lodz, Krakow and other places. Several hundred Jews stepped forth and they were told to sit in a special place. They were not permitted to stand. These people were already condemned and surrounded by the police. Now a break was called for.

Indeed, the various police formations began to drink and eat. They also put some old Jews on benches and made fun of them. The food and beverages finished, the show was over and back to work.

Up to this point, families were together. Now it was more systematic, rows of men, women and children were formed. To enforce the formation of rows, an SS man in uniform kept in hand a huge stick with a huge neck that grabbed or collared people into the proper row. Anyone protesting was immediately and brutally beaten with the stick and led to a special place to await death.

Presently, all male Jews were disposed of and a new break was called for. The police again began to eat and to drink. They also took some scared old Jews and mocked them. Time had come for the women and children. Here, brutality was boundless and used mercilessly. Breast–feeding children were torn away from their mothers, small infants were plucked from the arms of their mothers, the screams, the shouts and the beatings were endless. The piercing screams of the mothers penetrated every inch of the heart and every cell of the brain.

I looked at the sky and at the sun and saw no shame for the sun continued to shine as it did yesterday. Perhaps it was pleased with what was taking place under its domain? I was certain that the sun would cease to shine and the sky would darken us and the murderers. But I was wrong. The sun did not cease, it continued to shine as it did other days and other times and it also appeared to me as though it was laughing at it all.

I asked G–d where was justice, where was mercy, how can You stand by and look at it all? Do You want to deny Your own Torah? You who have emphasized so much humanity and pity! It is forbidden to remove the young birds from their nest while their mother flies about, the calf is not to be separated from her mother before the eighth day. All of these things in order not to inflict pain to the mother animal. The cow and her calf cannot be slaughtered the same day, yet You watched as infants were torn from their mothers arms. You watched mothers seeing their children led by the murderers to the trucks? What about the commandment of spilling blood? How can You sit by during this bloodbath? Is there no more G–d? I felt like I am going to lose my mind and this was very possible here. Let there be an end to it all. But it is not according to my will. The sun shines even brighter now, those rays are piercing our hearts.

It was now about 2 p.m. and another break of 15 minutes was called for. The police were served food and drinks and the entertainment was provided by the sorry lot of the scared Jews. The marked crowd was sitting on the ground, resigned to its fate. About 1,200 people: women, boys, girls and children. Now began the transfer of people to their assigned places. I am not capable of writing it down on paper, the human mind cannot comprehend it, how much cruelty exists in our world and all of it was unleashed right here in Zmigrod. Some of the people did not even make it alive to the trucks. The latter were going back and forth loaded with people. The trucks were crowded, which enabled some people to commit suicide while being driven to the slaughter, such as Frumet from the cigarette store and Sral [Israel] Merchower and family. They drank poison which Sheindzele [Sheindel Merchower] prepared in the pharmacy while working there. Children were tossed into the trucks as though they were logs. Over there [at Halbow] was a special unit that was armed with sticks, clubs and firearms. It kept pushing the arriving Jews into the huge pit. The children were pushed into the ditch alive in order to save bullets. When everyone in the ditch was killed, some barrels of lime were scattered above the ditch which was then covered with soil. Thus ended the lives of most Jews of Zmigrod.

The rest of us 400 Jews were told to bring 100,000 zlotys within 24 hours or else. We were then ordered to return home and to remain there. The Jews in the holding area were still awaiting their turn, for the trucks couldn't handle all the people at once. They were told to behave and to keep silent. We left the area and went home with a heavy heart. Some of us still had relatives, while others had none. Some homes had lights while others were totally dark. Nobody returned to these homes.

For five days we remained home and then a new order. All males aged 16– 45 were to report to the same square. We all obeyed and presented ourselves to the new chief of the Judenrat, Shmiel Weinstein, for the former one was killed. They selected about 150 people and put them immediately on trucks. They were not even permitted to say good–bye to their relatives or friends. They were sent to Plaszow [death camp on the outskirts of Krakow]. From these 150 people, about 18–20 survived the hell that was our lot, including the one of the writer.

I demand of myself daily: why the constant suffering? I will not write about my personal experiences since the suffering of the individual play a small role in the sea of troubles of the world. But I can ask myself whether I would not have been a happier person lying there with these saintly people? Why did I have to go from camp to camp not knowing whether I would survive it?

We started to work in camp. The pace was murder. Slacking was considered sabotage, which meant the bullet, death by shooting. After six weeks at camp, I received news that the remainder of the Jews at Zmigrod were assembled and sent to Belzec [death camp]. Thus ended Jewish life in Zmigrod.

I will not describe my personal experiences. Even this testimony is in short version.

Tutshe,

Please forgive me for summarizing the story. Some events did not even enter or were hardly mentioned. Believe me that the few things that were written down cost me a great deal of health. Pictures kept rushing into my mind and I began to visualize them. They rekindled the whole past and caused me great suffering and anguish. An entire parade of events kept marching by as though a motion picture was rolling and I did not know which scene to develop.

With these lines I am finishing my testimony. I wish you success in your endeavor.

[Signed] May G–d console us.

[Traditional religious signature on letters or documents that describe terrible afflictions imposed on the Jewish people.]

Names that appear in the testimony:

Berger, Heinech [Hanoch]
Birenbaum, Moshe Haim
Birnham, Haim Shia
Bobker, Shia [Yeshayahu]
Bromfeld, Yekel
Bronfeld, Naphtali
Buksbaum, Moshe Kalman
Buksbaum, Shia
Diamant, Yekel
Eisenberg, Hersh
Eisenberg, Reuven
Einsberg, Tuvia
Fessler, Miriam
Freund, Itzik
Freund, Kalman Mendel
Frumet
Ginzberg, Tuvia
Gross, Israel
Hozek, son of Israel Gross
Kanner, Golda
Krebs, Bela
Lang, Lea Dworah
Lang, Pinkas
Leizer, David
Merchower, Sral [Israel]
Merchower, Shindzele [Sheindel]
Parness, Nute
Pepper, Shulem
Rab, Fridka wife of Hersh Rab
Rab, Hersh
Rab, Shmerek, son of Hersh and
Frida Rab

Rab, Yudek, son of Hersh and Fridka Rab
Rimer, Shprincza, nicknamed the hunchback
Sheinwetter, Hersh
Shiff, Getzil
Shtrenger, Moshe
Tzanger, Ide's [Yehudit] son–in–law
Tzanger, Moshe Shia
Tzanger, Yudel
Tzanger, Zalman
Zimet, Sender
Tzimmet, Shia
Wahl, Shia
Weinstein, Shmiel
Zilber, Hersh David
Zilber, Shia

The document was written in Yiddish and translated into English by William Leibner

CHAPTER V
The Halberstam Rabbis

Rabbi Chaim Halberstam was born in the city of Tarnograd in 1793 when Poland was again partitioned. His father, Arieh Leibush, was a scholar and later assumed the post of dayan, or religious judge, of Przemysl, Poland. His mother was the daughter of a Rabbi Dawid of Brody, Galicia. On his father's side, he is a descendant of Rabbi Tzwi Hirsch, Rabbi of Halbershtadt, Germany; this is where the family name is derived from. According to tradition, the Rabbi changed his name to Halberstam in order not to grant recognition to a non-Jewish place. Rabbi Chaim traced his fatherly lineage to the great Rabbi Marshal, and on his mother's side to the great Rabbi Tzvi Ashkenazi of the 17th century.

He was a sick and lame child. The Hasidic tradition, however, told the story that the assistant teacher hit him on his leg, resulting in a permanent injury. As a young student, he already showed great intellect and erudition. He became fascinated by the Hasidic movement. His first Hasidic Rabbi was Yossel Halewi, a brother of the famous Rabbi "Hoze," or "Seer," of Lublin who lived in Tarnograd. On his insistence, the father, who was opposed to Hasidism, took him to see the Rabbi "Hoze" of Lublin.

He was so impressed by him that he continued to visit him until the "Hoze" passed away in 1814. Even after his death, Rabbi Chaim always honored the memory of the Rabbi of Lublin and frequently quoted him or his writings, and referred to him as our great saintly Rabbi of Lublin.

His great Torah idol was the Rabbi and head of the Yeshiva of Leipnik in Moravia, Czechoslovakia: Rabbi Baruch Teumim Frenkel, who later became world famous as the author of the "Baruch Teum" book.

Rabbi Chaim Halbershtam married, at the age of seventeen, the daughter of the Rabbi of Leipnik, Rachel. He lived with his father-in-law for a full year and studied at his yeshiva. At the home of the Leipniker Rabbi, Halbershtam developed a great interest in the book "More Nevuchim," a guide for the perplexed by the Jewish religious philosopher Rabbi Maimonides. He continued to study Maimonides and became very familiar with his rational philosophy.

At the age of eighteen, Rabbi Chaim Halbershtam was appointed Rabbi of Rudnik in central Galicia. The place was near the shtetl of Ropczyce, where the famous Rabbi Naphtali "Ropshitzer" lived. The relationship between the two rabbis was very smooth despite of the great age difference. The older Rabbi treated the young Rabbi as an equal. Rabbi Halbershtam fell under the spell of the Ropshitzer Rabbi and adopted many of his views, notably with regard to charity, and the combination of Hasidism with scholarship. All three elements are basic forms of the Sandzer Hasidic court. Rabbi Chaim always considered himself a student of the Ropshitzer Rabbi and always referred to him as "my saintly teacher and rabbi." He was imbued with the intelligence of the Ropshitzer court and borrowed from it many tunes that he brought to Sandz.

Following the death of the Ropshitzer Rabbi in 1827, Rabbi Halbershtam became restless and decided to leave the small hamlet of Rudnik. In 1828, he was invited to become "moyre tzedek," or righteous teacher, of Sandz. No community could have two official kehilla rabbis. If a community wanted someone desperately, they appointed him to the position of spiritual leader until the rabbi's seat became vacant. It is no accident that the invitation stipulated that the post being offered was that of "more tzedek," or righteous teacher, and not the position of rabbi, because Sandz had a Rabbi in the person of Baruch ben Moshe Dawid Landau. Rabbi Halberstam did not accept the invitation. He left Rudnik for the small shtetl of Zolin in the same area. Here he remained for a short period of time and moved to Kalow in Hungary where he remained rabbi for two years. He finally accepted, in 1830, the position of Rabbi of Sandz when the officiating rabbi passed away.

Rabbi Halberstam then remained his entire life in Sandz from 1830 to 1876, and became known throughout the world as "Rabbi Chaimel the Sandzer." Sandz became a center of Hasidism with the residence of Rabbi Halbershtam. Not only Hasidim of Galicia came to the court, but also Hasidim from all over Eastern Europe. Thousands of Hasidim came to the Rabbi on Saturday and holidays from Galicia, Slovakia, Carpathian-Russia, Hungary and the other parts of Poland. Together with the Hasidim also came famous rabbis and pious Jews, especially from the center of Galicia.

Rabbi Chaim Halberstam married three wives in succession. The first two were daughters of the Leipniker Rabbi mentioned above. He had a large family as one can see by looking at the genealogical chart. Most of his sons became rabbis in Galicia and his daughters married rabbis. The influence of the family was extremely powerful amongst the Jewish masses in Galicia. The Rabbi himself assumed the leadership of Hasidism in Galicia and shaped it into a powerful instrument of conservatism. In many aspects he accepted pragmatism; but when it came to religion or religious tradition, he would not budge an iota from the past.

He supported the cheder or traditional rote learning. He opposed general education and even Jewish education like Jewish history or bible study. He stressed Talmud study. Although himself an erudite scholar, he did not support such ideas for the majority. He insisted on absolute faith and devotion to it without hesitation. He wrote extensively and interpreted religious law. He answered and solved many theological questions that were written to him from many places. He has volumes of questions and answers that reveal a great deal of the period in question. He was accepted as a religious authority and as leader of the Jewish community of Galicia, especially the smaller townships. He passed away in Sandz in 1876. Rabbi Chaim Halberstam is buried at the cemetery, which is visited by Sandzer Hasidim to this day.

Yizkor Book of Nowy Zmigrod

The tombstone of Rabbi Chaim Halberstam in Sandz
(Picture donated by Jean Krieser of Paris, France)

As mentioned previously, Rabbi Chaim Halberstam had a number of sons and daughters. This is the tombstone for two of his sons: Rabbi Mordechai Ze'ev Halberstam and Rabbi Baruch Halberstam. The Latter became rabbi of the city of Rudnik where his father was once rabbi. He had several children and wanted them to be appointed as rabbis in Jewish communities in the region.

The post of rabbi of Zmigrod became available when the presiding rabbi passed away. Rabbi Baruch Halberstam and other Halberstam rabbis urged their followers to support Rabbi Sinai Halberstam, son of Rabbi Baruch and Pessel Halberstam to the post of Rabbi of Zmigrod. The Jewish community of Zmigrod was predominantly Hasidic and the majority were followers of the Sandzer Rabbi, Rabbi Chaim Halberstam. The kehilla considered it a great honor to have as rabbi a direct descendant of the famous rabbi, Chaim Halberstam . But there was some vocal opposition. Rabbi Barch Halberstam had to visit Zmigrod several times in order to get the appointment of Rabbi Sinai Halberstam. He was finally confirmed.

Rabbi Sinai Halberstam was born in 1869. He married Rukhama and they had the following children: Aaron, Yaakov, Dawid, Baruch, Chaim Juda, Awraham Yehezkel, Pessel, Israel and Arieh.

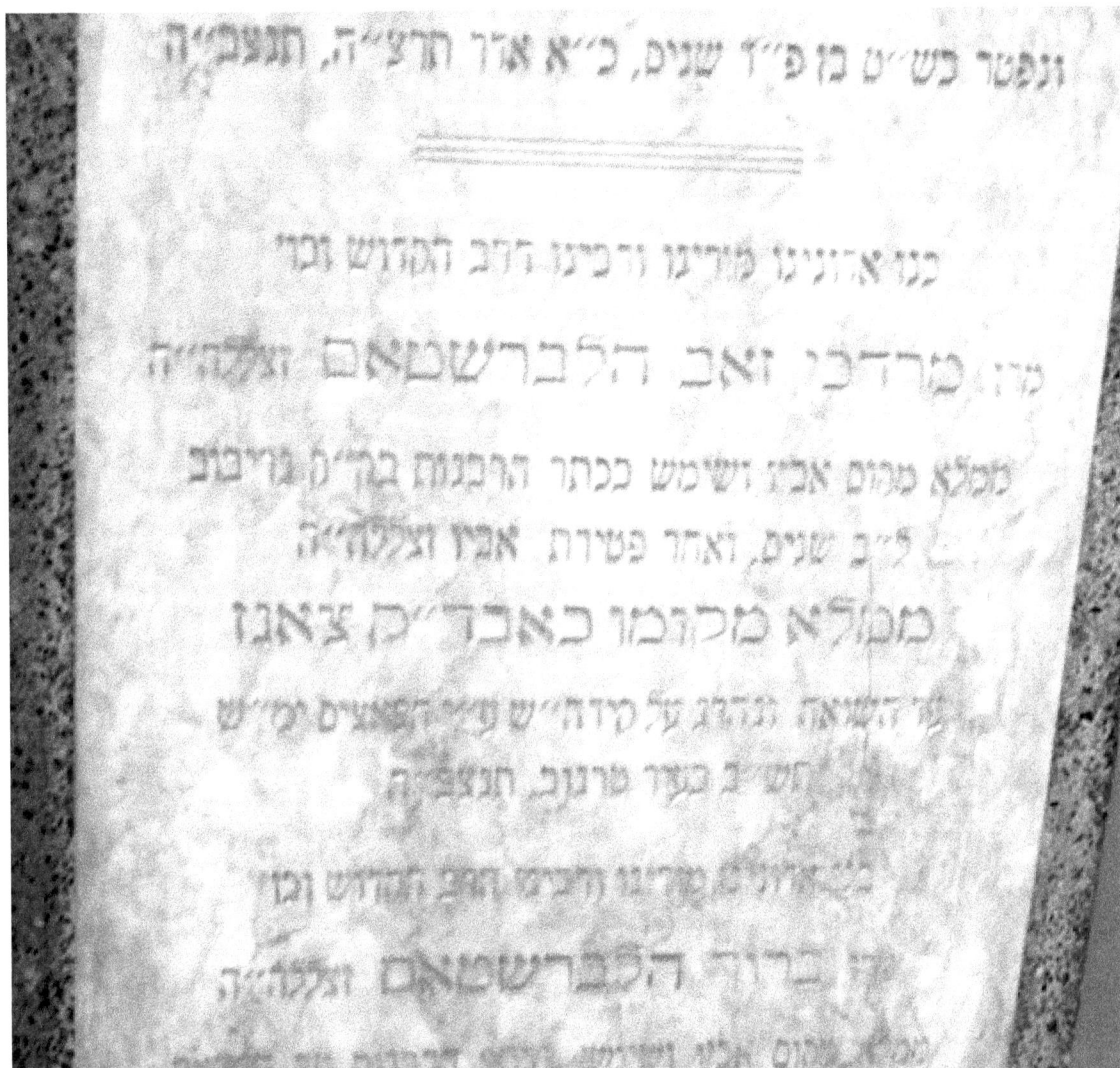

The tombstone of Rabbi Mordechai Ze'ev Halberstam and Rabbi Baruch Halberstam
(Picture donated by Jean Krieser of Paris, France)

The kehilla considered it a great honor to have as rabbi a direct descendant of the famous rabbi. He assumed his task and administered the spiritual needs of the community and the surrounding areas where Jews lived, namely the village of Osiek. Rabbi Halberstam followed in the footsteps of his grandfather and father, namely strict orthodoxy. He opposed the slightest of changes in spite of the great changes that faced Jews in Poland. Rabbi Halberstam had a large family and lived modestly for the community of Zmigrod was a relatively poor Jewish community.

The economic status of the Jews in Zmigrod was in a steady decline and the Polish government did everything in its power to speed up the process of Jewish pauperization. The community steadily lost young people in search of economic existence. Even Rabbi Sinai Halberstam left Zmigrod and appointed his son Aaron Halberstam to be rabbi of Zmigrod and Osiek. The latter shared the fate of the Jews of Zmigrod at Halbow with his entire family. Rabbi Sinai Halbershtam wound up in Russia during World War II, where he died of starvation. The Zmigroder society in New York always honored his memory. They even erected a memorial for him and his immediate family at the Zmigroder cemetery near New York City.

The Sandzer Hassidic movement split into several branches with time; namely Bobow-Sandz, Sadigora-Sandz, Klausenburg-Sandz and Zmigrod-Sandz. The latter branch continues to exist to the present.

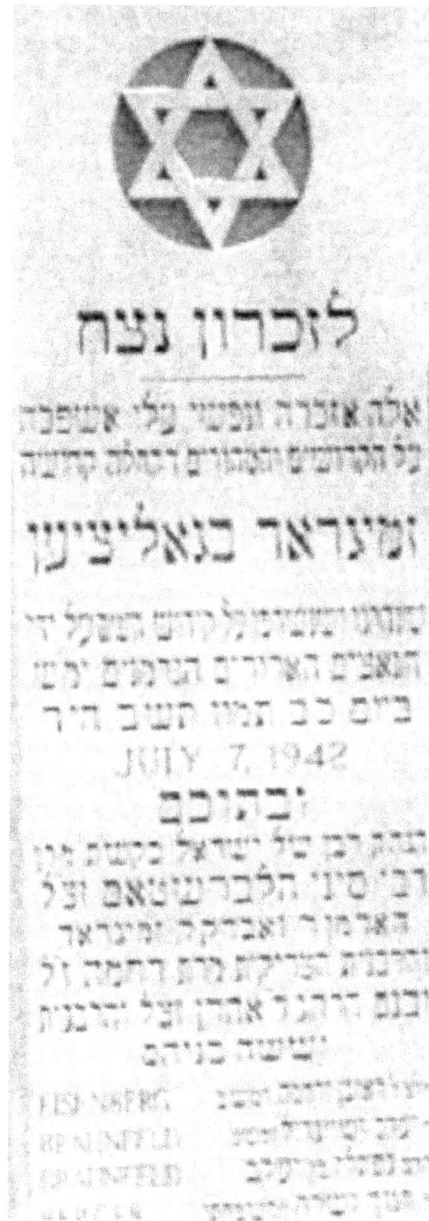

לזכרון נצח

אלה אזכרה ונפשי עלי אשפכה
על הקדושים הטהורים דקהלה קדושה

זמיגראר בנאליציען

נחנו ישמידו לל קדוש הכלל די
האצים הארירב הנעמס ידש
בים כב תמוז תשב היר
JULY 7, 1942

יבהוכם

הנהג רב של ישראל קשת אין
רב סיני הלברשטאם זצל
האדמור ואבדקה ימיצראר
ורבנת צדיקת מרת רתקה זל
יבנם דירגד אהרן זל ידובת
ששה בניהם

The Zmigroder Society in New York memorialized Rabbi Sinai Halberstam, his wife Rukhama, and his son Rabbi Aaron and his family

CHAPTER VI
Jewish Life in Pre–World War I Zmigrod
by Hersh Gross

סיפורי זכרונות שלי

נולדתי בשנת ע גליציה במערב קטנה הצ'בעיירה הגבול י' כי) זמיגרוד,(למשפחה
מיוחסת.

זקונים ובן במספר החמישי הייתי. גרוס נפתלי היה אבי(1858–1924) לבית שרה ואמי
אלסטר.

ילדים חמישה היו להוריי: משה, חיה, דוד, ואנכי רוזה. אלסטר אהרון בשם אח היה לאמא
ומינדל מלכה בשם ואחיות. אמרתי מיוחסת משפחה" ז ההורים מפי רק לנו נודע זה אך'ל.

הרמה במשפחה להתגאות הזדמנות בכל תמיד אהבה אמא, ר של בתו היתה כי' אלסטר משה
השנייה ז' מגורליצה ל, של ונכדה' כנר הרש) שמו על נקרא אני(, זץ כנר אביש רבי של לאחיו'ל, שכל
לרבנים נישאו בנותיו, הלברשטאם ברוך הצדיק הרב כמו) מסנץ הצדיק חיים הרבי בן) . השנייה
במיליץ הצדיק לרב נישאה,ביץ הצדיק לרב השלישית, ביסלו הצדיק לרב והרביעית.

הנ האחים ר'שני ל' ור אביש' כנר זץ הרש'גדולים עשירים גם אך גדולים צדיקים היו ל, אנשי– שם
ידועים. רבנים כולם היו אלסטר משפחת גם, מיוחסים מאוד דיינים.

ז אבי מפי'ייחוסו אודות הרבה שמענו לא ל, בדיבור וממעט נזהר מאד היה הוא כי, פעם אבל
גדול יותר שלו שהייחוס הדגיש משפחתי ויכוח בעת אחת, מהרמ יוחסין איגרת וברשותו'א.

מארצות אחת גליציה מדינת כידוע"אביון מלך" .בלי מרודה ענייה היתה גליציה מערב במיוחד
תחבורה ובלי כבישים, מסחר ובלי תעשייה בלי. ואויר חקלאות קצת רק

First page of the Hebrew original text

William Leibner wrote the brief introduction to help the reader understand the background of the story. He also translated it from Hebrew to English.

The author was born and lived in the small Galician hamlet named Zmigrod that is located in the Carpathian Mountains between the city of Jaslo and the Slovakian border. It was a very old Jewish community that once flourished on account of the wine trade between what would become Poland and Czechoslovakia. The trade declined with the building of railroads and highways. The economic situation steadily deteriorated, especially for Jews who depended on commerce. The non–existent economic opportunities forced many Jews of Zmigrod to seek opportunities elsewhere, even the writer and his family eventually left the hamlet where they lived for generations.

The early life story of the late Hersh Gross gives us a precious glimpse of Jewish life in the shtetl of Zmigrod prior to World War I. The material poverty of the Jewish population was beyond description. The author himself went hungry many a day since the family could not afford to buy the basic foods. Yet, the family considered itself privileged by the mere fact that it was related to some rabbis.

Religious tradition was embedded in the Jewish community and the rabbi was the dominant figure in the community. He was consulted on major personal issues and his decision was followed. The Jewish population strictly adhered to tradition and the synagogue dominated communal life. Religious education was stressed, especially the Talmud. Most Jews shied away from secular material and had the barest of contact with the surrounding non– Jewish population. Few Jews spoke German, the official language of the Austrian Empire, and even fewer spoke Polish; Yiddish was the language of the Jew in Zmigrod.

Hersh Gross (subsequently changed his name to Zvi Ram)

My Memories

I was born in 1894 in the West Galician small hamlet of Zmigrod, near the Czechoslovakian border (present day, Slovak border). The family consisted of my late father Naphtali Gross (1858–1924), my late mother Sarah Gross nee Alster and children: Moshe, Haya, David, Roza and Hersh. I was the fifth and youngest child in the family. My late mother had a brother named Aaron Alster and four sisters, two of whom were Malka and Mindel. Our parents considered themselves a prestigious family since they were connected to rabbis; we did not see it that way since poverty ruled our home and we frequently went hungry for lack of money to purchase basic foods.

Mother always liked to stress the importance and prestige of her family. Her father was Moshe Alster from Gorlice and she was the granddaughter of Hersh Kanner, for whom I am named. Hersh Kanner's brother was Rabbi Abish Kanner, whose daughters married famous and well knowny rabbis. The older daughter married Rabbi Baruch Halbershtam, the son of the famous hasidic Rabbi of Sandz, Rabbi Chaim Halbershtam. The second daughter married the Rabbi of Mielec; the third daughter married the rabbi of Biecz and the last daughter married the Rabbi of Jaslo.

The Kanner brothers were pious and rich people. The Kanner family produced distinguished Jewish leaders, mainly rabbis, and religious Jewish judges. We heard very little of our father's lineage for he was a quiet person and not given to boasting. Once he did mention that his family was related to Rabbi Moshe Iserlish of Krakow, one of the great Talmudic scholars of Polish Judaism. This statement stopped all further discussions, for few families in Poland could compete with such ancestry.

Zmigrod was located in Western Galicia, which was economically very poor. It had a primitive agriculture that consisted of small and crowded farms. The region boasted excellent air that blew from the Carpathian Mountains and wonderful natural views. The region lacked roads, highways, natural resources and industry. The only area of growth was the population sector.

Mother was orphaned prior to her marriage to my father. She was born in Gorlice but married in Zmigrod where she shared her house with her mother- in-law and her sister-in-law. The house was an old house that was handed down from father to son for generations. The house consisted of one room, an alcove, a storage room never restored following a fire whose signs were still visible, a garden, a huge basement and a piece of vacant land.

Father was a traveling jewelry salesman who also sold religious items, silver and gold articles. He traveled with his coachmen far and wide throughout the Austro–Hungarian Empire peddling his wares. He returned home for the holidays, and left when they finished. He would arrive a few days before Passover and help with the Passover preparations; namely, check the house for bread or bread products. Following the holiday he left and returned prior to the High Holidays and then left again at the end of the Sukkot Holiday. The pattern of life continued undisturbed, even the death of his mother did not alter his style of work.

Every two years the family was joined by a newcomer, but the income remained the same. Father received a very modest salary from the company that he worked for. The work pattern became a habit and he was unable to change his work, or perhaps there was nothing else available. The income had to cover the expenses of the coachman, the horse and his own expenses and, of course, the family. The entire burden of managing the household, raising the children, and keeping the place going fell on mother's shoulders and she successfully carried out this magnificent task of raising five healthy and orderly children.

We must add that father's work was not a pleasure trip. He traveled throughout the Empire but never slept in a hotel. He saved every penny, since his family depended on him. He saved and trimmed his expenses to the bare minimum. The coachman arranged the sleeping accommodations at the home of farmers. He also tended to the horse, the cart and even saw to it that father was kept warm during the long winter trips wearing a long fur coat and a big fur hat but was still cold during the blistering cold days. The savings that father accumulated were sent home by letters, where they were received with joy. Unfortunately, their numbers were limited.

We had almost no contact with our father's family in Zmigrod, although there were Grosses in town. Many people in the hamlet called my father "feter," uncle in Yiddish. We asked mother for an explanation. She told us that the nickname was due to his being overweight (a play of words in Yiddish; uncle in Yiddish means feter, and so does the word for a heavy male). Indeed he was an uncle to many nieces and nephews, since his brothers were much older.

We related much more to mother's family. Only one of her sisters still resided in Gorlice; two sisters moved to the USA with their families. The brother and one sister moved to Zmigrod. The brother Aaron kept his mother Rivka Alster in his house.

Our maternal grandmother, the daughter of Rabbi Hersh Kanner, lived in the house of Aaron Alster but mother tended to her. She also encouraged us children to visit her and bring her chicken soup and sweets. She was about 100 years old but her mind was still lucid. Still she needed care and mother provided it, for Aaron Alster and his wife Lea were too busy to care for grandmother. One Friday afternoon she bathed and changed clothing. She passed away the same evening.

Uncle Aaron sold leather soles to farmers and granted loans at high interest. He also sold and bought gold, silver, land, forests and real estate. His office was behind his wife's grocery, where he kept his supply of leather in the closet and the papers in a metal box. Lea Alster operated the grocery and also extended credit. Many people repaid in goods rather than in cash; the goods were then sold in the store. He kept all records and entered them in books.

Every Monday was market day in Zmigrod. The farmers crowded the Alster store; some came to buy soles, others borrowed money and still others came to repay loans and interest. The payments were frequently made in roosters, eggs, vegetables, etc. The uncle and the aunt got along very well with their customers. Everything was recorded in Yiddish in his books. He also used signs and symbols that only he understood. He used different pages for different transactions. These recordings took a great deal of time since it did not always involve cash but rather barter conversions to financial figures. On the table there was always a bottle of vodka and the customers were invited to partake, which smoothed the transactions.

The grocery was also busy and sold goods to farmers on credit. The aunt was very efficient and expedited her customers very rapidly. She also kept mental records and when she made mistakes, they were always in her favor. The loans were frequently repaid in goods that she sold in her store. The farmers loved her and her word was gospel to them.

Their financial success did not provide them total happiness, for they had no children. They gave birth to nine children who died in infancy. They kept their distance from us throughout the year except for the eve of Yom Kippur and Purim. On Purim day, we were invited to their house but we did not recognize them. On the table was a large container with different coins to be distributed to the poor people who came to the house. Food packages and donations were sent to the needy in the city. It was a known fact that on this day my uncle distributed charity; fundraisers and collectors of various charities visited the home and received contributions. The big table was set as befits a royal family. Vast amounts of food and drink were prepared by our aunt and placed on the table. We did not recognize our relatives.

On the eve of the holiest of days, our uncle would come to beg forgiveness. His conscience apparently bothered him, but this gesture did not ameliorate our economic situation. On the contrary, our condition worsened with every additional mouth. I was born in the month of January and there was no liquid water available since all the water froze. Snow was melted to provide water to clean me. Father returned from his trade route to celebrate the occasion. Indeed, the evening before the circumcision ceremony, a barrel of beer was ordered and consumed by the invited guests. The party was joyous and everybody was happy. The next day was the circumcision and following it, the guests received dried fruits since it was 15 days in the month of Shevat, the holiday of trees and plants.

We conducted ourselves as well–to–do people in spite of the fact that poverty was everywhere in the house. This was my mother's specialty, creating illusions. She stretched her resources to endless limits. She dressed, fed and cared for us children in the best possible manner and kept the place spotless. Every child received individual attention and she praised her children to the heavens.

At the age of three, I started to attend "cheder" or Hebrew religious school. There were two "cheders" for beginners in Zmigrod. One belonged to Chaim Lib and the other to Mechel Becker. I attended the second "cheder" and loved it. My older brother Moshe, who was 12 years old, carried me on his back to the classroom. The teacher lived in a two–room apartment. My brother dropped me at the threshold of the school and left me to face the new world that consisted of many noisy and restless children. I began to cry and insisted on going home. The assistant teacher came to my rescue and began to talk to me; he promised to teach me the alphabet if I stopped crying.

Slowly I became used to the school routine. I made some friends and most of the time we spent outside playing games. Most of my instruction I received from the assistant. Once he brought me face to face with the teacher. The latter sat me down next to him and I faced an open prayer book. On the table was a whip and I became terrified. Suddenly, I noticed that the teacher's fingers were joined (his entire family had the same problem). He examined me and I passed with flying colors. I acquired the command of the Hebrew alphabet very rapidly and passed on to study the dotted printed page.

I started to study the weekly Torah portion after attending the "cheder" for 18 months. My studies progressed well enough so that one Saturday when my father was home, the teacher was invited to examine me in front of invited guests. The Torah section for the week was "Vayikra." I was seated at the head of the table next to the rabbi. I read portions of the "humash," or bible, and recited orally a special speech for the occasion. My father was very proud and the members of the family kissed me following the presentation. Several bottles of seltzer water, a bottle of syrup, cakes and "rogalech" (pastry), prepared by mother, were brought up from the cellar and placed on the tables. The occasion was jovial and memorable. I continued my studies for about a year in this heder.

Then I went to a more adult "cheder" where I studied Torah with Rashi's (Rabenu Shlomo ben Itzhak) commentaries on the section

Of the Torah. The school day became longer and included evenings. We carried candleholders in the winter evenings to find our way home along the dark, muddy and cold streets. I never missed a school day. The cold winter was soon followed by the pleasant spring and summer. The cycle of life flowed and we always hoped for better days. Mother always told us that we had to study to be successful; then we would open a business and build a nice home. These so–called pipe dreams were repeated so often that we began to believe them, but in the meantime time we had to suffer.

We were relatively healthy in spite of the poor and insufficient food intake. The various childhood diseases passed us with relative ease. We, of course, suffered from the so–called "evil eye curses," and mother was a specialist in treating the disease. She would take a glass of water, add some salt, some breadcrumbs, and some burning coals and mix the concoction. We were then told to rinse the mouth with it and repeated the procedure three times a day. This prescription usually healed the problem. In more serious cases, assistance was asked of the teacher Zacharia Mandil.

He was a known "specialist" in curing serious evil eye cases. He repeatedly whispered holy phrases until the patient became totally bored and was sent home.

Years went by and the needs of the family increased, but the income remained static. Then suddenly letters stopped coming from father. We inquired daily at the post office, but there was no letter and we began to worry. Then the company that employed father informed us that he had been robbed and was heading home. He then told us the whole story. He used to have coachmen that worked for him for years until the latter decided to get married and work near the house. My father began to interview various drivers for his position and selected a Hungarian coachman who had excellent references, and the decision was also approved by the company. Father was pleased with the driver, who worked for him for two years. One time, he stopped to visit a local gentry, took with him some samples and left the coachman by the gate. On leaving the customer's house, he did not see his coach or the coachman. The latter vanished and left no trace.

My father looked all over but there was no trace. His anger turned to rage, but it was hopeless. People assembled and looked at my father in despair, but the event amused them. Some said the coach went there, others said it went that way, but nothing concrete. Finally he managed to reach the nearest hamlet where there was a police station and reported the event. The police dispatched telegrams to the nearest police stations, but father had to pay for them. He also sent one to the company and informed them of the incident. The thief was finally caught in the vicinity of Bremen where he intended to sail for America. Naturally he had sold everything but still had some money in his pocket that was seized and turned over to father. The thief was escorted to Hungary to face trial and jail.

Father returned home practically penniless and the jewelry was never recovered. At first the firm continued to pay a reduced salary to my father, but then they stopped all payments. They accused father of being careless and blamed him indirectly for their big loss. The company also reduced its business in the area and father lost his job. Soon he was offered another job by a local Jewish merchant with the initials D.T.Z., who sold agricultural machines. The job was easier, closer to home and involved less traveling.

A rich local merchant approached my father with the following proposition. He would pay for the construction of a brand new house instead of our old house. The new place would contain two flats and a store. The store and one flat would be his for 5 years. The other flat would be for our family. Father consulted specialists, builders and experts. All agreed that the proposal was sound. The merchant paid 500 kronen to father and a legal document was drawn up. Father was certain that he would make some money on the deal; instead he had to take loans to finish the building. We moved to a temporary place and building materials began to arrive at the site. Most of the materials consisted of wood, for the new house was a wooden home. Luck was with us when a fire started at Chawa Kolber's home, a few houses away and stopped in front of our construction site.

The house was finished and the tenant moved into the apartment and the store. He was pleased, for everything met his satisfaction. We also moved into a more spacious flat that had a kitchen separated from the main room and a corner where there was room for a bed for children. The place was also enclosed with a fence that gave us privacy. The old place was open and neglected, everybody used it and some even used it as their own storage place. Everything about the house was new and shining except for the stove that kept emitting smoke. All the repairs did not eliminate the problem.

Meanwhile, father started to complain about his legs and soon he had difficulty walking. At first the doctor thought it was rheumatism, but his prescriptions did not work. Other medications and prescriptions were bought, but they did not improve the situation. Father stopped leaving the house on account of the pains in his legs.

The old house was totally dismantled; no shred was left. The only room that remained intact was the basement. Two additional basements were added to the existing large basement. Within the large basement there was a dark hole that gave a sinister and frightful appearance. Whenever we tried to direct candlelight into the cave, the light extinguished. The old timers in Zmigrod stated that the hole was an extensive cave that led to the market square and it hid Jews during persecutions. I asked father to confirm the story but he did not reply; obviously he never bothered to check the place for fear.

I was determined to explore the cave and managed to obtain a lantern. Father and I began to descend the cave. At first I crawled downwards. I called my father but he did not hear me and decided to follow, so I helped him on the way down. The cave was full of debris that was scattered all over. We continued our journey and came upon stairs that led to a big clean empty room. At the end of the room there were again 9 large stairs that led to a smaller room. The walls were whitewashed, the floor consisted of large tiles and the ceiling consisted of concrete. Along the walls were man–made niches similar to baking ovens with dim protruding lights from above. I tried to light a match but to no avail. The place was immaculately clean but lacked oxygen. We immediately retreated to the big room and on the return trip collected some glass antiques, porcelains pieces and copper items. We started to climb up and the going was rough, especially for my father. I pushed him upwards and we finally made it back. We sold all the collected items to an antique dealer and received a fair price. I never ventured again into the cave.

The Empire required all children to attend school from the age of 6. Most Jewish children did not attend public school for one reason or another, and the authorities were not disturbed. Mother was too poor to arrange some deal so I had to attend school. The school was considered a Catholic institution similar to the church in Zmigrod. I began to attend school, although I was afraid since I never had contact with non–Jewish children and I was of small stature. The fact that I received chalk, a writing board, a pencil case holder and a school bag did not give me greater confidence. My older sister escorted me to school. She was in third grade and 2 years older than me. This was a radical change for me, since I was rather attached to my mother and went with her everywhere, including visiting her neighbors. I heard all the gossip and stories and later repeated them to my "cheder" friends. Now I became attached to my sister, we walked together to and from school and we also sat together during our free time. She loved me and I also liked her for she helped me with school matters. I was the only non–Polish speaker in the class and could not ask in Polish to leave the room.

My father had a very good friend named Sh. who was a well–to–do person, owned an inn and once headed the Jewish community. The friendship lasted already for several generations and began when both families were well to do. The family was enlightened and modern. They had a son who was unable to walk and stayed at home. We were the same age. My father urged me to befriend him. The friendship will be good for both of you, he told me. The boy speaks fluent Polish and you will be able to learn the language. I went to visit him and was received warmly by Mrs. Sh., who offered me candy and escorted me to her son's room.

We made our acquaintance, he in Polish and I in Yiddish. Although we did not have a common language, we remained friends. Generally I easily made friends, be it at "cheder" or at school. Once I was very angry when the "cheder" children threw rocks at a gentile neighbor. She charged into the "cheder" and screamed. The teacher told her that he could not punish the entire class due to the misbehavior of a few children. He told her to point to the children who threw the rocks. She pointed at me and I was punished innocently, while the culprits were standing by.

I never had a good ear for music and was not particularly attracted to the subject. During the music lesson I sat in the back of the room with the other 2 Jewish students and we talked. The teacher punished us by making us stand behind the blackboard, but we continued our conversations. She was furious and decided to punish us by whipping us. She pulled over a chair and we were supposed to lie on it facing down. I was the first to receive the punishment. By accident I tipped the chair and it fell on her foot. Apparently she had warts on her feet, for suddenly she screamed in pain. All the teachers in the school came to the rescue until they saw the scene. I was terrified and began to cry hysterically. I was then escorted to the principal. The crying intensified for I was terrified of the word "principal." The principal started to talk to me and calmed me. He was rather pleasant and had a beer barrel stomach. I was then sent home with the order to appear the next day with my mother. Of course, I was too embarrassed to tell the story at home. Soon the matter was forgotten. I finished the school year with a very good report card that consisted of good, very good and excellent grades. A Polish student named Pzycinek and I graduated with honors and were told to pick up special awards at the pharmacy where guests awaited us. The pharmacist, an ex–Jew, informed us that there was only one award per class and he gave it to the Polish student. He gave me two nuts and I was dumbfounded and speechless. Then the druggist practically pushed me out of the store.

The economic situation at home went from bad to worse. My oldest brother, presently 16, left for Germany to try his luck. Father's health deteriorated; he was barely able to move. Thus he did not work and there was no income. We took loans and signed notes but they had to be reimbursed and we did not have the money.

Things were so bad that mother placed pots with water on the stove to give the impression that she was cooking. Usually we bought wood, potatoes, cabbage for the winter but at present we had no money. Mother ceased to bake bread for she was embarrassed to ask the grocery store for further loans. We were terribly depressed and hopeless when the mailman suddenly appeared and showed a letter. The envelope had many stamps and it was difficult to decipher. We accepted the letter and my sister opened it and started to read it. It was written in Yiddish that was slightly different from our Yiddish. We even thought that the letter was not for us but she continued to read the letter and the signature. The letter was signed: "your sister Maltche." My father jumped up for joy on his painful legs and screamed "my dear sister Maltche is alive."

Here is the text of the letter: "My dear brother! Many years have elapsed since we communicated with each other and I shall not delve into the matter. Now that our economic situation is well established and we are fine, we thought of you. We urge you to give us a sign of your existence and we will help you. We remember that we owe you for a shipment of goods that we received and never paid for. We are willing to pay the bill with interest." My father then said: "I do not understand the world. You never know what happens the next moment." He never expected such a letter from his sister. We replied and received a nice money order that was immediately cashed. My father's health condition improved slightly and we began to eat again.

The sister's financial assistance enabled us to live. We continued to exchange lovely letters between the families. The debt has already been repaid several times over. My aunt married several years before my father married. Her husband had great visions and tried to start big. He faced many difficulties and began to wander to try his luck in different places. He reached Budapest where he tried his hand at business but failed, then Vienna and New York. He returned to Vienna where he opened a restaurant and a coffee shop, but he was not pleased with the results. He moved to London and then to Paris. The savings dwindled and he was in serious trouble. He soon noticed that prunes in Paris were very expensive and asked my father to send him some bags. Father took some of the money he received as wedding presents and sent him the merchandise.

For twenty years he never heard again from the man. Meanwhile, their son worked in a Parisian restaurant met a merchant who offered him a deal in Africa. He left for Africa where he earned money and returned to Paris and started a successful factory. The enterprise grew and he opened two additional factories in London. We can say one thing about this family: they did not develop snobbish attitudes but remembered their kin. They searched for their family members and assisted them wherever they were. The aunt also invited my father to come and visit her. My father was determined to see his sister and made serious efforts to improve his medical condition. As the saying goes, where there is a will there is a way.

My brother did not have luck in Germany and the hope that he would find work and support us failed. He tried his luck in several places but was unable to find a position. At last he found some remote place where he met some acquaintances and decided to move in with them. The place lacked kosher food. My brother and his co-residents decided to order from home two broiled ducks and sent the money. Mother went to the market and bought them; she then took them to the baker who broiled them. They emerged brownish and perfumed the area. We broiled ducks and dispatched them to him but kept the feathers, the intestines which provide some delicacies for us, and the fat. The ducks arrived and the fellows enjoyed the food. The experiment proved successful and continued for a long time. Mother even managed to make a small profit on these operations. Finally, there was good news: father improved and began to work a few hours a day with the store where he sold agricultural implements.

Our life began to normalize to some extent. Mother also hired a private teacher to teach us to write Yiddish and other subjects in order for us to be able to read and write, which she unfortunately did not. I continued my studies at school and at "cheder" where I already studied "Humash, Rashi and Talmud," or the bible with commentaries, and the Talmud. I was a good and serious student. The teacher selected me to help the weak students at the "cheder" and even assigned me to test them on Thursday, the usual test day in the "cheder", for which I often received some pennies. The students respected me whether for fear or achievement is difficult to say. The teacher tested the better students in the "cheder".

I hated public school with a passion. Once the teacher put me on his lap and reached for the scissors to clip my side curls. Of course this was a big joke, and in the process pinched me on the cheek for I was a lovable child and people liked to pinch me. I disliked pinching and hated the school. Many friends came to visit and play at the house.

My sisters, who were gentle souls and very obedient, also had many friends. They loved my mother and helped her with all her household chores.

My brother David was a poor student, and he absented himself often from the "cheder" and played with other boys who were not interested in school. He was called mischievous and punished, but to no avail. Sometimes he would stay away from home and we had to go search for him. At other times he asked for forgiveness and promised to be more obedient. He left home and went to a distant relative in Sandz, where he worked in a store. We missed his departure but were realistic enough to size up the situation. With our oldest brother, Moshe, his absence was felt deeper for he struggled in Germany to make a living. We all loved him and worshipped him like a saint. After two years in Germany, he announced that he would be coming home for Passover. Our joy was boundless and preparation began.

A week before Passover, he arrived and we went to meet him outside Zmigrod fully dressed. We received him with open arms and escorted him home. Already at the Sabbath table, he commented that father had some gray hair as a result of the miseries and shed some tears. He told us all about Germany and the places that he visited. We spent a pleasant Passover and sat and listened to his stories. We even suggested that he remain at home but he refused to listen. He disliked Poland. A week after Passover, he left us. We escorted him to the nearest railway station aboard the mail coach and there we separated. The separation was difficult and painful.

Spring followed Passover and summer followed spring. Our house was always busy with friends who played games. Mother sat on a bench near the house and gossiped with her neighbors. They also observed the street movements, for we lived in the street of the butchers in the center of the city near the square. Here you always heard the latest news and gossip in the hamlet. Thus, we heard that the local council decided to cancel this year the procession of the "Judash."

The shameful spectacle continued for years. A big doll of straw was dressed in old Jewish clothing, with a "shtreimel" or Jewish Hasidic hat and a belt of straw, it was paraded through Zmigrod to the church. The procession attracted the lowest elements of the hamlet and the vicinity that escorted the procession and walloped the straw doll with sticks. The procession was noisy and finally reached the church where it was hoisted to the tower and thrown out from the window. Here there was a prepared stage where the doll was burned. The anti–Jewish symbols were obvious in spite of the fact that the Jews represented almost 100 per cent of the city's population. A Jewish member of the local council managed to pass a resolution to cancel the procession this year. The proposal passed, but the procession still took place. Nobody protested, the Jews accepted this behavior as though it did not affect them.

On Fridays and during hot summer days, we went to the river to swim. We were always pelted with stones by gentile youngsters from the other side of the river. Sometimes we could not leave the river to get dressed due to the large number of stones, and we charged naked to the other side of the river and chased the stone throwers who also received a good beating. This was life in Zmigrod and nobody knew that it was called anti–Semitism. The Jew always had to lower his head even if he was the majority of the locality. He was raised with the saying that "Esau hates Jacob," meaning that gentiles always hate the Jew.

This was the period of the famous "Belis" trial (in which a Jew was accused of killing a Christian child for ritual purposes). Zmigrod had its own serious blood libel. One Saturday afternoon, the police arrived at the house of Yossef the cider maker and arrested him, his old wife, and his son–in–law, Sender, with his family. They placed them aboard a horse–drawn cart and escorted them to the nearest town. The police also brought a woman who claimed that these people had killed the child. The accused were secluded and kept in custody. The whole community was thunderstruck by the event. It was galvanized into action. Letters, petitions and prayer vigils were organized; emissaries were sent to all the great rabbis and finally the accused were released and the accuser was punished with a slight penalty.

In Zmigrod there were two bakeries and we were in the middle. On the right was the bakery of Leibish Tzigler, nicknamed the store of "Sara the wife of Leibish Tzigler." A good part of the Jewish population brought their bread, challah, cakes there and brought their cholent to be baked in her place. Leibish Tzigler was one of three brothers who were old–timers in the hamlet. They all lived in one courtyard next to our house. Leibish was the oldest and aged 93 years; his mother aged about 127 also lived with him. Occasionally she walked about the cemetery looking for her children that escaped the house.

The bakery on the left, about four homes from us, belonged to Shmuel Itzhak Findling and his wife Malka Chaya. She, too, ran a very good baking establishment and served hot coffee. Her place was very clean and attracted people. Suddenly their son Ephraim disappeared and left no trace. The parents thought that he may have traveled to see relatives; but as time passed, there was no trace of him. Nobody saw him and no trace, total silence. They asked for help at the local monastery but were refused admission. They also asked the police and the local officials for help, but these people ignored them. Slowly the parents became suspicious that their son was at the monastery. A gentile woman was sent to the place and she confirmed his presence there, but added that he wanted to convert to Christianity. Based on the evidence the parents seated themselves at the entrance to the monastery and begged the officials to release their son, but nothing helped. They were chased away. They intervened everywhere; their pleas even reached the Emperor's palace in Vienna. But the church stood its ground.

Then it was officially announced that Findling would convert the next Sunday in the local church. The Jews in Zmigrod assembled and declared a fast day. The owners left the bakery in the hands of neighbors and headed to see the famous rabbis of Sieniwa and Dzikow. As neighbors, we watched the place. A gentile "Pankistit" neighbor who lived next door and spoke Yiddish and German asked us "Why are you crying?," "You are waiting for the Messiah," and "He is already with the Messiah." She further stated that as a small girl she heard the Jews state that the "Jewish Messiah" is due to come and she was already 90 years of age and he still did not arrive, even if he walked as a turtle he should have been here. As a youngster I thought to myself, What do women know, it is forbidden to talk to them.

Saturday was a tragic and mournful day for the Jews of Zmigrod. The Findlings returned home Saturday night and immediately sat down to mourn their lost son. At midnight someone knocked at the door which was opened. Lo and behold, the lost son appeared out of breath. At the last moment he decided to return home and ran all the way fearful of being followed. The parents dispatched a messenger to a Jewish coach driver to get his coach ready. The same night Ephraim Findling was on his way to the house of the Rabbi of Sieniwa, for there was fear that someone may be looking for him. He arrived in the morning in Sieniwa and entered the house of the Rabbi, who fainted on seeing him. He then told the people that he and his late father prayed for the boy and the results were obvious. The boy remained at the rabbi's house and later married the sexton's (Zalman's) daughter. They settled in Nowy Sacz, where he worked as a tailor. They managed to reach Palestine with their children. One of them became a Rabbi in Haifa and the other one was a ritual slaughterer in the same city.

The Jews of Zmigrod went to bed depressed and bewildered but awakened in ecstasy on hearing the news of the night. Soon tragedy struck again as the old Rabbi Benyamin Zeew died without an heir. The leaders of the community decided to look for a rabbi and invited candidates to present themselves before the community. Usually, the contenders appeared on Saturday at the synagogue or at the study center where they delivered sermons. As usual, factions soon formed supporting one rabbi and others supported other rabbis.

Then Rabbi Sinai Halbershtam, the son of Rabbi Baruch Halbershtam, grandson of Rabbi Chaim Halbershtam appeared. He was selected overwhelmingly by the rulers of the Jewish community. There was some opposition that supported the son–in–law of the previous Rabbi, but it was swept aside by the wave of enthusiasm for the Sandzer Rabbi. He had a large family and his wife was the daughter of the Rabbi of Mielec and the granddaughter of Abish Kanner, who was related to our family. They rented a large apartment from G. Weinstein that was located two doors from us. Hasidim started to stream to Zmigrod to visit the Rabbi. The life of the city changed overnight. The Beith Hamidrash, or study hall, attracted large audiences. The wine blessing ceremonies (Kiddush), the lunches and the chants during the meals attracted large crowds. More and more people went to the Rabbi's house on Friday nights to hear him bless the wine and chant the meal songs that originated in Sandz.

The worshippers of the study center and the community decided to build a new and larger building with new furnishings. The old study center was dismantled and the worshippers were sent to two halls at the entrance of the synagogue until the new study center was finished. The old timers also received a 50% discount in purchasing seats in the new place. Most worshippers of the old study center received similarly positioned seats in the new building that was very modern and spacious. The building was constructed very rapidly and preparations were already being made for the dedication of the place. Many people, including non–residents, were invited to the ceremony. The Jews, dressed in their best Sabbath clothing, attended the ceremony. Many Rabbis were invited and they gave sermons. The local population liked the place and became attached to it. Here the students continued their studies and youngsters were impressed by the variety of books. Older Jews remembered spending days with these books. Children dreamed of sitting in front of their Talmud and studying by themselves, instead of the daily drudgery of the "cheder".

The study center towered next door to the synagogue that was very old and a national preserved monument in Poland. The entrance walls were two meters thick and reminded one of a fortress. In the hall entrance were two small opposite rooms called

"Kahal rooms," where the members of the "Hevra Kadisha Society," or burial society, prayed, and the other one served as a prayer hall for the old "Tehilim Zogers," or psalm readers. From the vestibule there were two heavy metal doors that lead to the actual prayer hall. The doors reached the ceiling and were locked by a heavy key. Ten steps led downwards to the actual hall of services where a large and beautiful carved "bima," or stage, stood in the middle. On the right side of the entrance were a few stairs leading to a bench where small children sat, and it was also used as a place to light candles in memory of the departed on the eve of Yom Kippur.

The place had no lighting except for candles and no heating. In the winter it was freezing, but in the summer it was pleasant and cool. There were small colored windows in the upper parts of the building and hanging lamps for candle inserts. Every worshipper there felt the presence of the Holy Spirit. On the High Holidays, children sat next to their fathers who wrapped them in their big talith. Sometimes I had difficulty breathing but I was close to father and heard him pray with a broken heart. He devoted himself to his prayers and lifted his head when they started selling the call–ups to the Torah. This custom seemed strange that on the Holiest day, the sexton would start auctioning business in the synagogue. Father then asked me whether I ate something, for I was only nine and was permitted to eat, which I did.

I still tremble when I remember the old Rabbi Benyamin Zeev walking from the mikvah to the synagogue hall where he put on the "kittel," or white robe, and then the prayer shawl. He began to walk in the direction of the prayer hall and uttered the first words of the prayer preceding the blowing of the shofar on Rosh Hashanah. A tremor seized the audience when the Rabbi began to blow the shofar from the stage. The instructions were read by the ritual slaughterer, Reb Sender. The sounds of the horn mesmerized and terrorized us; they forced us to think or take inventory of our lives. We almost had the impression that the high priest of Jerusalem was conducting the services. Heartbreaking implorations (is that a word?) were heard from the women's section.

The assistance from the aunt began to decline a bit and father decided to visit his sister. But he first made inquiries about the family in Paris. He was told that they were rich and the husband was the head of the synagogue. They had a "sukkah" and an "etrog" was seen on the table. All indications were that the family observed Jewish holidays and was religious. My father left Zmigrod and traveled through Germany where he stopped off to see his son. The latter bought him new clothes and helped him with his plan to continue his trip to Paris. He went directly to the business office and asked to see his sister. The door man looked at him suspiciously and offered him a donation. Father refused and insisted on seeing the owner. The son of the family called his mother and described the individual in Yiddish. Furthermore, he said that he is my uncle. The mother immediately told him to bring him home. The brother and sister met and cried. A nice table was set for the brother. They also exchanged his clothing for more befitting items, namely formal wear, a cylinder hat, striped pants, a waistcoat and lacquered shoes. They showed him many sites and spent time with him. After his stay of a few weeks, he left Paris. He came empty–handed and left (what does this mean? he left Paris with the goods? if so, then he wasn't empty–handed?) with packed suitcases of goods. The French family also promised to visit Zmigrod.

I already finished public school but did not receive my certificate. The rule was that school had to be attended for five years, the last year was optional. I decided to leave school after the fourth year and was happy since I disliked the school. My mother also hired a new teacher. The former Mr. Ingberg was a nice teacher but I needed a more advanced teacher and his name was Mr. Ringel. He taught bookkeeping, correspondence, translations and German. Religious studies I continued with Reb Zacharia Mandel from 5 a.m. to 9 a.m. Secular studies were from 10 a.m. to 1 p.m.; then from 3 p.m. until late in the evening I continued the studies at the heder.

Indeed I was a very busy student and rather successful in religious and secular studies for I neared my bar mitzvah. I was very conscious of my height; there was only one student shorter than myself. My bar mitzvah day was in the month of Shevat, about January, and my feet were covered with winter warts and I could not wear shoes. I barely made it to the synagogue where I put on for the first time the phylacteries and felt very important since I was now part of the minyan, or quorum, of men for services. I then received a pair of soft shoes and went to the house to bring the cookies and vodka to the worshippers at the synagogue; thus ended the bar mitzvah celebration.

The lease of five years for the store was up and we took over the store and moved to the larger apartment while the smaller one was rented. We decided to continue the grocery business that the previous owner operated. We had little cash to stock it but managed to loan (borrow?) some money and received some credit from wholesalers. We advertised and urged all our friends to patronize the store, but we did not have good luck. We provided excellent service, for the whole family worked in the store, but few customers visited our place. Still we were independent merchants and managed to eat.

My oldest brother remained in Germany for a long time since he could not return to Zmigrod. He was of draft age and had to appear before the army doctors. The Austrian military authorities drafted all people unless they failed the medical examination, then they were called back twice. If they failed all three times, they were discharged. The medical doctors in Galicia were stricter than the ones of the Austrian consulate in Germany. We received a note from Moshe that he would appear for the third time before a medical army board on the first day of the month of Nissan that will be on Shabbat. Mother immediately left for Rymanow to see the saintly rabbi and father went to pray at the tombstones of his ancestors. He barely managed to find them for it snowed heavily the previous days. He did locate his mother's grave and asked her to intercede with all ancestors on behalf of his son. Saturday afternoon, a granddaughter of Pearl, the wife of Yossef, distantly related to us, asked whether Moshe was scheduled to appear before a military commission. She dreamt that she saw grandmother Hendil in the women's section of the synagogue with a large package of cookies and cakes that she distributed to the worshippers on the discharge of her grandson Moshe. Pearl wanted to know whether this was a dream or reality. At the same time a telegram arrived from Germany, that my brother sent via a non–Jew, to the effect that he was discharged.

For Passover, my brother came home and we received him with open arms. Father contacted a marriage broker, Asher Stern, to start looking for a wife for Moshe. He soon found a potential candidate. Father had relatives check the background of the family and the reports substantiated the veracity of the information. Negotiations were brief between the families and they met half– way, at Styrzow, to finalize the engagement. My parents took along the wealthy Aaron Alster to provide the dowry for the groom's side. Moshe returned to Germany to assemble all his belongings and buy some gifts. As we mentioned earlier, he was not very successful but still managed to accumulate some savings. He returned to Zmigrod and all the preparations were being made for the wedding. Suddenly, the uncle demanded immediately the dowry money. My brother gave him back all the money and was left penniless. The family had to borrow and sign notes but went ahead with the wedding. The "aufruff," or call up to the Torah of the groom on Shabbat prior to the wedding, was held, followed by a nice reception. Later in the week we all dressed in our best clothing and headed to the wedding that took place in Tarnow. This was the first time that I traveled by train. Our wedding party included many relatives for whom we had to pay.

Every day somebody visited grandmother at Aaron Alster's home. On every Friday, my sister Hendil helped her bathe and change clothing and linen. She also set the candles next to her bed so that she could light them prior to Shabbat. Unfortunately that Friday afternoon she passed away prior to lighting the candles. We were all at home getting ready for Shabbat when the uncle burst into our place crying that his mother passed away. We also received information that father fell from the bench in the mikvah and broke a leg. We did not know which way to turn, to help father or to go to grandmother. Father soon limped home with some assistance and informed us that he did not break a leg. The Saturday was already strained for we loved grandmother who was about 96 years of age and her mind worked to the last moment. Uncle Aaron was forced to pay 400 silver pieces for the burial plot.

Father's sister Malka lived in Zmigrod, and her economic situation was poor. She returned from the United States and married a nice–looking man. Her savings helped them to open a hardware store that was not successful. They had a daughter and loved her. Her husband had a dream and next day he bought a lottery ticket. The number came in and he earned 1,800 kronen, a large sum of money. But their luck ran out and he defaulted. He left for Germany where he began to peddle. He became ill and returned home. He then went to his parents in Brzeszow, who took him to a professor in Krakow where he died at the railway station. Malka was left penniless and was forced to marry an elderly sick merchant who provided her with security and safety for the next few years.

My stingy uncle began to call on me to escort him on his distant trips in the countryside, since he feared to travel by himself. On busy days he asked me to help in the store, especially market or fair days. I soon got the hang of the business and with a little coaching from my relatives I was ready to enter the business world of Zmigrod. The owners were surprised by my rapid progress and delegated more and more commercial transactions to me. I received some pennies from my aunt and some from my uncle without telling his wife about it. My real intentions were to study business and to try to attract some clients to my family's store. Unfortunately, people liked to shop in stores that had large stocks; our store was clean but lacked goods since we did not have the money to stock it. The available merchandise was purchased on credit and had to be repaid. Every penny we had went to the creditors, even the checks we received from France. But the business did not grow; on the contrary, it kept declining and so did our finances.

The uncle from France informed us that they were coming to visit and we made great plans. I prepared a nice welcome sign that was posted at the entrance to the house. The uncle and aunt arrived in a special coach and we received them warmly.

They were pleased by the reception, but were disappointed that the appearance of Zmigrod had not changed an iota since they left it. The visitors remained but a few hours in our place. They were shocked by the terrible living conditions. Following a nice lunch they left Zmigrod and moved to the nearest town where conditions were slightly more modern, and invited all the relatives to visit them. We traveled to the city and he gave us a nice present prior to returning to France.

A letter soon arrived urging us to leave Zmigrod for England. The uncle suggested that he would rent an apartment and assist father in opening a factory that would sell the produced goods to my uncle. Father was tempted, although the idea of abandoning the ancestral home and friends worried him. He therefore consulted the Rabbi of Blazow; the latter placed a veto on the move. My father accepted the decision without further ado. The French relatives were angry and did not understand the decision. They had tried to help and were slapped in the face. The relationship cooled and although they still sent some support, it was obvious that they were hurt. Soon the assistance reduced itself to gifts before the High Holidays and Passover.

My brother Moshe, who worked in Germany, and his wife settled down in Tarnow and started to sell finished products. He tried to follow his brother–in–law, who was very successful in this line. The latter coached him and showed him how to purchase merchandise in Vienna and resell it in Tarnow. Moshe even asked my sister to stay with his wife during his trips to the capital to buy merchandise. His enterprise was not successful and the sister soon returned home with a beautiful coat. We did not know whether this was payment or a present for her stay. She was already of marriageable age and the uncle in France had left a dowry for her future wedding.

My brother David became a wood agent and traveled extensively even to Upper Silesia and to Berlin. He started to earn some money and sent us regularly small amounts. My sister Rosa also started working as a salesgirl in a big haberdashery store in town and brought home her entire earnings. These monies enabled us to survive.

I continued my studies and entered a new "cheder" that was instructed by a very good and bright teacher who was related to us by marriage. This brilliant man became a teacher for lack of opportunity. He had a small group of students, some older students, and instructed them in Talmud, commentaries, bible and theological Jewish jurisprudence. He also had another group of older and modern students where he elucidated the Hebrew language, Jewish scholarship and philosophy. This teacher also provided two hours of individual study at the study center. This is where (he sold cigarettes at the study center??) I became a peddler of cigarettes; I sold single cigarettes on credit as opposed to the tobacco store, an imperial monopoly, which sold for cash only. I earned some money and gave it to the house; I never spent it on myself. I saw some circus performances, listened to cantorial or vocal concerts, but never paid for tickets since I managed to enter the places without paying.

My Hebrew teacher, Ben Tzion Hacohen Rappaport, wrote articles and feature stories for the Zionist Hebrew newspaper "Hatzfira." The older Zionist students read and understood the articles of the paper. At first it was difficult to believe that this Hasidic person, who prayed at the rabbi's "minyan," or service, and often went to the mikvah, was capable of writing so fluently in modern Hebrew. Most rabbis wrote scholarly Talmudic Hebrew. The most surprising thing was that such a religious Jew was such a fervent Zionist. Orthodox Jews did not believe in Zionism and bitterly fought the Zionists.

I started to come earlier to the "cheder" and joined the older group. This continued for some time, and then the teacher gave me some articles to copy for the newspaper since I had a nice handwriting. He asked me if I wanted to continue and I replied positively, on the condition that I may be permitted to sit in on the Hebrew class. The deal was between the teacher and me. My business suffered but my education intensified. I kept copying for the teacher articles, poems and feature articles. I became familiar with the teacher's handwriting and copied rapidly his material.

The newspaper and other Hebrew written items began to circulate amongst the students. The teacher himself also distributed reading material that was not directly related to the religious texts that were supposedly being studied. The students faced big open Talmud books. Some of them placed the Zionist newspaper or articles under the book and glanced at them whenever it suited them.

While reading this material, a student heard someone approaching; he dropped the material on the floor and forgot about it. Chaim B. entered the room and saw the page on the floor. He picked it up and noticed that it was written in Hebrew. He assumed it was a letter so he could not read it since it was forbidden to read other people's mail. He started to make inquires about the letter and slowly the whole story unraveled.

It exploded on Saturday when the teacher was called up to the Torah, the letter-finder started to scream and shout that the person is a heretic, a non- believer, etc. A commotion started in the synagogue and our teacher was very offended. He closed the heder and decided to leave Zmigrod. He stated that this incident was a heavenly sign to leave the place. We lost a good teacher and said good–bye to him, his wife Sara and son Moshe. They left for Krakow where he became a principal of a Hebrew school and published several books on philosophy.

His students dispersed to various yeshivot. I continued to study at the study center, helped in the family store and also helped the aunt in the store and the uncle in the fields. The latter appointed me to supervise the harvesting of his fields. I hired the workers and settled their wages that required keeping records. Every dawn I walked to the village and took with me a half a loaf of bread with butter. This was my food for the day. The field hands brought me warm milk that was just milked or fruits to impress me so that I would not notice their lateness or goofing off on the job. The fresh air gave me a nice complexion. The records were in order and accepted by everybody. I was paid and brought it home.

Our home was always busy with friends coming and going. On Saturdays, we used to provide people with nuts and peanuts by the cup and on Sundays the bills were settled. Next door lived the friendly G. Weinstein family. This was a large well–to–do family that purchased all their needs at our store. Two of the sons seemed interested in my sisters and they constantly visited and spent time in our house. We were perturbed that the older sister was still single. True she did not have a large dowry, but she had other qualities. Finally the matchmaker, A. Stern, brought a match. The fellow studied in a Hungarian yeshiva and his family was prestigious. They lived in a village near the Hungarian border. The families met halfway, in the hamlet of Dukla, and discussed terms. The future bride and groom were attracted to each other and the engagement was written. My sister came home very happy. Father added to her dowry and the wedding took place.

Moshe's business in Tarnow went downhill and he was forced to close shop. He decided to return to Germany with his wife and daughter. They sold everything that they had including his expensive "shtreimel," or fur hat, for in Germany he could not wear it. This was a difficult decision for all of us, but we had to accept facts. He sent his wife and sick daughter to us in Zmigrod and he left for Germany where he met his old acquaintance Shlomo, who also recently married. Shlomo opened a store that sold old and used clothing and he was successful. My brother also decided to open a similar store that required a small investment and little expertise. He advertised that he bought old clothing, and merchandise flocked to his place. He developed a nice stock of clothing, shoes, dresses and also rented an apartment next door to the store. He fixed up the place for his family and requested that they join him in Germany. The store was making a modest profit but not what he expected. He claimed that the location was not suitable. He began to look and found a store in the street that Shlomo had his store. He leased it and now had two stores and needed help.

He asked our brother David, who was a wood agent in Berlin, to come to Duisburg to help him. The brother took vacation and left for Duisburg, where he managed a store. After several weeks David left and returned to his company and Moshe was left short again. He sent a letter home asking that I come to Germany to assist him. The letter reached us prior to Passover and he assured me that I would be able to continue my studies at the Baron de Hirsh School. I had already made preparations to leave for a yeshiva, but this letter with all the promises drew my attention. I cancelled my plans for the yeshiva and decided to leave for Germany. I so notified my brother and made arrangements to travel to him with a neighbor, B. Tzigler, the week after Passover. I did not reveal my plan to my friends but said good–bye to my neighbors and family. My parents escorted me to the railway station where we hugged and kissed. Parting was difficult for this was a distant separation. I cried like a baby in a corner of the train but eventually realized that I must face facts.

The train ride lasted two days. I arrived Thursday morning, had breakfast, rested, changed clothing and headed to the second store. David was sitting on pins and needles in the store that could not be closed for fear that a customer may appear. This was the reason that he did not meet me at home. He remained with me until the end of Shabbat. Sunday I was sent to open a store and was told that every item was marked. Stores were open for a few hours on Sunday. I had no experience in selling or buying in Germany and took the job with a great deal of apprehension. I opened the store and an elderly man saw a suitcase that did not have a price tag. I asked an outrageous sum and the man paid. I closed the store and went to my brother and told him the story. He told me I took six times the actual price. I returned to the store and soon a man asked to buy a suit with no price tag. I asked for a higher price and even gave the party a reduction. Again I went to my brother and he told me that I overcharged.

I began to manage the store, sold and bought items and made money. My brother was very pleased and left me alone. The store was making money and my brother would come only if he needed cash; otherwise, I was the boss in the store. My brother and sister–in–law were pleased with my financial activities and they also gave me all kinds of chores to perform; namely, to go the Jewish slaughterer, bring kosher milk, carry the niece, etc. I tended to all these tasks but was very angry at the way I was treated. I felt like a slave and was sorry that I came to Germany. I could not leave everything like David. The boiling point was reached when my sister was married and none of her brothers attended the wedding. This was the straw that broke the camel's back.

I then wrote a long letter home and explained the existing situation. My store was making money but the other store was a mess. I also suggested that my parents come to Germany, or send me carfare to return home while I was still on my feet. My parents were frightened by the letter and father traveled to the Rabbi of Blazow and showed him the letter. The latter told my father to leave immediately for Germany. Father was a bit surprised and asked the Rabbi politely why he was sending him now to Germany and before he stopped him from going to London. The answer was simple, said the Rabbi: "Before, your family was under your roof; now it needs you and this is where you should be. Furthermore, do not feel sad about leaving poor Galicia."

The Rabbi's decision was fully accepted and the news spread like wildfire throughout Zmigrod, even uncle Aaron came to verify the news and was shocked by it. The business was liquidated and the house was put up for sale. Our neighbor Shimon Eisenberg's daughter, Dworah, came and offered to match the highest bidder on the house. Father negotiated the sale and they paid in cash. All preparations were being made for the trip. Many items in the house were left to my older sister Roza and the rest was sold. They then left Zmigrod for Germany, where the business continued and flourished. My father passed away in 1924. With the arrival of the Nazis to power, I left Germany for Palestine in 1933 and settled in Petach Tikvah.

I returned to Poland in 1936 and stopped off to see my in– in Tarnow and then continued to Zmigrod where I met my uncle Aaron. He looked well and was tended by his second wife. I also visited our rabbi whose son lived in Jerusalem. He inquired about Palestine, the living conditions and the situation. I then asked him how he allowed his son to leave for Jerusalem. He answered that the Rabbis used to oppose the Zionist rebuilding of the country but now mortal dangers face the Jews, especially in Germany, thus the interest in Palestine. I enjoyed the conversation and continued to visit all the relatives and friends who seemed to have aged. It seemed to me that even the synagogue sunk a bit lower into the ground. The pleasant and saintly air filled the hall. I found my name inscribed on the bench of the study center.

Zmigrod has not changed. I saw all the places that I used to visit. The hamlet remained the same as I left it. The cool mountain air was refreshing. I decided to wash at the river where we used to wash on Fridays, but the river was no longer there. I went to the mikvah on the old rickety bridge through the old entrance and waited my turn. The steam room did not work; there were few tubs and ice cold water but it was very refreshing.

Saturday the hamlet took on a totally different aspect. The place was clean and the people were dressed in their Shabbat clothing. I prayed at the study center where my uncle grabbed me to sit next to him. I was asked to conduct the mussaf service and was bestowed with "maftir," or the last portion of the Torah reading. I spent a wonderful Shabbat with friends and relatives and urged them to think of moving to Palestine where Jews are safe. There were many questions that I tried to answer as best as I could. I told them that nobody starved in Palestine.

I then left Zmigrod and headed to Jaslo where I had relatives. They received me nicely and I was pleased with the visit. I even conducted the evening services at the synagogue since I recited "Kaddish" for my late mother. Someone tapped me on the shoulder and I immediately recognized the judicial rabbi Yehiel, the son of Iser, who used to live in Zmigrod and presently resided in Jaslo. He paid me a compliment and stated that he immediately recognized the Zmigroder manner of praying.

I left Poland with a heavy heart and returned home. I managed to bring my mother (the paragraph above says that his mother has already died. The chronology is confusing here) and sister Henia to Palestine. My brother David managed to reach the United States. My oldest brother Moshe and my sister Roza perished in the Shoah, as did most of the Jews of Zmigrod, Galicia, Poland and Europe.

This was written and signed by Zvi (Hersh Gross). The spelling of the first name was the author's.

P.S. Zvi Ram lived to the ripe old age of 87 and died in 1981 in Israel. He survived Hitler and his helpers who destroyed his old homestead with all the Jews. He left a testimony, namely a family and a written document of Jewish life in Zmigrod.

CHAPTER VII
Jewish Births in Zmigrod

Below are the birth records of the Zmigroder Jewish population for the years 1866-1889.

Missing are the following years: 1868, 1874, 1875 and 1876.

The Polish officials had a difficult time with the Yiddish or Hebrew names and frequently misspelled them, or just used the first name while the party had two first names. This created confusion in relating family members. Still, it is a priceless document of Jewish Zmigrod.

Jean Krieser who lived in Paris, France, did a wonderful job in obtaining these records that establish the names of Zmigroder Jews during the period.

Last Name	First Name	Maiden name	Birth date	Father	Mother	Gender
AIGER	Jacob		28/10/1869	Jude	Ziwe	M
ALSTER	Rachel		15/2/1879	Aaron		F
ALTHOLTZ	Elias		1/3/1867	Hersch	Frumet	M
ARDYSZYK	Miszket		26/10/1871	Berl	Pesel	F
ARDYSZYK	Pinkas		16/9/1872	Asher Benyamin	Perl	M
ARDYSZYK	Golde Riwa		1873	Asher Benyamin	Perl	F
AUMAN	Hersh		8/12/1879	Samuel Henech		M
AUMAN	Hudes		3/11/1881	Aaron Ber		F
AUMAN	Esther		2/8/1872	Abraham	Roze	F
AUMAN	Chaje Ziwje		2/8/1872	Abraham	Roze	F
AUMAN	Neche		15/11/1866	Aaron Ber	Ester	F
BER	Selig		17/3/1883	Aaron		M
BER	Sprince		3/4/1880	Aron		F
BERTIE	Efroim Hersch		27/2/1879	Aaron		M

BERGER	Reuven Yosef		23/7/1887	Mendel		M
BERGER	Rachel		20/7/1880	Israel		F
BERGER	Chane		5/5/1882	Israel		F
BERGER	Sara		20/10/1869	Alter	Gittel	F
BERGER	Bear		6/2/1876	Alter	Mindel	M
BERGER	Feivel Shmaje		1873		Breindel	M
BLOCH	Salomon		20/10/1871	Samuel	Neche	M
BLOCH	David Feivel		27/2/1879	Samuel		M
BLOCH	Benjamin Wolf		1873	Samuel	Reisel	M
BUCHER	Dewore		28/10/1869	Isaak	Mishket Chana	F
BUKSENABUM	Benjamin Wolf		1873	Isaac	Riwke	M
BUCHSBAUM	Schije		28/11/1871	Hendel	Riwa	M
CITRONENBAUM	Isaac		12/3/1872	Moses	Ester	M
DEUTSCHMAN	Samuel		15/2/1869	Mendel	Jides	M
DEUTCHMAN	Debora		14/7/1876	Mendel	Jides	F
EICHNER	Josef		28/10/1869	Moses Hersch	Chana Libes	M
EICHNER	Abraham		4/8/1866	Samuel Wolf	Itte	M
EISENBERG	Josef		15/6/1881	Hersch		M
EISENBERG	Mindel		12/6/1877	Jacob	Chana	F
EISENBERG	Shije		15/2/1867	Chaskel	Ides	M
EISENBERG	Samuel Markus		4/12/1871	Simon	Ruhel Leja	M
EISENBERG	Schyje		1/10/1876	Simon	Leia	M
ENGEL	Pesel		24/11/1869	Benjamin	Sara	F
ENGEL	Markus		2/21872	Benjamin	Sara	M
ERREICH	Cypre		18/7/1880	Mechel		F
ERREICH	Pessel		25/5/1883	Mechel		F

ERREICH	Jozef		23/8/1885			M
ERREICH	Sussel		3/11/1885	Mechel		F
ERREICH	Esther		30/7/1887	Mechel		F
ERREICH	Berl		18/9/1888	Feige Ruchel		M
ERREICH	Freidel		156/1883	Pinkas		F
ERREICH	Josef		5/11/1879	Leib		M
ERREICH	Abusz		30/9/1881	Mechel		M
ERRENREICH	Mawes		27/10/1871	Leibisch	Hendel	F
FACHER	Feige		13/1/1872	Mendel	Chaje	F
FEDER	Ester		11/8/1872	Hersch	Mindel	F
FENNIG	Riwka		23/1/1872	Lazar	Neche	F
FINDLING	Zlata		5/6/1883	Isaak		F
FINDLING	Jszeste		3/4/1880	Jacob		F
FINDLING	Abraham		27/3/1882	Jacob		M
FINDLING	Simche		25/5/1883	Jacob		M
FINDLING	Hicel		18/11/1879	Samuel Isaak		F
FINDLING	Perl		11/6/1881	Simche	Riwka	F
FINDLING	Berl		1873	Simche	Riwka	M
FINDLING	Hinda		14/9/1872			F
FINDLING	Israel Ber		26/7/1866	Efroim Hersch	Reisel	M
FINDLING	Chaim		4/10/1876	Simon	Gittel	M
FINDLING	Chaje		1873	Israel	Mishket	F
FINDLING	Dwore		1873	Israel	Mishket	F
FINDLING	Chaje Sche		18/1/1872	Hersch Dawid	Mishket	F
FINDLING	Samuel		17/1/1869	Isaac	Myszket	M
FINDLING	Jacob		15/4/1869			M
FINDLING	Isak		10/5/1869			M
FISCH	Rywka		8/4/1880	Jozef		F
FREUND	Laje		20/10/1885	Szyje		F
FRIEDMAN	Josef		29/9/1888	Hersch		M
GELLER	Scheindel		15/5/1882	Juda		F

GESTER	Nachman		22/8/1869	Elias	Sure	M
GETZLER	Marjem		12/3/1876	Wolf	Ester	F
GINZBERG	Ruban		11/4/1881	Isser		M
GOLD	Jona		26/8/1869	Leib	Miszket	M
GOLDMAN	Taube		10/6/1880	Isaak		F
GOLDWENDER	Chaje		8/1/1872	Naftali	Riwka	F
GOTTLIEB	Moses		1/11/1885	Mechel		M
GOTZLER	Isaak		19/7/1883	Hersch		M
GOTZLER	Chiel		23/12/1879	Samuel Henech		M
GOTZLER	Gittel		10/6/1867	Israel	Sussel	F
GOTZLER	Gittel		6/4/1869	Moses		F
GRAGER	Schifra		28/3/1872	Berisch		F
GREISSMAN	Isaak		2787/1869	Pinkas	Mindel	M
GROSS	Haje Hendel		27/12/1888	Naftali		F
GROSS	Moyszez Aaron		3/3/1879	Laiser		M
GROSS	Samiel		28/3/1881	Noe		M
GROSS	Isaak		22/7/1869	Berisch	Hinde	M
GROSS	Zwitche		12/3/1876	Ben Tzion	Rose	M
GROSS	Moses Nathan		21/1/1872	Baruch	Hinde	M
GROSSMAN	Chiel		12/3/1876	Isaac Mayer	Yete	M
HABER	Ides		15/3/1867	Semuel	Ester	F
HERSCHKOWITZ	Ette		1873	Shulem	Marjem	F
HIRSZ	Baroch		13/9/1872	Dawid	Yachne	M
HIRSZ	Wolf		9/11/1887	Simche		M
HERZ	Eisig		1873	Chaim	Yachne	M
HERZ	Isaac		18/3/1869	Dawid	Ester	M
HIRSCH	Kalman		24/1/1885	Markus		M
HIRSCH	Markus Wolf		16/3/1869	Salomon	Itte	M
HIRSCH	Alexander		20/8/1872	Salomon	Itte	M
HOLLENDER	Mindel		8/3/1883	Chaim Itsche		F
HONIG	Moses		1873			M

Yizkor Book of Nowy Zmigrod

| JUST | Gittel | | 13/6/1881 | Hersh Leib | | F |

JUST	Laser		20/2/1869	Berisch	Malke	M
KAHN	Markus		11/11/1879	Samiel		M
KAMIL	Hana		1873	Fischel	Navies	F
KAUFMAN	Marjem		5/7/1884	Israel		F
KEIL	Meier		5/12/1871			M
KELER	Mendel		15/7/1869	Hersch	Late	M
KELER	Hersch		19/11/1869	Simche Dawid	Dobre	M
KELLER	Frida		21/9/1881	Simche Baruch		F
KELLER	Keile		3/6/1867	Hersch	Beile	F
KESSLER	Feige		2/4/1872			F
KILIK	Dawid Fevel		2710/1879	Mojze		M
KINST	Mayer		18/3/1879	Isaak		M
KINZLER	Hersch		6/6/1876	Kalman	Kalman	M
KINZLER	Chaim Dawid		8/6/1876	Bear	Sussel	M
KINZLER	Salamon		1873	Isaac	Sussel	M
KIRKMAN	Freide Feige		8/6/1883	Samuel		F
KRILL	Moses		5/7/1884	Aaron		M
KLEIN	Moses Ezra		2710/1887	Chaim Fishel		M
KLEIN	Feige Gittel		13/10/1888	Chune		F
KLEIN	Oser		5/9/1872	Dawid	Leia	M
KLEINMAN	Josef Berl		7/7/1880	Mojszes Gershon		M
KOHN	Taube		29/3/1879	Leib		F
KOHN	Neche		20/3/1879	Jacob		F
KOHN	Hannah Sara		20/3/1879	Aaron		F
KOHN	Gittel		4/7/1887	Shaje		F
KOHN	Esther		18/9/1888	Josef		F
KOHN	Laje		20/6/1884	Hersch Leib		F
KOHN	Lippe		9/11/1884	Mayer Jozef		M
KOHN	Simche		22/5/1882	Chaim Awigdor		M

Yizkor Book of Nowy Zmigrod

KOHN	Abraham Isaak		29.3.1881	Moshe Josef			M
KOHN	Freidl		254/1881	Leib			F
KOHN	Abraham Kalman		14/8/1879				M
KOHN	Frida		18/6/1881	Moses			F
KOHN	Chaje		23/31882	Szyje			F
KOHN	Sara		1/6/1876	Markus Isser	Yente		F
KOHN	Hene		4/2/1876	Leib Hersh	Ruchel		F
KOHN	Isaac Leib		1873	Dawid	Blima		M
KOHN	Samiel Juda		14/1/1872	Shulem	Ruchel		M
KOHN	Josef		12/1/1872	Abraham Hirsch	Sure Freide		M
KOHN	Samiel		18/11/1869	Hersch Leib	Ides		M
KOHN	Eisig		4/11/1871	Hersch Leib	Eidel		M
KOHN	Ryfka		15/1/1885	Naftali			F
KOLBER	Marjem		10/11/1881	Markus			F
KOLBER	Rifka		12/7/1869	Lippe	Golde		F
KOLBER	Hersch		25/11/1866	Berl	Sima		M
KOLBER	Jacob		10/8/1866	Moses	Ryfka		M
KOLBER	Chaim		4/10/1876	Jacob	Blima		M
KOLBER	Chaim		1873	Moses	Chana		M
KOLBER	Abraam		14/3/1872	Berl	Sara		M
KOLBER	Leib		20/11/1869	Schije	Chawa		M
KORNFELD	Shaine		10/10/1888	Markus			M
	Ryfka						
KOWIE	Sara Dwore		17/8/1879	Shulem Hersh			F
KRATZER	Breindel		6/7/1869				F
KRATZER	Dewore		12/8/1866	Moses	Sara		F

KRATZER	Hirsch		12/9/1872	Moses	Sara	M
KRATZER	Sprince		12/5/1876	Chaim Aaron	Ester	F
KRATZER	Dwore		4/2/1872			F
KRAUSBLATT	Brucha Beila		24/8/1872	Josef Elle	Hitzel	F
KRAUSBLATT	Chane		24/8/1871			F
KREBS	Marjem		28/10/1871	Schmiel	Ruhel Leja	F
KREBS	Bear		8/2/1876	Smiel	Ruchel Chaje	M
KREMER	Izaak		12/9/1888		FeigeRuchel	M
KREMER	Berl		19/7/1883	Salomon		M
KRILL	Juda Leibisch		20/1/1872	Aaron	Ides	M
KRISCHER	Szyje		10/3/1879	Jacob Oinkas		M
KRISCHER	Joel		27/6/1880	Jacob Pinkas		M
KRISS	Leibisch		12/11/1866	Mendel	Chessia	M
KRZESZANER	David		28/7/1878	Abraham		M
KRZESZANER	Mosze		10/3/1885	Abraham		M
KURRIER	Benjamin Wolf		11/7/1887	Samuel		M
LAKS	Josef LeibLAKS		18/11/1883	Hersch		M
	Freide		30/10/1871	Naftali	Chana	F
LANDESMAN	Sara		2/9/1872	Sender	Mindel	F
LANG	Breindel		21/9/1881	Sender	Mindel	F
LANG	Marjem		25/4/1869			F
LANG	Michuel		15/2/1879	Juda		M
LANG	Laje		9/7/1887	Samuel		F
LANG	Leib Hersh		28/8/1869	Elias	Sara	M
LANG	Chaim		1/7/1867	Fivel	Dewore	M
LANG	Simon		2/4/1869	Juda Leibisch	Sara	M
LANG	Feige		26/10/1871	Fischel	Ruchel	M
LEIBNER	Saul Mendel		16/2/1876	Nathan	Rose	M

Yizkor Book of Nowy Zmigrod

LEIBNER	Rachel Witte		15/2/1879	Nathan	Rose	F
LEIBNER	Moses		18/2/1888	Isaak		M
LEWKOWICZ	Hinde		6/1/1872	Leiser	Sara	F
LORBER	Sara Riwka		25/10/1869	Leib	Sime	F
LUXENBERG	Eidel		25//9/1889	Zacharia		F
MOHRER	Malka Mirel		20/8/1887	Samuel		F
NARCISEN	Berl		25/8/1869	Hersz	Rywa	M
NEBEL	Moses		2/6/1867	Mandel	Ester	M
NEBEL	Chiel		4/2/1872	Jacob	Sime Ester	M
NEBEL	Benjamin		20/3/1869	Jacob	Ester Sie	M
NEBEL	Chaskel		26/3/1882	Hersch		M
NEBENTZAHL	Hendel		20/4/1869			F
OCHAWET	Benyamin		12/2/1876	Hersch	Ester	M
OCHAWET	Sara Chana		29/11/1879	Samuel Henech		M
PACHTER	Marjem		10/1/1869	Maier	Marjem	F
PENSAK	Szyje		10/3/1879	Jacob		M
PINKAS	Sara		8/3/1876	Josef	Tzerel	F
RABI	Jacob		5/12/1871	Hersch	Chaje	M
RABI	Rachel		26/3/1869	Aaron	Yides	F
RAUL	Leon		15/12/1879	Samuel Henech		M
REICH	Naftali		2/7/1869	Joseph	Dwora	M
REICHMAN	Moses Hirsz		28/10/1871	Joseph	Dwora	M
REICHMAN	Efroim		17/10/1884	Jozef	Dwora	M
REICHMAN	Pessel		5/4/1880	Josef	Dwora	F
REICHMAN	Samiel		16/11/1881	Josef	Dwora	M
REICHMAN	Franie		29/5/1882	Samuel Henoch		F
REICHMAN	Leje		1873	Berich	Beile	F
REINOLTZ	Elias		16/3/1876	Aaron	Feige	M

| RELIN | Juda | | 25/10/1871 | Isaac | Feige | M |

Yizkor Book of Nowy Zmigrod

RENDEL	Meilech		19/9/1888	Wolf		M
RETTIG	Riwke		10/4/1869	Gershon	Margule	F
RIKEL	Leibisch		8/9/1872	Gershon	Margule	M
RIKEL	Dawid Leib		15/6/1867	Hersch	Bracha	M
ROSENHAM	Salomon		2/3/1867			M
ROSNER	Moses Kalman		24/3/1869	Baroch	Reisel	M
ROSNER	Ruchel		3/2/1876	Bear	Laje	F
ROZENTHAL	Rachel		2/8/1885	Benyamin		F
SALOMON	Schyje		14/5/1876	Moes	Sera	M
SCHEINWETTER	Ester		1873			F
SCHERER	Michael Samuel		15/10/1887	Feivel		M
SCHIFF	Scheindl		20/9/1889	David		F
SCHIFF	Taube Laje		9/9/1889			F
SCHIFF	Leib Wolf		6/8/1887	Juda		M
SCHLOSS	Berl		5/7/1884	Chaim Fishel		M
SCHLOSS	Hinde		30/8/1878			F
SCHON	Fride		23/9/1881	Lieber		F
SEHACH	Hirsch		10/9/1872	Asher	Breindel	M
SHONFELD	Sara		11/8/1887	Moses David		F
SHREI	Beile		22/1/1885	Aaron Ber		F
SIMAN	Lenore		3/11/1881	Samuel		F
				Jacob		
SPERLING	Sara		1873	Schmiel	Gittel	F
SPERLING	Dawid Juda		25/10/1871	Chaim Eisig	Hicel	M
SPINER	Feige		20/11/1866	Sheije	Roze	F
SPIRA	Josef Meilech		11/9/1889	Seinwel		M
STECHER	Chajem		1/3/1885	Hersch		M
STECHER	Ester		16/7/1869	Mayer	Chaje	F
STECHER	Chaim		5/12/1871	Moses	Chaje	M

STECHER	Arje		4/3/1867			M
STEIN	Chiel		12/6/1876	Moses Schyje	Mortel	M

STEIN	Marjem		12/7/1876	Hersch	Hene	F
STEIN	Chaim Asher		6/10/1871	Moses Schyje	Masel	M
STEIN	Beile		14/4/1881	Moszes		F
STERN	Salamon Nathan		6/3/1885	Berl		M
STRENGER	Yosef Gedalia		15/10/1887	Yekel		M
TEITELBAUM	Tobe		8/2/1869	Meilech	Hudes	F
THALER	Breindel		1/4/1880	Chaim		F
TRACHMAN	Chaim		16/7/1867	Eisig	Breindel	M
TRACHMAN	Chane Selde		26/8/1872	Eisig	Breindel	F
TRACHMAN	Ester		6/3/1876	Samuel Chaim	Laje	F
TRACHMAN	Hiel		6/2/1872	Josef	Marjem	M
TRACHMAN	Chaje Sara		6/2/1869	Josef	Marjem	F
TRACHMAN	Benjamin Wolf		7/7/1880	Mayer		M
UNGER	Sheindel		10/2/1867	Marcus	Fraidel	F
UNGER	Sime Sussel	15/1/1885		Simche Baruch		F
WALTER	Freide		8/4/1881	Israel		F
WALTER	Chaje		15/3/1885	Israel		F
WALTER	Taube		21/3/1882			F
WALTER	Dawid		26/2/1867	Moses	Bejla	M
WEINTRAUB	Dwora		6/12/1871			F
WEINTRAUB	Marcus		18/1/1869	Kalman	Chaje Reisel	M
WEISSFELD	Rechel		11/3/1883	Wolf		F
WEISSMAN	Chana Malka		30/10/1885	Mechel		F
WILK	Reisel		8/7/1869			F
WINTER	Beile Riwka		15/1/1872	Mendel	Josef	F

Yizkor Book of Nowy Zmigrod

WINTER	Hersch		1/2/1888	David		M
WIST	Sara		3/11/1884	Lippe		F

WISTREICH	Riwke		3/4/1869	Berl	Bassa	F
WISTREICH	Natan		12/9/1888	Leib		M
WOHLMUTH	Lazar		1/8/1872	Pinkas	Sime	M
ZANGER	Araham		29/9/1871	Meilich	Chaje	M
ZANGER	Eidel		8/10/1887	Mayer		F
ZIEGLER	Rachel		3/11/188	Yosef		F
ZIEGLER	Sheindel		17/1/1885	Naftali		F
ZIEGLER	Freide		4/4/1881	Ruban		F
ZIEGLER	Serl		17/8/1878	Samuel Henech		F
ZIEGLER	Samuel		3/5/1881	Aaron Ber		M
ZIEGLER	Hene		25/8/1872	Berl	Malka Reisel	F
ZIEGLER	Meier		26/3/1872	Fishel	Feige	M
ZIMET	Chaje		4/6/1876	Fischel	Feige	F
ZIMET	Yoel		20/2/1879	Fischel	Feige	M
ZIMET	Roze		30/6/1882	Fishel	Feige	F
ZIMET	Matel		8/10/1887	Zacharia		F
ZIMET	Matel		28/6/1882	Sender		F
ZIMET	Ester		25/3/1885	Sender		F
ZIMET	David		9/11/1887	Sender		M
ZIMET	Efroim		28/12/1888	Mechel		M
ZIMET	Dawid		29/8/1869	Josef	Blima	M
ZIMET	Yemte		14/6/1876	Simon	Bayle	M
ZIMET	Hersch		26/1/1872	Simshon	Hinde	M
ZIMET	Hersch		18/3/1876		Pessel	M
ZISHIK	Zische		24/1/1872	Pinkas	Hitzel	M
ZWASS						

[Pages 199-226]

CHAPTER VIII
Destruction of Zmigrod

Testimony of Shimon Lang at Yad Vashem in Hebrew

Translation prepared by William Leibner. He also enclosed some pictures and documents to help understand events.

Shimon Lang, a native of Zmigrod who survived the Shoah

Document 03/9105

033C 4052

Yad Vashem in Jerusalem

Name of interviewee: Shimon Lang

Name of Interviewer: Elkana Matra

Date of interview: 5 October 1995

Typist: Ronit Mintz

Names of places that appear in the interview:

Zmigrod: near Jaslo, Galicia, Poland

Biezanow: village near Zmigrod

Pressburg: presently Bratislava, capital of Slovakia

Krakow: main city of Polish Galicia

Jaslo: Galician city east of Krakow

Plaszow: labor camp and then concentration camp near Krakow

Treblinka: deathcamp during World War II

Skarzysko–Kamienna: slave labor camp in Poland

Buchenwald: German concentration camp

Theresienstadt: German concentration camp located near Prague, Czechoslovakia

Question: I am interviewing Shimon Lang who was born in Zmigrod, Poland, in 1910. Please tell us something about yourself.

Answer: I was born in Zmigrod to a merchant family who owned a clothing store and tailor shop that employed two tailors. The shop operated from the end of World War I to the beginning of World War II. On Friday, September 1, 1939, the tailors were working. We went to the synagogue to pray and returned to resume our work loads. Suddenly planes flew over the hamlet, a rare sight in Zmigrod. The non–Jews said that these were Polish planes.

Question: Did you know that the war started?

Answer: No. We knew nothing at 5:30 in the morning. At 8 in the morning the German planes began to bomb the nearby rail lines. We then understood that the war started.

Question: Are you a native of the city?

Answer: My family are natives of Zmigrod. We have been Zmigroder for at least three generations.

Question: Both sides of the family?

Answer: Yes, both sides of the family. My family name is Lang. There are rumors in the family that my paternal great grandfather visited Zmigrod and fell in love with a local maiden. He married her and remained in Zmigrod.

Question: How many children were in the family?

Answer: There were three brothers and a sister. The sister was married with children and lived in the village of Biezanow.

Question: Please tell us something about your childhood, the local school, and life in general?

Answer: Zmigrod was a small place that consisted of about 350 Jewish families. Most were Hasidic families. There were also non–Hasidic Jews but religious.

Question: Were there non–Jews in Zmigrod?

Answer: Yes, the gentiles lived mostly outside of the city. There were a few gentile families in the city.

Question: How many synagogues were there in Zmigrod?

Answer: There was a big synagogue and a big study hall. At the entrance to the synagogue, there were wooden arms built into the wall where a condemned man was tied up for some time in public under the jurisdiction of the Jewish Committee of Four Lands that ruled Jewish community life between 1520–1764 in Poland. This committee not only collected taxes but also had legal power to impose corporal punishment. The Zmigroder synagogue was already in existence during the period. The thick walls and the steps leading down to the entrance of the synagogue indicated that it was a very old structure. The synagogue was used mainly for Sabbath services. The study center was used for services and for study. The study center was built when my father was a child.

Question: The study center was more modern?

Answer: The study center was more modern and taller. It had a few floors.

Question: Did people from the area come to the study center? Did youngsters visit the center?

Answer: Most of the people attending the services at the study center were Zmigroder. The same can be said for the people who studied there. The busy time for study occurred in the summer and the winter. Some Jews from the vicinity of Zmigrod attended the study centers.

Question: Did the study center also provide sleeping accommodations?

Answer: No. It was not the custom to sleep in the synagogue.

Question: Were there religious and non–religious Jews in Zmigrod?

Answer: No, nothing like today in Israel. I remember that one educated person did not wear a hat in Zmigrod. He also did not attend services.

Question: Only one person did not observe the religious laws?

Answer: Most of the population attended services. I do not know to what extent the Jews observed all the religious commandments but in public there was general acceptance of the Jewish religious tradition. Maybe there were Jews who ate pork in secret in the woods or smoked in secret on Sabbath, but in the home and certainly in public most Jews observed the Jewish tradition that was carried on for 2,000 years.

Question: How was your home?

Answer: My father was religious, even very religious. I was sent to "heder" or parochial school, then to the elementary Polish school. When I finished heder, I started to study the Talmud with the former head of the Pressburger yeshiva. We worked very hard at home. We had to learn a trade. We could not attend trade schools since they were open on Sabbath. Some Jewish students continued their studies despite Sabbath.

Question: Were there Jewish doctors or lawyers in Zmigrod?

Answer: There was a Jewish doctor but he studied in Vienna, Austria. Jews had a difficult time to be admitted to Polish universities that were very anti–Semitic. There was a gentile doctor in Zmigrod. I used him once at night. He came and did not ask whether we had money or not but attended to the sick. There were Jewish lawyers. We were always busy working in the store or in the workshop.

Question: What happened outside of school?

Answer: Outside of school and my religious studies, I was busy working.

Question: Did you play with other children?

Answer: Yes, some children played outside, but I did not have the time to play for there was so much work. Sometimes, other children went to the river to swim in the summer. I merely went swimming once, perhaps twice in my entire youth.

Question: Was there anti–Semitism in Zmigrod?

Answer: There was no lack of it. We lived near gentiles and there were hardly any ties; the gentiles had no love for us Jews.

Question: Did you have gentile friends?

Answer: Yes, I went with them to school. I had some friends. I can tell you that during the war there was an ad in the German paper that Jews would be sent to forced labor camps except those who worked in agriculture. My mother went to the one in charge and I was assigned to agricultural work.

Question: Where did you go to work?

Answer: I went to work near some village.

Question: Was it a gentile farm?

Answer: Yes. It was a gentile woman who had no husband. She had two small children and a baby daughter. My mother spoke to her and she accepted me as a worker. I worked there daily.

Question: How old were you?

Answer: I was about 26 or 27 years old. I was going to work with the wheel barrel next to the school. My Polish friend saw me and told me to stop the charade of working. This is not real. That's how the Poles reacted to Jewish workers and he was a friend who lived near my house. It pained him that I was working and maybe able to avoid being sent to a forced labor camp.

Question: Where was the labor camp next to Krakow?

Answer: Zmigrod is 140 kilometers east of Krakow. We worked very hard. My mother kept us very busy and did not permit us to waste time. She, of course, fed us well so that we had the energy to work. I can now say that this training perhaps helped me to survive the very difficult conditions in the concentration camps.

I had a sister who was about 18 or 19 years old who helped in the house. Then there was a brother aged 25 and another brother aged 17. Then my sister married and I had more work at home. I was the oldest child in the household. We always worked. There were rich Jews in Zmigrod, there were middle class Jews in Zmigrod and there were also Jews who did not have a slice of bread on Sabbath.

Question: Did the community help them?

Answer: The community did not help them, the community helped the rabbi, the cantor but not the poor Jews. Ordinary Jews made collections to help the poor Jews. Money or bread was collected and distributed. I remember collecting wood in the winter and then distributing the wood to poor Jewish homes so that they could have some heat. This was not a permanent solution but it helped for a time.

Question: The help was not organized?

Answer: Not in the modern way of a welfare organization.

Question: Were there youth movements in Zmigrod? Emissaries from Palestine?

Answer: The contacts with Palestine were very weak. Following the death of Marshal Pilsudski in 1935, a wave of anti–Semitism swept the country. Young Jews came to the "Hachshara,ʟ or training farm, to acquire agricultural skills that they would be able to use in Palestine. As the anti–Semitic ideology enveloped Poland, more and more Jews came to the training farm in Zmigrod. The young Jews were not only from Zmigrod but also from the vicinity. They spread the idea of Zionism. Youth movements like the Bnei Akiva, or religious Zionist youth group, began to appear and call the Jewish youth to join the movement.

Question: Did it occur to you to join such a training farm?

Answer: I was very busy at home and did not have the time to be involved. Furthermore, I belonged to the party known as Agudat Israel, or very religious anti–Zionist party, that was not interested in Zionism.

Question: Please tell what happened in 1939.

Answer: We lived until 1939. Those who were poor remained poor, those who were rich were rich and the middle class remained in the middle. The day of the outbreak of the war we knew that Jewish life that had existed in Europe ended. Some Jews hoped that the Germans would not kill all Jews as later happened. Some poor people even hoped that perhaps their poor economic situation would improve.

Question: They really thought that Hitler was going to save the poor people?

Answer: Nobody thought that Hitler would slaughter Jews en masse. It is easy to speculate after the fact, but the truth of the matter was that nobody believed that Hitler would kill Jews en masse. The Jews knew that they would not have it easy under Hitler but did not expect what happened. The rich Jews knew that times would be hard and the poor Jews who did not have a slice of bread for Sabbath hoped that maybe conditions would improve slightly.

Question: What happened September 1, 1939?

Answer: On September the first, the gentiles started to act up since the war caught them by surprise.

Question: Weren't they drafted?

Answer: Yes, they were drafted in the morning and returned home in the evening by truck. They drafted about 40 or 50 and sometimes 100 men and took them to the border. Zmigrod was about 4–5 kilometers from the border with Czechoslovakia that was already occupied by German forces. The Polish soldiers were drafted in August and traveled back and forth. The Polish soldiers looked at the German soldiers and vice–versa.

Question: Was this area of Czechoslovakia part of the Sudetenland?

Answer: No, this area was not part of the Sudetenland.

Question: Did the German soldiers recognize the Polish soldiers?

Answer: Yes, the German soldiers were placed along the Czech–Polish border prior to the beginning of the war. Even we could see the German soldiers at the border. With the outbreak of hostilities, the local Polish drafted soldiers abandoned their posts, changed to civilian clothing and came home.

Question: So the Polish soldiers were no longer in uniform?

Answer: Yes, they were already in civilian clothes. Besides, what could they do against a powerful German army equipped with tanks? It took them about a week to overrun Poland. During this week we made preparations. First, we took 40 Torahs from the synagogue and buried them at the Jewish cemetery in a big crate. We already felt sad but never anticipated what was to come. Friday morning about 10 A.M., I was standing by the window and noticed the first German soldiers had entered the city. The Jews were all at home behind locked doors. Nobody was on the street. The soldiers probably returned and reported that the city was clean of Polish soldiers. Then thousands of soldiers started to stream into Zmigrod. The stream continued to 10 in the evening. Most of the soldiers continued to move onward but some soldiers remained in Zmigrod. Jews and gentiles started to leave their homes and began to talk to the German soldiers and some even began to trade with the soldiers. Then the Germans shot a Pole. We soon realized that you could not do business with the Germans. The shooting took place one week prior to the Jewish New Year. The Germans continued to move.

Question: Through Zmigrod?

Answer: As long the German soldiers crossed Zmigrod, there were no disturbances. Problems started when they stayed in the city.

Question: What problems?

Answer: The problems started on Rosh Hashanah, or the Jewish New Year. Jews began to walk to the synagogue to pray. We were about 50 or 60 Jews at the synagogue. Two German soldiers entered the place and began to scream: "Out!" Of course, we started to leave and received slaps and kicks as we passed the soldiers on the way out. I reached home and told the family what had happened at the synagogue. There was then a house facing Main Street that was completely enclosed. Within the house there was a courtyard. Many Jews assembled there to pray. Suddenly, we were told that the Germans were looking for Jews to work. We started to run in all directions. The Germans spotted the Jews and entered the courtyard through the windows that they broke. They grabbed me, my brother and my father. A German took us and as we passed our home, he saw my mother with a "machsor," or a book with High Holiday prayers in her hands. He grabbed the book and threw it at the wall. He told her that in Austria they took care of the Jews by cutting their tongues and she still had the audacity to pray here. He took all three of us, beat us mercilessly along the road.

Question: Where did he lead you?

Answer: He led us to the estate to work.

Question: Was that a big estate?

Answer: Yes, the estate belonged to a rich Pole. The place had many German soldiers who slept on hay that was scattered along the floor. We saw many Jews at the estate. Our job was to assemble the hay and carry it to the fire where it was burned. This was our job. Every time I approached the fire with a bundle of hay, the German guard tried to push me toward the fire. We worked at this job the entire first day of the New Year. In the evening the Germans sent us home. Walking was difficult since the streets were full of German soldiers. Finally we reached home and made the blessing that we had survived the ordeal of the day. We managed to keep going until the Day of Atonement. We attempted to assemble and pray on the holiest of days for Jews, but again the Germans appeared and hunted the Jews to work. There was no rest from the manhunt. In November we had serious problems; every day the Germans came to look for Jewish workers and we worked every day.

Question: Did you work every day?

Answer: Yes, we worked daily. There was no organization like the "Judenrat" that would be created later. We dealt with German soldiers or, rather, they dealt with us.

Question: Did the Germans grab Jews off the street?

Answer: The Germans grabbed Jews wherever they found them. Since the houses of Zmigrod were low, they would break the entrance doors or the windows and appear in the homes and grab Jews. This continued until November. On November 20, I think, a pogrom took place.

Question: Who started the pogrom?

Answer: The pogrom started in the morning. In Zmigrod it was the custom to make public announcements by sending the town crier with a big drum who publicized the proclamation. The present order was that all Jews must open their stores and surrender their merchandise. Failing to do this would result in the death penalty. Jews who had stockpiles of merchandise were told to expose it. A half hour after the announcer was finished, gendarmes appeared.

Question: Were the gendarmes Germans?

Answer: Yes. The German gendarmes went from house to house and arrested all Jewish menfolk. They broke all household closets and chests. We were a bit naÃ¯ve and took out everything we had.

Question: Did they look for merchandise or other things?

Answer: They took everything. There were no haulers so they took the Jews who they apprehended, young and old, and ordered them to take everything outside the house and load it aboard trucks. They took all our possessions and left.

Question: Did they carry out everything?

Answer: They took apart entire rooms. Some Jews were left shirtless that day. This took place on November 20.

Question: Did they harm Jewish women?

Answer: They did not respect Jewish women. They took some Jewish women who separated the items they found. They kept them all day at this job.

Question: Were you also affected by the removal of merchandise?

Answer: We managed to hide some merchandise in the attic.

Question: What kind of merchandise?

Answer: We had some tissues but not too much.

Question: Did they also seize food items?

Answer: The Germans took everything.

Question: Did they take everything from you?

Answer: They took everything they saw. Some people were lucky that they did not see everything.

Question: Did the local population join the grabbing of material goods?

Answer: No. This was a purely German show. Tuesday evening they took all the plunder and drove it to the city of Jaslo, district headquarters. They returned on Friday and continued with the same searches. All the stores were then closed. The Germans then burned the Talmud books, the bible.

Question: How about the Torahs?

Answer: All Jews were ordered to take all their books out of the houses. I did not let my younger brother take the books, but I took them and delivered them to a German officer. He asked me if we had more books. I was afraid that they may search the house and answered in the affirmative. The German escorted me to the attic where I had some books. I took the books and left the house and followed the German. He led me to a square where a German officer took one book and opened the pages. He then told me to take the book and roll on the ground with the book to the fireplace where another German soldier told me to stand up and took the book from my hands and heaved it to the fire. I was then told to head home. I did not go home but went to the synagogue and took a small Torah from the Holy Ark. The Torah was very small but it was used in services. I took the Torah and left the synagogue. I decided to hide the small Torah with all our belongings. Later, we used the small Torah in a service we organized in the afternoon of the Day of Atonement, when things settled down a bit. After the service, I returned the small Torah to the hiding place at the house.

Question: Where did you hide the small Torah? In the attic?

Answer: No. Under one of the beds there was a hole in the ground that was dug up during World War I. The hole was covered with wood as though it was part of the floor, but it was accessible. It was used in emergencies. It was a small hole where we could put some merchandise, jewelry and other small valuables.

Question: Was this sort of a vault?

Answer: Yes. I thought I would be able to take the Torah out of the hiding place and use it for the services on"Simchat Torah," or the festival of the Torah holiday. Indeed, we organized a private service and I brought the Torah from hiding. While our service was taking place, the wife of one of the people praying with us entered the room and said,"Pray, for the Germans are burning the study hall!" I left the room and went to the next room that led to the store. I approached the window with hesitation and saw people with jerry cans of gas spraying the area and setting it on fire. Our house was situated between the synagogue and the local church.

Question: Were the torchers Germans?

Answer: I said to myself, if they are burning the synagogue then our house would also burn. I returned to the room with the hole in the floor and took a few things and also the Torah and headed to the courtyard of the neighboring church and buried all the items. I went back to the house to repeat the action but the Germans were all over the place looking for the so–called Jewish torchers.

Question: Did the Germans accuse the Jews of having torched their own synagogue?

Answer: Yes, the Germans kept looking for Jews and those found were roughed up.

Question: In your house?

Answer: No, I was in the churchyard returning to the house when the Germans entered our place. I waited until they left. I gave up the idea of carrying more stuff to the hiding place in the churchyard; instead I went to the attic. In the attic there was a niche. I went directly to the niche and found there a few people hiding. The niche had a slit that gave a view of the synagogue. The sight was beyond description. Jews were forced to carry buckets of water to the fire site where the flames were raging. The Jews were beaten mercilessly going and coming with the water buckets. The show lasted the entire night. The synagogue and the study hall were torched and only smoke columns could be seen from the place. In the morning I left my hiding place. The Germans soldiers left Zmigrod. They were replaced by the German police who remained permanently stationed in the city. The German police began daily searches and seizures at Jewish homes. Some Jews were arrested and sent to jail if there was the slightest suspicion against them. These activities continued for some time. Somewhat later, the Germans decided to form a "Judenrat," or Jewish council. They selected a party who was far from any involvement in community affairs. He was a crude man. The Germans were sure that he would do their bidding and they were not wrong. One cannot say that he did specifically bad things to the Jews of Zmigrod, but he certainly helped the Germans.

Question: Was he the middleman between the Jews and the Germans?

Answer: Yes, he was the go–between. This situation continued to 1942.

Question: What did you do in the meantime? You and your family?

Answer: My father did not work although he was not old. All Jews had to work at all kinds of local projects like shoveling snow, building roads, at the Steinbruch quarry. I decided to go to work at the quarry of Emil Ludwig Steinbruch. It was very hard work. This was not a labor. We went each morning and returned home each evening.

Question: Was this forced labor?

Answer: Yes, this was forced labor. Steinbruch paid a measly salary at the end of the month.

Question: Did they provide food at the work site?

Answer: We were not fed. At the end of the month we received a loaf of bread with jam. This continued until 1942.

Question: Did the family have food?

Answer: Hardly. We lived very economically. If you had a slice of bread, you knew that you cannot have another one. The food that I brought from Steinbruch was not only for myself but for the entire family.

Question: You were the sole worker in the family?

Answer: I was the only worker in the family who worked outside of Zmigrod. There was lots of work along the roads and shoveling snow.

Question: And your father?

Answer: My father worked but I worked outside the city and managed to get small quantities of food that I brought home.

Question: Did your father do any tailoring?

Answer: It was impossible to work since the gentiles did not dare to come to the center of the city. They were afraid for their lives. There was an occasional farmer who brought something to repair or bought a piece of merchandise, but fear prevailed everywhere.

Question: Did you know what was taking place in nearby communities; was there a newspaper or a radio?

Answer: We knew nothing. There was no newspaper nor radio. Slowly all communications with the outside were closed. We could not even reach the district city of Jaslo that was about 10 kilometers from Zmigrod. Only the head of the Judenrat had a valid pass that enabled him to travel to Jaslo in 1942.

Question: Did he travel in the spring or summer of 1942?

Answer: He traveled in the Hebrew month of Tamuz or July. The Germans demanded that the Jews make a contribution to Germany of 100,000 Polish zlotys. The Judenrat collected money and goods but could not reach the sum demanded by the Germans. The Judenrat managed to assemble 50,000 zlotys and the head of the Judenrat took the money to Jaslo. He told the Gestapo that this was all the money that could be collected from Zmigrod. This was on Friday. On Saturday a unit of the Gestapo visited a large pit in the area of Zmigrod. I think that the Germans already knew that the Jews would be killed.

Question: How did you know?

Answer: I was outside when the inspection commando returned from the site and was about to return to Jaslo. One of them made a sign.

Question: What kind of sign?

Answer: A sign that signified the end. (Probably a hand motion across the throat.) Then I understood that the pit was destined for us. On Sunday, Polish workers who used to work for the Polish arrived with heavy equipment in Zmigrod and continued to travel in the upper levels of the city in the direction of the pit.

Question: What happened then?

Answer: Sunday afternoon the Gestapo chief requested the list of Jewish residents of Zmigrod and their pictures from the head of the Judenrat. The Gestapo took these items and told him that all Jews must be ready on

Tuesday morning at the meadow that was outside Zmigrod. On Monday morning, the Gestapo chief called on the head of the Judenrat again and told him that all Jews must assemble at the meadow at 8 o'clock in the morning on Tuesday. Nobody was to be exempted.

Question: Everybody?

Answer: Everybody. Old people, young people, sick people, disabled people. We all started to walk to the meadow on Tuesday morning.

Question: You also joined the march?

Answer: Yes. We knew that things looked bad, but we did not realize that the Germans would take about 1,500 Jews to the meadow and select 1,200 of them to be killed. We all walked to the meadow. The Gestapo chief and his entourage soon arrived and proceeded to establish order. First they ordered all Jews aged 40 and over to head to a spot.

Question: Was this a selection?

Answer: Yes. Then the Jews themselves carried out another selection; many Jews were certain that Jews aged 40 would be sent home. So many younger Jews stepped over to the area. The Germans then drew a line between the aged–40 group and the rest of the Jewish population. No one was permitted to leave this group but any one could join the group. A Gestapo man with a big wooden club that ended in a hook began to walk among the Jews and placed the hook on the neck of Jews. Once the hook was placed on a Jew, he was ordered to join the aged group. This tedious process was going on and on. He then selected entire families with four children and sent them to the aged group. Also families with three children were doomed.

Question: And you?

Answer: I was standing with my father and brothers and my sister with her children. He ordered the sister with her two children to move to the aged group. I remained with my father and brothers.

Question: Was not your father supposed to join the aged group?

Answer: Yes, but he used his brains and was one of the few elderly people to survive that day.

Question: What about your mother?

Answer: My mother was next to my father. We all stood a certain distance away and huddled ourselves together after our sister and her children were removed. Then the real selection started among the remainder of the Jews of Zmigrod. The Gestapo chief sat himself down at a table and all the remaining Jews had to pass in front of him one at a time. He decided who returned home and who joined the aged group. My middle brother was the first to appear before the Gestapo men and he sent him to the aged group. Then I went and received a signed card that permitted me to go home. My younger brother also received a signed card. My father also received a signed card. Other people, younger than him, were however sent to the aged group. Once father received the signed card he edged over to mother and took her arm and they walked over to the site where people with cards were seated. They were soon sent home and my mother never received a card.

Question: He saved your mother?

Answer: Yes, he saved her that day. She, of course, died in the shoah as he did. But on this day he saved her. We returned home, my father, my mother, myself and my younger brother.

Question: What happened to the others?

Answer: Tuesday morning, the head of the Judenrat urged all Jews to make contributions to the Germans. He brought a sack and asked Jews to give everything they could. He said that maybe the contribution would lighten the German treatment of the Jews. The sack was half–full when the Jews reached the meadow. The Judenrat chief gave the sack to the Gestapo men. The Gestapo men told him:"You said that the Jews had no more money on Friday, yet now you suddenly found more money." He clubbed the Judenrat head on his head. Blood began to stream. He was forced to stand in the sun. The Gestapo chief told him that he would be the last Jew to be killed. Blood kept streaming from the open head wounds. Thus ended the saga of the Jews of Zmigrod onTuesday, July 7, 1942, or 22 days in the month of Tamuz, when bout 1,300 Jews were killed, When we reached our home in Zmigrod we already knew that most of the Zmigroder Jews were dead. No sooner did we arrive home when someone knocked at the door. We opened the door and saw a little girl of six or seven years. She was wrapped in a sheet and carried only a box with shoes in it. Her parents had a shoe store. She asked to be
permitted to enter the house. Apparently, her parents, seeing what was going on, told the girl to go to the river and hide. Nobody noticed her disappearance. She took advantage of the river that was flowing near the meadow to hide there.

Halbow near Zmigrod where most of the Jews of Zmigrod were killed on July 7, 1942

Question: Just the little girl survived?

Answer: Her parents and brothers aged 16 or 17 all were killed. Nobody remained alive. Her father was a Talmudic scholar and the girl brought with her box with the shoes.

Question: You took her in?

Answer: Yes, she remained with us to the end. On Friday we received orders to assemble at the same meadow. On Sunday about 200 people appeared including 50 people who worked for the Germans. The Germans selected about 150 people and sent them to Plaszow near Krakow.

Question: And you were among the transport to Plaszow?

Answer: Yes.

Question: And your brother?

Answer: He remained at home on Sunday. We were taken to the ghetto of Jaslo and then sent to the labor camp of Plaszow where we started to work.

Question: Was this a camp? Where did you live?

Answer: We lived in a barrack. Plaszow was a labor camp in 1942. I started to build a railway.

Question: Was this a new railway?

Answer: Actually we were building two parallel lines to circumvent the main railway station of Krakow that was jammed with traffic heading to the Russian front. Our group of 38 workers built the railway. Next to us was a German group that also worked along the railway line but they were paid in full. We received nothing, no food, no money. We built about 60 kilometers of track that enabled German trains to bypass the Krakow main railway station. We encountered there a huge amount of tools that served the railway.

A month after we left Zmigrod, the Gestapo chief wanted to complete his mission of erasing all the Jews from Zmigrod. He wanted to search every Jewish home.

Question: He wanted to search the homes?

Answer: He wanted to assemble all the goods and distribute them among the local population.

Question: Who was Dr. Gentz?

Answer: He sent all the good stuff to Germany and the rest was given to the local population. He cleared all the Jewish homes.

Question: What did they do with the rest of the Jews in Zmigrod?

Answer: After the transport left for Plaszow, very few Jews remained in Zmigrod, perhaps 10 people.

Question: Did your family also stay?

Answer: The Germans began to implement their policy of"Judenrein" or free of Jews in Zmigrod following our departure for Plaszow. My father stated that he was not willing to leave his house come what may. He preferred to die in his own bed if it came to it. The Germans brought carts drawn by horses and moved all the rest of the Jews to Jaslo. My father, mother and younger brother went to the niche in the attic where they met other Jews. The Ukrainians and Germans began a house–to–house search for Jews. The family was saved for the day. The searchers did not find the niche. They stayed while the rest were moved out of the city and sent to the death camp of Treblinka where they all perished.

German record of Shimon Lang's activities during World War II. Lang was arrested on April 1, 1940 and was assigned to forced labor. On July 1, 1942 he was sent to Plaszow labor camp. (The date is incorrect since the selection in Zmigrod took place on July 7, 1942. Lang was sent to Plaszow shortly thereafter.)
From Plaszow, he was sent to the Theresienstadt concentration camp on May 10, 1943. He was liberated on May 9, 1945.
(The index card failed to mention two concentration camps where Lang was, namely Skarzysko–Kamienna and Buchenwald.)
At the end of the war, Lang resided at the Landzberg D.P. camp

Question: And your family?

Answer: My family consisting of my father, mother and younger brother remained hidden in the attic. Later on I met my father once more and he told me the story. According to him, my brother decided that he had enough of the attic and left the hiding place. A shot was heard. My father knew that they killed his son. They were left in the attic. There were no Jews left in Zmigrod. There was only one Jew left who worked for the Germans. He cleared the Jewish apartments and the merchandise was sent to Jaslo. This party had a relative in the niche. He brought her bread.

Question: Did she share the bread with the others?

Answer: Yes. She was the sister of the cleaner. She had a baby with her. Every day the brother brought a bread that was shared among the people. There were about 10 people in hiding. One day, the brother announced to the sister that they were finishing the clearing operations and he did not know what would happen. He appeared the last day and brought a loaf of bread. He never showed again. The people started to ration the bread that they had. Each day they received smaller portions.

The great problem was water. These were summer days and the heat was unbearable in the niche. To wet their lips they resorted to their own urine for lack of water. Following two months in the attic, the rains started. Someone went downstairs to look for pots or pans to collect the rainwater. They had to be very careful not to be spotted. They finally collected some pots and placed them with the right inclination and the correct camouflage to gather some water.

Their misfortune was the marauding Ukrainians who were constantly lurking and searching the Jewish homes for goods. They noticed the pots and called the Gestapo. The latter came and at first saw nothing. Then they took apart the house and found the hiding place. Some people were killed instantly, others were taken away to the prison in Jaslo. My father's brother was shot. My father and mother they took to Jaslo. There they met other hidden Jews who were discovered in Zmigrod. One morning they decided to make a selection and sent a transport of Jews to Ostbahn near Plaszow. I was about one kilometer way from Ostbahn. During the selection, a Gestapo man pointed to my father and said, "This dog could go to work." Father was sent with the transport to Ostbahn.

Question: And your mother?

Answer: She was left in prison at Jaslo. She was then sent to the ghetto of Rzeszow. What happened later, I do not know. I later met people who were in the ghetto of Rzeszow and talked about a woman who resembled my mother. They even knew how to pronounce her name. Thus, I knew that they were talking about my mother. Father arrived at the Ostbahn camp that was near Plaszow. A Zmigroder Jew saw him. When I was returning from a work detail, the Jew yelled out to me that he saw my father. For the moment I could not believe my ears. But the man was an honest man and I took his word. In the evening we got our supper.

Question: What did it consist of?

Answer: They gave us soup. I then approached Odelman and I told him that I had nothing to give him but I promised him that I would repay him for the favor that I was about to ask of him. He was wearing a special hat and riding breaches that gave him the authority to walk freely within the Plaszow camp. He took to me to the fence that separated the Plaszow camp from the Ostbahn camp. There were about 500 Jews or more there, and at first I did not recognize my father. He did see me. I had not seen my father since I said goodbye to him in the attic on that Sunday when I left for the transport to Plaszow. He wore pants and a jacket. Now he was barely dressed. A prison guard along the way demanded his clothing. He had no choice but to give them. He was left with rags. He had not eaten for days. I barely recognized him. He told me hello. I told my father that I had nothing with me but I would see if I could arrange something in my camp.

In our camp, Obersharfuhrer Muller walked around from the morning to the evening with a rifle and stopped people and searched them. If he found any food or other things on them, he took them to the fence and shot them. I managed to get to the fence and collected some clothes from the dead bodies. I knew that my father was an excellent tailor and would be able to fix the clothing so that he would have something to wear.

The next day, I asked Odelman again to walk me to the fence and I gave my father the clothes. Of course, I did not have a needle and thread to give him. My father approached the supervisor of the tailor shop at the Ostbahn camp and asked him for needles and thread in exchange for repairing cloth for him. The German supervisor agreed. My father fixed his clothes and worked for the German, who fed him. The work was extra, since during the day he worked at hauling big boulders that weighed about 100 kilos.

One day they selected 18 people in my father's camp and brought them to Plaszow. My father was among them. He remained in Plaszow about a month, during which time he told me exactly what happened in the attic from my departure to their being discovered by the Germans. This is how I know what happened after my departure from Zmigrod. At the end of the month, the 18 people were returned to the Ostbahn camp, among them my father. I do not know how long he was there. One day, someone told me that my father was killed. With him 17 people were killed. After the war, the German that ordered the killing was later found guilty by a Polish court and hanged on the same area.

Question: The 18 people did something wrong?

Answer: No. There was a selection and they selected 18 people and my father was among them. This was in April or May. A serious epidemic of stomach typhus began. There was pressure on our supervisor to send us to work or to kill us. We hardly went to work. The entire camp population was infected. We were busy digging burial holes. Each day more holes. There seemed no end to it.

Question: Were you sick?

Answer: I was also sick. On this day, Muller told us that we must go to work or we would be shot. We went to work but soon the entire camp came down with the disease. Still, Muller insisted that we must work.

I dragged my feet for about 14 or 15 hours a day since we had to unload two rail cars. We were laying the rails on top of gravel. There were two rail cars with wood. The German supervisor told me to get on top of the cars and start unloading. I could barely stand on my feet. But blows were coming and finally I managed to climb the ladder to the top of the car. We were four people on top of the rail car. We formed two teams of two. Each team unloaded the wood on each side. My partner begged me to start working since he feared that the Germans would shoot him and me for slacking. I began to lift the wood and throw it down. We managed to finish the task that day.

I told my children later, that if I lived another 50 years I could not finish to tell about the events that took place. However, I must tell you this story. When I arrived at Plaszow, it was still a labor camp and not a concentration camp. The camp demanded a payment of 150 zlotys and in order to get the money, you could work in the camp for it and with the money you received, you could pay for the half a liter of soup and bread that you received.

We were paid at the end of the month and paid for the food that we received.

Every Monday we received a loaf of bread for the entire week. We had to divide the bread so that it would last for the entire week. I did not have money and begged a relative to have pity on me and grant me a loan of 150 zlotys. I told him that all my belongings were stolen and I had nothing left. He gave me a loan. I decided to write a letter home to Zmigrod. This was still possible.

Question: You asked the family to send you some money?

Answer: Yes. They sent me money and I paid back the loan. I got an extra job to clean the barbershop. I was paid and given bread. My problem was now how to save my bread from being stolen.

Question: What did you do?

Answer: I tied the bread to myself and carried it wherever I went. I could it even wash myself while the bread remained attached. I received my pay of 150 zlotys at the end of the month and a kilo of bread. I soon realized that I would not be able to survive on a kilo of bread and work so hard. Some workers could not resist the temptation and finished the kilo of bread and then starved of hunger.

I decided to buy and sell salami, as many other workers did in the camp. Gentiles used to come near the camp and sell bread and salami. The salami consisted of horse meat. Old horses were slaughtered and used to produce salami. I figured that I would earn some money and buy bread that would enable me to continue to live another day. I knew that this was not an ideal solution but I had to survive. I bought a salami from a female farmer and paid her. The transaction took place a small distance from the group of workers. They finished working and returned their tools to the tool shed.

They then crossed the rail line. I tried to catch up with them when a huge transport train loaded with soldiers and artillery blocked my passage. The train seemed never to end. Then the train stopped. I tried to crawl under a train car when I was spotted by a guard. He ordered me to stand and clear everything that I had. He saw the salami and asked to break it up in crumbs. Possibly he thought that it contained explosives. I executed the order. The guard was very nervous and took several steps backward. He loaded the rifle and misfired. He repeated the attempt twice more and gave up in disgust. He looked at me with unbelieving eyes. He asked me if I was protected by G–d. Then he told me to get my stuff and disappear. I said to myself, this soldier is going to fight the Russians. I crossed the track and joined my working crew that was waiting on the other side of the track

Question: Was that a miracle?

Answer: A miracle or luck. I had a hernia and dragged about while working on the rail lines. We were eight people. The Germans who worked with us were also eight people, but they had eight workers on each side while we were eight people who lifted the rail and put it on our shoulders. Once I decided to stand in the middle, but the German supervisor Schultz came over to me and told me never to do this again. He took me and placed me at the head of the crew that was lifting the rails. He even screamed at me to raise my shoulder so that the rail was evenly balanced.

Question: How long were you at this camp?

Answer: About a year, perhaps a year and a quarter. Then we left Plaszow and were shipped to Skarzysko–Kamienna.

Question: What was Skarzysko?

Answer: It was a camp where ammunition was produced.

Question: Where was it located?

Answer: It was in Southern Poland.

Question: Was it far from Plaszow?

Answer: I do not remember.

Question: Was this new place also a labor camp?

Answer: Yes, it was a labor camp and camp of death. There was less brutality and less shootings, but there were more dead people. They worked with acids and explosives.

Question: What did you do with these materials?

Answer: I did not work with ammunition. Anybody assigned to work with the ammunition soon turned greenish. Everything they touched turned green. Their clothing was shredded due to the acids. Even their bread turned green when they touched it.

Question: Was it poison?

Answer: Yes, it was poison.

Question: What work did you do?

Answer: I worked in the transport department. Our shift worked from six in the morning to ten o'clock in the evening.

Question: What exactly did you do?

Answer: We loaded and unloaded ammunition. Raw materials arrived and were unloaded. The finished ammunition was loaded. We started to work with a crew of 15 Jews and were soon reduced to 10. The work was hard and the watery soup and the slice of bread was not enough to sustain people. We worked in all kinds of weather, snow or rain. I had no clothing, certainly not for outside work. I was hungry, cold and tired. I returned from work exhausted and fell into bed. The beds were three stories high. No mattress. I slept on sawdust.

Question: You slept on sawdust?

Answer: Yes, we slept on sawdust without blankets, summer and winter. This was a typical labor camp that you do not see on TV.

Question: How long were you there?

Answer: I was there until 1944.

Question: Were you at camp with relatives or friends?

Answer: I had acquaintances.

Question: How close were they?

Answer: These two acquaintances were from Zmigrod. They survived the war and reside today in Canada. Our relationship was very limited since we had no time to talk. And what could I ask them? What would happen? We just did not have the time and the patience. The breaks at work were limited. People died right and left. Within a short time, we were 10 people then nine people and so on. Many were killed and some died. We knew when someone died when he did not join the group that was going to work. Then we knew that he was dead.

Question: When did you leave the place?

Answer: We knew already in 1944 that the Germans wanted to ship us out since the Russians had already crossed the Wisla River.

Question: Due to the Russian military advances?

Answer: We were a few Jews at Skarzysko and then a selection took place where they eliminated a third of the inmates. I survived the selection but I was almost naked. I did not know what would happen to me. Being a religious person, I believed that help would arrive since that was my destiny. That day, I was sent to bring the food from the main kitchen. I wheeled the barrel of soup that stood on a small trolley and was very careful not to spill it. I was very careful since I had to bring the soup to our group of workers.

Suddenly, there was an order to return to the camp immediately. The camp was dark and the selection was taking place among the Russians. I was permitted to cross the gate since I was bringing the food and I was naked. The other people were not permitted to cross the entrance gate. They decided to select the people at the entrance gate. Mass killings were taking place. I continued to walk with the food and did not dare to take some food, since I knew that this was the food for the entire group.

A new order was given to leave everything and proceed to the appel platz, or assembly mall. I opened the cover and took one portion and another portion of food. I swallowed everything very fast and ran to the assembly place. I realized that I was naked, so I ran to the barrack where there was a tailor. This tailor did repair work and always had some clothing. I begged him for some clothing and I managed to put on some clothes. The tailor survived the war. I ran to the assembly place and passed the selection. A small group of inmates was sent to Czestochowa, Poland, where we built anti–tank ditches. We arrived at the place and found a barn of straw that could provide shelter for about 100 people. We were about 500. Most of us had to stay outside and spend the night on the ground. We huddled together to keep warm. In the morning we went to work. This lasted for about a month.

Question: What did you eat?

Answer: We ate what they gave us, nothing in particular. We remained there for about one or two months. Then they took us to Buchenwald concentration camp. When we arrived at Buchenwald, we had to undergo a disinfection process. Two S.S. stood and watched as everybody undressed and had to immerse himself in a bath full of disinfectant material. This, of course, was also an occasion to examine all prisoners to see if they had hidden items on their bodies or in the body apertures. At the end of 1944, there were no longer shootings in the camps.

Question: What did you do in Buchenwald?

Answer: We were in Buchenwald for a short period of time.

Question: What did you do?

Answer: We went to work each day. We cleared the debris of the Allied bombings.

Question: Where next?

Answer: From Buchenwald they took us to Schliben in Germany, where there was a munitions factory that produced panzerfaust or anti–tank rockets. I did not work with ammunition. I was a construction worker.

Question: What did you build?

Answer: We did not build. We dug the ground. We worked there until the big explosion.

Date	23.8.1950/GG	Bu. No.	84914	Polid..Pole/Jude	
				GOC2/197/9	
Name	L A N G, Szymon		File	-IC/18-	
BD	1.6 1o	BP	Zmigrod	Nat	Polish Jew
Next of Kin					
Source of Information	Polit. Abt. Buchenwald, Neuzugänge v. SS-u.				
Last kn. Location	Polizeiführer Radom.			Date d 9.9.44.	
CC Buchenwald		Arr. 9.9.44.		lib.	
Transf. on		to			
Died on		in			
Cause of death					
Buried on		in			
Grave			D. C. No.		
Remarks	Page No.5, Curr. No.255				

Shimon Lang reached the Buchenwald concentration camp on September 9, 1944

Question: The explosion occurred as a result of an air attack?

Answer: No. There was a tremendous explosion during the night shift.

Question: Did the inmates blow up the factory?

Answer: Rumors had it that the man in charge of the factory set up the explosion, since the Russians were approaching the place rapidly. The first explosion occurred about 10 in the evening. I was sitting on my bed when the tremendous explosion shook me up. The second explosion followed and the debris hit our barrack. The place had so much ammunition that explosions continued to be heard throughout the night.

Question: Were people killed?

Answer: Next to our camp was a camp for women. When the explosions started, the women abandoned the barracks and headed to the gate of the camp. The guards refused to let them out. But the rush was so strong that the women pushed their way through the guards and walked out of their camp. We saw what happened and we also headed to the gate and broke out of our compound.

Question: Were these camps forced labor camps?

Answer: These were concentration camps. We ran in the opposite direction of the explosions. We gathered a small group and awaited news. We soon learned that the entire night work shift, with a few exceptions, was killed in the explosions. About 2,000 workers were killed. All the rail cars were loaded with ammunition. Nothing was left standing.

Question: Who remained alive?

Answer: Those who were not in the area, a handful survived. There were, of course, workers in deep bunkers who survived. We remained outside our compound in the large camp until the next day. Then a German came and led us back to our regular camp within the large concentration camp..

Question: What happened to the site of the explosion?

Answer: The site was a junkyard. We started to reconstruct the barracks. The Germans also took us out to other areas to clean the areas. The devastation was so huge that we barely managed to make a dent in the area. The area of destruction was immense and contained huge bunkers, rail lines and buildings that contained huge amounts of explosives. We had to clean the area. The Germans sent S.S soldiers each day to supervise the clearing of the areas.

Question: How long did you stay there?

Answer: We remained there for about two weeks. Then they took us to the Theresienstadt concentration camp.

Question: When in 1945?

Answer: In April 1945, we reached Theresienstadt. Along the way there was a cemetery.

Question: Did you walk?

Answer: No, we traveled by train but we received no food. Each railroad car had an assigned soldier. This soldier took from everybody whatever they had and shared it with the entire car. On occasion the soldier managed to get some food outside like cabbage, and brought it to us. Nothing substantial.

Question: Did you get to Theresienstadt?

Answer: When we arrived at the camp we received a slice of bread and I felt that was like eating sweetened bread. We remained in Theresienstadt for two weeks. Life was not easy. There was there an old winery where the food was dished out in cups. We arrived and were hungry like wolves, we pushed and shoved to get to the food. The hail of beatings did not stop us from trying to get to the food. Some people got food, others did not get any due to the pandemonium. The food situation did not change until the day we were liberated.

Question: How long did this last?

Answer: About two or three weeks.

Question: That means that you were liberated in May of 1945?

Answer: I was liberated May 10, 1945.

Question: Do you remember the day of liberation?

Answer: I remember. I was liberated on Saturday, May 10, 1945. Some inmates who were strong left the camp and started to enter German homes. Around the Theresienstadt concentration camp there was a large population that provided the logistical support for the camp. These homes were attacked by the camp inmates. They took whatever food or goods they saw. They brought the stuff back to the camp. I was too weak to move, but I decided that I must get something or I would starve. So next morning, I left the camp that was surrounded by Russian soldiers with rifles. I saw a German carrying a sack and I grabbed a corner of the sack. There began a tug of war. The German finally let go and left. I dragged the sack with all my energy to the road. I opened the sack and saw pictures of the man's wife. I left the sack and went to a few houses where I found a small bag of sugar, a loaf of bread and a can of meat. I had no opener but banged the can until it split at the top. I made a sandwich and sprinkled the sugar on top of it. I did not eat too much and started to walk back to the camp, but I did not feel good. I continued to walk and reached my barrack, whereupon I collapsed. I do not know what happened nor how long I was unconscious.

Question: Were you unconscious?

Answer: After a few days, I returned to my bed. Most of the inmates were gone. I rested on my bed. Two male nurses came and they were looking for me. Outside were dead bodies all over the place. Many of them died of dysentery. One of them brought me a glass of water with a biscuit. I remained in bed. Then the Russians entered the camp and began to make order. They separated the sick from the dead. They spread sheets on the beds like in a hospital. No food was given except for tea. A few days later they began to distribute biscuits that were hardened.

Question: Sort of dried toast?

Answer: Precisely. At first I could not do a thing since I was naked. But slowly as the kitchen was being organized, I got a job in the kitchen and things started to arrange themselves.

Question: Did you get clothes?

Answer: Yes. Some clothing. In the kitchen I received larger portions so I saved some of the food and managed to procure some clothing in exchange. We remained in Theresienstadt about a month and a half. There was one Jew in the camp who began to organize a group of Jewish survivors that would go to Palestine. The camp administration had a policy of urging all the survivors to return to their native lands. The camp administration told us that we must return home and then we can go to Palestine. But we knew what it meant to return to Poland. When I worked in Plaszow along the rail lines, we saw the transports of Jews that were heading to Treblinka.

Question: Did you know that these Jews would not return?

Answer: In Plaszow, when I worked along the rail lines, we were told not to look at the transports. Some transports stopped for some time. We were ordered to keep our noses to the ground. Anyone caught looking was removed and sent on the next transport or selection to the camps from where nobody returned. I remember an incident of a Jew who was begging for some water in exchange for all his possessions; his pleas were ignored and he was sent on a transport to the death camp.

Question: Who told you about the crematories or the gas chambers?

Answer: No. This we did not know.

Question: You did not want to go back to Poland?

Answer: I did not want to return to Poland and I did not return. There were 50 Jews who cleaned the ghetto of Zmigrod for the Germans. Only one person, named Adelman, survived. He was transported to the death camp but jumped the train. The Germans fired at him but it was night time and he lay on the ground until the train passed by. He managed to reach the city of Krakow, where he had a relative. Obviously the man had some money that he found while clearing the Jewish houses. He paid his way and reached his relative. But all the Jews of Krakow were in the ghetto or in Plaszow. He had to pay to get into the camp because on the outside he had no papers and no possibility of existence. It was difficult to get into the camp since they counted us in the morning when we left for work and repeated the counting when we returned to the Plaszow camp.

Question: Why did he want to go into the camp?

Answer: He had to go into the camp because there was no other place for a Jew. He had to pay to enter the camp and he must have paid a nice sum. Adelman had means and became an authority in the camp. He never hit people, but imposed himself on them. He was a practical man yet gentle enough, similar to his mother's family. He led the workers to their work place. He survived the war and is presently a multimillionaire in the USA. When he reached the USA, he met his mother and two brothers. He did not reach the USA empty–handed and became very rich in the USA. I never met him or talked to him, despite the fact that we were neighbors in Zmigrod. I went to cheder and he did not go to cheder nor to the public school. Yet he graduated university in the USA. He maintained contacts but not with me.

Question: When did you get to Israel?

Answer: I reached Palestine from Theresienstadt. I tried to influence all the Jewish survivors not to return to Poland where they would be killed. We were about 12 survivors. We decided not to return to Poland. I knew of a case where a survivor went to Poland and was killed by the neighbors. The Russians decided to close the camp. We were placed aboard a truck and started to travel. We traveled for hours and reached the Italian border. To enter Palestine, we needed certificates that we did not have. We therefore traveled back to Vienna, Austria, where there were many Ukrainians. We continued to travel until we reached the city of Landsberg in the American military zone of Germany. There we met Dr. Greengrass, who assigned us to rooms. We were six men in a room with bunk beds. We arrived at the Landsberg D.P. camp in June 1945.

Question: How long did you stay there?

Answer: When we arrived at Landsberg, the kitchen was already established. Each block received a food allotment that was then divided between the individuals. I felt very weak and barely walked.

Question: Did they operate on you in Landsberg?

Answer: In Landsberg there was a Jewish Polish hospital that had several good professors. One of them examined me and told me to return on a particular day. The professor made all the preparations. I appeared before the surgeons and they told me that they were doubtful whether the surgery would succeed. I told them that I was a sole survivor and nobody would shed tears if I did not emerge from the operation. They proceeded with the surgery and I remained bedridden for a long time. A German nurse nursed me for a month. I remained in the hospital for about eight or nine months. I could have left the hospital earlier, but the place where I lived was not to my liking so I stayed at the hospital. I left the hospital and started working in a tailor shop. I never learned how to sew. I asked my father years ago to let me attend a tailor training program but he never permitted it so I never learned sewing. This perhaps saved me, for in Plaszow the Gestapo came around looking for tailors. I later discovered they wanted to shoot Jews and were not interested in tailors. Lucky break for me that I did not know tailoring and could not volunteer for the work details. It seems my destiny protected me more than my intelligence.

Following the surgery I was very weak and it took me many months to recuperate. I continued to work at the shop and learned to become a good worker. In 1946 I met my wife and were married. We gave birth to a son.

Question: In Landsberg?

Answer: Yes, in Landsberg. He is today head of a department. He was born in 1947. I wanted to go to Palestine but my wife was busy looking for her relatives. Nobody of her family was left. She had five brothers and sisters. She kept saying,"How can I leave without them?" She also became pregnant and we had to postpone our planned trip to Palestine.

Interviewer: Thank you for the interview.

A group of Zmigrod survivors meet in Landsberg D.P. (Displaced Persons) camp in the American Zone of Occupation of Germany to memorialize the slaughter of the Jewish communities of Zmigrod and Osiek Jasielski.
(The picture was contributed by Selig Eisenberg)

The following survivors have helped to identify the survivors in the picture:
William Leibner, Zvi Keren, Max Findling and Shimon Lang. *(The Names have been updated as of June, 2000!)*
Seated (Bottom line), left to right: **Hanina Eisenberg/Stein, Lea Bronfeld, Baruch Krebs, Berish Krebs, Naftali Bronfeld and his wife, Jehshua Engel.**
Second line, left to right: **Malka Eisenberg, Shimon Lang, Lea Bronfeld's daughter, Jakob Leibner, Jechzkel/Chaskel Bobker**
Third line, left to right: **unknown, unknown, Reisel Kornfeld with her baby (Shimon), Heniek [Henoch] Krebs [Brish Krebs' son] standing, Izak Shaul/Szol Krisher standing**
Fourth Row, Standing: **Jechezkel Krisher, Selig Eisenberg and Chaim Kornfeld**

CHAPTER IX
Other Testimonies
Regarding Halbow

Testimony given by Moshe Einhorn, son of Shia Hersh and Shaindel
Einhorn. Born in 1905 in Nowy Zmigrod distict of Jaslo

On July 7th, 1942, the Germans ordered all the Jews to assemble at the sport place. Personally ordered to appear was Hersh Eisenberg, head of the Judenrat, and the entire family of Hersh Raab. The entire Gestapo contingent was present and headed by Muller and Genz. They started throwing beer bottles at Eisenberg until they killed him. Then they selected about 1,300 Jews and the Raab family and loaded them onto trucks that drove them to Halbow, 18 kilometers before Bardiow and 10 kilometers after Zmigrod. There in the forest of Halbow, a huge pit about 50 meters long was dug several days earlier by local workers. The pit was surrounded with people armed with machine guns that fired rounds at the lined up people. Each Jew received one bullet, and no more. The killed Jews fell into the pit. The Germans ordered the local men to cover the area which kept moving for the next three days.

The testimony was corroborated by my cousin, Pinkas Wohlmut, a merchant of Zmigrod who witnessed personally the killing of Eisenberg and the destruction of the Jews of the town. The public notary of the town also attested to this destruction as well as the carpenter Worawski and the farmer Winarski, a resident of Zmigrod.

To reach the above town, one has to travel to Jaslo and then by coach to Zmigrod and Halbow. The place is situated in a forest. The pit is devoid of fences and the animals graze there. Zmigrod itself is devoid of Jews.

Signed: Einhorn Moses mp.
Krakow, date, 17.1.1946.

William Leibner translated the above from Polish to English.

Testimony of the destruction of the Jews of Zmigrod by a Jew from Lodz

July 7th was the anniversary of the 1,060 Jews that were killed in Zmigrod, 18 kilometers from Jaslo, in 1942. 800 were older than 14 years and many were Jews from Lodz who were forced to leave their city in 1939. This township had about 1,500 Jews including the Jews of Lodz, Krakow and the surrounding areas.

It was a very hot summer day, the entire Jewish population marched five abreast to a special designated area. At 7 A.M., the executioners appeared. An order was barked: Attention! Everybody up! Then the first call, all those aged 60 over there to the right! The second call, the head of the J.S.S. and his family out! Now the entire Jewish population lined up in alphabetical order. An SS man with a big stick walked amongst the Jews and pulled people out of their row. He pushed them to the right and hit them with his stick. Groups were led into the forest of Halbow, 12 kilometers from Zmigrod. At 3 P.M., the head of the Judenrat, Hersh Eisenberg was called. He was brutally hit in the face and blood oozed all over his body. The district chief told him that he would be on the last truck and insisted that his blood stream in the sun. This lasted until 5 p.m. At 7 p.m. we saw the clothing that was returned. We were later told that children were buried alive. Then they asked the survivors for a contribution of 100,000 zlotys and gave three days to collect the amount. The payment was made in two installments. Four days later, 150 men were sent to Plaszow near Krakow. Six weeks later Zmigrod was Judenrein [free of Jews]. Some survived amongst those that were sent to Plaszow, the rest perished.

Thus was erased an old Jewish township of 800 years. The Jewish community should try to bury these saints in a proper Jewish burial place and not let them stay somewhere in a forest.

Signed: Matriharz Lodz, Pilsudskiego 74.

Translated from Yiddish to English by William Leibner

CHAPTER X
The Killers

The charge sheet against the killers of the Jews of Zmigrod. Osiek Jasielski and other Jews at the forest of Halbow, near Zmigrod, Galicia, Poland

Members of the Gestapo office of Jaslo, Galicia, Poland that included the hamlet of Zmigrod during the German occupation during WWII. The poster of the war criminals was displayed at the police station of Jaslo following WWII. Max Findling visited the place where he was incarcerated during the war and saw the poster. He photographed the poster that showed most of the Gestapo men in Jaslo.The document is presently displayed at the local museu

- 20 -

b) <u>Zmigrod (Fall II der Anklage)</u>

Vier Tage später als in Frystak, am 7.Juli 1942,
fand die große Vernichtungsaktion in <u>Zmigrod</u> statt.
Das südlich von Jaslo am Fuße der Beskiden ge-
legene Städtchen hatte 1942 nahezu 2000 jüdische
Einwohner, die den Stadtkern bewohnten. Zu ihnen
gehörten einige hundert Juden, die aus der Umge-
bung nach Zmigrod umgesiedelt worden waren. Die
wenigen polnischen Familien Zmigrods wohnten mei-
stens am Stadtrand und in den Außenbezirken. Auch
in Zmigrod durften die Juden ihren Wohnbezirk,
dessen Grenzen festgelegt waren, nicht ohne Er-
laubnis verlassen. Bei Zuwiderhandlungen drohte
ihnen die Todesstrafe.

Die Aktion selbst verlief ähnlich wie in Frystak,
doch waren die Befürchtungen der Juden viel größer,
weil sie inzwischen vom Schicksal der Menschen
im Wald bei Warzyce erfahren hatten. An den Judenrat erging der Befehl, dafür zu sorgen, daß
sich die jüdische Bevölkerung am genannten Tage
frühmorgens vollzählig auf einem am Ortsrand
gelegenen Platz versammelte. Der größte Teil der
Juden fand sich dementsprechend zwischen 6 und
7 Uhr früh auf dem sogenannten Balplatz ein, der
von <u>deutscher</u>, <u>polnischer</u> und <u>ukrainischer Polizei</u>
umstellt war. Als kurz darauf Dr.Gentz und die
Angehörigen des Greko Jaslo eintrafen, begann die
Selektion. Die familienweise aufgestellten Juden
mußten Geld und Wertsachen auf einer Decke auf
dem Platz niederlegen. Jüngere arbeitsfähige Leute
erhielten an einem Tisch einen Stempel in ihre
Arbeitspapiere und durften später den Platz verlassen. Alte Leute sollten zur Seite treten.
Sie waren die zuerst ausgewählten Opfer der geplanten
Vernichtungsaktion. Ihnen folgten Juden jeden
Alters und Geschlechts, die mehr oder weniger

*A page of the original charge sheet at the trial of Ansberg,
Germany.
Translated by William Leibner*

The picture originally appeared in the German press when the German government decided to prosecute German war criminals who committed heinous crimes during WWII in the area of Jaslo. The poster asked people who knew these criminals to step forth and give evidence. The poster and the request were reprinted in many countries. A number of Jewish survivors like Max Findling, Leo Rosner and others gave testimony. It took a long time to assemble all the incriminating evidence. Finally, the German prosecution was ready and presented the case to the court of of the city of Ansberg, Germany. The charge sheet was extensive and detailed. It listed most of the Gestapo men in Jaslo that included Zmigrod.

Dr. Walter Gentz, Kreishauptman, of the Jaslo district

Walter Gentz was born in Düsseldorf, Germany in 1907. He pursued his academic studies in the legal field, especially finance. He joined the Nazi party in 1928. He was awarded a doctorate in law. He advanced rapidly within the ranks of the Gestapo. In 1940, he was appointed finance inspector of the Polish district of Jaslo. that included and Zmigrod. In 1941 he was appointed "kreishauptman," district leader, of the Jaslo district that included Jaslo, Gorlice, Krosno and Zmigrod. He immediately began a process of Germanization of the city of Jaslo. He was determined to change Jaslo into a German city. He brutally persecuted Jews throughout his district. He participated in all actions aimed at the Jewish population in his ditrict. He actively participated in the selection of Jews in Zmigrod . His sadistic behaviour to innocent Jews is beyond description. Following the war, he managed to find work in Germany until he was arrested and brought to trial with some of his assistants. During the trial in Ansberg, Germany, he committed suicide in March of 1969.

Ludwig Losackers, S.S. Shturmbanfuhrer

Wilhelm Raschwitz, was a "Hauptsturmfuhrer" or chief of the Gestapo office I n Jaslo from 1941 to 1943. He was killed in battles with the partisans.

Ludwig Rommies

Salzer, Obersharffuhrer

Paul Baron, scharfuhrer

Laubenthal

Augustin

Walter Matheus

Albert Krischook

Theodor Drzyzga

Helmut Menz

Karl Hauch

Karl Hauch

Erich Kuschke

Leopold Backer

Franz Zalser

Aton Neuman

Gunter Gutsche

Ernest Meber

Wilhelm Schumacher

The charge

All of the above listed people were members of the Jaslo Gestapo office and responsible for the physical destruction of the Jewish communities in the Jaslo district. The case was a compounded case since all plans and actions aimed at the destruction of the Jewish communities started in the office of Jaslo. This office received the orders and implemented them. The trial was lengthy and the defense lawyers had a field day with some of the witnesses, especially with their memories. The following people appeared as witnesses for the prosecution; Joseph Findling, Max Findling, Eisenberg, Leo Rosner, Pinkas Wohlmut, Moshe Einhorn, and Israel Hal.

Zmigrod, Part II of the Charge

Four days after the Jews of Frystak were killed; it was the turn of the Jews of Zmigrod. The Jews of this community were killed on July 7,1942. Zmigrod is located south of Jaslo in the lower hills of the Beskiden mountains. The estimated Jewish population was about 2000 inclusive of several hundred Jews from the surrounding areas. The Jews lived in the center of town while some of the Polish families lived on the outskirts or in the outlying sections of town. In town itself, the Jews were limited to their section and needed a pass to leave their area. People that crossed without a pass faced death.

The action was similar to the one in Frystak, although the apprehension of the Jewish population was greater since it was aware of what happened in the forest of Warzyce [the killing site of the Jews in Frystak]. Thus the Judenrat of Zmigrod received an order in advance to see to it that every Jew appeared at the given time and place. Most of the Jews were there already between six and seven a.m. The so-called Bals place was surrounded with German, Polish and Ukrainian police. Shortly thereafter, Dr. Gentz and the leadership of the Jaslo Gestapo arrived and the selection began. The Jews were lined up with their families and they were told to drop all their belongings on a blanket that was spread out on the ground. Young able-bodied people received a special stamp in their work permit and were ordered to leave the area shortly thereafter. Old people were then selected to the right. They were the first victims of the planned extermination. They were soon followed by Jews of different ages and sexes that were pulled out of their rows by the Gestapo men as was in Frystak. These hungry, nervous and thirsty people stood and endured the hot summer day. They were beaten with sticks, pikes and weapons at the slightest infraction.

Dr. Gentz took an active role in these events. He roughed up the head of the Jewish Social Self-Help organization named Rab. The latter once complained to the Krakow office about the many refugees that were sent to Zmigrod and how they overcrowded the existing facilities. Dr. Gentz took the complaint personally and ordered Rab and his entire family to join the people condemned to death. Even worse was his behavior to the head of the Judenrat, Hersh Eisenberg. He was supposed to collect money before the action began but postponed it and claimed that the Jews were too poor. Dr. Gentz called him a liar. He and some

Gestapo men beat him with sticks, pikes and beer bottles. They insisted that he stand and watch the entire selection while blood flowed from his head. He joined the last transport. Different than in Frystak, the Gestapo men were under the influence of alcohol. Dr. Gentz ordered beer and schnapps to the selection site and the police helped themselves.

In Zmigrod, different than in Frystak, the Jews were transported by trucks to the killing site. Children and handicapped people who were unable to mount the trucks were simply tossed into them. The slightest resistance was met with sticks and rifle butts. The overloaded trucks drove from Zmigrod several kilometers south in the direction of Krempna to a place below the Krempna pass and above the village of Halbow. There, the Polish workers had dug a pit about 30 meters long, several meters wide and two to three meters deep. The Jews were told to undress and then pushed to the rim of the pit where they were shot. They fell into the pit. Several days later, the pit had to be covered again since the ground above the pit had risen. All together, on July 7th, 1942, at least 1,000 Jews and possibly 1,250 Jews of Zmigrod were killed at Halbow.

The trial proceeded at a slow pace due to the logistics of bringing witnesses from all over and providing translators. Assembling material was also a difficult task, as documents were scattered over many places. Still the proceedings took place and most of the killers were brought to the hall of justice. The judges were very lenient and most of the accused received very light sentences. The fact, however, remains that the perpetrators of these heinous crimes in Zmigrod were brought to light in a German courtroom, something the Gestapo men never dreamed would happen.

The murdered Jews at Halbow were not forgotten in some obscure forest in Poland. Their case was told and retold in the courtroom for some time. Their story was printed in the papers. The memorial of Halbow was rekindled. Jewish communities that lived for hundreds of years were wiped out by a few killers in a very short period of time for the simple reason that they were Jews. The Jewish community of Zmigrod and Osiek never revived following the war. The cemeteries in Zmigrod and Halbow are the only evidence of a past Jewish presence in these places.

CHAPTER XI
Bibliography

Andrzej Potoci, Zydzi w Podkarpackem. Wydanie I. Rzeszow, Poland, 2004

Samuel Rosenhan Written testimony in Yiddish of, a native of Osiek Jasielski, at Yad Vashem

Interviews with survivors from Osiek and Nowy Zmigrod notably Shimon Lang, Mordechai Findling, Jakob Leibner

Pinkas Hakehilot.

Central Historical Archives of the Jewish People in Jerusalem; HM/7921

Central Zionist Archives; Z-4/234-13

Book on Staszow, Tel Aviv, pp. 625-627

A. Rutkowski, "Zaglada Zydow w dystrykcie radomskim"

"Biuletyn ZIH," Warszawa 1955, no. 35, pp. 86, 164

"Nowy Dziennik" (newspaper), 18/5/1925. 16/2/1933, 18/1/1937

Yad Vashem Archives, TR-10/778;016/1764;M-1/E 728/602

Yad Vashem Archives, 021/16

YIVO Archives; ADRP 49H

Central Historical Archives of the Jewish People in Jerusalem; HM/712, HM/7101, HM/7099, HM/7096

Central Zionist Archives; Z-4/226-24; Z-3/178, Z-3/149

American Joint Archives; Poland, Reconstruction 399

Jaslo, Oskarza, Warszawa 1973, pp. 12, 59

"Hamitzpe" (newspaper ; 24/3/1905, 31/3/1905, 16/6/1905

"Hatzfira" (newspaper) 19/1/1906

"Kol Machzikei Hadath" (newspaper) 23/6/1905

"Divrei Akiva" 26/12/1936

"Chwila Wieczorna" (newspaper) 15/4/1935

"Noar Hatzioni" (newspaper) 17/11/1933, 26/6/1936

"Judishe Rundshau" (newspaper) 22/11/1918

"Monatsschrift der Oesterreichisch..." (newspaper) Wien, May 1905

"Nowy Dziennik" (newspaper) 14/12/1919, 24/1/1931, 28/1/1933, 11/2/1934, 5/1/1936, 8/1/1937, 20/5/1938, 23/5/1929, 4/6/1939

CHAPTER XII
Osiek Jasielski
near Jaslo, Galicia
(49°38' 21°29')

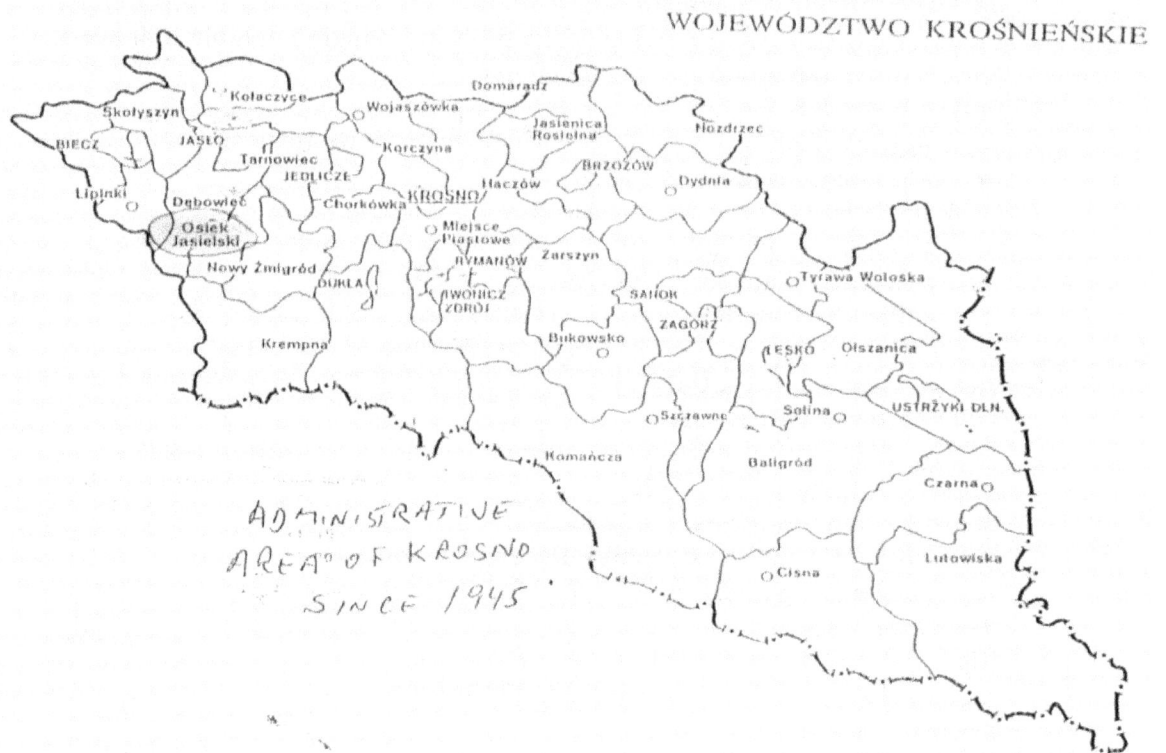

Administrative area of Krosno since 1945

Osiek Jasielski, Poland
(District of Jaslo, region of Krakow)
(Osiek is located East of Krakow, south of Jaslo and north
of Nowy Zmigrod. The place is officially called Osiek Jasielski)

Number of Jews	Total population	Year
1,880	965	232
1,900	882	247
1,921	813	213

Jewish Population chart in Osiek

Osiek Jasielski – Galicia, Poland

by William Leibner, **Jerusalem**

The hamlet Osiek, or Osiek Jasielski, as it is called in official documents, is located south of Jaslo and north of Nowy Zmigrod, Galicia, Poland. The Jews called the hamlet Osiek. There is another village of Osiek but it is located near Baranow in another region of Poland. This second Osiek also had a small Jewish population. We are concerned with the first hamlet called Osiek Jasielski.

We do not know the precise historical beginning of Osiek Jasielski, but it is mentioned for the first time as a village administered under the Magdenburg law. It formed part of the royal estate of the Polish Kings since 1365 and was granted the status of city already in 1502. In those days, it was an important place since it was strategically located along a commercial route that led across the Carpathian Mountains to Pressburg, or present–day Bratislawa, and Central Europe. A flourishing wine trade existed along this road that provided Poland with Hungarian wines. The fortunes of Osiek declined with the building of modern roads, and the appearance of the railways practically demolished the economy of the region, for it was much cheaper to ship wines or other products via rail instead of horse–drawn coaches. Osiek Jasielski never recovered from the economic blow and continued to decline economically; it even lost its municipal status. During the 19th and 20th centuries, it became well known for its horse fairs.

We do not know when the first Jewish families settled in Osiek, but in 1785 there were 9 Jewish families and in 1824 there were 31 Jews in Osiek. In the second half of the 19th century, there was already a Jewish population of 50 families. The nearby Jewish community of Zmigrod provided the religious needs of the early Jewish inhabitants including burial services. Eventually, the Jewish population organized a small kehilla that built a synagogue and a mikvah. The community even brought a rabbi, namely Rabbi Aaron Halbershtam, the oldest son of the Zmigroder Rabbi Sinai Halberstam, to administer the spiritual needs of the hamlet. The Jewish population consisted mainly of peddlers, small businessmen, artisans, farmers and horse dealers. Jews began to leave Osiek prior to World War I in search of economic opportunities. Ten to twenty Jewish families left the place between 1900 and 1921, some moved to bigger places and some left during World War One. The Russian army occupied Osiek and the

Russian Cossaks had a field day in robbing Jewish stores and homes. The Jewish community was pauperized.

The exodus continued during the war since the area was the scene of bitter fighting for control of the mountain passes. Few of the families that left returned to Osiek. The Jewish population continued to decline and sought better economic opportunities elsewhere. The Jewish population was basically very Orthodox, although there were some Zionist activities following World War One, especially among the Jewish youth. The Zionist activities became more widespread with the opening of a branch of the youth movement "Hanoar Hatzioni" in 1933 that attracted 40 youngsters. For the Zionist elections in 1935, the movement managed to sell 43 shekalim that entitled the purchasers to vote for delegates to the International Zionist Congress. The voters gave 42 votes to the list of the Palestinian working party and one vote to the General Zionist movement. In the local rural elections of 1939 in Osiek, four Jewish members were elected to the rural council that consisted of 20 members.

The local Christian population was very anti–Semitic and made life difficult for the Jews. Jewish children were harassed in the local public school; their peyot, or earlocks, were clipped or they were forced to kneel not far from a cross. During the anti–kosher slaughter campaign in Poland, the local authorities cancelled the license of the only Jewish kosher butcher shop in Osiek in 1937. Osiek accepted with joy the ban on ritual slaughter that closed the only kosher butcher shop in the hamlet. Thus, the Jews had to bring kosher meat from other places. The Jewish economic situation was very poor and the community could barely afford to maintain a rabbi. Rabbi Aaron Halberstam became rabbi of Zmigrod and Osiek. According to the Polish researcher, Andzej Potocki, the Jewish population of Osiek numbered about 300 souls in 1939.

The Germans occupied the hamlet and started to issue anti–Jewish orders, namely limiting Jewish mobility to the village itself. Jews were then forced to wear armbands. Their economic situation worsened from day to day. A branch of the J.S.S. (Jewish Self–Help) was activated that distributed warm meals to the needy and tended to the sick.

The German economic measures against the Jews hardened as the war progressed. The Jewish families were being pauperized while the German demands kept increasing. More Jewish forced laborers, more financial impositions and more edicts against the Jews. Then suddenly, Jews were being forced to leave Osiek Jasielski for Zmigrod, the nearby Jewish community. The process repeated itself several times until all the Jews of Osiek Jasielski and surrounding villages were driven to the ghetto of Zmigrod in the summer of 1942. The Jewish community of Osiek ceased to exist and became part of the Zmigrod Jewish community. This community would also soon disappear. Meanwhile conditions in Zmigrod became very crowded with the arrival of the Jews from the villages surrounding Zmigrod. Most of these Jews were not permitted to take with them but a few items. They arrived empty handed. The community organized help to provide these poor refuges with some basic necessities. The economic situation was hopeless. The younger Jews took on jobs but the elderly refugees were starving of hunger and disease. All the Jews in Zmigrod now shared the same fate. They will all march to the selection place at Bal's meadow and most of them would then be sent to Halbow where they would be murdered.

The Halbow forest near Zmigrod where most of the Jews of Zmigrod and Osiek would be murdered

The grave site of the Zmigroder and Osieker Jews killed on July 7, 1942 at Halbow near Zmigrod

Testimony Given by Shmuel Rosenhan

Born in 1928 in the Village Of Osiek

TESTIMONY GIVEN BY SHMUEL ROSENHAN

BORN IN 1928 IN THE VILLAGE OF OSIEK.

A page of the original text in Yiddish

The village of Osiek Jasielski is located on the outskirts of Zmigrod and was always part of the Jewish community of that township. We don't know the date of the testimony, although we assume that it was written some time after the war. The document was written in Yiddish. We don't know the specific date when the Jews of the village of Osiek were transferred to Zmigrod. We assume that it occurred in several phases, and by the summer of 1942 there were no more Jews in Osiek.

"The Germans entered our village between Rosh Hashanah and Yom Kippur (year?). Until 1941, when Germany attacked Russia, conditions remained somewhat calm. Then the Germans began to push the Jews out of Osiek and by July 1942, there were no Jews in Osiek. The Jews of Osiek were forced to enter the ghetto of Zmigrod. The two Jewish communities would now face the same fate.

On the 22nd day of the Jewish month of Tammuz, or the 7th of July, 1942, the Germans ordered all the Jews of Zmigrod (that included the Jews of Osiek and from all the surrounding villages and hamlets), to assemble at Bal's meadow in Zmigrod. Men, women and children were given identity cards which were already pre-marked. The young and able were marked for survival while the others were to be killed. They lined us up in a row in the big square below the town. The place was big and it was used to feed the animals. The older people and the small children were pulled from the rows and pushed in the direction of the waiting trucks guarded by the SS men. The latter bullied these people into the trucks which drove them to the forest of Halbow where they were lined up and killed. The small children up to the age of ten were killed with sticks. Each row of dead people would be covered with a layer of chalk and chlorine, then followed by another row of dead people. Thus layer followed layer; many people were only wounded or bruised but were nevertheless crushed or asphyxiated by the succeeding falling bodies. This process continued until the last truck with Jews arrived from Zmigrod. Then the Germans covered the pit with a thick coat of chalk, chlorine and then sand. Thus were killed about 1,650 Jews of Zmigrod and vicinity, as well as Jews from Krosno, Lodz and Krakow (Andzej Potocki, Polish researcher in the area, estimates that 1,257 Jews were killed at Halbow. The figure ranges from 1,650 to 1,200, depending on the witness).

The 450 survivors were asked to make a contribution of 100,000 zlotys (Polish currency) or they too would be shot. A collection was made and the sum was presented by the head of the "Judenrat" or Jewish community, Hersh Eisenberg, to the German Gestapo chief, Genz from Jaslo. The latter demanded more money as an excuse to get rid of the Judenrat head. Eisenberg informed the German that the people were broke and had no more money left.

The latter took Eisenberg and led him to the place where the selection had just taken place and ordered the SS men to work him over. They did their work with relish and blinded Hersh Eisenberg. His body was tossed onto one of the trucks and they dumped beer barrels on his body until he was killed.

All the survivors witnessed this brutal murder. His body was then driven out and buried with the rest of the Jewish community at the forest of Halbow. The entire action lasted from 6 A.M. until about 2 P.M. Two weeks later, all men were called to the same square and those aged 16–40 were sent to the death camp of Plaszow near Krakow. Two to three weeks later, the Germans surrounded the town and took all the Jews and sent them to the Belzec death camp.

My friend Yossi Kalb and myself escaped from Zmigrod the night before the final action. We wandered throughout the country until we reached the wooded areas where we met other Jews. Soon our group consisted of about 70–80 men. I was then about 13 years old. We remained with this partisan group for about six months. Then we were sent on a patrol to scout the area. Yossi Kalb and myself proceeded with our task and at some point left the forest. We were spotted by Polish policemen who surrounded us and took us prisoner. They removed our belts and shoelaces and took us to the village of Swardzik. Here they tied us and put us onto a horse–drawn carriage that took us to Zmigrod.

The meadow or Bal's place on the outskirts of Zmigrod where the big selection took place on July 7, 1942

The interrogations began immediately as to the whereabouts of the Jews in the forest. The interrogations and the tortures continued daily. We received daily about 50 grams of bread, some black coffee and some soup. This stay lasted about seven weeks. We didn't reveal the location of the partisan group and they decided to send us to the Jaslo police prison.

The Gestapo took over our case and tortured us daily.

At the prison, we met other Jews from our group in the forest. They told us that the entire partisan group was eliminated; some were killed in battle, others wounded and still others taken prisoner. The daily beatings, tortures and interrogations lasted for several weeks and then they stopped. Most of us were sent to the Ostbahn camp in Krakow, where I remained about 2–3 months. We were about 250 Jews divided into groups of four. Each group loaded four car loads of stones a day. The stones weighed between 10–50 kilograms. The pace of work was very fast and we were hardly fed. The exhaustion rate was alarming. The weak or sick workers were soon sent to Ghetto "B" in Krakow where they were shot. My turn soon came and I too was sent to this ghetto but I managed to escape. I wandered in town without papers for several days and returned to camp with one of the labor brigades that returned at night to camp Julek I in Krakow. Here, I met an acquaintance who introduced me to the SS commander of the base, named Miller. He gave me a job that lasted 14 days. I was then sent on a special work detail under the command of Kraus. We worked on the rail lines and built a bridge which still stands. We received a kilo of bread per week and some cabbage soup. I worked for several months until I became infected with typhus. I was too weak to work and rested. I was caught and received 25 lashes with a leather whip for each day that I was absent. The beatings were administered by Jewish kapos. They then sent me to the death camp of Plaszow.

At the camp, I was assigned to a work gang that laid rails. Each crew of four people carried rails weighing about 300 kilos. We finished the rail work; then we were assigned to build barracks. We formed a formation and marched in the direction of the work site. At the gate stood an SS man named Krakow, and he told me to step aside. I was lined up with the weak and sick workers. We were about 60 Jews and the day was Yom Kippur [the holiest day in Judaism]. We were led to the famous hill called "Huyawa Gurka." Or cursed hill We were always threatened with the name but we never saw it. Now the black Ukrainians (Ukrainian guards wearing black uniforms) assisted by Jewish kapos like Finkelstein who was later shot trying to escape and Kerner who was arrested after the war and sent to a Krakow Polish prison. On the hill, already stood Amon Goeth, sadistic commander of Plaszow, and Wahn. They told us to undress and proceed to the other side of the hill.

While the group undressed, I escaped and ran in the direction of the camp while bullets chased me. I was lucky, I entered the camp. One day later, Finkelstein appeared at 1 or 2 P.M. and called my name. He led me to the room of the kapos where Wahn waited for me. They tied my hands and feet to a bench and gave me 75 lashes. They used 9–10 buckets of cold water to keep me alive since I kept passing out. I managed to return to my barrack where I remained for one month without being able to sit or lay on my back. I then saw

Dr. Gross, a Jew, and asked for an exemption from work. He chased me out of the office and threatened to send me to the "Hill." I refused to work and hid under the sleeping shelf in the barrack that accommodated many sleepers. Once, I even saw SS men searching the area for people to fill their quota for the killing list, but I was well hidden. I had been told that there would be an action and took the necessary precaution. Wahn walked about with his dog and his pistol but didn't get me.

Shortly thereafter, I heard that a work group was forming of 210 men for work at the enamel factory in Krakow. I went to register but the Jewish camp leader, Hilewicz, refused to accept me since I was on the death list. I stepped aside, waited until he left, then presented myself again and was accepted.

We left the camp and headed to the factory where I rested 14 days. When I arrived at the factory I was a "musulman," a candidate for the cemetery. The rest enabled me to recuperate. I then started to work on plane parts and regained my strength. That enabled me to survive the war. We were about 1,100 Jews and conditions were very good. I worked there about 8–9 months. Later in 1944, I returned to Plaszow where I remained four weeks. I was then assigned to a work group that went to the quarry in Bierzanow near Krakow. Meanwhile, we heard that the Plaszow camp was closed (about December 1944).

We were soon sent to Germany in a boxcar that contained 110 bodies. We traveled three days and on the fourth day arrived in Shachwitz near Dresden. More than half of the inmates were sick and the other ones had fainted. We were immediately sent to work and many died of typhus and related diseases. The weak inmates were sent by rail to Leitmeritz near Prague, in Czechoslovakia; the healthy ones marched for two weeks until we reached the camp. Many marchers, especially weak ones, were shot along the way or killed in wooded areas. We arrived at Leitmeritz and were ushered into the barrack like a bunch of sheep. We fell one on top of each other and remained there for eight days. Then we were sent to Theresienstadt concentration camp to be killed. The Jewish leadership bribed the SS commander of the camp and he sent all the SS men to the front, which gave him free rein in the camp. The Swiss Jews promised him that on their liberation they would take him, his wife and children to Switzerland. Indeed, following the liberation of the camp, they fulfilled their promise.

Thanks to this arrangement, we survived until May 9, 1945, when the area was liberated by the Russian army. On May 8, 1945, the camp was shelled and fired upon by a unit of retreating German soldiers. Many Jews were killed by the fire but the Germans didn't enter the camp. We were finally free and many inmates went on a food binge, which caused many of them to become sick and even to die. We were issued weapons by the Russian army and I took my revenge on the Germans. My vengeance, however, did not pacify me, for my pain was deep. My entire people, my entire family — parents, sisters and brothers consisting of about 80 people —were killed. I was a sole survivor, a total orphan since the age of 13. I am now aged 18."

Signed: Shmuel Rosenhan

A copy of the testimony was given to me by Shimon Lang of Zmigrod who was a friend of Shmuel Rosenhan. I translated it from the Yiddish script to English.

Jews of Osiek prior to and during WWII

Below is a partial list of Osieker Jews that we managed to obtain from Yad Vashem files and from the list of residents in Plaszow labor camp and from interviews with Jewish survivors, including Shimon Lang

Sources:

YA	Yad Vashem Testimony
T	Testimony materials
BD	Business Directory
JSS	Jewish self help
P	Personal research, letters, family interviews
JG	JewishGen list of Zmigrod

(NOTE: In the following table, the Gender of each individual is shown in the First Name(s) column by either an M (for Male) or F (for Female))

Family name	First name(s)	Maiden name	Birth date	Birth place	Residence	Father	Mother	Source
APPELBAUM	Mosze (M)			Osiek	Osiek			YA
BIENSTOCK	Wilma (F)			Osiek	Osiek			YA
BIENSTOCK	Wera (F)			Osiek	Osiek			YA
DENMARK	Josef (M)			Osiek	Osiek			YA
DENMARK	Liwa (F)			Osiek	Osiek			YA
DERSHEWITZ	Moshe (M)			Osiek	Osiek			P
FEDER	Maja (F)			Osiek	Osiek			YA
FEDER	Sheindel (F)			Osiek	Osiek			P
FEDER	Lebush (M)			Osiek	Osiek			P

Family name	First name(s)	Maiden name	Birth date	Birth place	Residence	Father	Mother	Source
FEDER	Leizer (M)			Osiek	Osiek			P
FEIER	Leib (M)			Osiek	Zmigrod			JSS
FEIER	Ryfka (F)		1917	Osiek	Zmigrod			JSS
FEIER	Isak (M)			Osiek	Zmigrod	Leib	Ryfka	JSS
FEIER	Rwka (F)			Osiek	Zmigrod			JG
FEIER	Isaac (M)		1908	Osiek	Zmigrod			JG
FEIER	Leib (M)		1907	Osiek	Zmigrod			JG
FEIER	Taube (F)		1904	Osiek	Zmigrod			JG
FEIER	Moses (M)		1902	Osiek	Osiek			BD
FEIER	Ben (M)			Osiek	Osiek			JG
FELD	Shmuel (M)			Osiek	Osiek			P
FELLER	Hers (M)			Osiek	Osiek			P
FELLER	Natan (M)			Osiek	Osiek			P
FELLER	Israel (M)			Osiek	Osiek			P
FISH	Suskind (M)			Osiek	Osiek			P
GROSHAUS	Dasa (F)			Osiek	Osiek			YA
GROSHAUS	Lewi (M)			Osiek	Osiek			YA
GRUBER	Izruel (M)			Osiek	Osiek			YA
GRUBER	Mozes (M)			Osiek	Osiek			YA
GRUBER	Serla (F)			Osiek	Osiek			P
GRUBER	Shmuel (M)			Osiek	Osiek			P

Yizkor Book of Nowy Zmigrod

Family name	First name(s)	Maiden name	Birth date	Birth place	Residence	Father	Mother	Source
HABER	Aaron (M)			Osiek	Osiek			YA
HAGLER	Izak (M)			Osiek	Osiek			YA
HAHN	Tibor (M)			Osiek	Osiek			P
HAHN	Hersh (M)			Osiek	Osiek			P
HELLER	Yossi (M)			Osiek	Osiek			P
KALB	David (M)			Osiek	Osiek			P
KALB	Bina (F)			Osiek	Osiek			P
KALB	Harry (M)			Osiek	Osiek			P
KALB	Zalman (M)		1871	Osiek	Osiek	Josef		YA
KALB	Yossi (M)			Osiek	Osiek			YA
KAPEL	Alter (M)			Osiek	Osiek			P
HESTER	Josef (M)			Osiek	Osiek			YA
KLEINER	Josef (M)			Osiek	Osiek			YA
KOHEN	Symcha (M)			Osiek	Osiek			YA
KOHEN	Mayer (M)			Osiek	Osiek			YA
KOHEN	Frida (F)			Osiek	Osiek			YA
KOHEN	Hina (F)			Osiek	Osiek			YA
KOHEN	Aaron (M)			Osiek	Osiek			YA
KOLBER	Yossef (M)			Osiek	Osiek			P
KRANZ	Abraham		1878	Osiek	Osiek			P

Family name	First name(s)	Maiden name	Birth date	Birth place	Residence	Father	Mother	Source
	(M)							
KRAZ	Biima (F)	ROSENHAND		Osiek	Osiek			P
KRAUS	Ilonka (F)			Osiek	Osiek			YA
KURSCHNER	Samuel (M)			Osiek	Osiek			P
KURSCHNER	Rachel (F)	ROSENHAND		Osiek	Osiek			P
LANDGARTEN	Awraham (M)			Osiek	Osiek			YA
LANGFELDER	Rachel (F)			Osiek	Osiek			YA
LANGFELDER	Wlli (M)			Osiek	Osiek			YA
LANGFELDER	Terejia (F)			Osiek	Osiek			YA
LANGFELDER	Elza (F)			Osiek	Osiek			YA
LEIBGARD	Salomon (M)			Osiek	Osiek			P
LEIBGARD	Chaja (F)			Osiek	Osiek			P
LEIBGARD	Marcus (M)		1873	Osiek	Korncyza	Salomon		P
LERMAN	Hersh (M)		1868	Osiek	Osiek			P
LERMAN	Ryfka (F)	ROSENHAND		Osiek	Osiek			P
LERMAN	Aiga (F)			Osiek	Osiek			YA
LERMAN	Moses (M)			Osiek	Osiek			YA
LERMAN	Blima (F)			Osiek	Osiek			YA
LERMAN	Rosa (F)			Osiek	Osiek			YA
LERMAN	Marcus (M)			Osiek	Osiek			YA

Yizkor Book of Nowy Zmigrod

Family name	First name(s)	Maiden name	Birth date	Birth place	Residence	Father	Mother	Source
LERMAN	Marcus (M)			Osiek	Osiek			JSS
LERMAN	Mendel (M)			Osiek	Osiek			JSS
LERMAN	Szymon (M)			Osiek	Osiek			JSS
LERMAN	Cila (F)			Osiek	Osiek			JG
LERMAN	Ita Lea (F)			Osiek	Osiek			JG
LERMAN	Yehezkel (M)			Osiek	Osiek			P
LERMAN	Mordechai (M)			Osiek	Osiek			P
LERMAN	Dawid Lewi (M)			Osiek	Osiek			P
LERMAN	Awraham (M)			Osiek	Osiek			P
LERMAN	Hersh Leib (M)			Osiek	Osiek			P
LERMAN	Tuwia (M)			Osiek	Osiek			P
LERMAN	Yeheskel (M)			Osiek	Osiek			JG
LERMAN	Chaim (M)			Osiek	Osiek			YA
LERMAN	Gittel (F)		1921	Osiek	Osiek			YA
LICHTENTAL	Juliana (F)			Osiek	Osiek			YA
LICHTENTAL	Elena (F)			Osiek	Osiek			YA
LICHTENTAL	Ermina (F)			Osiek	Osiek			YA

Family name	First name(s)	Maiden name	Birth date	Birth place	Residence	Father	Mother	Source
MAJEROWICZ	Moshe (M)			Osiek	Osiek			P
MESSINGER	Bela (F)			Osiek	Osiek			YA
MITZNER	Dawid Elim (M)			Osiek	Osiek			P
MONTILJO	Shlomo (M)			Osiek	Osiek			YA
NEGGER	Menashe (M)			Osiek	Osiek			P
PELLER	Chaim (M)			Osiek	Osiek			JSS
PELLER	Nachum (M)			Osiek	Osiek			YA
PELLER	Chaim (M)			Osiek	Osiek			YA
PELLER	Nachum (M)			Osiek	Osiek			YA
POPER	Hilda (F)			Osiek	Osiek			YA
POPER	Lea (F)			Osiek	Osiek			YA
PUCH	Feige (F)			Osiek	Osiek			P
REIFER	Eliezer (M)			Osiek	Osiek			YA
REIFER	Adela (F)			Osiek	Osiek			YA
REIFER	Bela (F)			Osiek	Osiek			YA
REIFER	Etel (F)			Osiek	Osiek			YA
REIFER	Tzwi (M)			Osiek	Osiek			YA
REIFER	Samuel (M)			Osiek	Osiek			YA
REIFER	Frydel (F)			Osiek	Osiek			YA

Family name	First name(s)	Maiden name	Birth date	Birth place	Residence	Father	Mother	Source
REIFER	Moshe (M)			Osiek	Osiek			YA
REIFER	Meir (M)			Osiek	Osiek			YA
REIFER	Miriam (F)			Osiek	Osiek			YA
REIFER	Idel (M)			Osiek	Osiek			YA
ROSENHAN	Chaim Lei (M)			Osiek	Osiek			JSS
ROSENHAN	Hersh Leib (M)			Osiek	Osiek			JSS
ROSENHAN	Marcus Daw (M)			Osiek	Osiek			JSS
ROSENHAN	Szymon (M)			Osiek	Osiek			JSS
ROSENHAN	Mania (F)			Osiek	Osiek			YA
ROSENHAN	Anna (F)			Osiek	Osiek			YA
ROSENHAN	Awraham (M)			Osiek	Osiek			YA
ROSENHAN	Chaja (F)		1917	Osiek	Osiek			YA
ROSENHAN	Awraham (M)			Osiek	Osiek			JSS
ROSENHAN	Hershel (M)			Osiek	Osiek			YA
ROSENHAN	Ita (F)		1920	Osiek	Osiek			YA
ROSENHAN	Rachel (F)		1912	Osiek	Zmigrod	Awraham		YA
ROSENHAN	Sara (F)		1916	Osiek	Zmigrod	Awraham		JG

Family name	First name(s)	Maiden name	Birth date	Birth place	Residence	Father	Mother	Source
ROSENHAN	Riwk (F)		1891	Osiek	Zmigrod			JG
ROSENHAN	Mindla (F)		1886	Osiek	Zmigrod	Marcus	Ruchla	YA
ROSENHAND	Awrum (M)			Osiek	Osiek			P
ROSENHAND	Rachel (F)			Osiek	Osiek			P
ROSENHAND	Mendel (M)		1879	Osiek	Osiek			P
ROSENHAND	Ita (F)			Osiek	Osiek			P
ROSENHAND	Mortdechai (M)			Osiek	Osiek			P
ROSENHAND	Shmuel (M)			Osiek	Osiek			P
ROSENHAND	Marcus (M)			Osiek	Osiek			P
ROSENHAND	Ruchla (F)	HAUSNER		Osiek	Osiek			P
ROSENHAND	Eliezer (M)			Osiek	Osiek			YA
ROSENHAND	Awraham (M)			Osiek	Osiek			YA
ROSENHAND	Rachel (F)			Osiek	Osiek	Eliezer		JSS
ROSENHAND	Riwka (F)		1912	Osiek	Osiek	Awraham		JSS
ROSENHAND	Hershel (M)		1918	Osiek	Osiek	Awraham		JSS
ROSENHAND	Ita (F)		1920	Osiek	Osiek	Awraham		JSS
ROSENHAND	Hencia (F)			Osiek	Osiek			YA
ROSENHAND	Hannah (F)		1905	Osiek	Osiek			P
ROSENHAND	Rachel (F)			Osiek	Osiek			YA
ROSENHAND	Asher (M)			Osiek	Osiek			P

Yizkor Book of Nowy Zmigrod

Family name	First name(s)	Maiden name	Birth date	Birth place	Residence	Father	Mother	Source
ROSENHAND	Lewi (M)		1903	Osiek	Osiek			YA
ROSENHAND	Josef D (M)		1900	Osiek	Osiek			YA
ROSENHAND	Bluma (F)		1914	Osiek	Osiek			YA
ROSENHAND	Mendel (M)		1909	Osiek	Osiek			YA
ROSENHAND	Haja (F)		1917	Osiek	Osiek	Lewi		JSS
ROSENHAND	Hancha (F)	LERMAN		Osiek	Osiek			P
ROSENHAND	Solomon (M)			Osiek	Osiek			P
ROSENHAND	Wolf (M)			Osiek	Osiek			P
ROSENTHAL	Chaim (M)			Osiek	Osiek			P
ROZENTZWEIG	Lea (F)			Osiek	Osiek			P
ROZENTZWEIG	Hela (F)		1926	Osiek	Osiek	Chaim	Lea	YA
ROZENTZWEIG	Lea (F)		1895	Osiek	Osiek	Chaim	Lea	YA
ROZENTZWEIG	Simcha (M)		1928	Osiek	Osiek	Chaim	Lea	JG

CHAPTER XIII
Jews Who Lived in Zmigrod Prior and During World War Two

Sources

YA	Yad Vashem Testimony
T	Testimony materials
BD	Business Directory
JSS	Jewish self help
P	Personal research, letters, family interviews
JG	JewishGen list of Zmigrod
R	Rapoport History of Jews in Jaslo
JR	Jean Krieser papers

Yizkor Book of Nowy Zmigrod

Family name	First name(s)	Maiden name	Birth date	Birth place	Residence	Father	Mother	Gender	Spouse	Source	Remarks
ABRAMSON	Julius				Zmigrod			M		P	Holocaust
ADELSON	Max			Zmigrod	Zmigrod			M		P	USA
AIGER	Jude			Zmigrod	Zmigrod			M		JR	
AIGER	Ziwe			Zmigrod	Zmigrod			F	Jude	JR	
AIGER	Jacob			Zmigrod	Zmigrod			M		JR	
ALSTER	Rivka		1877	Gorlice	Zmigrod			F		P	died
ALSTER	Aaron			Gorlice	Zmigrod		Rivka	M		P	
ALSTER	Lea			Gorlice	Zmigrod			F	Aaron	P	died
ALSTER	Rachel			Zmigrod	Zmigrod			F		JR	
ALTHOLTZ	Hersch			Zmigrod	Zmigrod			M		JR	
ALTHOLTZ	Frumet			Zmigrod	Zmigrod			F	Hersch	JR	
ALTHOLTZ	Towia H		1866	Zmigrod	Zmigrod			F		JR	
ALTHOLTZ	Elias		1867	Zmigrod	Zmigrod	Hersch	Frumet	M		P	died
ALTSCHULER	Leibl			Zmigrod	Zmigrod			M		P	Holocaust
ALTSCHULER	Pessah			Zmigrod	Zmigrod			M		P	Holocaust
ARDYSZYK	Berl			Zmigrod	Zmigrod			M		JR	
ARDYSZYK	Pesel			Zmigrod	Zmigrod			F	Berl	JR	
ARDYSZYK	Miszket		1871	Zmigrod	Zmigrod	Berl	Pesel	F		JR	
ARBELES	Hersh			Zmigrod	Zmigrod			M		P	
ARMSTEIN	Baruch			Zmigrod	Zmigrod			M		JG	USA
ARMSTEIN	Esther		1869	Zmigrod	Zmigrod			F		JG	USA
ARMSTEIN	Chaim		1872	Zmigrod	Zmigrod			M		JG	USA
ARMSTEIN	Regina		1870	Zmigrod	Zmigrod			F		JG	USA

Yizkor Book of Nowy Zmigrod

Family name	First name(s)	Maiden name	Birth date	Birth place	Residence	Father	Mother	Gender	Spouse	Source	Remarks
ARMSTEIN	Joseph		1904	Zmigrod	Zmigrod			M		JG	USA
ARMSTEIN	Asher		1902	Zmigrod	Zmigrod			M		JG	USA
ASHENBERG	Rachel		1883	Zmigrod	Zmigrod			F		JG	survived
ASHER	Moses D		1887	Zmigrod	Zmigrod			M		JR	
ASHER	Sara			Zmigrod	Zmigrod	Moses D		F		JR	
ASHER	Benyamin			Zmigrod	Zmigrod			M		JR	
ASHER	Perl			Zmigrod	Zmigrod			F	Benyamin	JR	
ASHER	Pinkas		1872	Zmigrod	Zmigrod	Benyamin	Perl	M		JR	
ASHER	Golda R		1873	Zmigrod	Zmigrod	Benyamin	Perl	F		JR	
AUERBACH	Mriam		1895	Zmigrod	Zmigrod	Hersh		F		YA	Holocaust
AUMAN	Beile		1885	Zmigrod	Zmigrod			F		JG	
AUMAN	Aron Ber			Zmigrod	Zmigrod			M		JR	
AUMAN	Esther			Zmigrod	Zmigrod			F	Aron Ber	JR	
AUMAN	Neche		1886	Zmigrod	Zmigrod	Aron B	Esther	F		JG	
AUMAN	Hudes		1881	Zmigrod	Zmigrod			F			
AUMAN	Awraham			Zmigrod	Zmigrod			M		JR	
AUMAN	Rose			Zmigrod	Zmigrod			F	Awraham	JR	
AUMAN	Esther		1872	Zmigrod	Zmigrod	Awraham	Rose	F		JR	
AUMAN	Chaje Zi		1872	Zmigrod	Zmigrod	Awraham	Rose	F		JR	
AUMAN	Sara Sh			Zmigrod	Zmigrod	Awraham	Rose	F		JR	
AUMAN	Samuel H			Zmigrod	Zmigrod			M		JR	
AUMAN	Hersch		1879	Zmigrod	Zmigrod	Samuel H		M		JR	

Yizkor Book of Nowy Zmigrod

Family name	First name(s)	Maiden name	Birth date	Birth place	Residence	Father	Mother	Gender	Spouse	Source	Remarks
BARACHAN	Wigdor				Zmigrod			M		JSS	
BARACHAN	Peril				Zmigrod			F	Wigdor	JSS	
BARACHAN	Moses				Zmigrod	Wigdora	Peril	M		JSS	Plaszow
BARACHAN	E.				Zmigrod			M		JSS	
BARTERER	Shimon Z			Zmigrod	Zmigrod			M		P	Holocaust
BARTERER	Hannah			Zmigrod	Zmigrod			F		P	Holocaust
BECK	Dawid			Zmigrod	USA			M		JG	USA
BECK	Mendel Y				Zmigrod			M		P	
BER	Riwka			Zmigrod	Zmigrod			F	Shimon Z	JG	
BER	David Lippa			Zmigrod	Zmigrod			M		JG	
BER	Feiga R			Zmigrod	Zmigrod			F	David L	JG	
BER	Moshe			Zmigrod	Zmigrod			M		JG	
BER	Yaacov			Zmigrod	Zmigrod			M		JG	survived
BER	Leiser			Zmigrod	Zmigrod			M		JSS	
BER	F			Zmigrod	Zmigrod			M		BD	
BER	Aron			Zmigrod	Zmigrod			M		JR	
BER	Shprince		1880	Zmigrod	Zmigrod	Aron		F		JR	
BER	Selig		1883	Zmigrod	Zmigrod	Aron		M		JR	
BERG	Mendel							M		P	
BERG	Malka	BERGER		Zmigrod				F	Mendel	P	
BERG	Rachel		1877			Mendel	Malka	F		P	
BERG	Ester		1880			Mendel	Malka	F		P	
BERG	Sara		1881			Mendel	Malka	F		P	

Family name	First name(s)	Maiden name	Birth date	Birth place	Residence	Father	Mother	Gender	Spouse	Source	Remarks
BERG	Reywen Y		1887			Mendel	Malka	M		P	
BERTIE	Aron Ber			Zmigrod	Zmigrod			M		JR	
BERTIE	Efroim H		1879	Zmigrod	Zmigrod	Aron B		M		JR	
BEKER	Mechel			Zmigrod	Zmigrod			M		P	
BERGER	Asher			Zmigrod	Zmigrod			M		JG	
BERGER	David		1888	Zmigrod	Zmigrod			M		JG	
BERGER	Mendel			Zmigrod	Zmigrod			M		JR	
BERGER	Reuven Y		1887	Zmigrod	Zmigrod	Mendel		M		JG	
BERGER	Rachel		1880	Zmigrod	Zmigrod			F		JG	
BERGER	Izrael			Zmigrod	Zmigrod			M		P	
BERGER	Perla	HOEFLICH		Zmigrod	Zmigrod			F	Izrael	P	
BERGER	Michael S		1878	Zmigrod	Zmigrod	Izrael	Perla	M		P	
BERGER	Rachel		1880	Zmigrod	Zmigrod	Izrael	Perla	F		P	
BERGER	Chaim		1882	Zmigrod	Zmigrod	Izrael	Perla	M		P	
BERGER	Mojzesz			Zmigrod	Zmigrod			M		P	
BERGER	Rywka	PENCAK		Zmigrod	Zmigrod			F	Mojzesz	JR	
BERGER	Leje		1879	Zmigrod	Zmigrod	Mojzesz	Rywka	F		JR	
BERGER	Henech		1882	Zmigrod	Zmigrod	Mojzesz	Rywka	M		JR	
BERGER	Jossef		1888	Zmigrod	Zmigrod	Mojzesz	Rywka	M		JR	
BERGER	Marcus D			Zmigrod	Zmigrod			M		JR	
BERGER	Chaje R	KAUFMAN		Zmigrod	Zmigrod			F		JR	
BERGER	Michael Sh		1877	Zmigrod	Zmigrod			M		JR	
BERGER	Salomon		1880	Zmigrod	Zmigrod			M		JR	

Yizkor Book of Nowy Zmigrod

Family name	First name(s)	Maiden name	Birth date	Birth place	Residence	Father	Mother	Gender	Spouse	Source	Remarks
BERGER	Hadassah			Zmigrod				F	HFriedman	JR	
BERGER	Leja			Zmigrod				F	IGertner	JR	
BERGER	Matel			Zmigrod				F	M Weiberger		
BERGER	Rachel			Zmigrod				F	N Orenstein	P	
BERGER	Malka			Zmigrod	Zmigrod			F	M Berg	P	
BERGER	Yehoshua			Zmigrod	Zmigrod			M		JG	
BERGER	Brandel	MORGENSTERN		Zmigrod	Zmigrod			F	Yehoshua		
BERGER	Isaac S		1875	Zmigrod	Zmigrod	Yehoshua	Brandel	F		P	
BERGER	Golde		1877	Zmigrod	Zmigrod	Yehoshua	Brandel	M		P	
BERGER	Abraham		1879	Zmigrod	Zmigrod	Yehoshua	Brandel	M		P	
BERGER	Seinwel		1882	Zmigrod	Zmigrod	Yehoshua	Brandel	M		P	
BERGER	Wolf		1884	Zmigrod	Zmigrod	Yehoshua	Brandel	M		P	
BERGER	Mozes		1888	Zmigrod	Zmigrod	Yehoshua	Brandel	M		P	
BERGER	Berish			Zmigrod	Zmigrod			M		JG	
BERGER	Chaim			Zmigrod	Zmigrod			M		JG	
BERGER	Chawa			Zmigrod	Zmigrod			F		JG	
BERGER	Itche			Zmigrod	Zmigrod			M		JG	
BERGER	Yona			Zmigrod	Zmigrod			M		JG	
BERGER	Sasha			Zmigrod	Zmigrod			F		JG	
BERGER	Jakob		1878	Zmigrod	Zmigrod			M		WS	USA
BERGER	Alter			Zmigrod	Zmigrod			M		JR	

Family name	First name(s)	Maiden name	Birth date	Birth place	Residence	Father	Mother	Gender	Spouse	Source	Remarks
BERGER	Mindel			Zmigrod	Zmigrod			F	Alter	JR	
BERGER	Bear		1876	Zmigrod	Zmigrod	Alter	Mindel	M		JR	
BERGER	Alter			Zmigrod	Zmigrod			M		JR	
BERGER	Chana G	EISENBERG		Zmigrod	Zmigrod			F	Alter	JR	
BERGER	Sarah		1869	Zmigrod	Zmigrod	Alter	Chana Git	F		JR	
BERGER	Chaim		1871	Zmigrod	Zmigrod	Alter	Chana Git	M		P	
BERGER	Dworah		1876	Zmigrod	Zmigrod	Alter	Chana Gittel	F		P	
BERGER	Heinech		1878	Zmigrod	Zmigrod	Alter	Chana Gittel	M		P	
BERGER	Dawid		1880	Zmigrod	Zmigrod	Alter	Chana Gittel	M		P	
BERGER	Hersh Tz		1885	Zmigrod	Zmigrod	Alter	Chana Gitt	M		YA	Holocaust
BERGER	Ester	RIEGER		Zmigrod	Zmigrod			F	Hersh Tzvi	P	
BERGER	Yosef		1887	Zmigrod	Zmigrod	Alter	Chana Gitt	M		P	
BERGER	Bertha		1905	Zmigrod	Zmigrod	Alter	Chana Git	F	Gertner	JG	
BERGER	Yentel		1907	Zmigrod	Zmigrod	Alter	Chana Git	F	A.Landau		
BERGER	Moshe		1907	Zmigrod	Zmigrod	Yossel,	Yentel	M		YA	Holocaust
BERGER	Sheindel		1912	Zmigrod	Zmigrod	Naphtali		F	Moshe	P	Holocaust
BERGER	Heinech			Zmigrod	Zmigrod			F		P	Holocaust
BERGLASS	Izaak Beer				Zmigrod			M		JG	

Yizkor Book of Nowy Zmigrod

Family name	First name(s)	Maiden name	Birth date	Birth place	Residence	Father	Mother	Gender	Spouse	Source	Remarks
BERGLASS	Gitla	STEIN		Zmigrod	Zmigrod			F	I Beer	JG	
BERGLASS	Markus		1887	Zmigrod	Zmigrod	Izaak B	Gitla	M		JG	
BERGLASS	Mindela	ROSENTHAL	1886	Zmigrod	Zmigrod			F	Markus	JG	USA
BERGLASS	Yenta				Zmigrod			F		P	Holocaust
BERGMAN	Bil Abraha				Zmigrod			M		JG	USA
BERGMAN	Auba				Zmigrod			F		JG	
BERGMAN	Yaakow			Zmigrod	Zmigrod			M		P	survived
BERNHOLTZ	Manfred				Zmigrod			M		P	Holocaust
BERNSTEIN	Jacob Is		1887	Zmigrod	Zmigrod			M		JG	survived
BESZANER	Baruch									P	
BESZANER	Chaim									P	
BIGAIER	Harry			Zmigrod				M		T	
BINDER	Sally				Zmigrod			F		P	Holocaust
BINDER	Yehezkel				Zmigrod			M		P	
BIRENBAUM	Moshe H				Zmigrod			M		YA	Zmigrod
BIRNBACH	Mosze			Zmigrod		Shlomo		M		JG	
BIRNBACH				Zmigrod				F		YA	
BIRNBACH	Szalom		1903	Zmigrod	Lublin	Moshe		M		JG	
BIRNBACH								F		YA	Holocaust
BIRNBACH	Hella		1938	Zmigrod	Zmigrod	Shulem		F		YA	Holocaust
BIRNBACH	Riwka		1909	Zmigrod	Germany	Moshe		F		YA	Holocaust
BIRNBACH	Chana		1916	Zmigrod	Zmigrod	Moshe		F		YA	Holocaust
BIRNBACH	Chaya		1917	Zmigrod	Zmigrod	Moshe		F		YA	Holocaust

Yizkor Book of Nowy Zmigrod

Family name	First name(s)	Maiden name	Birth date	Birth place	Residence	Father	Mother	Gender	Spouse	Source	Remarks
BIRNBACH	Herna		1935	Zmigrod	Zmigrod	Eliezer		F		JSS	Holocaust
BIRNBACH	Mendel				Zmigrod			M		JG	
BIRNBACH	Ch				Zmigrod			M		T	
BIRNBACH	Haim S				Zmigrod			M		JG	
BIRNHAM	Chaim S				Zmigrod			M		P	
BLANK	Aron			Zmigrod	Zmigrod			M		JG	
BLANK	Zelde Lea			Zmigrod	Zmigrod			F	Aron	JG	
BLANK	Aron			Zmigrod	Zmigrod			M		JG	
BLANK	Gitel	FEUER	1884	Zmigrod	Zmigrod			F	Aron	YA	Holocaust
BLANK	Zelda			Zmigrod	Jaslo	Arieh		F		JG	USA
BLANK	Joseph		1882	Zmigrod	Zmigrod			M		JG	USA
BLATT	Rose			Zmigrod	Zmigrod			F		JG	
BLAU	Moses			Zmigrod	Zmigrod			M		P	Holocaust
BLAUGRUND	Lea			Zmigrod	Zmigrod			F		JG	
BLAUGRUND	Dolish			Zmigrod	Zmigrod			F		JG	
BLAUGRUND	Haya			Zmigrod	Zmigrod			F		JG	
BLAUGRUND	Menasche C			Zmigrod	Zmigrod			M		BD	
BLAUGRUND	Hersh			Zmigrod	Zmigrod			M		JSS	Plaszow
BLAUGRUND	Joel				Zmigrod			M		JSS	Plaszow
BLAUGRUND	Pesil				Zmigrod			F	Menashe	JSS	
BLAUGRUND	Leib		1905	Zmigrod	Zmigrod	Manasche	Pesil	M		JSS	
BLAUGRUND	Natan				Zmigrod			M		JSS	Plaszow
BLEDER	Saul				Zmigrod			M		JSS	Plaszow

Yizkor Book of Nowy Zmigrod

Family name	First name(s)	Maiden name	Birth date	Birth place	Residence	Father	Mother	Gender	Spouse	Source	Remarks
BLEDER	Henryk				Zmigrod			M		JSS	Plaszow
BLOCH	Samuel H			Zmigrod	Zmigrod			M		JR	
BLOCH	Neche			Zmigrod	Zmigrod			F	Samuel H	JR	
BLOCH	Salomon		1871	Zmigrod	Zmigrod	Samuel H	Neche	M		JR	
BLOCH	Dawid F		1879	Zmigrod	Zmigrod	Samuel H	Neche	M		JR	
BLOCH	Samuel			Zmigrod	Zmigrod			M		JR	
BLOCH	Reisel			Zmigrod	Zmigrod			F	Samuel	JR	
BLOCH	Benjamin W		1873	Zmigrod	Zmigrod	Samuel	Reisel	M		JR	
BOBKER	Arieh			Zmigrod	Zmigrod			M		T	Holocaust
BOBKER	Serka	BEILES		Zmigrod	Zmigrod			F	Arieh	P	Holocaust
BOBKER	Malka			Zmigrod	Zmigrod	Arieh	Serka	F		P	Holocaust
BOBKER	Yosef M			Zmigrod	Zmigrod	Arieh	Serka	M		P	Holocaust
BOBKER	Mozes Abra			Zmigrod	Zmigrod			M		JG	
BOBKER	Esther			Zmigrod	Zmigrod	Mozes Ab	Esther	F	Mozes A	JG	
BOBKER	Malke		1875	Zmigrod	Zmigrod			F		JG	
BOBKER	Heinech			Zmigrod	Zmigrod			M		JG	
BOBKER	Feiga			Zmigrod	Zmigrod			F	Moshe A.	JG	
BOBKER	Shia			Zmigrod	Zmigrod			M		JG	
BOBKER	Yehezkel			Zmigrod	Zmigrod			M		JG	
BOBKER	Yosef			Zmigrod	Zmigrod			M		JG	survived
BOBKER	Golda			Zmigrod	Zmigrod			F		P	
BOBKER	Itzhak			Zmigrod	Zmigrod			M		P	
BOBKER	Hersh			Zmigrod	Zmigrod			M		JG	

Family name	First name(s)	Maiden name	Birth date	Birth place	Residence	Father	Mother	Gender	Spouse	Source	Remarks
BRAND	Matityahu				Zmigrod			M		P	
BRANDEIS	Abraham		1917			Isak	Jdes	M		JG	
BRAUNFELD	Yaakow							M		JG	
BRAUNFELD	Scheindel		1875	Zmigrod	Zmigrod	Baruch		F	Yaakow	P	Holocaust
BRAUNFELD	Shalamon		1902	Zmigrod	Zmigrod	Yaakow		M		P	Holocaust
BRAUNFELD	Jcchak		1909	Zmigrod	Zmigrod	Yaakow		M		P	Holocaust
BRAUNFELD	Sara		1913	Zmigrod	Zmigrod	Yaakow		F		YA	Holocaust
BRAUNFELD	Naphtali			Zmigrod	Zmigrod	Yaakow		M		P	survived
BRAUNFELD	Lea			Zmigrod	Zmigrod			F		P	survived
BRAUNFELD	Yekel				Zmigrod			M		T	
BRENNER	Dawid		1869		Zmigrod			M		JG	USA
BROCHA	Moshe Y				Zmigrod			M		JG	
BRZEGOWSKI	Elias				Zmigrod			M		JSS	Plaszow
BUCHER	Isaak			Zmigrod	Zmigrod			M		JR	
BUCHER	Miszket C			Zmigrod	Zmigrod			F	Isaak	JR	
BUCHER	Dewore		1869	Zmigrod	Zmigrod	Isaak	Miszket Ch	F		JR	
BUKSBAUM	Itzhak			Zmigrod	Zmigrod			M		JG	
BUKSBAUM	Riwka			Zmigrod	Zmigrod			F	Itzhak	YA	
BUKSBAUM	Shia			Zmigrod	Zmigrod	Itzhak	Riwka	M		T	
BUKSBAUM	Benyamin W		1873	Zmigrod	Zmigrod	Itzhak	Riwka	M		P	Holocaust
BUKSBAUM	Feige				Zmigrod	Shia	Feige	F	Shia		
BUKSBAUM	Liebe				Zmigrod	Shia	Feige	F		P	Holocaust

Yizkor Book of Nowy Zmigrod

Family name	First name(s)	Maiden name	Birth date	Birth place	Residence	Father	Mother	Gender	Spouse	Source	Remarks
BUKSBAUM	Riwa			Zmigrod	Zmigrod			F		JR	
BUKSBAUM	Schije		1871	Zmigrod	Zmigrod		Riwa	M		JR	
BUKSBAUM	Lea			Zmigrod	Zmigrod			F		P	Holocaust
BUKSBAUM	Sara			Zmigrod	Zmigrod			F		P	
BUKSBAUM	Haim			Zmigrod	Zmigrod			M		JG	survived
BUKSBAUM	Moshe K			Zmigrod	Zmigrod			M		JG	
BUKSBAUM	Osias		1922	Zmigrod	Zmigrod			M		JG	
BUKSBAUM	Chawa			Zmigrod	Zmigrod			F		P	Holocaust
BUKSBAUM	Yehuda				Zmigrod			M		P	
BURNERKRAND	Shlomo		1874	Zmigrod	Zmigrod			M		JG	
BURNERKRAND	Hersch E			Zmigrod	Zmigrod			M		JG	
CITRONENBAUM	Zishe			Zmigrod	Zmigrod			M		P	
CITRONENBAUM	Moses			Zmigrod	Zmigrod			M		JR	
CITRONENBAUM	Ester			Zmigrod	Zmigrod			F	Moses	JR	
CITRONENBAUM	Isaak		1872	Zmigrod	Zmigrod	Moses	Ester	M		JR	
COHEN	Nathan			Zmigrod	Zmigrod			M		JG	USA
CUKERMAN	Josef		1890		Zmigrod	Menachem		M		YA	Holocaust
CZIESZANOWER	Naftali				Zmigrod			M		JSS	Plaszow
CZIESZANOWER	Jakob				Zmigrod			M		JSS	Plaszow
CZIESZANOWER	Tziporah				Zmigrod			F		P	
CZIESZANOWER	Awraham			Zmigrod	Zmigrod			M		YA	
CZIESZANOWER	Hela	EHRLICH		Zmigrod	Zmigrod			F	Awraham	YA	

Family name	First name(s)	Maiden name	Birth date	Birth place	Residence	Father	Mother	Gender	Spouse	Source	Remarks
CZIESZANOWER	Lea	KRIEGER		Zmigrod	Zmigrod	Mordechai	Yentel	F		YA	Belzec
DAM	Leib		1800	Zmigrod	Zmigrod			M		JG	
DANTZIGER	Benjamin				Zmigrod			M		P	
DENEN	Samuel			Zmigrod	Zmigrod			M		JG	
DEUTCHMAN	Hene		1851	Zmigrod	Zmigrod			F		JG	USA
DEUTSCHMAN	Deborah		1886	Zmigrod	Zmigrod			F		JG	
DEUTSCHMAN	Mendel			Zmigrod	Zmigrod			M		JG	
DEUTSCHMAN	Hudes	STECHER	1835	Zmigrod	Zmigrod			F	Mendel	JG	died 1921
DEUTSCHMAN	Ryfka		1867	Zmigrod	Zmigrod	Mendel	Hudes	F		JG	
DEUTSCHMAN	Samuel		1869	Zmigrod	Zmigrod	Mendel	Hudes	M		JG	
DEUTSCHMAN	Sophie	HOCHNER		Zmigrod	Zmigrod			F	Samuel	JG	
DEUTSCHMAN	Deborah		1876	Zmigrod	Zmigrod	Mendel	Hudes	F		JR	
DEUTSCHMAN	Ben		1879	Zmigrod	Zmigrod	Mendel	Hudes	M		JG	
DEUTSCHMAN	Mais	KORN		Zmigrod	Zmigrod			M		JG	
DEUTSCHMAN	Tzeite		1881	Zmigrod	Zmigrod	Mendel	Hudes	F	Ben	JG	
DEUTSCHMAN	Mayer		1888	Zmigrod	Zmigrod	Mendel	Hudes	M		JG	
DIAMANT	Esther				Zmigrod			F		JG	
DIAMANT	Yekel				Zmigrod			M		T	
DIAMANT	Leib		1923	Zmigrod		Yaakow		M		YA	Holocaust
DOBRES	Shmuel C				Zmigrod			M		P	
DRUCKER	Mayer		1883	Zmigrod	Zmigrod			M		JG	
DZERDZEWIC	Mozes				Zmigrod			M		JSS	Plaszow
EDELSTEIN	Hannah			Zmigrod	Zmigrod			F		JG	

Yizkor Book of Nowy Zmigrod

Family name	First name(s)	Maiden name	Birth date	Birth place	Residence	Father	Mother	Gender	Spouse	Source	Remarks
EFRATI	Sarah			Zmigrod	Zmigrod			F		JG	
EICHNER	Moses H			Zmigrod	Zmigrod			M		JR	
EICHNER	Chana L			Zmigrod	Zmigrod			F	Moses H	JR	
EICHNER	Josef			Zmigrod	Zmigrod	Moses	Chana Lie	M		JR	
EICHNER	Aron			Zmigrod	Zmigrod			M		JG	
EICHNER	Debora		1876	Zmigrod	Zmigrod			F	Aron	JG	
EICHNER	Chaim S			Zmigrod	Zmigrod			M		JG	
EICHNER	Esther	MUTZNER		Zmigrod	Zmigrod			F	Chaim		
EICHNER	Brucha			Zmigrod	Zmigrod			F	Dawid	JG	
EICHNER	Dawid			Zmigrod	Zmigrod			M		JG	
EICHNER	Berta	SCHMIER		Zmigrod	Zmigrod			F	Dawid	P	
EICHNER	Perla		1905	Zmigrod	Zmigrod	Dawid	Berta	F		JG	
EICHNER	Jacob son		1905	Zmigrod	Zmigrod	Dawid	Berta	M		JG	
EICHNER	Chana			Zmigrod	Zmigrod			F	Dawid	JG	
EICHNER	Teme			Zmigrod	Zmigrod	Dawid	Chana	F		JG	
EICHNER	Isak			Zmigrod	Zmigrod			M		JG	
EICHNER	Sara	ROSENBERG		Zmigrod	Zmigrod			F	Isak	JG	
EICHNER	Hersh			Zmigrod	Zmigrod	Isak	Sara	M		JG	
EICHNER	Aron			Zmigrod	Zmigrod	Isak	Sara	M		JG	
EICHNER	Moses			Zmigrod	Zmigrod			M		JG	
EICHNER	Ides,			Zmigrod	Zmigrod			F	Moses	JG	

Family name	First name(s)	Maiden name	Birth date	Birth place	Residence	Father	Mother	Gender	Spouse	Source	Remarks
EICHNER	Joseph		1869	Zmigrod	Zmigrod	Moses	Ides,	M		JG	
EICHNER	Markus W		1878	Zmigrod	Zmigrod	Moses	Ides,	M		JG	
EICHNER	Nachmen		1876	Zmigrod	Zmigrod	Moses	Ides,	M		JG	
EICHNER	Moses			Zmigrod	Zmigrod			M		JG	
EICHNER	Esther		1869	Zmigrod	Zmigrod	Moses	Esther	F	Moses	JG	
EICHNER	Tzudik		1869	Zmigrod	Zmigrod	Moses	Esther	M		JG	
EICHNER	Nachmen		1871	Zmigrod	Zmigrod	Moses	Esther	M		JG	
EICHNER	Chaje T			Zmigrod	Zmigrod	Moses	Esther	F		JG	
EICHNER	Samuel W			Zmigrod	Zmigrod	Moses	Esther	M		JG	
EICHNER	Nachmen			Zmigrod	Zmigrod			M		JG	
EICHNER	Zywia	WACHS		Zmigrod	Zmigrod			F	Nachmen	JG	
EICHNER	Chaje		1880	Zmigrod	Zmigrod	Nachmen	Zywia	F		JG	
EICHNER	Israel		1875	Zmigrod	Zmigrod	Nachmen	Zywia	M		JG	
EICHNER	Sara		1886	Zmigrod	Zmigrod	Nachmen	Zywia	F		JG	
EICHNER	Shmuel			Zmigrod	Zmigrod			M		JG	
EICHNER	Perl	HORLAUBER		Zmigrod	Zmigrod			F	Shmuel	JG	
EICHNER	m.		1885	Zmigrod	Zmigrod	Shmuel	Perl	M		JG	
EICHNER	Israel		1882	Zmigrod	Zmigrod	Shmuel	Perl	M		JG	
EICHNER	Sara		1886	Zmigrod	Zmigrod	Shmuel	Perl	F		JG	
EICHNER	Salomon		1888	Zmigrod	Zmigrod	Shmuel	Perl	M		JG	
EICHNER	Isak		1899	Zmigrod	Zmigrod	Shmuel	Perl	M		JG	
EICHNER	Dawid		1891	Zmigrod	Zmigrod	Shmuel	Perl	M		JG	
EICHNER	Feiga		1896	Zmigrod	Zmigrod	Shmuel	Perl	F		JG	

Yizkor Book of Nowy Zmigrod

Family name	First name(s)	Maiden name	Birth date	Birth place	Residence	Father	Mother	Gender	Spouse	Source	Remarks
EICHNER	Chaje		1904	Zmigrod	Zmigrod	Shmuel	Perl	F		JG	
EICHNER	Samuel			Zmigrod	Zmigrod			M		JG	
EICHNER	Ite			Zmigrod	Zmigrod			F	Samuel	JG	
EICHNER	Abraham		1886	Zmigrod	Zmigrod	Samuel	Ite	M		JG	
EICHNER	Nachmen		1872	Zmigrod	Zmigrod	Samuel	Ite	M		JG	
EICHNER	Feige		1877	Zmigrod	Zmigrod	Samuel	Ite	F		JG	
EICHNER	Tema		1879	Zmigrod	Zmigrod	Samuel	Ite	F		JG	
EICHNER	Rifka			Zmigrod	Zmigrod	Samuel	Ite	F		JG	
EICHNER	Wolf		1885	Zmigrod	Zmigrod	Samuel	Ite	M		JG	
EICHNER	Chana M	SCHMIER		Zmigrod	Zmigrod			F	Wolf	JG	
EICHNER	Alter		1885	Zmigrod	Zmigrod	Wolf	Chana Matel			JG	
EICHNER	Sara B		1887	Zmigrod	Zmigrod	Wolf	Chana Matel			JG	
EICHNER	Isak				Zmigrod			M		JSS	Plaszow
EICHNER	Sala				Zmigrod			F		JSS	
EICHNER	S				Zmigrod			M		JG	
EMER	Jula	ENGELHARDT		Zmigrod	Zmigrod			F		YA	
EINHORN	Josef			Zmigrod	Zmigrod			M		JSS	Plaszow
EINHORN	Shia H			Zmigrod	Zmigrod			M		JG	
EINHORN	Sheindel			Zmigrod	Zmigrod			F	Shia H	JG	
EINHORN	Moshe			Zmigrod	Zmigrod	Shia H.	Sheindel	M		JG	
EINHORN	Dworah			Zmigrod	Zmigrod			F		P	
EINHORN	Bluma			Zmigrod	Zmigrod			F		P	

Family name	First name(s)	Maiden name	Birth date	Birth place	Residence	Father	Mother	Gender	Spouse	Source	Remarks
EINHORN	Yaakow			Zmigrod	Zmigrod			M		P	
EINHORN	Nate			Zmigrod	Zmigrod			M		P	
EINHORN	Eliezer			Zmigrod	Zmigrod			M		P	
EISENBACH	Oscar			Zmigrod	Zmigrod			M		JG	USA
EISENBACH	Yetta			Zmigrod	Zmigrod			F		JG	USA
EISENBACH	Hanina			Zmigrod	Zmigrod			M		JG	
EISENBACH	Malka			Zmigrod	Zmigrod			F		JG	survived
EISENBACH	Zelig			Zmigrod	Zmigrod			M		JG	survived
EISENBERG	Moses		1885	Zmigrod	Zmigrod			M		JSS	Plaszow
EISENBERG	Braindel		1884	Zmigrod	Zmigrod			F		JG	
EISENBERG	Chaim		1887	Zmigrod	Zmigrod			M		P	Holocaust
EISENBERG	Chiel			Zmigrod	Zmigrod			M		JG	
EISENBERG	Hanina			Zmigrod	Zmigrod			M		JG	
EISENBERG	Henoch			Zmigrod	Zmigrod			M		JG	survived
EISENBERG	Hersh			Zmigrod	Zmigrod			M		T	
EISENBERG	Chaskel			Zmigrod	Zmigrod			M		JR	
EISENBERG	Ides,			Zmigrod	Zmigrod	Chaskel	Ides,	F	Chaskel	JR	
EISENBERG	Shje		1867	Zmigrod	Zmigrod	Hersh		M		JR	
EISENBERG	Josef		1871	Zmigrod	Zmigrod			M		Jjr	
EISENBERG	Isser			Zmigrod	Zmigrod			M		JG	
EISENBERG	Malka			Zmigrod	Zmigrod			F		JG	
EISENBERG	Jacob							M		JR	
EISENBERG	Chana							F	Jacob	JR	

Yizkor Book of Nowy Zmigrod

Family name	First name(s)	Maiden name	Birth date	Birth place	Residence	Father	Mother	Gender	Spouse	Source	Remarks
EISENBERG	Mindel		1867	Zmigrod	Zmigrod	Jacob	Chana	F		JG	
EISENBERG	Reuven			Zmigrod	Zmigrod			M		P	Holocaust
EISENBERG	Hadasah				Zmigrod			F	Reuven	Holocaust	
EISENBERG	Schia		1867	Zmigrod	Zmigrod			M		JG	
EISENBERG	Tuvia			Zmigrod	Zmigrod			M		T	
EISENBERG	Zelig			Zmigrod	Zmigrod			M		JG	
EISENBERG	Moses				Zmigrod			M		JSS	Plaszow
EISENBERG	Itzhak				Zmigrod			M		BD	
EISENBERG	Shimon			Zmigrod	Zmigrod			M		JR	
EISENBERG	Leja			Zmigrod	Zmigrod			F	Shimon	JR	
EISENBERG	Samuel M		1871	Zmigrod	Zmigrod	Shimon	Leja	F		JR	
EISENBERG	Schyje		1876	Zmigrod	Zmigrod	Shimon	Leja	F		JR	
EISENBERGER	Asher				Zmigrod			M		P	
EISENBERGER	Simon				Zmigrod			M		P	
EISENBERGER	Dworah			Zmigrod	Zmigrod	Simon		F		P	
EISENBERGER	Taube				Zmigrod			F		P	
EKIERT	J				Zmigrod			M		BD	
ELLERT	Neche		1897	Zmigrod	Zmigrod	Elie		F		YA	Auschwitz
EMER	Isak			Jaslo	Zmigrod	Arieh Leib		M		YA	Holocaust
EMMER	Jula		1907		Zmigrod	Avraham		F		YA	Holocaust
ENDEL	Melchior				Zmigrod			M		P	
ENDZWEIG	Mechel		1879	Zmigrod	Zmigrod			M		JG	

Yizkor Book of Nowy Zmigrod

Family name	First name(s)	Maiden name	Birth date	Birth place	Residence	Father	Mother	Gender	Spouse	Source	Remarks
ENDZWEIG	Ida				Zmigrod			F		P	Holocaust
ENGEL	Mark		1879	Zmigrod	Zmigrod			M		JG	
ENGEL	Feiga			Zmigrod	Zmigrod			F		JG	survived
ENGEL	Nehemia			Zmigrod	Zmigrod			F		JG	survived
ENGEL	Yehoshua			Zmigrod	Zmigrod			M		JG	
ENGEL	Benjamin			Zmigrod	Zmigrod			M		JR	
ENGEL	Sara			Zmigrod	Zmigrod			F	Benjamin	JR	
ENGEL	Pesel		1869	Zmigrod	Zmigrod	Benjamin	Sara	F		JR	
ENGEL	Markus		1872	Zmigrod	Zmigrod	Benjamin	Sara	M		JR	
ENGEL	Nachum		1882	Zmigrod	Zmigrod	Benjamin	Sara	M		YA	Holocaust
ENGEL	Mordechai		1880	Zmigrod	Zmigrod	Benjamin	Sara	M		YA	
ENGEL	Leiser				Zmigrod	Mordechai		M		YA	
ENGEL	Riwka		1917		Zmigrod	Mordechai		F		YA	Holocaust
ENGEL	Reisel		1920		Zmigrod	Mordechai		F		YA	Holocaust
ENGEL	Jehoshua			Zmigrod	Zmigrod			M		JG	
ENGEL	Yehiel			Zmigrod	Zmigrod			M			
ENGEL	Gittel	EISENBERG		Zmigrod	Zmigrod			F	Yehiel		
ENGEL	Oser		1893	Zmigrod	Jaslo	Yehiel	Gittel	M		R	
ENGEL	Moshe			Zmigrod	Jaslo	Yehiel	Gittel	M		R	
ENGELHARDT	Awraham			Zmigrod	Zmigrod			M		YA	
ENGELHARDT	Yete			Zmigrod	Zmigrod			F	Awraham	YA	
ENGELHARDT	Julia			Zmigrod	Zmigrod	Awraham	Yete	F		YA	

Yizkor Book of Nowy Zmigrod

Family name	First name(s)	Maiden name	Birth date	Birth place	Residence	Father	Mother	Gender	Spouse	Source	Remarks
ENGELHARDT	Moshe			Zmigrod	Zmigrod			M		JG	
ENGELHARDT	Neche			Zmigrod	Zmigrod			F	Moshe	YV	
ENGELHARDT	Mendel				Zmigrod			M		P	
ENGELHARDT	Hersh				Zmigrod			M		P	
ERBICH	Ryfke			Zmigrod	Zmigrod			F		JSS	
ERBSTEIN	Nachman		1880		Zmigrod			M		JG	USA
ERBSTEIN	Leie		1887		Zmigrod			F	Nachman	JG	USA
ERBSTER	Yona			Zmigrod	Zmigrod			M		P	Holocaust
ERBSTER	Mindel			Zmigrod	Zmigrod			M		P	Holocaust
ERREICH	Taube Laje		1889	Zmigrod	Zmigrod			F		JG	
ERREICH	Mechel			Zmigrod	Zmigrod			M		JR	
ERREICH	Mosze		1860	Zmigrod	Zmigrod	Mechel		M		YA	Auschwitz
ERREICH	Chyfre		1880	Zmigrod	Zmigrod	Mechel		F		JG	
ERREICH	Pessel		1883	Zmigrod	Zmigrod	Mechel		F		JR	
ERREICH	Josef		1885	Zmigrod	Zmigrod	Mechel		M		JR	
ERREICH	Sussel		1885	Zmigrod	Zmigrod	Mechel		F		JR	
ERREICH	Ester		1887	Zmigrod	Zmigrod	Mechel		F		P	
ERREICH	Chaim		1890	Zmigrod	Zmigrod	Moshe		F		YA	Auschwitz
ERREICH	Noam				Zmigrod			M		JSS	Plaszow
ERREICH	Mordecke				Zmigrod			M		JSS	Plaszow
ERREICH	Aron		1892	Zmigrod	Zmigrod			M		JSS	
ERREICH	Ryfka			Zmigrod	Zmigrod			F	Aron	JSS	Plaszow
ERREICH	Salomon		1905	Zmigrod	Zmigrod	Aron	Ryfka	M		JSS	Plaszow

Family name	First name(s)	Maiden name	Birth date	Birth place	Residence	Father	Mother	Gender	Spouse	Source	Remarks
ERREICH	Riwka M			Zmigrod	Zmigrod	Aron	Ryfka	F		P	Holocaust
ERREICH	Michael			Zmigrod	Zmigrod	Aron	Ryfka	M		P	Holocaust
ERREICH	Buse			Zmigrod	Zmigrod	Abraham		F	Abraham	JG	
ERREICH	Moshe		1868	Zmigrod	Zmigrod	Abraham	Buse	M		JG	survived
ERREICH	Taube		1871	Zmigrod	Zmigrod			F		JG	
ERREICH	Bracha		1868	Zmigrod	Zmigrod			F		JG	
ERREICH	Wolf		1905	Zmigrod	Zmigrod			M		JG	survived
ERREICH	Moses K			Zmigrod	Zmigrod			M		JG	
ERREICH	Golde			Zmigrod	Zmigrod			F	Moses K	JG	
ERREICH	Hersh L		1868	Zmigrod	Zmigrod	Moses K	Golde	M		JG	
ERREICH	Avraham		1892	Zmigrod	Zmigrod	Moshe		M		YA	Auschwitz
ERREICH	Jicchak		1896	Zmigrod	Zmigrod	Moshe		M		YA	Auschwitz
ERREICH	Slomo		1894	Zmigrod	Zmigrod	Moshe		M		YA	Auschwitz
ERREICH	Feige R			Zmigrod	Zmigrod			F		JR	
ERREICH	Abisch		1881	Zmigrod	Zmigrod		Feige Ruchel	M		JR	
ERREICH	Berl		1888	Zmigrod	Zmigrod		Feige Ruc	M		JR	
ERREICH	Pinhas			Zmigrod	Zmigrod			M		JR	
ERREICH	Freidel		1883	Zmigrod	Zmigrod	Pinhas		F		JR	
ERREICH	Leib			Zmigrod	Zmigrod			M		JR	
ERREICH	Josef			Zmigrod	Zmigrod	Leib		M		JR	
ERTESZEK	Meir		1878	Zmigrod	Zmigrod	Berish		M		YA	Plaszow
FACHER	Abraham		1868	Zmigrod	Zmigrod			M		JG	
FACHER	Mendel			Zmigrod	Zmigrod			M		JG	

Yizkor Book of Nowy Zmigrod

Family name	First name(s)	Maiden name	Birth date	Birth place	Residence	Father	Mother	Gender	Spouse	Source	Remarks
FACHER	Sime	EICHNER		Zmigrod	Zmigrod			F	Mendel	JG	
FACHER	Feige		1872	Zmigrod	Zmigrod	Mendel	Sime	F		JG	
FACHER	Masche		1876	Zmigrod	Zmigrod	Mendel	Sime	F		JG	died 1879
FACHER	Salomon		1879	Zmigrod	Zmigrod	Mendel	Sime	M		JG	
FACHER	Annie		1886	Zmigrod	Zmigrod	Mendel	Sime	F		JG	
FACHER	David		1891	Zmigrod	Zmigrod	Mendel	Sime	M		JG	
FACHER	Idel			Zmigrod	Zmigrod			M		YA	
FACHER	Sara			Zmigrod	Zmigrod			F	Idel	YA	
FASSER	Noach				Zmigrod			M		P	
FEDER	Hersch			Zmigrod	Zmigrod			M		JR	
FEDER	Mindel			Zmigrod	Zmigrod			F	Hersch	JR	
FEDER	Esther		1872	Zmigrod	Zmigrod	Hersch	Mindel	F		JR	
FEDER	Chaim				Zmigrod			M		JSS	Plaszow
FEDER	Izak				Zmigrod			M		JSS	Plaszow
FEDER	Pepka				Zmigrod			F		JSS	
FEDER	Shimshon				Zmigrod			M		BD	
FEFERBERG	Miriam				Zmigrod			F		P	
FEIBEL	Herman		1895		Zmigrod			M		JG	USA
FEIER	Leib			Osiek	Zmigrod			M		JSS	
FEIER	Ryfka			Osiek	Zmigrod			F	Leib	JSS	
FEIER	Isak		1905	Osiek	Zmigrod	Leib	Ryfka	M		JSS	Plaszow
FEIER	Riwka		1871		Zmigrod			F		JG	USA
FEIER	Isaac		1908		Zmigrod			M		JG	USA

Yizkor Book of Nowy Zmigrod

Family name	First name(s)	Maiden name	Birth date	Birth place	Residence	Father	Mother	Gender	Spouse	Source	Remarks
FEIER	Leie		1907		Zmigrod			F		JG	USA
FEIER	Taube		1904		Zmigrod			F		JG	USA
FEIER	Moses		1902		Zmigrod			M		BD	
FEIER	Ben			Zmigrod				M		JG	USA
FEIER	Tillie		1877	Zmigrod				F		JG	USA
FEIGENBLUM	Abraham			Zmigrod				M		JG	USA
FEIGENBLUM	Dora			Zmigrod				F		JG	USA
FELD	Salamon				Zmigrod			M		JSS	Plaszow
FELDSTEIN	Awraham				Zmigrod			M		BD	
FELDSTEIN	Israel		1892		Zmigrod			M		JG	USA
FELDSZTAJN	Mosze		1904	Zmigrod	Zmigrod	Yehuda		M		YA	USA
FELLER	Israel	OSIEK		Zmigrod	Zmigrod			M		JG	survived
FELS	Shyja H			Zmigrod	Zmigrod			M		JG	
FELS	Shifre			Zmigrod	Zmigrod			F	Shyja H	JG	
FENNIG	Hersch				Zmigrod			M		JSS	
FENNIG	Lazar			Zmigrod	Zmigrod			M		JSS	Plaszow
FENNIG	Neche			Zmigrod	Zmigrod			F	Lazar	JR	
FENNIG	Riwka		1872	Zmigrod	Zmigrod	Lazar	Neche	F		JG	
FENNIG	Ester		1878	Zmigrod	Zmigrod			F		JG	
FENNIG	Hersch			Zmigrod	Zmigrod			M		JG	
FENNIG	Reisel		1882	Zmigrod	Zmigrod			F		JG	
FENNIG	Berish			Zmigrod	Zmigrod			M		P	
FENNER	Max		1868	Zmigrod				M		P	USA

Yizkor Book of Nowy Zmigrod

Family name	First name(s)	Maiden name	Birth date	Birth place	Residence	Father	Mother	Gender	Spouse	Source	Remarks
FERBER	Ryfka		1880		Zmigrod			F		JG	USA
FERBER	Jacob		1901		Zmigrod			M		JG	USA
FERYSZKA	Meir Sha		1920	Zmigrod	Zmigrod			M		P	USA
FESSLER	Miriam			Zmigrod	Zmigrod			F	Awraham	JG	
FEUER	Szymon			Zmigrod	Zmigrod			M		JG	
FEUER	Chaja T	EICHNER		Zmigrod	Zmigrod			F	Szymon		died 1921
FEUER	Sara C		1881	Zmigrod	Zmigrod	Szymon	Chaja Tema	M		JG	
FEUER	Zudik		1883	Zmigrod	Zmigrod	Szymon	Chaja Tema	M		JG	
FEUER	Wolf B		1887	Zmigrod	Zmigrod	Szymon	Chaja Tema	M		JG	
FEUER	Abraham		1887	Zmigrod	Zmigrod	Szymon	Chaja Tema	M		JG	
FEUER	Cerel		1889	Zmigrod	Zmigrod	Szymon	Chaja Tema	M		JG	
FEUER	Ben			Zmigrod	Zmigrod			M		JG	
FEUER	Tillie	STECHER	1877	Zmigrod	Zmigrod	Ben	Tillie	F	Ben	JG	
FEUER	Gitel		1884	Zmigrod	Zmigrod			F		JG	
FILLER	Bluma			Zmigrod				F		JG	USA
FINDLING	Hersh			Zmigrod	Zmigrod	Shimshon	Gittel	M		P	
FINDLING	Esther			Zmigrod	Zmigrod			F	Hersh	P	
FINDLING	Leopold			Zmigrod	Zmigrod	Hersh	Esther	M		P	
FINDLING	Samuel			Zmigrod	Zmigrod	Hersh	Esther	M		P	

Yizkor Book of Nowy Zmigrod

192

Family name	First name(s)	Maiden name	Birth date	Birth place	Residence	Father	Mother	Gender	Spouse	Source	Remarks
FINDLING	Ella			Zmigrod	Zmigrod	Hersh	Esther	F		P	
FINDLING	Shprincze R.			Zmigrod	Zmigrod	Shimshon	Gittel	F		P	
FINDLING	Avraham			Zmigrod	Zmigrod	Shimshon	Gittel	M		P	
FINDLING	Pearl		1880	Zmigrod	Zmigrod			F	Avraham	Holocaust	
FINDLING	Leon				Zmigrod	Avraham	Pearl	M		P	
FINDLING	Shimshon		1912		Zmigrod	Avraham	Pearl	M		P	Holocaust
FINDLING	Eliezer				Zmigrod	Avraham	Pearl	M			survived
FINDLING	Feige		1916		Zmigrod	Avraham	Pearl	F		P	Holocaust
FINDLING	Haim		1917		Zmigrod	Avraham	Pearl	M		P	Holocaust
FINDLING	Miriam		1906		Zmigrod			F		P	Holocaust
FINDLING	Shlomo		1937		Zmigrod		Miriam	M		P	Holocaust
FINDLING	Chaim			Zmigrod	Zmigrod	Shimshon	Gittel	M		P	
FINDLING	Gittel	KOCH		Zmigrod	Zmigrod			F	Chaim	P	
FINDLING	Feige R			Zmigrod	Zmigrod	Shimshon	Gittel	F		P	
FINDLING	Yehiel			Zmigrod	Zmigrod	Shimshon	Gittel	M		P	
FINDLING	Shprincze	DAREKEWITZ		Zmigrod	Zmigrod	Yehiel	Shprincze	F	Yehiel	P	
FINDLING	Shimshon			Zmigrod	Zmigrod	Yehiel	Shprincze	M		P	
FINDLING	Itzhak			Zmigrod	Zmigrod	Shimshon	Gittel	M		P	
FINDLING	Rachel			Zmigrod	Zmigrod			F	Itzhak	P	

Yizkor Book of Nowy Zmigrod

Family name	First name(s)	Maiden name	Birth date	Birth place	Residence	Father	Mother	Gender	Spouse	Source	Remarks
FINDLING	Yaacov			Zmigrod	Zmigrod	Itzhak	Rachel	M		P	
FINDLING	Motel			Zmigrod	Zmigrod	Itzhak	Rachel	M		P	survived
FINDLING	Gittel			Zmigrod	Zmigrod	Itzhak	Rachel	F		P	
FINDLING	Chiel Her		1877	Zmigrod	Zmigrod			M		P	survived
FINDLING	Sima			Zmigrod	Zmigrod	Chiel Her		F	Chiel Her	P	survived
FINDLING	Simon			Zmigrod	Zmigrod	Chiel Her	Sima	M		P	survived
FINDLING	Abraham			Zmigrod	Zmigrod			M		P	
FINDLING	Lea			Zmigrod	Zmigrod			F	Abraham	P	
FINDLING	Moshe A			Zmigrod	Zmigrod	Abraham	Lea	M		P	
FINDLING	Hinde	ZATLER		Zmigrod	Zmigrod			F	Moshe A	P	
FINDLING	Herman			Zmigrod	Zmigrod	Moshe A	Hinde	M		P	
FINDLING	Adele			Zmigrod	Zmigrod	Moshe A	Hinde	F		P	
FINDLING	Rachel G			Zmigrod	Zmigrod	Moshe A	Hinde	F		P	
FINDLING	Zlatte			Zmigrod	Zmigrod	Moshe A	Hinde	F		P	
FINDLING	Avraham		1880	Zmigrod	Zmigrod			M		P	
FINDLING	Abraham		1888	Zmigrod	Zmigrod			M		P	
FINDLING	Berl			Zmigrod	Zmigrod			M		P	
FINDLING	Rela	IZRAEL		Zmigrod	Zmigrod			F	Berl	P	
FINDLING	Samuel		1886	Zmigrod	Zmigrod	Berl	Rela	M		P	
FINDLING	Simche			Zmigrod	Zmigrod			M			
FINDLING	Riwka			Zmigrod	Zmigrod			F	Simche		
FINDLING	Perl		1871	Zmigrod	Zmigrod	Simche	Riwka	F			
FINDLING	Berl		1873	Zmigrod	Zmigrod	Simche	Riwka	M		P	

Yizkor Book of Nowy Zmigrod

Family name	First name(s)	Maiden name	Birth date	Birth place	Residence	Father	Mother	Gender	Spouse	Source	Remarks
FINDLING	Berl		1881	Zmigrod	Zmigrod			M		P	
FINDLING	Bika		1927	Zmigrod	Zmigrod			M		P	
FINDLING	Breindel		1881	Zmigrod	Zmigrod			F		P	
FINDLING	Gittel			Zmigrod	Zmigrod			F	Simon	JR	
FINDLING	Hershel		1873	Zmigrod	Zmigrod	Simon	Gittel	M		P	Holocaust
FINDLING	Esther		1878	Zmigrod	Zmigrod	Hershel		F	Hershel	P	Holocaust
FINDLING	Simon			Zmigrod	Zmigrod	Hershel	Esther	M		JR	Holocaust
FINDLING	Leopold			Zmigrod	Zmigrod	Hershel	Esther	M		P	
FINDLING	Shprincze	RUCHEL		Zmigrod	Zmigrod	Simon	Gittel	F		P	
FINDLING	Chaim		1876	Zmigrod	Zmigrod	Simon	Gittel	M		P	
FINDLING	Gittel	KOCH		Zmigrod	Zmigrod			F	Chaim	P	
FINDLING	Sima			Zmigrod	Zmigrod	Chaim	Gittel	F		P	
FINDLING	Rachel			Zmigrod	Zmigrod	Chaim	Gittel	F		P	
FINDLING	Awraham			Zmigrod	Zmigrod	Chaim	Gittel	F		P	
FINDLING	Haya			Zmigrod	Zmigrod	Chaim	Gittel	F		P	
FINDLING	Moshe			Zmigrod	Zmigrod	Chaim	Gittel	F		P	
FINDLING	Shimshon			Zmigrod	Zmigrod	Chaim	Gittel	F		P	
FINDLING	Awraham			Zmigrod	Zmigrod	Simon	Gittel	M		P	
FINDLING	Pearl	ZAWISHLAG		Zmigrod	Zmigrod			F	Awraham	P	
FINDLING	Leon			Zmigrod	Zmigrod	Awraham	Pearl	M		P	
FINDLING	Shimshon			Zmigrod	Zmigrod	Awraham	Pearl	M		P	
FINDLING	Eliezer			Zmigrod	Zmigrod	Awraham	Pearl	M		P	
FINDLING	Chaim			Zmigrod	Zmigrod	Awraham	Pearl	M		P	

Yizkor Book of Nowy Zmigrod

Family name	First name(s)	Maiden name	Birth date	Birth place	Residence	Father	Mother	Gender	Spouse	Source	Remarks
FINDLING	Tova			Zmigrod	Zmigrod	Awraham	Pearl	F		P	
FINDLING	Tziporah			Zmigrod	Zmigrod	Awraham	Pearl	F		P	
FINDLING	Gittel			Zmigrod	Zmigrod	Awraham	Pearl	F		P	
FINDLING	Feige R			Zmigrod	Zmigrod	Simon	Gittel	F			
FINDLING	Sima			Zmigrod	Zmigrod	Simon	Gittel	F			
FINDLING	Hiel H			Zmigrod	Zmigrod			M	Hiel Hersh		
FINDLING	Simon			Zmigrod	Zmigrod	Hiel H	Sima	M			
FINDLING	Chaim		1886	Zmigrod	Zmigrod			M		P	
FINDLING	Chaim S			Zmigrod	Zmigrod			M		P	
FINDLING	Ester	MITZNER		Zmigrod	Zmigrod			F	Chaim S	P	
FINDLING	Simche		1883	Zmigrod	Zmigrod	Chaim S	Ester	M		P	
FINDLING	Chaje		1871	Zmigrod	Zmigrod			F		P	
FINDLING	Chane		1875	Zmigrod	Zmigrod			F		P	
FINDLING	Chiel		1887	Zmigrod	Zmigrod			M		P	
FINDLING	Chiel		1920	Zmigrod	Zmigrod			M		P	
FINDLING	Hersch			Zmigrod	Zmigrod			M		P	
FINDLING	Chana	STACHEL		Zmigrod	Zmigrod			F	Hersch	P	
FINDLING	Moses D		1868	Zmigrod	Zmigrod	Hersch	Chana	M		P	
FINDLING	Chypre		1880	Zmigrod	Zmigrod			F		P	
FINDLING	Dwora		1884	Zmigrod	Zmigrod			F		P	
FINDLING	Dwora		1875	Zmigrod	Zmigrod			F		P	
FINDLING	Shmuel I			Zmigrod	Zmigrod			M		P	
FINDLING	Malka C			Zmigrod	Zmigrod			F	Shmuel It	P	

Family name	First name(s)	Maiden name	Birth date	Birth place	Residence	Father	Mother	Gender	Spouse	Source	Remarks
FINDLING	Hicel			Zmigrod	Zmigrod	Shmuel I	Malka Chaya	M		JR	
FINDLING	Efroim		1886	Zmigrod	Zmigrod	Shmuel I	Malka Chaya	M		P	
FINDLING	Efroim		1881	Zmigrod	Zmigrod			M		P	
FINDLING	Eisig		1919	Zmigrod	Zmigrod			M		P	
FINDLING	Eisig		1888	Zmigrod	Zmigrod			M		P	
FINDLING	Freidel		1880	Zmigrod	Zmigrod			F		P	
FINDLING	Freudel		1889	Zmigrod	Zmigrod			F		P	
FINDLING	Gele		1888	Zmigrod	Zmigrod			F		P	
FINDLING	Genendel		1884	Zmigrod	Zmigrod			F		P	
FINDLING	Gitel		1921	Zmigrod	Zmigrod			F		P	
FINDLING	Hersh,			Zmigrod	Zmigrod			M		P	
FINDLING	Chana	STACHEL		Zmigrod	Zmigrod			F	Hersh,	P	
FINDLING	Moses		1878	Zmigrod	Zmigrod	Hersh,	Chana	M		P	
FINDLING	Hillel		1872	Zmigrod	Zmigrod			M		P	
FINDLING	Hinda		1882	Zmigrod	Zmigrod			F		P	
FINDLING	Hinde		1889	Zmigrod	Zmigrod			F		P	
FINDLING	Ides		1870	Zmigrod	Zmigrod			M		P	
FINDLING	Isak			Zmigrod	Zmigrod			F	Isak	P	
FINDLING	Malka	BOBKER	1906	Zmigrod	Zmigrod	Isak	Malka	M		P	
FINDLING	Mozes			Zmigrod	Zmigrod			M		JR	
FINDLING	Jacob		1880	Zmigrod	Zmigrod	Jacob		F		JR	
FINDLING	Este										

Yizkor Book of Nowy Zmigrod

Family name	First name(s)	Maiden name	Birth date	Birth place	Residence	Father	Mother	Gender	Spouse	Source	Remarks
FINDLING	Awraham		1883	Zmigrod	Zmigrod	Jacob		M		JR	
FINDLING	Simche		1883	Zmigrod	Zmigrod	Jacob		M		JR	
FINDLING	Itte		1886	Zmigrod	Zmigrod			F		P	
FINDLING	Izak			Zmigrod	Zmigrod			M		P	
FINDLING	Sara	ROSENBERG		Zmigrod	Zmigrod			F	Izak	P	
FINDLING	Sosche C		1872	Zmigrod	Zmigrod	Izak	Sosche Ch	F		P	
FINDLING	Jakob		1870	Zmigrod	Zmigrod			M		P	
FINDLING	Jacob		1919	Zmigrod	Zmigrod			M		P	
FINDLING	Jacob W			Zmigrod	Zmigrod			M		P	
FINDLING	Ita	MEISNER	1885	Zmigrod	Zmigrod	Jacob W	Ita	F	Jacob W	P	
FINDLING	Seinwel			Zmigrod	Zmigrod	Jacob W	Ita	F		P	
FINDLING	Sima			Zmigrod	Zmigrod	Jacob W	Ita	F		P	married 1920
FINDLING	Joel		1878	Zmigrod	Zmigrod			M		P	
FINDLING	Josef		1882	Zmigrod	Zmigrod			M		P	
FINDLING	Leib		1877	Zmigrod	Zmigrod			M		P	
FINDLING	Mirjam		1872	Zmigrod	Zmigrod			F		P	
FINDLING	Markus		1917	Zmigrod	Zmigrod			M		P	
FINDLING	Markus		1923	Zmigrod	Zmigrod			M		P	
FINDLING	Matel		1877	Zmigrod	Zmigrod			M		P	
FINDLING	Meyer		1867	Zmigrod	Zmigrod			M		P	
FINDLING	Mendel			Zmigrod	Zmigrod			M		P	married 1931

Yizkor Book of Nowy Zmigrod

Family name	First name(s)	Maiden name	Birth date	Birth place	Residence	Father	Mother	Gender	Spouse	Source	Remarks
FINDLING	Moses			Zmigrod	Zmigrod			M		P	
FINDLING	Feige	EICHNER		Zmigrod	Zmigrod			F	Moses	P	
FINDLING	Samuel Y		1870	Zmigrod	Zmigrod	Moses	Feige	M		P	
FINDLING	Sara			Zmigrod	Zmigrod			F		P	
FINDLING	Mozes			Zmigrod	Zmigrod			M		P	
FINDLING	Mojzes		1911	Zmigrod	Zmigrod			M		P	
FINDLING	Nachmen			Zmigrod	Zmigrod			M		P	
FINDLING	Zywie	WACHS		Zmigrod	Zmigrod			F	Nachmen	P	
FINDLING	Syma		1904	Zmigrod	Zmigrod	Nachmen	Zywie	F		P	
FINDLING	Salmen		1889	Zmigrod	Zmigrod			M		P	
FINDLING	Simon			Zmigrod	Zmigrod			M		P	
FINDLING	Rywka	TZIMET		Zmigrod	Zmigrod			F	Simon	P	
FINDLING	Joel		1878	Zmigrod	Zmigrod	Simon	Rywka	M		J	
FINDLING	Pearl		1884	Zmigrod	Zmigrod	Simon	Rywka	F		J	
FINDLING	Mozes		1914	Zmigrod	Zmigrod			M		P	
FINDLING	Isaac			Zmigrod	Zmigrod			M		P	
FINDLING	Zlata		1883	Zmigrod	Zmigrod	Isaac		F		JR	
FINDLING	Samuel			Zmigrod	Zmigrod			M		P	
FINDLING	Perl			Zmigrod	Zmigrod	Samuel		F	Samuel	P	
FINDLING	Chana		1882	Zmigrod	Zmigrod	Samuel	Perl	F		P	
FINDLING	Wigdor		1877	Zmigrod	Zmigrod	Samuel	Perl	M		P	
FINDLING	Sima		1923	Zmigrod	Zmigrod	Samuel	Perl	F		P	
FINDLING	Samuel W			Zmigrod	Zmigrod			M		P	

Yizkor Book of Nowy Zmigrod

Family name	First name(s)	Maiden name	Birth date	Birth place	Residence	Father	Mother	Gender	Spouse	Source	Remarks
FINDLING				Zmigrod	Zmigrod			F	Samuel W	P	
FINDLING	Simon		1921	Zmigrod	Zmigrod	Samuel W		M		P	
FINDLING	Wolf			Zmigrod	Zmigrod			M		P	
FINDLING	Chana M	SCHMIER		Zmigrod	Zmigrod			F	Wolf	P	
FINDLING	Simson		1916	Zmigrod	Zmigrod	Wolf	Chana Ma	M		P	
FINDLING	Izrael			Zmigrod	Zmigrod			M		P	
FINDLING	Chaje S	KATZ		Zmigrod	Zmigrod			F	Izrael	P	
FINDLING	Neche		1879	Zmigrod	Zmigrod	Izrael	Chaje Sar	F		P	
FINDLING	Pinkas		1886	Zmigrod	Zmigrod	Izrael	Chaje Sar	M		P	
FINDLING	Perl		1881	Zmigrod	Zmigrod	Izrael	Chaje Sar	F		P	
FINDLING	Sara		1884	Zmigrod	Zmigrod	Izrael	Chaje Sar	F		P	
FINDLING	Reisla		1905	Zmigrod	Zmigrod	Izrael	Chaje Sar	F		P	
FINDLING	Samuel			Zmigrod	Zmigrod	Izrael	Chaje Sar	M		P	married 1914
FINDLING	Natan			Zmigrod	Zmigrod	Izrael	Chaje Sar	M		P	
FINDLING	Moshe H			Zmigrod	Zmigrod			M		P	
FINDLING	Simson		1905	Zmigrod	Zmigrod	Chiel		M		P	
FINDLING	Jakub		1905	Zmigrod	Zmigrod			M		P	Plaszow
FINDLING	Eisik				Zmigrod			M		P	
FINDLING	Aron		1885	Zmigrod	Zmigrod			M		P	
FINDLING	Baile			Zmigrod	Zmigrod			F	Aron	P	

Family name	First name(s)	Maiden name	Birth date	Birth place	Residence	Father	Mother	Gender	Spouse	Source	Remarks
FINDLING			1885	Zmigrod	Zmigrod			M		P	
FINDLING	Avraham			Zmigrod	Zmigrod			M		P	
FINDLING	Sima			Zmigrod	Zmigrod			F	Avraham	P	
FINDLING	Lea			Zmigrod	Zmigrod			F		JG	
FINDLING	Leibish			Zmigrod	Zmigrod	Avraham	Sima	M		P	
FINDLING	Lea			Zmigrod	Zmigrod	Leibish		F	Leibish	P	
FINDLING	Lea		1853	Zmigrod	Zmigrod	Leibish		F		P	died 1936.
FINDLING	Chaim			Zmigrod	Zmigrod	Leibish		M		P	
FINDLING	Zissel	TZIGER		Zmigrod	Zmigrod			F	Chaim	P	
FINDLING	Marc			Zmigrod	Zmigrod	Chaim	Zissel	M		P	
FINDLING	Nathan			Zmigrod	Zmigrod	Leibish		M		P	
FINDLING	Avraham			Zmigrod	Zmigrod	Leibish		M		P	
FINDLING	Shprintze			Zmigrod	Zmigrod	Leibish		F		P	
FINDLING	Dwora			Zmigrod	Zmigrod	Leibish		F		P	
FINDLING	Sima			Zmigrod	Zmigrod	Leibish		F		P	
FINDLING	Nathan			Zmigrod	Zmigrod	Avraham	Sima	M		P	
FINDLING	Shimon			Zmigrod	Zmigrod	Avraham	Sima	M		P	
FINDLING	Yaacov			Zmigrod	Zmigrod	Avraham	Sima	M		P	
FINDLING	Hendel	DEUTSCHMANN		Zmigrod	Zmigrod			M		P	
FINDLING	Malka	DILLER		Zmigrod	Zmigrod			F	Yaacov	P	
FINDLING	Fraidel			Zmigrod	Zmigrod	Yaacov	Hendel	F		P	
FINDLING	Ita			Zmigrod	Zmigrod	Yaacov	Hendel	F		P	
FINDLING	Moses D		1868	Zmigrod	Zmigrod	Yaacov	Hendel	M		P	

Yizkor Book of Nowy Zmigrod

Family name	First name(s)	Maiden name	Birth date	Birth place	Residence	Father	Mother	Gender	Spouse	Source	Remarks
FINDLING				Zmigrod	Zmigrod			F	Moses D		
FINDLING	Tzeite			Zmigrod	Zmigrod	Moses D		F		P	
FINDLING	Idel Leib			Zmigrod	Zmigrod	Moses D		M		P	
FINDLING	Mendel			Zmigrod	Zmigrod	Moses D		M		P	
FINDLING	Sole			Zmigrod	Zmigrod	Moses D		F		P	
FINDLING	Ester			Zmigrod	Zmigrod	Moses D		F		P	
FINDLING	Mechel			Zmigrod	Zmigrod	Moses D		M		P	
FINDLING	Yaacov			Zmigrod	Zmigrod	Moses D		M		P	
FINDLING	Naphtali			Zmigrod	Zmigrod	Moses D		M		P	USA
FINDLING	Jo			Zmigrod	Zmigrod	Moses D		M		P	
FINDLING	Shimshon			Zmigrod	Zmigrod	Avraham	Sima	M		P	
FINDLING	Gittel	WALTER		Zmigrod	Zmigrod			F	Shimshon	P	
FINDLING	Joseph			Zmigrod	Zmigrod	Shimshon	Gittel	M		JG	USA
FINDLING	Abraham			Zmigrod	Zmigrod	Shimshon	Gittel			J	
FINDLING	Seinwel L		1885	Zmigrod	Zmigrod	Shimshon	Gittel	M		J	
FINDLING	Chiel		1887	Zmigrod	Zmigrod	Shimshon	Gittel	M		J	
FINDLING	Eisik		1888	Zmigrod	Zmigrod	Shimshon	Gittel	M		J	
FINDLING	Isaac			Zmigrod	Zmigrod	Shimshon	Gittel	M		JR	
FINDLING	Myszket			Zmigrod	Zmigrod			F	Isaac	JR	

Family name	First name(s)	Maiden name	Birth date	Birth place	Residence	Father	Mother	Gender	Spouse	Source	Remarks
FINDLING	Samuel		1869	Zmigrod	Zmigrod	Isaac	Myszket	M		JR	
FINDLING	Jacob		1869	Zmigrod	Zmigrod	Isaac	Myszket	M		JR	
FINDLING	Isaac		1869	Zmigrod	Zmigrod	Isaac	Myszket	M		JR	
FINDLING	Hersch D			Zmigrod	Zmigrod			M		JR	
FINDLING	Miszket		1872	Zmigrod	Zmigrod			F	Hersch D	JR	
FINDLING	Chaja S			Zmigrod	Zmigrod	Hersch D	Miszket	F		JR	
FINDLING	Efroim H			Zmigrod	Zmigrod			M		JR	
FINDLING	Reisel			Zmigrod	Zmigrod	Efroim H		F	Efroim H	JR	
FINDLING	Israel B		1866	Zmigrod	Zmigrod	Efroim H	Reisel	M		JR	
FINDLING	Israel			Zmigrod	Zmigrod			M		JR	
FINDLING	Miszket			Zmigrod	Zmigrod			M	IBeer	JR	
FINDLING	Chaje		1873	Zmigrod	Zmigrod	Israel B	Miszket	M		JR	
FINDLING	Dwore		1873	Zmigrod	Zmigrod	Israel B	Miszket	M		JR	
FINK	Mayer			Zmigrod	USA			M		JG	USA
FINK	Genia		1885		Zmigrod			F		JG	USA
FISH	Moyszes			Zmigrod	Zmigrod			M		JR	
FISH	Rywka		1880	Zmigrod	Zmigrod	Moyszes Ar		F		JR	
FISCHER	Yaacov			Zmigrod	USA			M		P	USA
FISHLER				Zmigrod	Zmigrod			M		JG	
FISHLER	Mendel		1884	Zmigrod	Zmigrod			M		JG	
FRACHMAN	Leib		1892	Zmigrod	Zmigrod			M		JG	USA
FRENKIL	Moshe				Zmigrod			M		P	
FREUND	Szyje			Zmigrod	Zmigrod			M		JR	

Yizkor Book of Nowy Zmigrod

Family name	First name(s)	Maiden name	Birth date	Birth place	Residence	Father	Mother	Gender	Spouse	Source	Remarks
FREUND	Laje		1885	Zmigrod	Zmigrod	Szyje		F		JR	
FREUND	Kiwe Leib		1887	Zmigrod	Zmigrod			M		JG	
FREUND	Kalman M		1858	Zmigrod	Zmigrod			M	Alte	JG	
FREUND	Osias		1858		Zmigrod			M		JG	USA
FREUND	Alte		1858		Zmigrod			F	Osias	WS	USA
FREUND	Baruch		1897		Zmigrod			M		WS	USA
FREUND	Samuel		1895		Zmigrod			M		WS	USA
FREUND	Itzik				Zmigrod			M		T	
FREUND	Chaim I				Zmigrod			M		P	
FREUND	Yente				Zmigrod			F			
FRICHSON	Jozef			Zmigrod	Zmigrod			M		JG	
FRICHSON	Gitla	WEINREICH		Zmigrod	Zmigrod			F	Jozef	JG	
FRICHSON	Sara			Zmigrod	Zmigrod	Jozef	Gitla	F		JG	
FRIEDMAN	Hersch			Zmigrod	Zmigrod			M		BD	
FRIEDMAN	Hadassah	BERGER		Zmigrod				F		P	
FRIEDMAN	Sura		1882			Hersch	Hadassah	F	Hersch	P	
FRIEDMAN	Suessel		1885			Hersch	Hadassah	F		P	
FRIEDMAN	Yossef		1888			Hersch	Hadassah	M		P	
FRIEDMAN	Josef		1888	Zmigrod	Zmigrod	Hersch		M		JR	
FRIEDMAN	Hanah		1869		Zmigrod			F		JG	USA
FRIEDMAN	Frime		1900		Zmigrod			F		JG	USA
FRIEDMAN	Zofia		1903		Zmigrod			F		JG	USA
FRIHILING	Miszkat		1888	Zmigrod	Zmigrod			M		JG	

Family name	First name(s)	Maiden name	Birth date	Birth place	Residence	Father	Mother	Gender	Spouse	Source	Remarks
FRUMET					Zmigrod			M		T	
FUSENFEST	Icek				Zmigrod			M		JSS	Plaszow
GALANTY	Arieh			Zmigrod	Zmigrod			M			
GALANTY	Matel	SIDWERTS	1898	Dukla	Zmigrod	Shmuel		F	Arieh	YS	Holocaust
GALER	Gitel			Zmigrod				F		YA	
GARNREICH	Roman				Zmigrod			M		JSS	Plaszow
GELB	Gittel		1887	Zmigrod	Zmigrod			F	Yehezkel	JSS	
GELB	Yaacov			Zmigrod	Zmigrod			M		P	Holocaust
GELB	Tilie			Zmigrod	Zmigrod			F	Yaacov	JSS	
GELB	Yehezkel			Zmigrod	Zmigrod			M		JSS	
GELB	Mechel				Zmigrod			M		JSS	
GELB	Freidel				Zmigrod			F	Mechel	JSS	
GELB	Alter		1905	Zmigrod	Zmigrod	Mechel	Frieda	M		JSS	Plaszow
GELB	Rachel				Zmigrod			F		JSS	
GELB	Joseph				Zmigrod			M		JG	USA
GELB	Hersh				Zmigrod			M		P	
GELLER	Juda			Zmigrod	Zmigrod			M		JR	
GELLER	Scheindel		1882	Zmigrod	Zmigrod	Juda		F		JR	
GELLER	Benjamin		1867		Zmigrod			M		JG	USA
GELLER	Rosa		1903		Zmigrod			F		JG	USA
GELLER	Abraham		1893		Zmigrod			M		JG	USA
GELLER	Sala				Zmigrod			F		P	
GENSTERMAN	Ester		1877	Zmigrod	Zmigrod			F		JG	

Yizkor Book of Nowy Zmigrod

Family name	First name(s)	Maiden name	Birth date	Birth place	Residence	Father	Mother	Gender	Spouse	Source	Remarks
GESTER	Elias			Zmigrod	Zmigrod			M		JR	
GESTER	Sure			Zmigrod	Zmigrod			F	Elias	JR	
GESTER	Nachman		1869	Zmigrod	Zmigrod	Elias	Sure	M		JR	
GETTENBERG	Eisik				Zmigrod			M		JSS	Plaszow
GETTENBERG	Beila			Zmigrod	Zmigrod			F		JSS	
GETZ	Shmuel			Zmigrod	Zmigrod			M		P	survived
GETZ	Yaakow I			Zmigrod	Zmigrod			M		P	survived
GETZEL	Nahum Y				Zmigrod			M		P	
GETZEL	Hersh				Zmigrod			M		P	
GETZLER	Yitzhak		1887	Zmigrod	Zmigrod	Zeew		M		YS	Plaszow
GETZLER	Moses			Zmigrod	Germany	Pinhas		M		P	Holocaust
GETZLER	Zeev W			Zmigrod	Germany	Moses		M		P	Holocaust
GETZLER	Ester			Zmigrod	Germany			F	Zeev Wolf	JR	
GETZLER	Marjem		1876	Zmigrod	Germany	Zeev W	Ester	F		JR	
GETZLER	Moses		1895		Zmigrod			M		JG	USA
GETZLER	Regina		1889		Zmigrod			F		JG	USA
GETZLER	Fieda		1882	Zmigrod	Zmigrod			F		JG	
GETZLER	Gittel		1867	Zmigrod	Zmigrod			F		JG	
GETZLER	Henia			Zmigrod	Zmigrod			F		JG	survived
GETZLER	Itzhak J		1883	Zmigrod	Zmigrod			M		JG	
GETZLER	Jacob		1883	Zmigrod	Zmigrod			M		JG	
GETZLER	Markus		1882	Zmigrod	Zmigrod			M		JG	
GETZLER	Moses		1867	Zmigrod	Zmigrod			M		JG	

Yizkor Book of Nowy Zmigrod

Family name	First name(s)	Maiden name	Birth date	Birth place	Residence	Father	Mother	Gender	Spouse	Source	Remarks
GETZLER	Alter			Zmigrod	Zmigrod			M		P	Holocaust
GETZLER	Mordechai			Zmigrod	Zmigrod			M		P	
GETZLER	Moshe M			Zmigrod	Zmigrod			M		P	
GINZBERG	Tuvia			Zmigrod	Zmigrod			M		JG	
GINZBERG	Isser		1881	Zmigrod	Zmigrod	Isser		M		JR	
GINZBERG	Ruben			Zmigrod	Zmigrod			M		JR	
GLANTZ	Israel			Zmigrod	Zmigrod			M		JSS	Plaszow
GLASER	Hermann			Zmigrod	Zmigrod						
GLASER	Roman		1905	Zmigrod	Zmigrod	Herman	Epstein	M		JG	
GLEICH	Leib		1885	Zmigrod	Zmigrod			M		JG	
GLEZER	Yehudit			Zmigrod	Zmigrod			F		JG	
GLEZER	Yehudah			Zmigrod	Zmigrod			M		JG	
GLEZER	Yehudah			Zmigrod	Zmigrod	Yehudah		M		JG	
GOETZ	Osiah			Zmigrod	Zmigrod			M		JG	
GOETZ	Sheindel	STECHER		Zmigrod	Zmigrod			F	Osiah	JG	
GOETZ	Jankel		1916	Zmigrod	Zmigrod	Osiah	Sheindel	M		JG	
GOETZ	Shimshe			Zmigrod	Zmigrod	Osiah	Sheindel	M		JG	
GOETZ	Naftuli J			Zmigrod	Zmigrod	Osiah	Sheindel	M		JG	
GOETZ	Chin			Zmigrod	Zmigrod	Osiah	Sheindel	M		JG	
GOETZ	Itchie			Zmigrod	Zmigrod	Osiah	Sheindel	M		JG	
GOLD	Leib			Zmigrod	Zmigrod			M		JR	
GOLD	Miszket			Zmigrod	Zmigrod			F	Leib	JR	
GOLD	Jona		1869	Zmigrod	Zmigrod	Leib	Miszket	M		JR	

Yizkor Book of Nowy Zmigrod

Family name	First name(s)	Maiden name	Birth date	Birth place	Residence	Father	Mother	Gender	Spouse	Source	Remarks
GOLDBERG	Malke		1886	Zmigrod	Zmigrod			F		JSS	Holocaust
GOLDBERG	Ita		1908	Zmigrod	Zmigrod	Lewy		F		JSS	Plaszow
GOLDBERG	Israel				Zmigrod			M		JG	USA
GOLDBLATT	Annie			Zmigrod				F		JSS	
GOLDBLATT	Hadassah			Zmigrod	Zmigrod			F		P	survived
GOLDFARB	Gittel Dwo			Zmigrod	Zmigrod			F	Awraham	P	Holocaust
GOLDFARB	Sz.				Zmigrod			M		JG	
GOLDFINGER	Lea		1884	Zmigrod	Zmigrod			F		JG	survived
GOLDMAN	Awshalom				Zmigrod			M		P	
GOLDMAN	Isaak		1879	Zmigrod	Zmigrod			M		YA	Holocaust
GOLDMAN	Miryam			Zmigrod	Zmigrod	Naphtali		F		YA	Belzec
GOLDMAN	Naftali		1914	Zmigrod	Zmigrod	Avraham		M		JG	USA
GOLDMAN	Harry			Zmigrod				M		JG	
GOLDMAN	Isaac			Zmigrod	Zmigrod			M		JR	
GOLDMAN	Taube		1880	Zmigrod	Zmigrod	Isaac		F		JR	
GOLDSTEIN	Freidel		1887	Zmigrod	Zmigrod			F		YA	Auschwitz
GOLDSZTEJN	Chana		1900	Zmigrod	Berlin	Wolf		F		JSS	Plaszow
GOLDWASSER	Isek				Zmigrod			M		JSS	Plaszow
GOLDWENDER	Isser				Zmigrod			M		JG	
GOLDWENDER	Ozer C		1877	Zmigrod	Zmigrod			M		JG	
GOLDWENDER			1888	Zmigrod	Zmigrod			M		JG	
GOLDWENDER	Naftali			Zmigrod	Zmigrod			M		JG	
GOLDWENDER	Ryfka			Zmigrod	Zmigrod			F	Naftali	JG	

Family name	First name(s)	Maiden name	Birth date	Birth place	Residence	Father	Mother	Gender	Spouse	Source	Remarks
GOLDWENDER	Chaje		1872	Zmigrod	Zmigrod	Naftali	Ryfka	F		JR	
GOLDWENDER	Neche		1884	Zmigrod	Zmigrod	Naftali	Ryfka	F		JG	
GOLDWENDER	Moshe		1874	Zmigrod	Zmigrod			M		JG	
GOLDWENDER	Chawa			Zmigrod	Zmigrod			F		P	
GOTTLIEB	Joseph		1885	Zmigrod	Zmigrod	Joseph		M		JR	
GOTTLIEB	Moses			Zmigrod	Zmigrod			M		BD	
GOTZ	Itzhak			Zmigrod	Zmigrod			M		JG	
GOTZ	Sheindel			Zmigrod	Zmigrod			F		JG	
GOTZ	Shmuel			Zmigrod	Zmigrod			M		JG	
GOTZ	Chana		1868	Zmigrod	Zmigrod			F		JG	
GOTZ	Markus D			Zmigrod	Zmigrod			M		JG	
GOTZ	Ceril			Zmigrod	Zmigrod			F	Markus D		
GOTZ	Chaskel		1922	Zmigrod	Zmigrod	Markus D	Ceril	M		JG	
GOTZ	Moshe L			Zmigrod	Zmigrod			M		JG	
GOTZ	Ryfka Ro	WEISS		Zmigrod	Zmigrod			F	Moshe Li		
GOTZ	Naphtali		1908	Zmigrod	Zmigrod	Moshe L	Ryfka Ro	M		JG	
GOTZ	Nachum J.		1894	Zmigrod	Zmigrod	Moshe L	Ryfka Ro	M		JG	
GOTZ	Sara	WEINFELD	1886	Zmigrod	Zmigrod			F	Nachum J.		
GOTZ	Chaskel		1922	Zmigrod	Zmigrod	Nachum J.	Sara	M		JG	
GOTZ	Feige		1924	Zmigrod	Zmigrod	Nachum J.	Sara	F		JG	
GOTZ	Saul D		1929	Zmigrod	Zmigrod	Nachum J.	Sara	M		JG	

Yizkor Book of Nowy Zmigrod

Family name	First name(s)	Maiden name	Birth date	Birth place	Residence	Father	Mother	Gender	Spouse	Source	Remarks
GOTZ	Naphtali		1908	Zmigrod	Zmigrod			M		JG	
GOTZ	Sara	LEIZER	1906	Zmigrod	Zmigrod			F	Naphtali		
GOTZ	Hersh		1934	Zmigrod	Zmigrod	Naphtali	Sara	M		JG	
GOTZ	Roiza Ry		1936	Zmigrod	Zmigrod	Naphtali	Sara	F		JG	
GOTZ	Oizer			Zmigrod	Zmigrod			M		P	Holocaust
GOTZ	Sheindel	STECHER		Zmigrod	Zmigrod			F	Oizer	P	Holocaust
GOTZ	Naphtali J		1905	Zmigrod	Zmigrod	Oizer	Sheindel	M		P	Holocaust
GOTZ	Shmuel			Zmigrod	Zmigrod	Oizer	Sheindel	M		P	Holocaust
GOTZ	Shimon			Zmigrod	Zmigrod	Oizer	Sheindel	M		P	Holocaust
GOTZ	Mina			Zmigrod	Zmigrod			F		JG	
GOTZ	Nahum			Zmigrod	Zmigrod			M		P	Holocaust
GOTZ	Yehudit			Zmigrod	Zmigrod			F	Nahum	P	Holocaust
GOTZ	Ozer				Zmigrod			M		BD	
GOTZ	Scheindla	STECHER			Zmigrod			F	Ozer	JG	
GOTZ	Mojzes L				Zmigrod			M		JG	
GOTZ	Ryfka	WEISS			Zmigrod			F	Mojzes L	JG	
GOTZLER	Hersch			Zmigrod	Zmigrod			M		YA	Auschwitz
GOTZLER	Isaac		19/7/1 883	Zmigrod	Zmigrod	Hersch		M		JR	
GOTZLER	Elias			Zmigrod	Zmigrod			M		JR	
GOTZLER	Chiel		1879	Zmigrod	Zmigrod	Elias		M		JR	
GOTZLER	Israel			Zmigrod	Zmigrod			M		JR	
GOTZLER	Sussel			Zmigrod	Zmigrod			M	Israel	JR	

Yizkor Book of Nowy Zmigrod

Family name	First name(s)	Maiden name	Birth date	Birth place	Residence	Father	Mother	Gender	Spouse	Source	Remarks
GOTZLER	Gittel		1887	Zmigrod	Zmigrod	Israel	Sussel	F		JR	
GOTZLER	Moses			Zmigrod	Zmigrod			M		JR	
GOTZLER	Gittel		1869	Zmigrod	Zmigrod			F		JR	
GRABER	Franai		1889	Zmigrod	Zmigrod	Shmerl		F		P	survived
GRABER	Yehezkel			Zmigrod	Zmigrod			M		P	
GRABER	Dawid			Zmigrod	Zmigrod			M		P	
GRAJER	Abraham		1868	Zmigrod				M		P	USA
GRAJER	Szerka		1866	Zmigrod				F		JG	
GRAGER	Chaja			Zmigrod	Zmigrod			F		JG	
GRAGER	Asher			Zmigrod	Zmigrod			M		JG	
GRAGER	Taube	WEIN		Zmigrod	Zmigrod			F	Asher	JG	
GRAGER	Leib		1879	Zmigrod	Zmigrod	Asher	Taube	M		JG	
GRAGER	Hersh		1877	Zmigrod	Zmigrod	Asher	Taube	M		JG	
GRAGER	Rachel		1877	Zmigrod	Zmigrod	Asher	Taube	F		JG	
GRAGER	Beril			Zmigrod	Zmigrod			M		JG	
GRAGER	Sara	HENDLER		Zmigrod	Zmigrod			F	Beril	JG	
GRAGER	Menashe		1875	Zmigrod	Zmigrod	Beril	Sara	M		JG	
GRAGER	Liba		1879	Zmigrod	Zmigrod	Beril	Sara	F		JG	
GRAGER	Berish			Zmigrod	Zmigrod			M		JG	
GRAGER	Menashe			Zmigrod	Zmigrod			M	Berish	JG	
GRAGER	Schiffra		1872	Zmigrod	Zmigrod	Berish		F		JG	
GRAGER	Menashe		1875	Zmigrod	Zmigrod	Berish		M		JG	
GRAGER	Rochama		1906	Zmigrod	Zmigrod			F		JG	

Yizkor Book of Nowy Zmigrod

Family name	First name(s)	Maiden name	Birth date	Birth place	Residence	Father	Mother	Gender	Spouse	Source	Remarks
GRAGER	Moses		1879	Zmigrod	Zmigrod			M		JG	
GRAGER	Neche	GOLDWENDER		Zmigrod	Zmigrod			F	Moses	JG	
GREIDIGER	Froim		1923	Zmigrod	Zmigrod			M		YA	
GREISMAN	Pinkas			Zmigrod	Zmigrod			M		JR	
GREISMAN	Mindel			Zmigrod	Zmigrod			F	Pinkas	JR	
GREISMAN	Isaac		27/7/1869	Zmigrod	Zmigrod	Pinkas	Mindel	M		JR	
GRIN	Motel		1870	Zmigrod	Zmigrod	Dawid		M		JG	Holocaust
GRIN	Abraham H		3/9/1886	Zmigrod	Zmigrod			M		JG	
GRINSPAN	Simon			Zmigrod	Zmigrod			M		JG	
GRINSPAN	Rywka	PENZER		Zmigrod	Zmigrod			F	Simon	JG	
GRINSPAN	Avraham		1877	Zmigrod	Zmigrod	Simon	Rywka	M		JG	
GRINSPAN	Ides	MEISNER		Zmigrod				F	Avraham	JG	
GRINSPAN	Chaim			Zmigrod		Avraham	Ides	M		JG	
GROMET	Sarah	TZINGER	1890	Zmigrod	Jaslo	Zale z	Hantche	F		YV	
GROSFELD	J.			Zmigrod	Zmigrod			M		YA	Holocaust
GROSS	Hersh			Zmigrod	Zmigrod	Hersh		M		P	died
GROSS	Naphtali		1858	Zmigrod	Zmigrod			M		P	
GROSS	Sarah	ALSTER		Zmigrod	Zmigrod		Rivka	F	Naphtali	P	survived
GROSS	Moshe			Zmigrod	Zmigrod	Naphtali	Sarah	M		P	Holocaust
GROSS	Haya		1888	Zmigrod	Zmigrod	Naphtali	Sarah	F		P	survived
GROSS	David			Zmigrod	Zmigrod	Naphtali	Sarah	M		P	survived
GROSS	Roza			Zmigrod	Zmigrod	Naphtali	Sarah	F		P	Holocaust

Family name	First name(s)	Maiden name	Birth date	Birth place	Residence	Father	Mother	Gender	Spouse	Source	Remarks
GROSS	Hersh			Zmigrod	Zmigrod	Naphtali	Sarah	M		P	survived
GROSS	Maltshe			Zmigrod	Paris	Hersh		F		P	
GROSS	Malka			Zmigrod	Zmigrod	Hersh		F		P	
GROSS	Ester		1914	Zmigrod	Zmigrod	Dawid		F		YA	Auschwitz
GROSS	Moses		1884	Zmigrod	Zmigrod	Naphtali		M		YA	Holocaust
GROSS	Naftali			Zmigrod	Zmigrod	Srul		M		JG	Holocaust
GROSS	Chaya		1884	Zmigrod	Zmigrod			F		JG	
GROSS	Chaja		1883	Zmigrod	Zmigrod			F		JG	
GROSS	Dawid			Zmigrod	Zmigrod			M		JG	
GROSS	Izrael			Zmigrod	Zmigrod			M		JG	
GROSS	Leja Ft		1882	Zmigrod	Zmigrod			F		JG	
GROSS	Mechel			Zmigrod	Zmigrod			M		JG	
GROSS	Meir			Zmigrod	Zmigrod			M		JG	survived
GROSS	Mali			Zmigrod	Zmigrod			F		JG	survived
GROSS	Salomon		1887	Zmigrod	Zmigrod			M		P	Holocaust
GROSS	Esther			Zmigrod	Zmigrod			F	Salomon	P	Holocaust
GROSS	Wigdor			Zmigrod	Zmigrod			M		JG	
GROSS	Shlomo			Zmigrod	Zmigrod	Awigdor		M		P	Holocaust
GROSS	Seril	LEIBNER		Zmigrod	Zmigrod			F	Shlomo	Holocaust	
GROSS	Wolf			Zmigrod	Korczyna			M		YA	Holocaust
GROSS	Israel			Zmigrod	Zmigrod			M		T	
GROSS	Reisel			Zmigrod	Zmigrod			F	Israel	YV	
GROSS	Joseph		1895	Zmigrod	Zmigrod	Israel	Reisel	M		YA	Holocaust

Yizkor Book of Nowy Zmigrod

Family name	First name(s)	Maiden name	Birth date	Birth place	Residence	Father	Mother	Gender	Spouse	Source	Remarks
GROSS	Irena			Zmigrod	Zmigrod			F	Joseph	YA	
GROSS	Leiser		1897	Zmigrod	Zmigrod	Israel	Reisel	M		YA	Holocaust
GROSS	Naftali		1893	Zmigrod	Zmigrod	Israel	Reisel	M		BD	Holocaust
GROSS	Laiser		1879	Zmigrod	Zmigrod			M		JR	
GROSS	Mojszes A			Zmigrod	Zmigrod	Laiser		M		JR	
GROSS	Noe			Zmigrod	Zmigrod			M		JR	
GROSS	Samiel		1881	Zmigrod	Zmigrod	Noe		M		JR	
GROSS	Berisch			Zmigrod	Zmigrod	Noe		M		JR	
GROSS	Hinde			Zmigrod	Zmigrod	Noe		F	Berisch	JR	
GROSS	Isaac		1869	Zmigrod	Zmigrod	Berisch	Hinde	F		JR	
GROSS	Ben Tzion			Zmigrod	Zmigrod			M		JR	
GROSS	Rose		1876	Zmigrod	Zmigrod	Ben Tzion	Rose	F	Ben Tzion	JR	
GROSS	Tzwi Itche			Zmigrod	Zmigrod			M		JR	
GROSS	Baruch			Zmigrod	Zmigrod			M		JR	
GROSS	Hinde			Zmigrod	Zmigrod			F	Baruch	JR	
GROSS	Moses N		1872	Zmigrod	Zmigrod	Baruch	Hinde	M		JR	
GROSS	Mechel				Zmigrod			M		BD	
GROSS	S				Zmigrod			M		JG	USA
GROSS	Benjamin		1874		Zmigrod			M		JG	USA
GROSS	Schaji		1888		Zmigrod			M		JG	USA
GROSS	Hendel		1888		Zmigrod			M		JG	USA
GROSS	Tobe		1894		Zmigrod			F		BD	
GROSS	Fraida				Zmigrod			F		P	survived

Family name	First name(s)	Maiden name	Birth date	Birth place	Residence	Father	Mother	Gender	Spouse	Source	Remarks
GROSS	Hozek,				Zmigrod			M		JG	
GROSSER	Hersh				Zmigrod			F		BD	
GROSSFELD	J				Zmigrod			M		JSS	Plaszow
GROSSHAUS	Shalom				Zmigrod			M		P	Holocaust
GROSSHAUS	Sheinde;				Zmigrod			F		P	Holocaust
GROSSMAN	Isaac M			Zmigrod	Zmigrod			M		JR	
GROSSMAN	Yete			Zmigrod	Zmigrod			F	I Meyer	JR	
GROSSMAN	Chiel		1876	Zmigrod	Zmigrod	Isaac M	Yete	M		JR	
GRUBER	Leib				Zmigrod			M		JSS	Plaszow
GRUBER	Nuchem				Zmigrod			M		JSS	Plaszow
GRUN	Matel		1871	Zmigrod	Zmigrod	Dawid		F		JSS	Plaszow
GRUNBAUM	Leon				Zmigrod			M		JSS	
GRUNBAUM	Lea				Zmigrod			F		JSS	
GRUNIS	Natan				Zmigrod			M		JSS	
GRUNIS	Mali				Zmigrod			F	Natan	JSS	Plaszow
GRUNIS	Henryk				Zmigrod	Natan	Mali	M		JSS	Plaszow
GUTWEIN	Isak				Zmigrod			M		P	
GUTWEIN	Samuel			Zmigrod	Korczyna			M		P	
GUTWEIN	Esther			Zmigrod	Korczyna			F		JG	USA
GUTWEIN	Shlomo L				Zmigrod			M		P	
GUZIK	Adolph		1892		Zmigrod			M		JG	USA
GUZIK	Fani		1868		Zmigrod			F		JG	USA
GUZIK	Mariem		1903		Zmigrod			F		JG	USA

Yizkor Book of Nowy Zmigrod

Family name	First name(s)	Maiden name	Birth date	Birth place	Residence	Father	Mother	Gender	Spouse	Source	Remarks
GUZIK	Gusta		1897		Zmigrod			F	David	JG	
HABER	Sara			Zmigrod	Zmigrod			F		JG	
HABER	Chajem Juda			Zmigrod	Zmigrod			M		JG	
HABER	Reizla	ZOLL	1877	Zmigrod	Zmigrod			F	Chajem J	JG	
HABER	Sheindel H			Zmigrod	Zmigrod	Chajem J	Reizla	F		JG	
HABER	Noe			Zmigrod	Zmigrod			F	Noe	JG	
HABER	Mashe	FASCHER		Zmigrod	Zmigrod			F		JG	
HABER	Feiga		1903	Zmigrod	Zmigrod	Noe	Noe	F		JG	
HABER	Ozias			Zmigrod	Zmigrod			M		JG	
HABER	Helene	GETZLER		Zmigrod	Zmigrod			F	Ozias	JG	
HABER	Zygmunt		1933	Zmigrod	Zmigrod	Ozias	Helene	M		JG	
HABER	Simcha		1903	Zmigrod	Zmigrod			M		JG	
HABER	Ita Lea	LERMAN		Zmigrod	Zmigrod			F	Simcha	JG	
HABER	Ryfka		1936	Zmigrod	Zmigrod	Simcha	Ita Lea	F		JG	
HABER	Roza		1899	Zmigrod	Zmigrod			F		JG	
HABER	Hela			Zmigrod	Zmigrod			F		JG	
HABER	Thelma			Zmigrod	Zmigrod			F		JG	
HABER	Dawid			Zmigrod	Zmigrod			M		JG	
HABER	Chaim J			Zmigrod	Zmigrod			M		JG	
HABER	Henia	GETZLER		Zmigrod	Zmigrod			F	Chaim J	JG	
HABER	Semuel			Zmigrod	Zmigrod			M		JR	
HABER	Ester			Zmigrod	Zmigrod			F	Semuel	JR	

Family name	First name(s)	Maiden name	Birth date	Birth place	Residence	Father	Mother	Gender	Spouse	Source	Remarks
HABER	Ides		1867	Zmigrod	Zmigrod	Semuel	Ester	F		JR	
HAK	Szymon		1898	Zmigrod	Zmigrod			M		P	
HALBERSHTAM	Sinai		1869	Sandz	Zmigrod	Baruch	Pessel	M		P	
HALBERSHTAM	Ruchama							F	Sinai	P	
HALBERSHTAM	Aaron			Sandz	Osiek	Sinai	Ruchama	M		P	Holocaust
HALBERSHTAM	Yaakow			Sandz	Zmigrod	Sinai	Ruchama	M		P	
HALBERSHTAM	Dawid			Sandz	Zmigrod	Sinai	Ruchama	M		P	
HALBERSHTAM	Baruch			Sandz	Zmigrod	Sinai	Ruchama	M		P	
HALBERSHTAM	Chaim J			Sandz	Zmigrod	Sinai	Ruchama	M		P	
HALBERSHTAM	Abraham			Sandz	Zmigrod	Sinai	Ruchama	M		P	
HALBERSHTAM	Yehezkel			Zmigrod	Zmigrod	Sinai	Ruchama	M		P	
HALBERSHTAM	Pesel			Zmigrod	Zmigrod	Sinai	Ruchama	F		P	
HALBERSHTAM	Israel			Zmigrod	Zmigrod	Sinai	Ruchama	M		P	
HALBERSHTAM	Arieh			Zmigrod	Zmigrod	Sinai	Ruchama	M		P	
HALBERSHTAM	Leibel			Zmigrod	Zmigrod	Sinai,	Ruchama	M		JG	USA
HAMMER	Fannie			Zmigrod				F		JG	
HANDLER	Juda			Zmigrod	Zmigrod			M		JG	
HANDLER	Sheindel	TRACHMAN		Zmigrod	Zmigrod			F	Juda	JG	
HANDLER	Ephroim		1881	Zmigrod	Zmigrod	Juda	Sheindel	M		JG	
HANDLER	Wolf		1888	Zmigrod	Zmigrod	Juda	Sheindel	M		JG	
HASELBECK	Lowe		1882	Zmigrod	Zmigrod			M		JG	
HASENFELD	Israel		1884	Zmigrod	Zmigrod			M		JG	
HASENTZER	Moshe				Zmigrod			M		P	*

Yizkor Book of Nowy Zmigrod

Family name	First name(s)	Maiden name	Birth date	Birth place	Residence	Father	Mother	Gender	Spouse	Source	Remarks
HECHTER	Marjem		1880	Zmigrod	Zmigrod			F		JG	
HENDLER	Simon			Zmigrod	Zmigrod			M		JG	
HENDLER	Ite			Zmigrod	Zmigrod			F	Simon	JG	
HENDLER	Sara			Zmigrod	Zmigrod			F		JG	
HERBACH	Soura			Zmigrod	Zmigrod			F		JG	
HERBST			1878	Zmigrod	Zmigrod			M		JG	
HERBST			1887	Zmigrod	Zmigrod			M		JSS	Plaszow
HERBSTMAN	Awraham				Zmigrod			M		P	
HEREN	Izydor				Zmigrod			M		JG	USA
HERSZ	Dawid			Zmigrod	Zmigrod			M		JR	
HERSZ	Yachne			Zmigrod	Zmigrod			F	Dawid	JR	
HERSZ	Baroch		1871	Zmigrod	Zmigrod	Dawid	Yachne	M		JR	
HERSZ	Simche			Zmigrod	Zmigrod			M		JR	
HERSZ	Wolf		1887	Zmigrod	Zmigrod	Simche		M		JR	
HERSCHFELD	Helene		1889	Zmigrod	Zmigrod			F		JSS	Plaszow
HERSHBERG	Natan				Zmigrod			M		P	
HERSHLIKOWITZ	Izak				Zmigrod			M		JG	
HERSHLIKOWITZ	Shulem			Zmigrod	Zmigrod			M		JR	
HERSHLIKOWITZ	Marjem			Zmigrod	Zmigrod			F	Shulem	JR	
HERSHLIKOWITZ	Ette		1873	Zmigrod	Zmigrod	Shulem	Marjem	F		JR	
HERSHTEL	Benyamin			Zmigrod	Zmigrod			M		P	Holocaust
HERSHTEL	Lea			Zmigrod	Zmigrod			F	Benyamin	P	Holocaust
HERZ	Markus		1887	Zmigrod	Zmigrod			M		BD	

Yizkor Book of Nowy Zmigrod

Family name	First name(s)	Maiden name	Birth date	Birth place	Residence	Father	Mother	Gender	Spouse	Source	Remarks
HERZ	D				Zmigrod			M		JG	
HERZ	Regina				Zmigrod			F		P	
HERZ	Chaim			Zmigrod	Zmigrod			M		JR	
HERZ	Yachne			Zmigrod	Zmigrod			F	Chaim	JR	
HERZ	Eisig		1873	Zmigrod	Zmigrod	Chaim	Yachne	M		JR	
HERZ	Dawid			Zmigrod	Zmigrod			M		JR	
HERZ	Ester			Zmigrod	Zmigrod			M	Dawid	JR	
HERZ	Isaac		1869	Zmigrod	Zmigrod	Dawid	Ester	M		JR	
HILLER	Pinhas			Zmigrod	Zmigrod			M		J	
HILLER	Hendel	KRILL		Zmigrod	Zmigrod			F	Pinhas	J	
HILLER	Beile F		1881	Zmigrod	Zmigrod	Pinhas	Hendel	F		J	
HILLER	Beile F		1881	Zmigrod	Zmigrod	Pinhas	Hendel	M		J	
HILLER	Shyje		1883	Zmigrod	Zmigrod	Pinhas	Hendel	F		J	
HILLER	Rachel		1884	Zmigrod	Zmigrod	Pinhas	Hendel	F		J	
HILLER	Seinwel		1886	Zmigrod	Zmigrod	Pinhas	Hendel	M		J	
HILLER	Scheindel			Zmigrod	Zmigrod	Pinhas	Hendel	F		J	
HILLER	Naphtali H.				Zmigrod			M			
HILLER	Esther				Zmigrod			F		JG	
HILLER	Abraham A		1926	Zmigrod	Zmigrod			M		JG	
HILLER	Izrael		1924	Zmigrod	Zmigrod			M		JG	
HILLER	Shmuel			Zmigrod	Zmigrod			M		P	Holocaust
HILLER	Itta			Zmigrod	Zmigrod			F	Shmuel	P	Holocaust
HIRSCH	Markus			Zmigrod	Zmigrod			M		JR	

Yizkor Book of Nowy Zmigrod

Family name	First name(s)	Maiden name	Birth date	Birth place	Residence	Father	Mother	Gender	Spouse	Source	Remarks
HIRSCH	Kalman		1885	Zmigrod	Zmigrod	Markus		M		JR	
HIRSCH	Salomon			Zmigrod	Zmigrod			M		JR	
HIRSCH	Itte			Zmigrod	Zmigrod			F	Salomon	JR	
HIRSCH	Markus W		1869	Zmigrod	Zmigrod	Salomon	Itte	M		JR	
HIRSCH	Alexander		1872	Zmigrod	Zmigrod	Salomon	Itte	M		JR	
HIRSCHBERG	Eisig			Zmigrod	Zmigrod			M		JR	
HIRSCHBERG	Chaim S		1895	Zmigrod	Zmigrod	Eisig		M		JG	
HIRSCHBERG	Leo		1898	Zmigrod	Zmigrod	Eisig		M		JG	
HIRSCHBERG	Nathan			Zmigrod	Zmigrod			M		YA	Plaszow
HIRSCHBERG	Lewy			Zmigrod	Zmigrod			M		P	
HIRSCHBERG	Lucla			Zmigrod		Lewy		F		JSS	Plaszow
HIRSCHBERG	Adolph			Zmigrod	Zmigrod			M		JSS	Plaszow
HIRSCHBERG	Menashe			Zmigrod	Zmigrod			M			
HIRSCHBERG	Sheine			Zmigrod	Zmigrod			F	Menashe		
HIRSCHBERG	Natan		1905	Zmigrod	Zmigrod	Menashe	Sheine	M		JSS	
HIRSCHBERG	Leib			Zmigrod	Zmigrod			M		JSS	Plaszow
HIRSCHBERG	Lea			Zmigrod	Zmigrod			F		JG	USA
HOCHEISER	Abraham			Zmigrod				M		JG	USA
HOCHEISER	Ides			Zmigrod				F		JG	
HOLLANDER	Chaim Itche			Zmigrod	Zmigrod			M		JR	
HOLLANDER	Mindel		1883	Zmigrod	Zmigrod	Chaim Itche		F		JR	
HOLLANDER	Shmiel			Zmigrod	Zmigrod			M		JG	

Family name	First name(s)	Maiden name	Birth date	Birth place	Residence	Father	Mother	Gender	Spouse	Source	Remarks
HOLLANDER	Laje		1885	Zmigrod	Zmigrod			F		JG	
HOLLANDER	Chaim			Zmigrod	Zmigrod			M		P	Holocaust
HOLLANDER	Yehezkel			Zmigrod	Zmigrod			M		P	Holocaust
HOLLANDER	Bila			Zmigrod	Zmigrod			F		P	
HOLLOSHUETZ	Bender		1884	Zmigrod	Zmigrod			M	Chaim	JG	
HONOG	Moses		1873	Zmigrod	Zmigrod			M		JR	
HORLOBER	Israel			Zmigrod	Zmigrod			M		JG	
HORLOBER	Estera			Zmigrod	Zmigrod			F	Israel	JG	
HORLOBER	Pearl			Zmigrod	Zmigrod	Israel	Estera	F		JG	
HOROWITZ	ReiselSar			Zmigrod	Zmigrod	Sinai	Ruchama	F		P	
INGBER	Elisha			Zmigrod	Zmigrod			M		JG	
INGBER	Towa			Zmigrod	Zmigrod			M		P	Holocaust
INGBER	Eller			Zmigrod	Zmigrod			M		JSS	Plaszow
INGBER	Eliyahu				Zmigrod			M		P	
ISRAEL	Hersh L				Zmigrod			M		P	
ISTER	Moses				Zmigrod			M		JG	
JAKUBOWICZ	Aron		1887	Zmigrod	Zmigrod			F	Elisha	P	Holocaust
JAKUBOWICZ	Isaak D		1885	Zmigrod	Zmigrod			M		JG	
JAKUBOWICZ	Malke		1882	Zmigrod	Zmigrod			F		JG	
JAKUBOWICZ	Neche		1879	Zmigrod	Zmigrod			F		JSS	Plaszow
JUST	Josef				Zmigrod			M		JSS	
JUST	Edna				Zmigrod			F		BD	
JUST	Ch				Zmigrod			M		JG	

Yizkor Book of Nowy Zmigrod

Family name	First name(s)	Maiden name	Birth date	Birth place	Residence	Father	Mother	Gender	Spouse	Source	Remarks
JUST			1877	Zmigrod	Zmigrod			M		JG	
JUST	Baruch		1883	Zmigrod	Zmigrod			M		JG	
JUST	Berl		1879	Zmigrod	Zmigrod			M		JG	
JUST	Chaje		1879	Zmigrod	Zmigrod			F		JG	
JUST	Jozef D		1885	Zmigrod	Zmigrod			M		JG	
JUST	Shmuel				Zmigrod			M		P	
JUST	Elisheva	NUSSBAUM			Zmigrod			F	Shmuel	P	
JUST	Jides		1881	Zmigrod	Zmigrod			F		JG	
JUST	Risze		1887	Zmigrod	Zmigrod			M		P	
JUST	Naphtali			Zmigrod	Zmigrod			M		JG	
JUST	Moses			Zmigrod	Zmigrod			M		JR	
JUST	Hersch L			Zmigrod	Zmigrod			M		JR	
JUST	Gittel		1881	Zmigrod	Zmigrod	Hersch L		F		JR	
JUST	Berisch			Zmigrod	Zmigrod			M		JR	
JUST	Malka			Zmigrod	Zmigrod			M	Berisch	JR	
JUST	Laser		1869	Zmigrod	Zmigrod	Berisch	Malka	F		JR	
KAHN	Samiel			Zmigrod	Zmigrod			M		JR	
KAHN	Markus		1879	Zmigrod	Zmigrod	Samiel		M		JR	
KAHN	Mechel			Zmigrod	Zmigrod			M		P	
KAHN	Sarah			Zmigrod	Zmigrod			F		P	
KALB	Yossi,			Osiek	Zmigrod			M		JG	
KALB	David			Zmigrod	Zmigrod			M		P	Holocaust
KALB	Bina			Zmigrod	Zmigrod			F	David	P	Holocaust

Family name	First name(s)	Maiden name	Birth date	Birth place	Residence	Father	Mother	Gender	Spouse	Source	Remarks
KALB	Harry B.			Zmigrod	Zmigrod			M		P	USA
KALB	Zalman		1871	Zmigrod	Jaslo	Yossef		M		JSS	Plaszow
KALB	Jozef			Zmigrod	Zmigrod			M		JG	USA
KALB	Josef			Zmigrod	Zmigrod			M		JSS	Plaszow
KALB	Brandel		1890		Zmigrod			F		JG	USA
KALB	Dawid		1867		Zmigrod			M		JSS	Plaszow
KALB	Itzhak				Zmigrod			M		P	
KALBER	Hava			Zmigrod	Zmigrod			F		P	
KALINSKI	Mozes				Zmigrod			M		JSS	Plaszow
KAMIL	Fischel			Zmigrod	Zmigrod			M		JR	
KAMIL	Mawes			Zmigrod	Zmigrod			M	Fischel	JR	
KAMIL	Hana		1873	Zmigrod	Zmigrod	Fischel	Mawes	M		JR	
KAMPF	Chaskel				Zmigrod			M		JSS	
KAMPF	Jta				Zmigrod			M		YA	
KANAREK	Aaron		1905	Zmigrod		Awigdor		F		JG	Holocaust
KANNER	Yossef		1924	Zmigrod	Zmigrod			M		YA	Holocaust
KANNER	Lida			Zmigrod	Zmigrod	Motel		M		JSS	Plaszow
KANNER	Naftatali			Zmigrod	Zmigrod			M		JSS	
KANNER	Golda			Zmigrod	Zmigrod			M		JG	
KANNER	Naphtali Y			Zmigrod	Zmigrod			M		P	
KANNER	Shlomo			Zmigrod	Zmigrod			F		P	
KANNER	Golda			Zmigrod	Zmigrod			F		P	
KANNER	Mania			Zmigrod	Zmigrod			F		JG	

Yizkor Book of Nowy Zmigrod

Family name	First name(s)	Maiden name	Birth date	Birth place	Residence	Father	Mother	Gender	Spouse	Source	Remarks
KANNER	Naftali			Zmigrod	Zmigrod			M		JG	USA
KANNER	Sheindel		1903	Zmigrod	USA			F	Israel	P	USA
KANNER	Irving			Zmigrod				M		YV	
KASTENBAUM	Aron			Zmigrod	Zmigrod			M		JG	
KATZ	Ite			Zmigrod	Zmigrod			F	Aron	JG	
KATZ	Chaja S		1924	Zmigrod	Zmigrod	Aron	Ite	F		JG	
KATZ	Deborah			Zmigrod	Zmigrod			F		JG	
KATZ	Hersch			Zmigrod	Zmigrod			M		JG	
KATZ	Chana	STACHEL		Zmigrod	Zmigrod			F	Hersch	JG	
KATZ	Isaak		1895	Zmigrod	Zmigrod	Hersch	Chana	M		JG	
KATZ	Malka	BOBKER		Zmigrod	Zmigrod			F	Isaak	JG	
KATZ	Mania born	BOBKER		Zmigrod	Zmigrod			F		JSS	Plaszow
KATZ	Abraham			Zmigrod	Zmigrod			M		JG	
KATZ	Esther	MIN		Zmigrod	Zmigrod			F		P	Holocaust
KAUFMAN	Israel			Zmigrod	Zmigrod			M		JR	
KAUFMAN	Marjem		5/7/18 84	Zmigrod	Zmigrod	Israel		F		JR	
KAUFMAN	Haim			Zmigrod	Zmigrod			M		JG	
KAUFMAN	Ryfke		1888	Zmigrod	Zmigrod			F		BD	
KAUFMANN	Szymon				Zmigrod			M		JG	USA
KAUFMANN	Yehiel		1894		Zmigrod			M		JG	USA
KAUFMANN	Simon		1891		Zmigrod			M		JG	USA
KAUFMANN	Jacob			Zmigrod				M		P	USA

Yizkor Book of Nowy Zmigrod

Family name	First name(s)	Maiden name	Birth date	Birth place	Residence	Father	Mother	Gender	Spouse	Source	Remarks
KAUFMANN	Wolf				Zmigrod			M		P	
KAUFMANN	Ascher		1910	Zmigrod	Zmigrod	Tzwi		M		YA	Holocaust
KEIL	Meier			Zmigrod	Zmigrod			M		JR	
KELLER	Hersch			Zmigrod	Zmigrod			M		JR	
KELLER	Lata		1869	Zmigrod	Zmigrod	Hersch		F	Hersch	JR	
KELLER	Mendel			Zmigrod	Zmigrod	Hersch	Lata	M		JR	
KELLER	Simche D			Zmigrod	Zmigrod			M		JR	
KELLER	Dobre			Zmigrod	Zmigrod			F	Simche D	JR	
KELLER	Hersch		1869	Zmigrod	Zmigrod	Simche D	Dobre	M		JR	
KELLER	Simche B			Zmigrod	Zmigrod			M		JR	
KELLER	Frida		1881	Zmigrod	Zmigrod	Simche B		F		JR	
KELLER	Hirsch		1887	Zmigrod	Zmigrod	Asher		M		YA	Holocaust
KELLER	Mchael		1912	Zmigrod	Zmigrod	Asher		M		YA	Holocaust
KELLER	Markos		1901	Zmigrod	Gorlice	Asher		M		JSS	Plaszow
KELLER	Jozef				Zmigrod			M		JSS	Plaszow
KELLER	Mechel				Zmigrod			M		JSS	
KELLER	Hena				Zmigrod			F		BD	
KELLER	Jacob				Zmigrod			M		JG	Holocaust
KELLER	Rivka			Zmigrod	Zmigrod			F	Zvi Yaacov	died 1991	
KELLER	Yechezkel S			Zmigrod	Zmigrod	Zvi Yaacov	Rivka	M		JG	
KELLER	Asher			Zmigrod	Zmigrod	Zvi Yaacov	Rivka	M		JG	Holocaust
KELLER	Miriam			Zmigrod	Zmigrod			F	Asher	YA	

Yizkor Book of Nowy Zmigrod

Family name	First name(s)	Maiden name	Birth date	Birth place	Residence	Father	Mother	Gender	Spouse	Source	Remarks
KELLER	Zvi Y			Zmigrod	Zmigrod	Asher	Miriam	M		JG	
KELLER	Michal			Zmigrod	Zmigrod	Zvi Y	Rivka	M		JG	Holocaust
KELLER	Mordechai			Zmigrod	Zmigrod	Zvi Y	Rivka	M		JG	Holocaust
KELLER	Rachel L			Zmigrod	Zmigrod	Zvi Y	Rivka	F		JG	Holocaust
KELLER	Hersch			Zmigrod	Zmigrod			M		JR	
KELLER	Beile			Zmigrod	Zmigrod			F	Hersch	JR	
KELLER	Keile		1867	Zmigrod	Zmigrod	Hersch	Beile	F		JG	
KELLER	Emanuel			Zmigrod	Zmigrod			M		JSS	Plaszow
KELLER	Salomon			Zmigrod	Zmigrod			M		JG	
KESERLAUF	Beile			Zmigrod	Zmigrod			F		YA	Holocaust
KESSLER	Chaim		1877	Zmigrod	Zmigrod	Shmuel		M		BD	Holocaust
KESSLER	Chaim I			Zmigrod	Zmigrod			M		JG	USA
KESSLER	Gitel		1890	Zmigrod	Zmigrod			F		JG	USA
KESSLER	Mendel		1884	Zmigrod	Zmigrod			M		JG	
KESSLER	Feige		1872	Zmigrod	Zmigrod			F		JR	
KIGEL	Wigdor		1889	Zmigrod	Zmigrod			M		JG	
KILIK	Sarah			Zmigrod	Zmigrod			F		JG	
KILIK	Moyszes			Zmigrod	Zmigrod			M		JR	
KILIK	Dawid F			Zmigrod	Zmigrod	Moyszes		M		JR	
KINDERMAN	Majer		1879	Zmigrod	Zmigrod			M		JG	
KINST	Isaac			Zmigrod	Zmigrod			M		JR	
KINST	Mayer		1879	Zmigrod	Zmigrod	Isaac		M		JR	
KINZLER	Leibish			Zmigrod	Jaslo			M		P	

Family name	First name(s)	Maiden name	Birth date	Birth place	Residence	Father	Mother	Gender	Spouse	Source	Remarks
KINZLER	Moshe			Zmigrod	Jaslo			M		P	
KINZLER	Itzhak			Zmigrod	Zmigrod			M		P	Holocaust
KINZLER	Moshe				Zmigrod			M		P	
KINZLER	Kalman			Zmigrod	Zmigrod			M		JR	
KINZLER	Mirl		1876	Zmigrod	Zmigrod	Kalman	Mirl	F	Kalman	JR	
KINZLER	Hersch			Zmigrod	Zmigrod	Kalman	Mirl	M		JR	
KINZLER	Bear			Zmigrod	Zmigrod			M		JR	
KINZLER	Sussel			Zmigrod	Zmigrod			F	Bear	JR	
KINZLER	Chaim D		1876	Zmigrod	Zmigrod	Bear	Sussel	M		JR	
KINZLER	Isaac			Zmigrod	Zmigrod			M		JR	
KINZLER	Sussel			Zmigrod	Zmigrod			F	Isaac	JR	
KINZLER	Salomon		1873	Zmigrod	Zmigrod	Isaac	Sussel	M		JR	
KIRKMAN	Samuel			Zmigrod	Zmigrod			M		JR	
KIRKMAN	Freide F		1883	Zmigrod	Zmigrod	Samuel		F		JR	
KLAGSBAD	Hersh L			Zmigrod	Zmigrod			M		P	Holocaust
KLEIN	Liebe	BUKSBAUM	1897	Zmigrod	Zmigrod			F	Hersh L	P	Holocaust
KLEIN	Moshe		1917	Zmigrod	Zmigrod	Hersh L	Liebe	M		P	survived
KLEIN	Chana		1919	Zmigrod	Zmigrod	Hersh L	Liebe	F		P	survived
KLEIN	Golde		1924	Zmigrod	Zmigrod	Hersh L	Liebe	F		P	Holocaust
KLEIN	Neche		1927	Zmigrod	Zmigrod	Hersh L	Liebe	F		P	survived
KLEIN	Rywka		1930	Zmigrod	Zmigrod	Hersh L	Liebe	F		JG	
KLEIN	Itzhak			Zmigrod	Zmigrod			M		BD	
KLEIN	Chune				Zmigrod			M		JG	USA

Yizkor Book of Nowy Zmigrod

Family name	First name(s)	Maiden name	Birth date	Birth place	Residence	Father	Mother	Gender	Spouse	Source	Remarks
KLEIN	Feige Gi		1884	Zmigrod	Zmigrod	Chune		F		JR	
KLEIN	Dawid			Zmigrod	Zmigrod			M		JR	
KLEIN	Leja		1872	Zmigrod	Zmigrod	Dawid		F	Dawid	JR	
KLEIN	Ozer		1872	Zmigrod	Zmigrod	Dawid	Leja	M		JR	
KLEIN	Chaim F		1887	Zmigrod	Zmigrod			M		JR	
KLEIN	Moses E		1887	Zmigrod	Zmigrod	Chaim F		M		JR	
KLEIN	Issel		1887	Zmigrod	Zmigrod			M		YA	
KLEIN	Pauline	LEIBNER		Zmigrod	Zmigrod			F		P	
KLEIN	Sabina		1900	Lopon	Zmigrod	Awigdor		F		JG	Holocaust
KLEINBERGER	Adela				Zmigrod			F		P	Holocaust
KLEINMANN	Moses G				Zmigrod			M		JG	
KLEINMANN	Dwora	MARKOWICZ			Zmigrod			F	Moses G	JG	
KLEINMANN	Jozef Berl		1880	Zmigrod	Zmigrod	Moses G.	Dwora	M		JG	
KLEINMANN	Reisel		1882	Zmigrod	Zmigrod	Moses G.		F		JG	
KLEINMANN	Chaim		1883	Zmigrod	Zmigrod			M		JG	USA
KLEINMANN	Deborah		1891		Zmigrod			F		JG	USA
KNOBEL	Adolph		1913		Zmigrod			M		JG	
KNOBEL	Gittel				Zmigrod			F		P	
KOCH	Awraham				Zmigrod			M		P	
KOCHANOWER	Gittel		1881	Zmigrod	Zmigrod			F		YA	
KOHN	Frimet		1905	Zmigrod	Zmigrod	Asher		F		YA	Holocaust
KOHN	Laya		1895	Zmigrod	Zmigrod	Avraham		F		JSS	Plaszow
KOHN	Avraham			Zmigrod	Zmigrod	Shimon		M		YA	Holocaust

Yizkor Book of Nowy Zmigrod

Family name	First name(s)	Maiden name	Birth date	Birth place	Residence	Father	Mother	Gender	Spouse	Source	Remarks
KOHN	Shimon				Zmigrod	Yossef		M		JSS	Holocaust
KOHN	Symche			Zmigrod	Zmigrod			M		P	
KOHN	Frieda				Zmigrod			F			Plaszow
KOHN	Chaim			Zmigrod	Zmigrod	Symche	Frieda	M		JG	JSS
KOHN	Zwi			Zmigrod	Zmigrod	Symche	Frieda	M		P	
KOHN	Tuvia			Zmigrod	Zmigrod	Symche	Frieda	M		P	
KOHN	Zipporah			Zmigrod	Zmigrod	Symche	Frieda	F		BD	
KOHN	J			Zmigrod	Zmigrod			M		BD	
KOHN	M				Zmigrod			M		JG	USA
KOHN	Jossel		1893		Zmigrod			M		JG	USA
KOHN	Moses		1890		Zmigrod			M		JSS	Plaszow
KOHN	Leiser			Zmigrod	Zmigrod			M		JG	
KOHN	Shimon							M		P	
KOHN	Myriam	KREISER		Zmigrod	Zmigrod	Shimon		F	Shimon	P	
KOHN	Reisel				Zmigrod	Shimon	Myriam	F		P	
KOHN	Leib		1879	Zmigrod	Zmigrod			M		JR	
KOHN	Taube		1879	Zmigrod	Zmigrod	Leib		F		JR	
KOHN	Freidil		1881	Zmigrod	Zmigrod	Leib		F		JR	
KOHN	Jacob			Zmigrod	Zmigrod			M		JR	
KOHN	Neche		1879	Zmigrod	Zmigrod	Jacob		F		JR	
KOHN	Aron			Zmigrod	Zmigrod			M		JR	
KOHN	Hannah S		1879	Zmigrod	Zmigrod	Aron		F		JR	
KOHN	Shaje		1879	Zmigrod	Zmigrod			M		JR	

Yizkor Book of Nowy Zmigrod

Family name	First name(s)	Maiden name	Birth date	Birth place	Residence	Father	Mother	Gender	Spouse	Source	Remarks
KOHN	Abraham K		1879	Zmigrod	Zmigrod	Shaje		M		JR	
KOHN	Chaje		1882	Zmigrod	Zmigrod	Shaje		F		JR	
KOHN	Gittel		1887	Zmigrod	Zmigrod	Shaje		F		JR	
KOHN	Naftali		1885	Zmigrod	Zmigrod	Naftali		M		JR	
KOHN	Ryfka		1885	Zmigrod	Zmigrod	Naftali		F		JR	
KOHN	Moses J			Zmigrod	Zmigrod			M		JR	
KOHN	Abraham I		1881	Zmigrod	Zmigrod	Moses J		M		JR	
KOHN	Esther		1888	Zmigrod	Zmigrod	Moses J		F		JR	
KOHN	Hersch L			Zmigrod	Zmigrod			M		JR	
KOHN	Ides			Zmigrod	Zmigrod	Hersch L		F	Hersch L	JR	
KOHN	Samiel		1869	Zmigrod	Zmigrod	Hersch L	Ides	M		JR	
KOHN	Laje		1884	Zmigrod	Zmigrod	Hersch L	Ides	F		JR	
KOHN	Mayer J			Zmigrod	Zmigrod			M		JR	
KOHN	Lippe			Zmigrod	Zmigrod	Mayer J		M		JR	
KOHN	Chaim A			Zmigrod	Zmigrod			M		JR	
KOHN	Simche		1882	Zmigrod	Zmigrod	Chaim A		M		JR	
KOHN	Markus Is			Zmigrod	Zmigrod			M		JR	
KOHN	Yente			Zmigrod	Zmigrod	Markus I		F		JR	
KOHN	Sara		1876	Zmigrod	Zmigrod	Markus I	Yente	F	Markus I	JR	
KOHN	Leib H			Zmigrod	Zmigrod			M		JR	
KOHN	Ruchel			Zmigrod	Zmigrod			F	Leib Hersh		
KOHN	Hene		1876	Zmigrod	Zmigrod	Leib H	Ruchel	F		JR	
KOHN	Dawid			Zmigrod	Zmigrod			M		JR	

Family name	First name(s)	Maiden name	Birth date	Birth place	Residence	Father	Mother	Gender	Spouse	Source	Remarks
KOHN	Blima			Zmigrod	Zmigrod			F	Dawid	JR	
KOHN	Isaac L		1873	Zmigrod	Zmigrod	Dawid	Blima	M		JR	
KOHN	Riwe			Zmigrod	Zmigrod			M		JR	
KOHN	Sara		1873	Zmigrod	Zmigrod			F	Riwe	JR	
KOHN	Chaskel			Zmigrod	Zmigrod	Riwe	Sara	M		JR	
KOHN	Shulem			Zmigrod	Zmigrod			M		JR	
KOHN	Ruchel			Zmigrod	Zmigrod			F		JR	
KOHN	Shmuel J		1872	Zmigrod	Zmigrod	Shulem	Ruchel	M	Shulem	JR	
KOHN	Abraham H			Zmigrod	Zmigrod			M		JR	
KOHN	Sure F			Zmigrod	Zmigrod			F	Abraham H		
KOHN	Josef		1872	Zmigrod	Zmigrod	Abraham H	Sure Frei	M		JR	
KOHN	Hersch L			Zmigrod	Zmigrod			M		JR	
KOHN	Eidel			Zmigrod	Zmigrod			F	Hersch L	JR	
KOHN	Eisig		1871	Zmigrod	Zmigrod	Hersch L	Eidel	M		JR	
KOLBER	Chaim			Zmigrod	Zmigrod			M		JG	
KOLBER	Hersch		1880	Zmigrod	Zmigrod			M		JG	
KOLBER	Jitel		1879	Zmigrod	Zmigrod			F		JG	
KOLBER	Josef			Zmigrod	Zmigrod			M		JG	USA
KOLBER	Itche			Zmigrod	Zmigrod			M		YA	Belzec
KOLBER	Chaya		1887	Zmigrod	Zmigrod	Naphtali		F		JSS	Plaszow
KOLBER	Abraham				Zmigrod			M		JSS	Plaszow
KOLBER	Jakob				Zmigrod			M		JSS	Plaszow

Family name	First name(s)	Maiden name	Birth date	Birth place	Residence	Father	Mother	Gender	Spouse	Source	Remarks
KOLBER	Joel				Zmigrod			M		JSS	Plaszow
KOLBER	Moses			Zmigrod	Zmigrod			M		JG	
KOLBER	Ryfka			Zmigrod	Zmigrod			F		JSS	
KOLBER	Josef		1905	Zmigrod	Zmigrod	Moses	Ryfka	M		JSS	
KOLBER	Mordechai		1889	Zmigrod	Zmigrod			M		JG	
KOLBER	Blume		1887	Zmigrod	Zmigrod			F		JG	
KOLBER	Chaje S		1887	Zmigrod	Zmigrod			F		JG	
KOLBER	Hersch		1886	Zmigrod	Zmigrod			M		JG	
KOLBER	Jacob		1886	Zmigrod	Zmigrod			M		JG	
KOLBER	Jides		1881	Zmigrod	Zmigrod			F		JG	
KOLBER	Markus		1887	Zmigrod	Zmigrod			M		YA	
KOLBER	Rachel		1905	Zmigrod	Zmigrod	Asher		F		JG	
KOLBER	Markus			Zmigrod	Zmigrod			M		JR	
KOLBER	Marjem		1881	Zmigrod	Zmigrod	Markus		F		JR	
KOLBER	Lippe			Zmigrod	Zmigrod			M		JR	
KOLBER	Golde			Zmigrod	Zmigrod			F	Lippe	JR	
KOLBER	Rifka		1869	Zmigrod	Zmigrod	Lippe	Golde	F		JR	
KOLBER	Berl			Zmigrod	Zmigrod			M		JR	
KOLBER	Sima			Zmigrod	Zmigrod			F	Berl	JR	
KOLBER	Hersch		1866	Zmigrod	Zmigrod	Berl	Sima	M		JR	
KOLBER	Awraham		1872	Zmigrod	Zmigrod	Berl	Sima	M		JR	
KOLBER	Moses			Zmigrod	Zmigrod			M		JR	
KOLBER	Ryfla			Zmigrod	Zmigrod			F	Moses	JR	

Yizkor Book of Nowy Zmigrod

Family name	First name(s)	Maiden name	Birth date	Birth place	Residence	Father	Mother	Gender	Spouse	Source	Remarks
KOLBER	Jacob		1886	Zmigrod	Zmigrod	Moses	Ryfla	M		JR	
KOLBER	Jacob			Zmigrod	Zmigrod			M		JR	
KOLBER	Blima			Zmigrod	Zmigrod			F	Jacob	JR	
KOLBER	Chaim		1876	Zmigrod	Zmigrod	Jacob	Blima	M		JR	
KOLBER	Moses			Zmigrod	Zmigrod			M		JR	
KOLBER	Chana			Zmigrod	Zmigrod			F	Moses	JR	
KOLBER	Chaim		1873	Zmigrod	Zmigrod	Moses	Chana	M		JR	
KOLBER	Schije			Zmigrod	Zmigrod			M		JR	
KOLBER	Chawa			Zmigrod	Zmigrod			F	Schije	JR	
KOLBER	Leib		1869	Zmigrod	Zmigrod	Schije		M		JR	
KORN	Alter			Zmigrod				M		P	
KORN	Lea			Zmigrod	Zmigrod	Tzwi Y	Rivka	F	Alter	YV	
KORN	Pinhas			Zmigrod	Zmigrod	Alter	Lea	M		YV	
KORN	Haim			Zmigrod	Zmigrod			M		JG	
KORNFELD	Markus			Zmigrod	Zmigrod			M		JR	
KORNFELD	Shayne R		1888	Zmigrod	Zmigrod	Markus		F		JR	
KORNFELD	Reisel			Zmigrod	Zmigrod			F		JG	
KORNFELD	Zelig			Zmigrod	Zmigrod			M		YA	
KORZENIK	Lea			Zmigrod	Zmigrod			F	Zelig	YA	
KORZENIK	Mosze		1898	Zmigrod	Zmigrod	Zelig	Lea	M		YA	
KORZENIK	Acher		1881	Zmigrod	Zmigrod			M		JG	
KOSCHER	Chaim			Zmigrod	Zmigrod			M		JG	
KOSCHER	Fryderke		1898	Zmigrod	Zmigrod			F		JG	

Yizkor Book of Nowy Zmigrod

Family name	First name(s)	Maiden name	Birth date	Birth place	Residence	Father	Mother	Gender	Spouse	Source	Remarks
KOSCHER	Libe		1883	Zmigrod	Zmigrod			F		JG	
KOSCHER	Henryk		1889	Zmigrod	Zmigrod			M		YS	
KOZNER	Itzo			Zmigrod	Germany	Yehuda		M		JG	
KOWIE	Shulem H			Zmigrod	Zmigrod			M		JR	
KOWIE	Sara D		1866	Zmigrod	Zmigrod			F	Shulem H	JR	
KRAJZER	Dwore			Zmigrod	Zmigrod			F		JSS	Plaszow
KRAKER	Yehiel			Zmigrod	Zmigrod			M		P	Holocaust
KRAMER	Reisel			Zmigrod	Zmigrod			F		P	Holocaust
KRAMER	Mates				Zmigrod			M		JSS	
KRAMER	Hiel			Zmigrod	Zmigrod			M		JSS	
KRAMER	Reisel			Zmigrod	Zmigrod	Hiel	Reisel	F	Hiel	JSS	Plaszow
KRAMER	Salomon		1880	Zmigrod	Zmigrod			M		JG	
KRAMER	Efroim Se		1885	Zmigrod	Zmigrod			M		JG	
KRAMER	Malke		1886	Zmigrod	Zmigrod			F		JG	
KRAMER	Chiel		1883	Zmigrod	Zmigrod			M		JG	
KRAMER	Feige		1882	Zmigrod	Zmigrod			F		JG	
KRAMER	Izak		1888	Zmigrod	Zmigrod			M		JG	
KRAMER	Sara		1889	Zmigrod	Zmigrod			F		JG	
KRAMER	Ryfka		1901	Zmigrod	Zmigrod			F		JG	
KRAMER	Rachel		1883	Zmigrod	Zmigrod			F		JG	USA
KRAMER	Salomon			Zmigrod	Zmigrod			M		JR	
KRAMER	Feige R			Zmigrod	Zmigrod			F	Salomon	JR	
KRAMER	Berl		1882	Zmigrod	Zmigrod	Salomon	Feige Ruc	M		JR	

Yizkor Book of Nowy Zmigrod

Family name	First name(s)	Maiden name	Birth date	Birth place	Residence	Father	Mother	Gender	Spouse	Source	Remarks
KRAMER	Izaak		1888	Zmigrod	Zmigrod	Salomon	Feige Ruc	M		JR	
KRANZ	Emilie		1878		Zmigrod			F		JG	USA
KRANZ	Leon		1878		Zmigrod			M		P	
KRANZ	Benyamin				Zmigrod			M		P	
KRANZ	Frieda		1903		Zmigrod	Joshua	Sheva	F		YA	survived
KRANZER	Pessah		1898	Zmigrod		Yossef		M		JG	Holocaust
KRATZER	Abraham M		1889	Zmigrod	Zmigrod			M		JG	
KRATZER	Josef			Zmigrod	Zmigrod			M		JR	
KRATZER	Sara			Zmigrod	Zmigrod	Josef		F		JR	
KRATZER	Moses			Zmigrod	Zmigrod			M		JR	
KRATZER	Sara			Zmigrod	Zmigrod			F	Moses	JR	
KRATZER	Dewora			Zmigrod	Zmigrod	Moses	Sara	F		JR	
KRATZER	Breindel		1869	Zmigrod	Zmigrod	Moses	Sara	F		JR	
KRATZER	Hersch		1872	Zmigrod	Zmigrod	Moses	Sara	F		JR	
KRATZER	Chaim A			Zmigrod	Zmigrod			M		JR	
KRATZER	Ester			Zmigrod	Zmigrod			F	Chaim Aron		
KRATZER	Dwore			Zmigrod	Zmigrod	Chaim A	Ester	F		JR	
KRATZER	Sprince		1876	Zmigrod	Zmigrod	Chaim A	Ester	F		JR	
KRAUSBLATT	Josef E			Zmigrod	Zmigrod			M		JR	
KRAUSBLATT	Hitzel			Zmigrod	Zmigrod			F	Josef Elie	JR	
KRAUSBLATT	Brucha B		1871	Zmigrod	Zmigrod	Josef E	Hitzel	F		JR	
KRAUSBLATT	Chane		1871	Zmigrod	Zmigrod	Josef E	Hitzel	F		JR	
KREBS	Smiel			Zmigrod	Zmigrod			M		JR	

Yizkor Book of Nowy Zmigrod

Family name	First name(s)	Maiden name	Birth date	Birth place	Residence	Father	Mother	Gender	Spouse	Source	Remarks
KREBS	Ruxhel C			Zmigrod	Zmigrod			M	Smiel	JR	
KREBS	Marjem		1871	Zmigrod	Zmigrod	Smiel	Ruxhel Chaje	M		JR	
KREBS	Ber		1876	Zmigrod	Zmigrod	Smiel	Ruxhel Chaje	M		JR	
KREBS	Baruch			Zmigrod	Zmigrod			M		JG	
KREBS	Sonia			Zmigrod	Zmigrod			F	Baruch	JG	
KREBS	Bela			Zmigrod	Zmigrod			F		JG	
KREBS	Berish			Zmigrod	Zmigrod			M		JG	
KREBS	Berish			Zmigrod	Zmigrod			M	Berish	JG	
KREBS	Heineh			Zmigrod	Zmigrod	Berish		F		JG	
KREBS	Yehudit			Zmigrod	Zmigrod	Berish		F		JG	
KREBS	Edith			Zmigrod	Zmigrod			F		JG	
KREBS	Itzhak			Zmigrod	Zmigrod			M		JG	
KREBS	Mosh			Zmigrod	Zmigrod			M		JG	
KREBS	Sheindel			Zmigrod	Zmigrod			F		JG	
KREBS	Shprincza			Zmigrod	Zmigrod			F		JG	
KREBS	Yeshiahu			Zmigrod	Zmigrod			M		JSS	Plaszow
KREBS	Pinkas				Zmigrod			M		BD	
KREBS	F				Zmigrod			M		BD	
KREBS	Ch				Zmigrod			M		T	
KREBS	Bela				Zmigrod			F		YA	
KREBS	Moshe			Zmigrod	Jaslo			M			
KREBS	Moshe			Zmigrod		Yehuda		M		JSS	Plaszow

Family name	First name(s)	Maiden name	Birth date	Birth place	Residence	Father	Mother	Gender	Spouse	Source	Remarks
KREISER	Salomon		1920	Zmigrod	Zmigrod	Chiel	Reisel	M		JSS	Plaszow
KREMER	Jakob		1905		Zmigrod			M		BD	
KRIEGER	Meir			Zmigrod	Zmigrod			M		P	
KRILL	Aron			Zmigrod	Zmigrod			M		P	
KRILL	Judes	KRIEGER	1872	Zmigrod	Zmigrod			F	Aron	P	
KRILL	Juda L		1872	Zmigrod	Zmigrod	Aron	Judes	M		P	
KRILL	Benjamin W		1875	Zmigrod	Zmigrod	Aron	Judes	M		P	
KRILL	Chaim		1878	Zmigrod	Zmigrod	Aron	Judes	M			
KRILL	Chancze S		1879	Zmigrod	Zmigrod	Aron	Judes	F		P	
KRILL	Chana		1881	Zmigrod	Zmigrod	Aron	Judes	F		P	
KRILL	Moses		1884	Zmigrod	Zmigrod	Aron	Judes	M		P	
KRILL	Sprincze		1885	Zmigrod	Zmigrod	Aron	Judes	F		P	
KRILL	Fishel		1888	Zmigrod	Zmigrod	Aron	Judes	M		P	
KRILL	Chana I		1887	Zmigrod	Zmigrod	Aron	Judes	F		P	
KRILL	Fishel			Zmigrod	Zmigrod			M		P	
KRILL	Sara M	GROSSMAN		Zmigrod	Zmigrod	Fishel		F	Fishel	P	
KRILL	Hersh		1870	Zmigrod	Zmigrod	Fishel	Sara Malka	M		P	
KRILL	Ester		1873	Zmigrod	Zmigrod	Fishel	Sara Malka	F	Moshe	P	
KRILL	Hendel		1875	Zmigrod	Zmigrod	Fishel	Sara Malka	F		P	
KRILL	Shulem		1871	Zmigrod	Zmigrod	Fishel	Sara Malka	M		P	
KRILL	Jacob		1880	Zmigrod	Zmigrod	Fishel	Sara	M		P	

Yizkor Book of Nowy Zmigrod

Family name	First name(s)	Maiden name	Birth date	Birth place	Residence	Father	Mother	Gender	Spouse	Source	Remarks
KRILL	Joseph		1883	Zmigrod	Zmigrod	Fishel	Sara Malka	M		P	USA
KRILL	Moses		1885	Zmigrod	Zmigrod	Fishel	Sara Malka	M		P	
KRILL	Leib Wolf		1887	Zmigrod	Zmigrod	Fishel	Sara Malka	M		P	USA
KRILL	Aron			Zmigrod	Zmigrod			M		P	
KRILL	Niche			Zmigrod	Zmigrod			F	Aron	P	
KRILL	Mayer		1871	Zmigrod	Zmigrod	Aron	Niche	M		P	
KRILL	Sara	ERREICH		Zmigrod	Zmigrod			F	Mayer	P	
KRILL	Josef		1903	Zmigrod	Zmigrod	Mayer	Sara	M		P	
KRILL	Leibish		1876	Zmigrod	Zmigrod			M		P	
KRILL	Nissim			Zmigrod	Zmigrod			M		JG	USA
KRILL	Ite		1893	Zmigrod	Zmigrod			F		JG	emigrated
KRILL	Yeheskel			Zmigrod	Zmigrod			M		YA	
KRILL	Hendel			Zmigrod	Zmigrod			F	P Hiller	J	
KRISCHER	Touba		1915	Zmigrod	Gorlice	Moshe		F		YA	Holocaust
KRISCHER	Yoel		1885	Zmigrod	Jaslo	Yaakow		M		YA	Holocaust
KRISCHER	Nehemia		1890	Zmigrod	Zmigrod	Hersh		F		YA	Holocaust
KRISCHER	Moshe			Zmigrod	Zmigrod			M		P	
KRISCHER	Elka		1920	Zmigrod	Zmigrod	Moshe		F		JSS	Plaszow
KRISCHER	Chaskel			Zmigrod	Zmigrod			M		JSS	
KRISCHER	Moshe			Zmigrod	Zmigrod			M		YV	

Family name	First name(s)	Maiden name	Birth date	Birth place	Residence	Father	Mother	Gender	Spouse	Source	Remarks
KRISCHER	Necha	NEBENTZAHL			Zmigrod			F	Moshe	YV	Holocaust
KRISCHER	Sara		1918	Zmigrod	Zmigrod	Moshe	Necha	F		YA	emigrated
KRISCHER	Dawid		1890	Zmigrod	Zmigrod			M		JG	
KRISCHNER	Itzhak			Zmigrod	Zmigrod			M		JG	
KRISHNER	Tova			Zmigrod	Zmigrod			F		JG	
KRISHNER	Yaakow P			Zmigrod	Jaslo			M		P	
KRISHNER		CITRONENBAUM		Zmigrod	Zmigrod	Mordechai		F	Yaakow P	P	
KRISHNER	Yehuda S		1879	Zmigrod	Zmigrod	Yaakow P		M		P	
KRISHNER	Joel		1880	Zmigrod	Zmigrod	Yaakow P		M		JR	
KRIESER	Samuel			Zmigrod	Zmigrod			M		JG	
KRIESER	Yehuda Tzwi			Sandz		Samuel		M		P	
KRIESER	Sara S	AUMAN		Zmigrod	Zmigrod				Samuel	P	
KRIESER	Itzhak E		1890	Sandz	Zmigrod	Yehuda Tz	Sara Shprince			P	Holocaust
KRIESER	Miriam			Zmigrod	Zmigrod					P	
KRIESER	Aron		1901	Zmigrod	Zmigrod					P	
KRIESER	Ryfka	TUCHFELD		Zmigrod	Zmigrod					P	
KRIESER	Mendel			Zmigrod	Zmigrod			M		JR	
KRIESER	Cherssia			Zmigrod	Zmigrod			F	Mendel	JR	
KRIESER	Leibisch		1866	Zmigrod	Zmigrod	Mendel	Cherssia	M		JR	
KROON	Sara	TRACHMAN		Zmigrod	Zmigrod			F	Samuel	JG	
KROON	Hinde		1882	Zmigrod	Zmigrod			F		JG	
KRZESZANER	Marjem		1887	Zmigrod	Zmigrod			F		JG	

Yizkor Book of Nowy Zmigrod

Family name	First name(s)	Maiden name	Birth date	Birth place	Residence	Father	Mother	Gender	Spouse	Source	Remarks
KRZESZANER	Abraham			Zmigrod	Zmigrod			M		JR	
KRZESZANER	Mosze		1885	Zmigrod	Zmigrod	Abraham		M		JR	
KRZESZANER	Dawid		1878	Zmigrod	Zmigrod	Abraham		M		JR	
KUGEL	Mendel		1884	Zmigrod	Zmigrod			M		YA	
KUGEL	Kalman		1887	Zmigrod		Hersh		M		YA	Holocaust
KUNSTLER	Klaman		1888	Zmigrod		Tzwi		M		JSS	Plaszow
KUNSTLER	Mendel			Zmigrod	Zmigrod			M		JSS	Plaszow
KURSCHNER	Samuel			Zmigrod	Zmigrod			M		JG	
KURRIER	Samuel			Zmigrod	Zmigrod			M		JR	
KURRIER	Benjamin W		1887	Zmigrod	Zmigrod	Samuel		M		JR	
KURZMANN	Mindel	THALER		Zmigrod	Zmigrod			F	Samuel	JG	
KURZMANN	Hersch		1887	Zmigrod	Zmigrod	Samuel	Mindel	M		JG	
KURZMANN	Sara		1879	Zmigrod	Zmigrod	Samuel	Mindel	F		JG	
KURZMANN	Izaak		1881	Zmigrod	Zmigrod	Samuel	Mindel	M		JG	
KURZMANN	Freidel F		1883	Zmigrod	Zmigrod	Samuel	Mindel	F		JG	
KURZMANN	Chaim A		1885	Zmigrod	Zmigrod	Samuel	Mindel	M		JG	
KURZMANN	Benjamin W.		1887	Zmigrod	Zmigrod	Samuel	Mindel	M		JG	
KURZMANN	Mozes		1889	Zmigrod	Zmigrod	Samuel	Mindel	M		JG	
KURZMANN	Shmerl			Zmigrod	Zmigrod			M		JG	
KURZMANN	Hizel			Zmigrod	Zmigrod			M	Shmerl	JG	
KURZMANN	Beik Chjk		1869	Zmigrod	Zmigrod	Shmerl	Hizel	M		JG	
KURZMANN	Ruchel		1877	Zmigrod	Zmigrod	Shmerl	Hizel	F		JSS	Plaszow

Yizkor Book of Nowy Zmigrod

Family name	First name(s)	Maiden name	Birth date	Birth place	Residence	Father	Mother	Gender	Spouse	Source	Remarks
KURZMANN	Mates				Zmigrod			M		BD	
KWASSER	Freidil				Zmigrod			F		JG	USA
LAKS	Feige R		1892		Zmigrod			F		JSS	survived
LAKS	Naftali				Zmigrod			M		JSS	
LAKS	Ryfka				Zmigrod			F		YA	
LAKS	Mendel			Zmigrod	Zmigrod	Chaim		M		JG	Holocaust
LAKS	Hendel		1888	Zmigrod	Zmigrod			F		JG	
LAKS	David			Zmigrod	Zmigrod			M		P	Holocaust
LAKS	Esther			Zmigrod	Zmigrod			F		JG	
LAKS	Idel		1887	Zmigrod	Zmigrod			F		P	died 1938
LAKS	Dawid			Zmigrod	Zmigrod			M		P	Holocaust
LAKS	Riwka			Zmigrod	Zmigrod			F	Dawid	P	survived
LAKS	Nathan			Zmigrod	Zmigrod	Dawid	Riwka	M		P	survived
LAKS	Bertha			Zmigrod	Zmigrod	Dawid	Riwka	F		P	survived
LAKS	Golda			Zmigrod	Zmigrod	Dawid	Riwka	F		P	survived
LAKS	Mania			Zmigrod	Zmigrod	Dawid	Riwka	F		P	USA
LAKS	Chana M			Zmigrod	Zmigrod	Dawid	Riwka	F		JG	
LAKS	Naftali			Zmigrod	Zmigrod	Naftali		M		JR	
LAKS	Joseph			Zmigrod	Zmigrod	Naftali		M		JR	
LAKS	Sara			Zmigrod	Zmigrod			F		YA	Holocaust
LAKS	Frieda			Zmigrod	Zmigrod	Naphtali		F		YA	Holocaust
LAKS	Perl		1875		Zmigrod	Michael		F		YA	
LAKS	Ryfka		1887		Zmigrod	Naphtali		F		JG	Holocaust

Yizkor Book of Nowy Zmigrod

Family name	First name(s)	Maiden name	Birth date	Birth place	Residence	Father	Mother	Gender	Spouse	Source	Remarks
LAKS	Chaim			Zmigrod	Zmigrod			M		YV	
LAKS	Serl			Zmigrod	Zmigrod			F		YV	
LAKS	Shukem			Zmigrod	Zmigrod			M		YV	Auschwitz
LAKS	Wolf			Zmigrod	Zmigrod			M		JSS	Plaszow
LAMBIK	Salomon		1887	Zmigrod	Zmigrod			M		P	
LANDESMAN	Chaskel		1889	Zmigrod	Zmigrod			M		P	
LANDESMAN	Naftali			Zmigrod	Zmigrod			M		JR	
LANDESMAN	Chana			Zmigrod	Zmigrod			F	Naftali	JR	
LANDESMAN	Freide		1871	Zmigrod	Zmigrod	Naftali	Chana	F		JR	
LANG	David			Zmigrod	Zmigrod			M		P	
LANG	Hannah			Zmigrod	Zmigrod			F		P	
LANG	Hinde Jen		1887	Zmigrod	Zmigrod			F		P	
LANG	Laje		1887	Zmigrod	Zmigrod			F		P	
LANG	Nathan		1887	Zmigrod	Zmigrod			M		P	
LANG	Pinhas			Zmigrod	Zmigrod			M		P	
LANG	Lea D			Zmigrod	Zmigrod			F	Pinhas	P	
LANG	Pinhas			Zmigrod	Zmigrod			M		P	
LANG	Braindla			Zmigrod	Zmigrod			F	Pinhas		
LANG	Sarah D		1885	Zmigrod	Zmigrod			F		P	
LANG	Shimon			Zmigrod	Zmigrod			M		P	
LANG	Shimon			Zmigrod	Zmigrod			M	Shimon	P	
LANG	Yehuda			Zmigrod	Zmigrod			M		P	
LANG	Dworah			Zmigrod	Zmigrod			F	Yehuda	P	

Yizkor Book of Nowy Zmigrod

Family name	First name(s)	Maiden name	Birth date	Birth place	Residence	Father	Mother	Gender	Spouse	Source	Remarks
LANG	Eliyahu			Zmigrod	Zmigrod	Yehuda	Dworah	M		P	
LANG	Hannah	GOLDMAN		Zmigrod	Zmigrod			F	Eliyahu	P	
LANG	Esther	SCHACHNER		Zmigrod	Zmigrod			F		P	
LANG	Benjamin			Zmigrod	Zmigrod	Eliyahu	Hannah	M		P	
LANG	Sarah	MALTZ		Zmigrod	Zmigrod			F	Benjamin	P	
LANG	Helen			Zmigrod	Zmigrod	Eliyahu	Hannah	F		P	
LANG	Nelly			Zmigrod	Zmigrod	Eliyahu	Hannah	F		P	
LANG	Sara			Zmigrod	Zmigrod	Eliyahu	Hannah	F		P	
LANG	Mimi			Zmigrod	Zmigrod	Eliyahu	Hannah	F		P	
LANG	Abraham			Zmigrod	Zmigrod	Eliyahu	Hannah	M		P	
LANG	Hilda			Zmigrod	Zmigrod	Eliyahu	Hannah	F		P	
LANG	Michuel		1879	Zmigrod	Zmigrod	Yehuda	Dworah	M		JR	
LANG	Haim			Zmigrod	Zmigrod	Yehuda	Dworah	M		P	
LANG	Feiga Rei.	FINDLING		Zmigrod	Zmigrod	Haim	Feiga Rei.	F	Haim	P	
LANG	Abraham			Zmigrod	Zmigrod	Haim	Feiga Rei.	M		P	
LANG	David			Zmigrod	Zmigrod	Haim	Feiga Rei.	M		P	
LANG	Seril			Zmigrod	Zmigrod	Haim	Feiga Rei.	F		P	
LANG	Pinhas		1888	Zmigrod	Zmigrod	Yehuda	Dworah	M		P	Holocaust
LANG	Reisel	TZIMET		Zmigrod	Zmigrod			F	Pinhas	Holocaust	
LANG	Gittel		1910	Zmigrod	Zmigrod	Pinhas	Reisel	F	Baruch	P	Holocaust
LANG	Baruch			Zmigrod	Zmigrod			M		P	Holocaust
LANG	Yehuda			Zmigrod	Zmigrod	Baruch	Gittel	M		P	Holocaust
LANG	Efroim F.			Zmigrod	Zmigrod	Baruch	Gittel	M		P	

Yizkor Book of Nowy Zmigrod

Family name	Maiden name	First name(s)	Birth date	Birth place	Residence	Father	Mother	Gender	Spouse	Source	Remarks
LANG		Shimon		Zmigrod	Israel	Pinhas	Reisel	M		P	survived
LANG	JASKEL	Dinah						F	Shimon	P	Holocaust
LANG		Naphtali		Zmigrod	Zmigrod	Pinhas	Reisel	M		P	Holocaust
LANG		Efroim F.	1926	Zmigrod	Zmigrod	Pinhas	Reisel	M		P	Holocaust
LANG		Yosef	1876	Zmigrod	Zmigrod	Yehuda	Dworah	M		P	Holocaust
LANG	PENSIG	Hava		Zmigrod	Zmigrod			F	Yosef	Holocaust	
LANG	LANG	Reisel	1903	Zmigrod	Zmigrod	Yosef	Hava	F		P	Holocaust
LANG		Itzhak	1903	Zmigrod	Zmigrod	Shimon	Hule	M		P	Holocaust
LANG		Baruch		Zmigrod	Zmigrod	Itzhak	Reisel	M		P	Holocaust
LANG		Hersz	1905	Zmigrod	Gorlice	Yosef	Hava	M		P	Holocaust
LANG								M	Hersh Ber	Holocaust	
LANG		Hitzel	1910	Zmigrod	Zmigrod	Yosef	Hava	F		YA	
LANG		Baruch		Zmigrod	Jaslo	Yossef	Hava	M		P	
LANG		Gittel		Zmigrod	Zmigrod	Baruch	Gittel	F	Baruch	P	
LANG		Yehuda		Zmigrod	Zmigrod	Baruch	Gittel	M		P	
LANG		Ephraim F	1913	Zmigrod	Zmigrod	Yossef	Hava	M		YA	Auschwitz
LANG		Michael		Zmigrod	Zmigrod	Yosef	Hava	M		P	Holocaust
LANG		Shimon		Zmigrod	Zmigrod	Yosef	Hava	M		P	Holocaust
LANG		Sara		Zmigrod	Zmigrod	Yosef	Hava	F	Itzhak	P	survived
LANG		Itzhak		Zmigrod	Zmigrod			M		P	survived
LANG		Shimon		Zmigrod	Zmigrod			M		YA	Holocaust

Family name	Maiden name	First name(s)	Birth date	Birth place	Residence	Father	Mother	Gender	Spouse	Source	Remarks
LANG		Chula	1885	Zmigrod	Gorlice	Yehuda	Dworah	M		P	Holocaust
LANG		Esther		Zmigrod	Zmigrod	Shimon	Hila	F	Benjamin	P	
LANG		Benjamin		Zmigrod	Zmigrod			M		P	
LANG		Sima		Zmigrod	Zmigrod	Benjamin	Esther	F		P	
LANG		Sara		Zmigrod	Zmigrod	Benjamin	Esther	F		YA	
LANG		Dawid		Zmigrod	Zmigrod	Shimon	Hila	M		P	Holocaust
LANG		Itzhak		Zmigrod	Zmigrod	Shimon	Hila	M		P	
LANG		Reisel		Zmigrod	Zmigrod	Itzhak	Reisel	F	Itzhak	P	Holocaust
LANG		Sara		Zmigrod	Zmigrod	Itzhak	Reisel	F		P	Holocaust
LANG		Baruch		Zmigrod	Zmigrod	Itzhak	Reisel	M		P	Holocaust
LANG		Shimon Y.		Zmigrod	Zmigrod	Itzhak	Reisel	M		P	Holocaust
LANG		Moshe		Zmigrod	Zmigrod	Yehuda	Dworah	M		P	Holocaust
LANG	KELLER	Yetta Ita		Zmigrod	Zmigrod	Yehuda	Dworah	F	Moshe	P	
LANG		Shlomo		Zmigrod	Zmigrod	Yehuda	Dworah	M		P	
LANG	GOLDBLAT	Hadassah		Zmigrod	Zmigrod	Shimon		F	Shlomo	P	
LANG		Itzhak L.		Zmigrod	Zmigrod	Shimon		M		P	
LANG				Zmigrod	Zmigrod	Itzhak L.		F	Itzhak L.		
LANG		Shlomo		Zmigrod	Zmigrod	Itzhak L.		M		P	
LANG		Seril		Zmigrod	Zmigrod	Itzhak L.		F		P	
LANG		Reisel		Zmigrod	Zmigrod	Itzhak L.		F		P	
LANG		Shmuel		Zmigrod	Zmigrod			M		P	
LANG	STECHER	Reisel		Zmigrod	Zmigrod			F	Shmuel	P	
LANG		Szymon	27/4/1884	Zmigrod	Zmigrod			M		YA	Auschwitz

Yizkor Book of Nowy Zmigrod

Family name	First name(s)	Maiden name	Birth date	Birth place	Residence	Father	Mother	Gender	Spouse	Source	Remarks
LANG	Hela		1904	Zmigrod	Zmigrod	Yossef		F		P	Holocaust
LANG	Sime	LEHR	1879	Zmigrod	Zmigrod			F		YA	Holocaust
LANG	Czala		1914	Zmigrod	Zmigrod	Yossef		M		YA	Holocaust
LANG	Roza		1903	Zmigrod	Zmigrod	Yossef		F		YA	Auschwitz
LANG	Tzwi		1903	Zmigrod	Gorlice	Yossef		M		YA	Holocaust
LANG	Sala			Zmigrod	Zmigrod	Yossef		F		YA	Auschwitz
LANG	Szymon		1911	Zmigrod	Zmigrod	Yossef		M		YA	Holocaust
LANG	Serl		1909	Zmigrod	Zmigrod	Yossef		F		P	Holocaust
LANG	Michael			Zmigrod	Zmigrod	Yosef	Hava	M		YA	Majdanek
LANG	Izak		1903	Zmigrod	Gorlice	Shimon		M		YA	Auschwitz
LANG	Roza		1901	Zmigrod	Gorlice	Sassetz		F		YA	Auschwitz
LANG	Dawid		1906	Zmigrod	Gorlice	Aaron		M		YA	Auschwitz
LANG	Shimon		1924	Zmigrod	Gorlice	Itzhak		M		YA	Auschwitz
LANG	Sara		1921	Zmigrod	Zmigrod	Itzhak		F		YA	Holocaust
LANG	Esther			Zmigrod	Zmigrod	Shimon		F		YA	Holocaust
LANG	Rosalia			Zmigrod	Zmigrod	Ephraim		F		YA	Holocaust
LANG	Sara			Zmigrod	Gorlice	Itzhak		F		JSS	Plaszow
LANG	Yossef			Zmigrod	Gorlice			M		YA	
Hana	Hana	FINDLING		Zmigrod	Gorlice			F	Yossef	YA	
Hana	Michael				Zmigrod	Yossef	Hana	M		JSS	Plaszow
LANG	Szymon			Zmigrod	Zmigrod			M		YA	
LANG	Hersh			Zmigrod	Gorlice			M		YA	Holocaust
LANG	Mindel			Gorlice	Gorlice			F	Hersh	YA	Holocaust

Family name	First name(s)	Maiden name	Birth date	Birth place	Residence	Father	Mother	Gender	Spouse	Source	Remarks
LANG	Sara				Gorlice			F		YA	Holocaust
LANG	Reisel			Zmigrod	Gorlice			F		YA	Holocaust
LANG	Dawid			Zmigrod	Gorlice			M		YA	Holocaust
LANG	Sara Br			Zmigrod	Gorlice			F		BD	Holocaust
LANG	Jehuda				Zmigrod			M		BD	
LANG	Pinhas				Zmigrod			M		BD	
LANG	S				Zmigrod			M		JG	USA
LANG	Isak		1865		Zmigrod			M		JG	USA
LANG	Leizer		1893		Zmigrod			M		JG	USA
LANG	Samuel				Zmigrod			M		JG	USA
LANG	Nathan		1891		Zmigrod			M		JG	USA
LANG	Nute		1883		Zmigrod			M		T	Holocaust
LANG	Lea D				Zmigrod			F		YS	
LANG	Yossef			Zmigrod	Zmigrod			M		P	Holocaust
LANG	Dworah			Zmigrod	Zmigrod			F		P	Holocaust
LANG	Raphael				Zmigrod			M		P	
LANG	Sender			Zmigrod	Zmigrod			M		JR	
LANG	Breindel		1881	Zmigrod	Zmigrod	Sender		F		JR	
LANG	Mindel			Zmigrod	Zmigrod			F	Sender	JR	
LANG	Sara			Zmigrod	Zmigrod	Sender	Mindel	F		JR	
LANG	Marjem		1869	Zmigrod	Zmigrod			F		JR	
LANG	Samuel			Zmigrod	Zmigrod			M		JR	
LANG	Laje		1887	Zmigrod	Zmigrod	Samuel		F		JR	

Yizkor Book of Nowy Zmigrod

Family name	First name(s)	Maiden name	Birth date	Birth place	Residence	Father	Mother	Gender	Spouse	Source	Remarks
LANG	Elias			Zmigrod	Zmigrod			M		JR	
LANG	Sara			Zmigrod	Zmigrod			F	Elias	JR	
LANG	Leib H		1869	Zmigrod	Zmigrod	Elias	Sara	M		JR	
LANG	Feivel			Zmigrod	Zmigrod			M		JR	
LANG	Dwore		1867	Zmigrod	Zmigrod			F	Feivel	JR	
LANG	Chaim			Zmigrod	Zmigrod	Feivel	Dwore	M		JR	
LANG	Juda L			Zmigrod	Zmigrod			M		JR	
LANG	Sara			Zmigrod	Zmigrod			F	Juda L	JR	
LANG	Simon		1869	Zmigrod	Zmigrod	Juda L	Sara	M		JR	
LECH	Fischel			Zmigrod	Zmigrod			M		JR	
LECH	Ruchel			Zmigrod	Zmigrod	Fischel		F	Fischel	JR	
LECH	Simon			Zmigrod	Zmigrod	Fischel	Ruchel	M		JR	
LAPPMAN	Mendel		1896	Zmigrod	Zmigrod	Chaim		M		JSS	
LAX	Kappel				Zmigrod			M		JG	USA
LAZAR	Nathan			Zmigrod				M		JG	USA
LEFF	Sarah			Zmigrod				F		JG	USA
LEFF	Leonard				Zmigrod			M		JG	USA
LEHR	Hortense				Zmigrod			F		JG	USA
LEHR	Harvey				Zmigrod			M		BD	USA
LEHR	Leon				Zmigrod			M		JSS	Plaszow
LEHRMAN	Rubin				Zmigrod			M		JSS	Plaszow
LEIBER	Josef				Zmigrod			M		P	Holocaust
LEIBER	Marcus				Zmigrod			M		P	USA

Family name	First name(s)	Maiden name	Birth date	Birth place	Residence	Father	Mother	Gender	Spouse	Source	Remarks
LEIBNER	Nathan N		1844	Korczyna	Zmigrod	Shragai F	Sheindel	M		P	died 1929
LEIBNER	Pearl R	TZIMET		Zmigrod	Zmigrod			F		P	died 1874
LEIBNER	Ephraim		1868		Korczyna	Nathan N	Pearl Ruch	M		P	Holocaust
LEIBNER	Sprince R	FINDLING	1879	Zmigrod	Zmigrod	Ephraim	Sprince	F	Ephraim	P	Holocaust
LEIBNER	Pearl		1900	Zmigrod	USA	Ephraim	Sprince			P	survived
LEIBNER	Sima		1903	Zmigrod		Ephraim	Sprince			P	Holocaust
LEIBNER	Serl			Zmigrod	Zmigrod	Ephraim	Sprince			P	Holocaust
LEIBNER	Yaakov		1905	Zmigrod		Ephraim	Sprince			P	survived
LEIBNER	Moshe			Zmigrod	Zmigrod	Ephraim	Sprince			P	Holocaust
LEIBNER	Shimshon		1914	Zmigrod	Zmigrod	Ephraim	Sprince			P	Holocaust
LEIBNER	Reisel			Zmigrod	Zmigrod	Ephraim	Sprince			P	Holocaust
LEIBNER	Mania			Zmigrod	Zmigrod	Ephraim	Sprince			P	died 1918
LEIBNER	Sheindel		1873	Zmigrod	Zmigrod	Nathan	Pearl	F		P	USA
LEIBNER	Reisel	ACHTSAM	1833	Zmigrod	Zmigrod	Moyszes	Fania	F	Nathan	USA	
LEIBNER	Menachem		1876	Zmigrod	Zmigrod	Nathan	Reisel	M		P	USA
LEIBNER	Rachel W		1879	Zmigrod	Zmigrod	Nathan	Reisel	F		P	USA
LEIBNER	Baruch L		1881	Zmigrod	Zmigrod	Nathan	Reisel	M		P	died 1881
LEIBNER	Joseph		1885	Zmigrod	Zmigrod	Nathan	Reisel	M		WS	USA
LEIBNER	Emma-S		1886	Zmigrod	Zmigrod	Nathan	Reisel	F		WS	USA
LEIBNER	Esther			Korczyna	Zmigrod	Shragai F	Sheindel	F		P	died 1922
LEIDEN	Dawid				Zmigrod			M		JSS	
LEISER	Eva				Zmigrod			F		JSS	
LEISER	Necha				Zmigrod			F		BD	

Yizkor Book of Nowy Zmigrod

Family name	First name(s)	Maiden name	Birth date	Birth place	Residence	Father	Mother	Gender	Spouse	Source	Remarks
LEISER	P				Zmigrod			M		JG	USA
LEISER	Joseph			Zmigrod				M		T	
LEITNER	David				Zmigrod			M		JG	
LEIZER	Hirsch			Zmigrod	Zmigrod			M		JG	
LEIZER	Perl	STERN		Zmigrod	Zmigrod			F	Hirsch	JG	
LEIZER	Yehiel			Zmigrod	Zmigrod			M		JG	
LEIZER	Kalman				Zmigrod			M		P	
LEIZER	Wol		1887	Zmigrod	Zmigrod			M		BD	
LEMBIG	Asher			Zmigrod	Zmigrod			M		P	Holocaust
LEMPEL	Feige	GETZLER		Zmigrod	Zmigrod			F	Asher	P	Holocaust
LEMPEL	Chaim				Zmigrod			M		JSS	Plaszow
LERMAN	Markus			Osiek	Zmigrod			M		JSS	Plaszow
LERMAN	Mendel				Zmigrod			M		JSS	Plaszow
LERMAN	Szymon				Zmigrod			M		JSS	Holocaust
LERMAN	Cila				Zmigrod			F		JG	
LERMAN	Ita Lea			Zmigrod	Zmigrod			F		JG	
LERMAN	Yeheskel			Osiek	Zmigrod			M		JG	Holocaust
LERMAN	Chaim			Zmigrod	Zmigrod			M		YA	
LERNER	Gittel		1921	Zmigrod	Zmigrod	Chaim		F		YA	Holocaust
LERNER	Israel		1914	Zmigrod	Zmigrod	Chaim		M		YA	Holocaust
LERNER	Ita		1886	Zmigrod	Zmigrod	Yaakow		F		JSS	Holocaust
LERNER	Mendel			Lodz	Zmigrod			M		JSS	
LESLAU	Ester			Lodz	Zmigrod			F	Mendel	JSS	Plaszow

Family name	First name(s)	Maiden name	Birth date	Birth place	Residence	Father	Mother	Gender	Spouse	Source	Remarks
LESLAU	Jakub		19/03/1905	Lodz	Zmigrod	Mendel	Ester	M		JSS	Plaszow
LESLAU	Genia				Zmigrod			F		JSS	Plaszow
LESLAU	Chaim			Zmigrod	Zmigrod			M		P	
LEWKOWICZ	Isaac			Zmigrod	Zmigrod			M		JR	
LEWKOWICZ	Moses		1888	Zmigrod	Zmigrod	Isaac		M		JR	
LIB	Benjamin				Zmigrod			M		JSS	Plaszow
LIBERMAN	Moses				Zmigrod			M		JSS	
LIBERMAN	Lea				Zmigrod			F		JSS	
LIBERMAN	Niche				Zmigrod			F		JSS	Plaszow
LIBERMAN	Dawid				Zmigrod			M		JG	
LICHTIG	Jakob		1887	Zmigrod	Zmigrod			M		JG	
LICHTIG	Samuel		1881	Zmigrod	Zmigrod			M		JG	
LICHTIG	Wigdor	SENDER	1880	Zmigrod	Zmigrod			M		JSS	Plaszow
LICHTIG	Leib				Zmigrod			M		YA	
LIERDERBAUM	Hitzel			Zmigrod	Sandz	Yossef		F		WS	USA
LIPSCHITZ	Adele		1884		Zmigrod			F		JG	USA
LISKER	Max			Zmigrod	Zmigrod			M		YA	
LORBER	Leiser			Zmigrod	Zmigrod			M		JR	
LORBER	Sara			Zmigrod	Zmigrod			F	Leiser	JR	
LORBER	Hinde		1905	Zmigrod	Zmigrod	Leiser	Hinde	F		JR	
LUDNER	Israel		1880	Zmigrod	Zmigrod	Dawid		M		JG	Holocaust
LUXEMBURG	Leib			Zmigrod	Zmigrod			M		JR	
LUXEMBURG	Sime			Zmigrod	Zmigrod			F	Leib	JR	

Yizkor Book of Nowy Zmigrod

Family name	First name(s)	Maiden name	Birth date	Birth place	Residence	Father	Mother	Gender	Spouse	Source	Remarks
LUXEMBURG	Sara R		1869	Zmigrod	Zmigrod	Leib	Sime	F		JR	
MAJEROVICZ	Awraham		1901		Zmigrod			M		JG	USA
MALZ	Sarah		1933	Zmigrod	Zmigrod			F	Avraham	P	Holocaust
MALZ	Berl		1853	Zmigrod	Zmigrod			M		P	Holocaust
MALZ	Dwojra		1887	Zmigrod	Zmigrod			F		JG	
MALZ	Laje			Zmigrod	Zmigrod			F		JG	
MALZ	Salomon			Zmigrod	Zmigrod			M		JG	
MALZ	Sema	SPIRE		Zmigrod	Zmigrod			F	Salomon	JG	
MALZ	Haim		1907	Zmigrod	Zmigrod	Salomon	Sema	M		JG	
MALZ	Chaje	EICHNER		Zmigrod	Zmigrod			F	Haim	JG	
MALZ	Samuel H		1885	Zmigrod	Zmigrod			M		JG	USA
MALZ	Dawid			Zmigrod				M		YA	
MALZ	Zacharia			Zmigrod	Zmigrod			M		P	
MANDIL	Frederyka		1890	Zmigrod	Sandz	Zigmunt		F		JG	USA
MANNES	Chaim		1884		Zmigrod			M		JSS	Plaszow
MARCHOMANN	Israel				Zmigrod			M		JG	
MARGULES	Josef Ber			Zmigrod	Zmigrod			M		JG	
MARKOWICZ	Dwojra	HORN		Zmigrod	Zmigrod			F	Josef Ber	JG	
MARKOWICZ	Reisel		1883	Zmigrod	Zmigrod	Josef B	Dwojra	F		JG	
MARKOWICZ	Hersch		1886	Zmigrod	Zmigrod	Josef B	Dwojra	M		JG	
MARKOWICZ	Reisel		1883	Zmigrod	Zmigrod			F		JG	USA
MARKOWICZ	Chana		1904		Zmigrod			F		JG	USA
MARKOWITZ	Bernard		1892		Zmigrod			M		JG	USA

Yizkor Book of Nowy Zmigrod

Family name	First name(s)	Maiden name	Birth date	Birth place	Residence	Father	Mother	Gender	Spouse	Source	Remarks
MEHER	Samuel		1907	Zmigrod	Zmigrod			M		JG	
MEHL	Chaim		1889	Zmigrod	Zmigrod			M		JG	USA
MEHL	Feige		1886	Zmigrod	Zmigrod			F		JG	
MEHR			1887	Zmigrod	Zmigrod			M		JG	
MEISNER	Berl			Zmigrod	Zmigrod			M		JG	
MEISNER	Gittla	IZRAEL		Zmigrod	Zmigrod			F	Berl	JG	
MEISNER	Mozes		1896	Zmigrod	Zmigrod	Berl	Gittla	M		JG	
MEISNER	Feiga	EICHNER		Zmigrod	Zmigrod			F	Mozes	JG	
MEISNER	Israel J.		1925	Zmigrod	Zmigrod	Mozes	Feiga	M		JG	
MEISNER	Salomon		1929	Zmigrod	Zmigrod	Mozes	Feiga	M		JG	
MEISNER	Gerzon		1905	Zmigrod	Zmigrod			M		JG	
MEISNER	Israel		1840	Zmigrod	Zmigrod			M		JG	
MEISNER	Sara C	KATZ		Zmigrod	Zmigrod			F	Israel	JG	
MEISNER	Ides		1876	Zmigrod	Zmigrod	Israel	Sara Chaj	F		JG	
MEISNER	Lipa		1871	Zmigrod	Zmigrod	Israel	Sara Cha	M		JG	
MEISNER	Sara	GALLER		Zmigrod	Zmigrod	Lipa		F	Lipa	JG	
MEISNER	Esther			Zmigrod	Zmigrod	Lipa	Sara	F	Lipa	JG	
MEISNER	Rajsel		1874	Zmigrod	Zmigrod			F		JG	died 1934
MEISNER	Chajem		1879	Zmigrod	Zmigrod			M		JG	
MEISNER	Cyrel		1880	Zmigrod	Zmigrod	Chajem		F		JG	
MEISNER	Itte		1880	Zmigrod	Zmigrod	Chajem		F		JG	
MEISNER	Rachel		1885	Zmigrod	Zmigrod		Itte	F		JG	
MEISNER	Reisel		1889	Zmigrod	Zmigrod		Itte	F		JG	

Family name	First name(s)	Maiden name	Birth date	Birth place	Residence	Father	Mother	Gender	Spouse	Source	Remarks
MEISNER	Samuel		1882	Zmigrod	Zmigrod		Itte	M		JG	
MEISNER	Mozes			Zmigrod	Zmigrod			M		JG	
MEISNER	Feiga	EICHNER		Zmigrod	Zmigrod			F	Mozes	JG	
MEISNER	Izrael		1925	Zmigrod	Zmigrod	Mozes	Feiga	M		JG	
MEISNER	Solomon		1929	Zmigrod	Zmigrod	Mozes	Feiga	M		JG	
MEISNER	Mozes			Zmigrod	Zmigrod			M		JG	
MEISNER	Sara			Zmigrod	Zmigrod			F		JSS	
MEISNER	Sara				Zmigrod			F		BD	
MEISNER	Shmuel				Zmigrod			M		T	
MELAMET	Aaron			Zmigrod	Zmigrod			M		P	Holocaust
MELDER	Sara			Zmigrod	Zmigrod			F		P	Holocaust
MELDER	Hershel				Zmigrod			F		P	
MENTZLER	Sral				Zmigrod			M		T	
MERCHOWER	hindzele [				Zmigrod			F		JG	USA
MERCHOWER	J.Morris			Zmigrod	Zmigrod			M		JG	USA
MILLER	Chaim		1887	Zmigrod	Zmigrod			M		JG	
MOHR	Israel I		1850	Zmigrod	Zmigrod			M		JG	
MOHRER	Shlomo			Zmigrod	Zmigrod			F	Israel I		
MOHRER	Shlomo		1869	Zmigrod	Zmigrod	Israel Is		M		JG	
MOHRER	Feiga	KINZLER	1872	Zmigrod	Zmigrod			F	Shlomo	JG	
MOHRER	Alexander		1893	Zmigrod	Zmigrod			M		JG	
MOHRER	Moritz			Zmigrod	Zmigrod	Alexander Z.		M		JG	

Yizkor Book of Nowy Zmigrod

Family name	First name(s)	Maiden name	Birth date	Birth place	Residence	Father	Mother	Gender	Spouse	Source	Remarks
MOHRER	Rosa			Zmigrod	Zmigrod	Alexander Z.		F		JG	
MOHRER	Ida				Zmigrod	Alexander Z.		F		JG	
MOHRER	Sabine			Zmigrod	Zmigrod	Alexander Z.		F		JG	
MOHRER	Markus			Zmigrod	Zmigrod			M		JSS	Plaszow
MOHRER	Natan			Zmigrod	Zmigrod			M		JG	
MOHRER	Zacharia			Zmigrod	Zmigrod			M		JR	
MOHRER	Eidel		1889	Zmigrod	Zmigrod	Zacharia		F		JR	
MOLAKIN	Moses			Zmigrod	Zmigrod			M		JG	
MORGENSTERN	Feiga	GOLDBERGER		Zmigrod	Zmigrod			F	Moses	JG	
MORGENSTERN	Jenta		1905	Zmigrod	Zmigrod	Moses	Feiga	F		JG	USA
MORGENSTERN	Rosa			Zmigrod	Zmigrod			F		P	
MUND	Yehiel			Zmigrod	Germany			M		YA	
MUND	Roza	GROSS		Zmigrod	Germany	Naphtali	Sarah	F	Yehiel	YA	
MUND	Ruth			Zmigrod				F		YA	Auschwitz
NALKIN	Yaakow		1885	Zmigrod		Shmuel		M		JSS	Plaszow
NARCISEN	Samuel			Zmigrod	Zmigrod			M		JR	
NARCISEN	Malka M		1887	Zmigrod	Zmigrod	Samuel		F		JR	
NARCISENFELD	Dawid				Zmigrod			M		JSS	Plaszow
NAUMAN	Nutek				Zmigrod			M		JG	
NAUTASCH	Ben Tzio				Zmigrod			M			Holocaust
NEBEL	Hersch			Zmigrod	Zmigrod			M		JR	
NEBEL	Rywa			Zmigrod	Zmigrod			F	Hersch	JR	

Yizkor Book of Nowy Zmigrod

Family name	First name(s)	Maiden name	Birth date	Birth place	Residence	Father	Mother	Gender	Spouse	Source	Remarks
NEBEL	Ben Tzio			Zmigrod	Zmigrod	Hersch	Rywa	M		JG	USA
NEBEL	Berl		1869	Zmigrod	Zmigrod			M		JR	
NEBEL	Mendel			Zmigrod	Zmigrod			M		JR	
NEBEL	Ester			Zmigrod	Zmigrod			F	Mendel	JR	
NEBEL	Moses		1867	Zmigrod	Zmigrod	Mendel	Ester	M		JG	
NEBEL	Rachel		1877	Zmigrod	Zmigrod			F	Hersch	JG	
NEBEL	Jacob			Zmigrod	Zmigrod			M		JR	
NEBEL	Sime E			Zmigrod	Zmigrod			F	Jacob	JR	
NEBEL	Benyamin		1869	Zmigrod	Zmigrod	Jacob	Sime Ester	M		JR	
NEBEL	Chiel		1872	Zmigrod	Zmigrod	Jacob	Sime Ester	M		JR	
NEBEL	Moses			Zmigrod	USA			M		YS	Holocaust
NEBEL	Leiser		1890	Zmigrod	Zmigrod	Hersh		M		JG	
NEBENZAHL	Hersh		1850	Zmigrod	Zmigrod			M		JG	USA
NEBENZAHL	Taube wife	GOTZLEN		Zmigrod	Zmigrod			F	Hersh	JG	
NEBENZAHL	Sender		1876	Zmigrod	Zmigrod	Hersh	Taube	M		JG	
NEBENZAHL	Bina			Zmigrod	Zmigrod	Hersh	Taube	M		JG	
NEBENZAHL	Hansche			Zmigrod	Zmigrod	Hersh	Taube	F		JG	
NEBENZAHL	Neche		1881	Zmigrod	Zmigrod	Hersh	Taube	F		JG	
NEBENZAHL	Chaskel		1882	Zmigrod	Zmigrod	Hersh	Taube	M		JR	died 1935
NEBENZAHL	Leib			Zmigrod	Zmigrod	Hersh	Taube	M		JG	
NEBENZAHL	Neche	BALSAM		Zmigrod	Zmigrod			F	Leib	JG	
NEBENZAHL	Josef		1887	Zmigrod	Zmigrod			M		JG	

Family name	First name(s)	Maiden name	Birth date	Birth place	Residence	Father	Mother	Gender	Spouse	Source	Remarks
NEBENZAHL	Josef		1904	Zmigrod	Zmigrod			M		BD	
NEBENZAHL	H				Zmigrod			M		JG	USA
NEBENZAHL	Malka		1871		Zmigrod			F		JG	USA
NESSLE	Mirla		1903	Zmigrod	Zmigrod			F		JG	USA
NESSLE	Mozko		1906	Zmigrod	Zmigrod			M		YA	
NESSLE	Esther		1895	Zmigrod		Avraham		F		JSS	Plaszow
NEUBAUER					Zmigrod			M		JSS	
NEUGER	Hersh Lei				Zmigrod			M		P	
NEULITZKER	Tema				Zmigrod			F		BD	
NEUMAN	Dawid		1914	Zmigrod	Zmigrod			M		JG	
NEUMAN	Noe			Zmigrod	Zmigrod			F		JG	
NEUMAN	Mascha	EICHNER		Zmigrod	Zmigrod			F		JG	
NEUMAN	Eliasz			Zmigrod	Zmigrod			M		JG	
NUSSBAUM	Sara	LANDAU		Zmigrod	Zmigrod			F	Eliasz	JG	
NUSSBAUM	Shimon L.			Zmigrod	Zmigrod			M		JG	
NUSSBAUM	Rochama	ENGLARD		Zmigrod	Zmigrod			F	Shimon L.	JG	
NUSSBAUM	Ryfka Cha		1932	Zmigrod	Zmigrod			F		JG	
NUSSBAUM	Shulim		1930	Zmigrod	Zmigrod			M		JG	
NUSSBAUM	Feiga		1873	Zmigrod	Zmigrod	Hirsch	Sara Ester	F		BD	
OCHWAT	Markus		1885	Zmigrod	Zmigrod			M		JG	
OCHWAT	Chaje		1887	Zmigrod	Zmigrod			F		JG	
OCHWAT	Hirsch			Zmigrod	Zmigrod			M		JG	
OCHWAT	Sara E	GREGER		Zmigrod	Zmigrod			F	Hirsch	JG	died 1942

Yizkor Book of Nowy Zmigrod

Family name	First name(s)	Maiden name	Birth date	Birth place	Residence	Father	Mother	Gender	Spouse	Source	Remarks
OCHWAT	L				Zmigrod			M		JSS	
OCHWAT	Eliezer				Zmigrod			M		P	
OCHWAT	Hersch			Zmigrod	Zmigrod			M		JG	
OCHWAT	Ester			Zmigrod	Zmigrod			F	Hersch	JR	
OCHWAT	Hendel		1869	Zmigrod	Zmigrod	Hersch	Ester	F		JR	
OCHWAT	Benjamin		1876	Zmigrod	Zmigrod	Hersch	Ester	M		JR	
ORGLER	Natan		1878	Zmigrod	Zmigrod			M		JG	USA
ORNSTEIN	Natan							M		P	
ORNSTEIN	Rachel	BERGER	1877	Zmigrod				F	Natan	P	
ORNSTEIN	Marcus					Natan	Rachel	M		P	
ORNSTEIN	Salomon		1871		Zmigrod			M		JG	USA
PACHTER	Isaac		1879	Zmigrod	Zmigrod			M		JR	
PACHTER	Sara C			Zmigrod	Zmigrod			F		JR	
PACHTER	Feige	TRACHMAN	1873		Zmigrod			F	Salomon	JG	USA
PACHTER	Naftuli		1908		Zmigrod	Salomon	Feige	M		JG	USA
PACHTER	Sara		1909		Zmigrod	Salomon	Feige	F		JG	USA
PACHTER	Wolf		1905		Zmigrod	Salomon	Feige	M		JG	USA
PACHTER	Schlomo		1892		Zmigrod			M		T	
PACHTER	Leibush				Zmigrod			M		P	
PACHTER	Nute				Zmigrod			M		YA	Holocaust
PARNESS	Yossef				Zmigrod			M		JSS	
PELLER	Breindel		1918		Zmigrod	Yossef		F		YA	Holocaust
PELLER	Jek		1913		Zmigrod	Yossef		M		JSS	Plaszow

Family name	First name(s)	Maiden name	Birth date	Birth place	Residence	Father	Mother	Gender	Spouse	Source	Remarks
PELLER	Szlomo		1913		Zmigrod	Yossef		M		JSS	Plaszow
PELLER	Chaim			Osiek	Zmigrod	Hersh		M		JSS	Plaszow
PELLER	Nachum			Osiek	Zmigrod	Hersh		M		YA	
PELLER	Izak				Zmigrod			M		JSS	
PELLER	Israel				Zmigrod			M		JSS	
PELLER	Gimpel				Zmigrod			M		JG	
PELLER	Leib			Zmigrod	Zmigrod			M		JG	
PENZAK	Maier			Zmigrod	Zmigrod			M		JR	
PENZAK	Reisel			Zmigrod	Zmigrod			F	Maier	JR	
PENZAK	Marjem		1869	Zmigrod	Zmigrod	Maier	Reisel	F		JR	
PENZAK	Rachel			Zmigrod	Zmigrod	Leib		F	Leib	JG	
PENZAK	Rywka			Zmigrod	Zmigrod	Leib	Rachel	F		T	
PENZAK	Lezer				Zmigrod			M		JG	USA
PFENIG	Moise		1876		Zmigrod			M		JG	USA
PHEFERBERG	Beile		1896		Zmigrod			F		JG	USA
PHEFERBERG	Shulem			Zmigrod	Zmigrod			M		JSS	Plaszow
PHEFFER	Lea			Zmigrod	Zmigrod			F	Shulem	P	Holocaust
PHEFFER	Leiser				Zmigrod			M		JG	USA
PHEFFER	Hermann		1870		Zmigrod			M		BD	
PHEFFER	Shlomo				Zmigrod			M		JSS	Plaszow
PHEFFER	Samuel		1882		Zmigrod			M		JG	
PIETEK	Majer		1877	Zmigrod	Zmigrod			M		JG	USA
PINCZOWSKI	Lina		1887		Zmigrod			F		JG	USA

Yizkor Book of Nowy Zmigrod

Family name	First name(s)	Maiden name	Birth date	Birth place	Residence	Father	Mother	Gender	Spouse	Source	Remarks
PINKAS	Jacob			Zmigrod	Zmigrod			M		JR	
PINKAS	Szyje		1879	Zmigrod	Zmigrod	Jacob		M		JR	
PLATNER	Bertrand			Zmigrod				M		JG	
POLIANSKI	Leibush		1887		Zmigrod			M		P	
PORETS	Shyje			Zmigrod	Zmigrod			M		JG	
POSTRUNG	Esther M wife b.15/11/18 84	STEICHER		Zmigrod	Zmigrod			F		JG	
POSTRUNG	Marjem		1882	Zmigrod	Zmigrod			F		JG	
POSTRUNG	Miszket		1884	Zmigrod	Zmigrod			M		JG	
POSTRUNG	Moshe M		1879	Zmigrod	Zmigrod			M		JG	
POSTRUNG	Sara D		1886	Zmigrod	Zmigrod			F		JSS	Plaszow
POSTRUNG	Chaskel			Zmigrod	Zmigrod			M		JSS	Plaszow
POSTRUNG	Bela			Zmigrod	Zmigrod			F		JG	
PRINTZ	Yaacov			Zmigrod	Zmigrod			M		JG	
RABI	Josef			Zmigrod	Zmigrod			M		JR	
RABI	Tzerel			Zmigrod	Zmigrod			F	Josef	JR	
RABI	Sara		1876	Zmigrod	Zmigrod	Josef	Tzerel	F		JR	
RABI	Jacob			Zmigrod	Zmigrod			M		JR	
RABI	Chaje			Zmigrod	Zmigrod			F	Jacob	JR	
RABI	Hersh			Zmigrod	Zmigrod	Jacob	Chaje	M		JG	
RABI	Fridka			Zmigrod	Zmigrod			F	Hersh son,head of JSS		

Yizkor Book of Nowy Zmigrod

Family name	First name(s)	Maiden name	Birth date	Birth place	Residence	Father	Mother	Gender	Spouse	Source	Remarks
RABI	Shmerek			Zmigrod	Zmigrod	Hersh son,head of JSS	Fridka	M		JG	
RABI	Yude			Zmigrod	Zmigrod	Hersh son,head of JSS	Fridka	M		JG	
RABI	Mojzes			Zmigrod	Zmigrod			M		JG	
RABI	Blume			Zmigrod	Zmigrod	Mojzes		F	Mojzes	JG	
RABI	Feiga		1879	Zmigrod	Zmigrod		Blume	F		YA	Holocaust
RABI	Yaakow		1872	Biecz	Zmigrod	Shulem		M		JG	USA
RABI	Franz		1884	Zmigrod	Zmigrod			M		JG	USA
RAFF	Jacob W		1888	Zmigrod	Zmigrod	Eisik		M		JG	USA
RAFF	Yetta	MEISNER		Zmigrod	Zmigrod			F	Jakob W	JG	USA
RAFF	Ida			Zmigrod	Zmigrod	Jakob W	Yetta	M		JG	USA
RAFF	Ike/Itzhak			Zmigrod	Zmigrod	Jakob W	Yetta	F		JG	USA
RAFF	Srul/J			Zmigrod	Zmigrod	Jakob W	Yetta			P	USA
RAFF	Itzhak			Zmigrod	Zmigrod			M		YA	
RAFF	Yozef		1898	Zmigrod	Zmigrod	Leibish		M		P	Holocaust
RAND	Ben Zio			Zmigrod	Zmigrod			M		JSS	Holocaust
RAPPOPORT	Sara			Zmigrod	Zmigrod	Ben Zion		F	Ben Zion	P	
RAPPOPORT	Moshe			Zmigrod	Zmigrod	Ben Zion	Sara	M		P	
RAPPOPORT	Yehezkel			Lodz	Zmigrod			M		JSS	
RAUL	Aron			Zmigrod	Zmigrod			M		JR	
RAUL	Yides			Zmigrod	Zmigrod			F	Aron	JR	
RAUL	Rachel		1869	Zmigrod	Zmigrod	Aron	Yides	F		JR	

Yizkor Book of Nowy Zmigrod

Family name	First name(s)	Maiden name	Birth date	Birth place	Residence	Father	Mother	Gender	Spouse	Source	Remarks
REDLICH	Scheindel			Lodz	Zmigrod			F	Yehezkel	JSS	
REDLICH	Szulim		1905	Lodz	Zmigrod	Yehezkel	Scheindel	M		JG	
REDLICH	B			Zmigrod	Zmigrod			M		JG	
REICH	Samuel H		1879	Zmigrod	Zmigrod	Samuel H		M		JR	
REICH	Leon			Zmigrod	Zmigrod			M		JR	
REICHMAN	Jozef			Zmigrod	Zmigrod			M		JR	
REICHMAN	Dwora			Zmigrod	Zmigrod			F	Jozef	JR	
REICHMAN	Naftali		1869	Zmigrod	Zmigrod	Jozef	Dwora	M		JR	
REICHMAN	Moses H		1871	Zmigrod	Zmigrod	Jozef	Dwora	M		JR	
REICHMAN	Pessel		1880	Zmigrod	Zmigrod	Jozef	Dwora	F		JR	
REICHMAN	Samuel		1881	Zmigrod	Zmigrod	Jozef	Dwora	M		JR	
REICHMAN	Efroim		1884	Zmigrod	Zmigrod	Jozef	Dwora	M		JR	
REICHMAN	Samuel H			Zmigrod	Zmigrod			M		JR	
REICHMAN	Fania		1882	Zmigrod	Zmigrod	Samuel H		F		JR	
REICHMAN	Sali		1877	Zmigrod	Zmigrod			F		JSS	
REICHMAN	A.				Zmigrod			M		JG	USA
REICHMAN	Helene		1873		Zmigrod			F		JG	USA
REICHMAN	Cilla		1894		Zmigrod			F		JG	USA
REICHMAN	Babeth		1896		Zmigrod			F		JG	USA
REICHMAN	Samuel		1897		Zmigrod			M		JSS	Plaszow
REICHMAN	Izkela			Lodz	Zmigrod			M		JSS	
REIDLICH	Scheindel			Lodz	Zmigrod			F		JSS	
REIDLICH	Schulem		1905	Lodz	Zmigrod	Izkela	Scheindel	M		YA	Holocaust

Yizkor Book of Nowy Zmigrod

Family name	First name(s)	Maiden name	Birth date	Birth place	Residence	Father	Mother	Gender	Spouse	Source	Remarks
REIDLICH	Mojze		1898		Zmigrod	Mordechai		M		YA	Holocaust
REINHOLTZ	Berisch			Zmigrod	Zmigrod			M		JR	
REINHOLTZ	Beile			Zmigrod	Zmigrod			F	Berisch	JR	
REINHOLTZ	Leje		1873	Zmigrod	Zmigrod	Berisch	Beile	F		JR	Holocaust
REISS	Basia			Zmigrod	Zmigrod	Henoch		F		JG	survived
REISS	Pavel				Zmigrod			M		JG	survived
REISS	Fula							F		JSS	
REISS	Naftali			Zmigrod	Zmigrod			M		JG	
RELIN	Aron			Zmigrod	Zmigrod			M		JR	
RELIN	Feige			Zmigrod	Zmigrod			F	Aron	JR	
RELIN	Eliasz		1876	Zmigrod	Zmigrod	Aron	Feige	M		JR	
RENDEL	Isaac			Zmigrod	Zmigrod			M		JR	
RENDEL	Feige			Zmigrod	Zmigrod			F	Isaac	JR	
RENDEL	Juda			Zmigrod	Zmigrod	Isaac	Feige	M		JR	
RETFELD	Marcus		1889	Zmigrod	Zmigrod			M		JG	
RETTIG	Wolf			Zmigrod	Zmigrod			M		JR	
RETTIG	Meilech		1888	Zmigrod	Zmigrod	Wolf		M		JG	
RETTIG	Shprincza			Zmigrod	Zmigrod			F		BD	
RIEMER	Gittel				Zmigrod			F		P	
RIEMER	Gershon				Zmigrod			M		P	
RIKEL	Gershon			Zmigrod	Zmigrod			M		JR	
RIKEL	Margalit			Zmigrod	Zmigrod			F	Gershon	JR	
RIKEL	Riwke		1869	Zmigrod	Zmigrod	Gershon	Margalit	F		JR	

Yizkor Book of Nowy Zmigrod

Family name	First name(s)	Maiden name	Birth date	Birth place	Residence	Father	Mother	Gender	Spouse	Source	Remarks
RIKEL	Leibisch		1872	Zmigrod	Zmigrod	Gershon	Margalit	M		JR	
RIMGEL	Stan				Zmigrod			M		JG	USA
RINGENBERG	Shimen		1871	Zmigrod	Zmigrod			M		JG	
ROSDEITCHER	Lipa			Zmigrod	Zmigrod			M		JG	
ROSENBERG	Beila	KESSLER		Zmigrod	Zmigrod			F	Lipa	BD	
ROSENBERG	Lipa			Zmigrod	Zmigrod			M		JG	USA
ROSENBERG	Michael			Zmigrod				M		JG	
ROSENBERG	Dawid			Zmigrod	Zmigrod			M		JG	
ROSENBLUT	David Leib		1867	Zmigrod	Zmigrod			M		JG	
ROSENHAM	Hersch			Zmigrod	Zmigrod			M		JR	
ROSENHAM	Bracha			Zmigrod	Zmigrod			F	Hersch	JR	
ROSENHAM	Dawid L		1867	Zmigrod	Zmigrod	Hersch	Bracha	M		JR	
ROSENHAM	Avraham			Zmigrod	Zmigrod			M		P	Holocaust
ROSENHAM	Yehudit			Zmigrod	Zmigrod			F	Avraham	P	Holocaust
ROSENHAM	Esther			Zmigrod	Zmigrod	Avraham	Yehudit	F		JG	
ROSENHAM	Riwka			Zmigrod	Zmigrod	Avraham	Yehudit	F		P	Holocaust
ROSENHAM	David A			Zmigrod	Zmigrod			M		P	Holocaust
ROSENHAM	Feiga			Zmigrod	Zmigrod	David Ari	Feiga	F	David A	P	Holocaust
ROSENHAN	Rivkah			Zmigrod	Zmigrod			F		JG	
ROSENHAN	Shmuel			Osiek	Zmigrod			M		JG	
ROSENHAN	Markus			Zmigrod	Zmigrod			M		JG	
ROSENHAN	Ruchla	HAUSNER		Zmigrod	Zmigrod			F	Markus	JSS	Plaszow
ROSENHAN	Dawid Y			Zmigrod				M			

Family name	First name(s)	Maiden name	Birth date	Birth place	Residence	Father	Mother	Gender	Spouse	Source	Remarks
ROSENHAN	Feiga			Zmigrod				F	Dawid Y		
ROSENHAN	Yossef			Zmigrod				M			
ROSENHAN	Chaim L				Zmigrod			M		JSS	Plaszow
ROSENHAN	Hersh L				Zmigrod			M		JSS	Plaszow
ROSENHAN	Markus D				Zmigrod			M		JSS	Plaszow
ROSENHAN	Szymon				Zmigrod			M		JSS	
ROSENHAN	Mania				Zmigrod			F		JSS	
ROSENHAN	Ana				Zmigrod			F		YA	Holocaust
ROSENHAN	Avram			Osiek	Zmigrod	Eliezer		M		YA	Holocaust
ROSENHAN	Haja		1917	Zmigrod	Zmigrod	Lewy		F		YA	Holocaust
ROSENHAN	Avraham			Osiek	Zmigrod			M		JSS	
ROSENHAN	Hershel		1918	Osiek	Zmigrod	Avraham		M		YA	Holocaust
ROSENHAN	Ita		1920	Osiek	Zmigrod	Avraham		M		YA	Holocaust
ROSENHAN	Rachel		1912	Osiek	Zmigrod	Avraham		F		YA	Holocaust
ROSENHAN	Rivka		1916	Osiek	Zmigrod	Avraham		F		JG	USA
ROSENHAN	Sara		1891		Zmigrod			F		JG	
ROSENHAN	Mindla		1886	Zmigrod	Zmigrod	Markus	Ruchla	F		YA	Auschwitz
ROSENTHAL	Chaim				Zmigrod			M			
ROSENTHAL	Ber			Zmigrod	Zmigrod			M		JR	
ROSENTHAL	Laje			Zmigrod	Zmigrod			F	Ber	JR	
ROSENTHAL	Ruchel		1876	Zmigrod	Zmigrod	Ber	Laje	F		JR	
ROSENTZWEIG	Lea	KURTZMAN		Zmigrod	Zmigrod	Chaim		F	Chaim		
ROSENTZWEIG	Bela		1926	Zmigrod	Zmigrod	Chaim	Lea	F		YA	Auschwitz

Yizkor Book of Nowy Zmigrod

Family name	First name(s)	Maiden name	Birth date	Birth place	Residence	Father	Mother	Gender	Spouse	Source	Remarks
ROSENTZWEIG	Lea		1895	Zmigrod	Zmigrod	Shmuel	Lea	F		YA	Auschwitz
ROSENTZWEIG	Simcha		1928	Zmigrod	Zmigrod	Chaim	Lea	M		JG	USA
ROSENTZWEIG	Chaim L				Zmigrod			M		P	
ROSENTZWEIG	Leon			Zmigrod				M		JG	USA
ROSNER	Aaron			Zmigrod				M		JSS	Plaszow
ROSNER	Israel			Zmigrod	Zmigrod			M		JSS	Plaszow
ROSNER	Moses D			Zmigrod	USA			M		JSS	USA
ROSNER	Yaacov			Zmigrod	USA			M		P	USA
ROSNER	Sabine				Zmigrod			F			
ROSNER	Ester				Zmigrod			F	Mordechai	BD	
ROSNER	M				Zmigrod			M		JG	
ROSNER	Chawa		1902	Zmigrod	Zmigrod			F		JG	
ROSNER	Israel		1889	Zmigrod	Zmigrod			M		JG	
ROSNER	Salomon		1867	Zmigrod	Zmigrod			M		JG	
ROSNER	Chaim		1884	Zmigrod	Zmigrod			M		JG	
ROSNER	Chaje Cz		1905	Zmigrod	Zmigrod			F		JG	
ROSNER	Feiga		1866	Zmigrod	Zmigrod			F		JG	
ROSNER	Freidel		1885	Zmigrod	Zmigrod			F		JG	
ROSNER	Hendel		1870	Zmigrod	Zmigrod			F		JG	
ROSNER	Israel		1889	Zmigrod	Zmigrod			M		JG	
ROSNER	Josef		1866	Zmigrod	Zmigrod			M		JG	
ROSNER	Lazar H		1889	Zmigrod	Zmigrod			M		JG	
ROSNER	Markus H			Zmigrod	Zmigrod			M		JG	

Family name	First name(s)	Maiden name	Birth date	Birth place	Residence	Father	Mother	Gender	Spouse	Source	Remarks
ROSNER	Baruch			Zmigrod	Zmigrod			M		JR	
ROSNER	Reisel			Zmigrod	Zmigrod			F	Baruch	JR	
ROSNER	Moses K		1870	Zmigrod	Zmigrod	Baruch	Reisel	M		JG	
ROSNER	Reisel		1887	Zmigrod	Zmigrod			F		JG	
ROSNER	Samuel		1895	Zmigrod	Zmigrod			M		P	
ROSNER	Froim			Zmigrod	Zmigrod			M		JG	
ROSNER	Yakow			Zmigrod	Zmigrod			M		BD	
ROSSLER	Isak			Zmigrod	Zmigrod			M		JSS	
ROTH	Hela			Zmigrod	Zmigrod			F		JG	
ROTH	Breindel		1880	Zmigrod	Zmigrod			F		JG	
ROTH	Marjem S		1878	Zmigrod	Zmigrod			F		JG	
ROTH	Meir			Zmigrod	Zmigrod			M		P	Holocaust
ROTHENBERG	Feitsche			Zmigrod	Zmigrod			F	Meir	P	Holocaust
ROTHENBERG	S				Zmigrod			M		JSS	Plaszow
ROTHENBERG	Chaim			Zmigrod	Zmigrod			M		JG	
RUBENFELD	Asher			Zmigrod	Zmigrod			M		YA	Auschwitz
RUBIN	Michael		1882	Zmigrod	Zmigrod	Avraham		M		JG	
RUBIN	Hannah			Zmigrod	Zmigrod			F		JG	
RUBINSTEIN	Haskel			Zmigrod	Zmigrod			M		JG	
SALOMON	Benjamin			Zmigrod	Zmigrod			M		JR	
SALOMON	Rachel		1885	Zmigrod	Zmigrod	Benjamin		F		JR	
SALZ	Esther	STECHER	1880	Zmigrod	Zmigrod	Hakel		F	Haskel	JG	
SALZ	Tillie		1877	Zmigrod	Zmigrod	Hakel	Esther	F		JG	

Yizkor Book of Nowy Zmigrod

Family name	First name(s)	Maiden name	Birth date	Birth place	Residence	Father	Mother	Gender	Spouse	Source	Remarks
SALZ	Leib			Zmigrod	Zmigrod			M		JG	
SAUER	Lieber			Zmigrod	Zmigrod			M		JG	
SCHACHNER	Lieber			Zmigrod	Zmigrod			M		JR	
SCHACHNER	Fride	FINDLING	1881	Zmigrod	Zmigrod	Lieber		F		JR	
SCHACHNER	Lea			Zmigrod	Zmigrod			F		JG	
SCHACHNER	Avrahan S		1879	Zmigrod	Zmigrod	Lieber	Lea	M		JG	
SCHACHNER	Yenta	BERGLASS		Zmigrod				F	Avrahan S	JG	
SCHACHNER	Itche		1881	Zmigrod	Zmigrod	Lieber	Lea	M		JG	
SCHACHNER	Chajem		1884	Zmigrod	Zmigrod	Lieber	Lea	M		JG	died 1951
SCHACHNER	Selig		1887	Zmigrod	Zmigrod	Lieber	Lea	M		JG	
SCHACHNER	Raisel L.	UNGER		Zmigrod	Zmigrod			F	Selig	JG	
SCHACHNER	Shprince		1889	Zmigrod	Zmigrod	Lieber	Lea	F		JG	
SCHACHNER	Moritz		1895	Zmigrod	Zmigrod	Lieber	Lea	M		JG	died 1958
SCHACHNER	Leon M		1920	Zmigrod	Zmigrod			M		JG	
SCHACHNER	Rosa	EISENBERG		Zmigrod	Zmigrod			F	Leon M	JG	
SCHACHNER	Rachel		1/1/18 85	Zmigrod	Zmigrod			F		JG	USA
SCHACHNER	Perl		1893		Zmigrod			F		JG	USA
SCHACHNER	Baruch		1892		Zmigrod			M		JG	USA
SCHACHNER	Lina		1905		Zmigrod			F		JG	USA
SCHACHNER	Anna		1896		Zmigrod			F		JG	
SCHACHNER	Aaron			Zmigrod	Zmigrod			M		JG	
SCHAKER	Yettte	TRACHMAN		Zmigrod	Zmigrod			F		JSS	

Yizkor Book of Nowy Zmigrod

Family name	First name(s)	Maiden name	Birth date	Birth place	Residence	Father	Mother	Gender	Spouse	Source	Remarks
SCHAKER	Chaim			Zmigrod	Zmigrod			M		JSS	
SCHEINDLINGER	Chana			Zmigrod	Zmigrod			F	Chaim	JSS	Plaszow
SCHEINDLINGER	Izak		1913	Zmigrod	Zmigrod	Chaim	Chana	M		JSS	Plaszow
SCHEINDLINGER	Moses				Zmigrod			M		JSS	Plaszow
SCHEINDLINGER	Naftali				Zmigrod			M		JSS	
SCHEINDLINGER	Elenski				Zmigrod			F		BD	
SCHENK					Zmigrod			M		JG	USA
SCHERER	Sara		1896		Zmigrod			F		JG	USA
SCHERER	Oscar				Zmigrod			M		JG	
SCHERER	Chana R			Zmigrod	Zmigrod			F		JG	
SCHERER	Josef			Zmigrod	Zmigrod			M		JG	
SCHERER	Feiga	HABER		Zmigrod	Zmigrod			F		JG	
SCHERER	Szymon		1922	Zmigrod	Zmigrod			M		YA	
SCHERER	Itzhak				Zmigrod			M		P	
SCHIFF	Feivil			Zmigrod	Zmigrod			M		JR	
SCHIFF	Michael		1887	Zmigrod	Zmigrod	Feivil		M		JR	
SCHIFF	Aaron		1880	Zmigrod	Zmigrod	Shragai		M		JG	Holocaust
SCHIFF	Getzil			Zmigrod	Zmigrod			M		P	Holocaust
SCHIFF	Blumah			Zmigrod	Zmigrod			F	Getzil	P	Holocaust
SCHIFF	Malka Gross			Zmigrod	Zmigrod			F		JG	
SCHIFF	Samuel		1883	Zmigrod	Zmigrod			M		P	
SCHIFF	Samuel		1879	Zmigrod	Zmigrod			M		JG	
SCHIFF	Sheinedl		1869	Zmigrod	Zmigrod			F		T	

Yizkor Book of Nowy Zmigrod

Family name	First name(s)	Maiden name	Birth date	Birth place	Residence	Father	Mother	Gender	Spouse	Source	Remarks
SCHIFF	Dawid				Zmigrod			M		JSS	Plaszow
SCHIFF	Sheindil			Zmigrod	Zmigrod			F	Dawid	JR	
SCHIFF	Taube L		1889	Zmigrod	Zmigrod	Dawid	Sheindil	F		JR	
SCHIFF	Getzil				Zmigrod			M		P	
SCHIFF	Hershel		1896		Zmigrod			M		JSS	Plaszow
SCHILDWACH	Moses				Zmigrod			M		JSS	
SCHILDWACH	Henoch				Zmigrod			M		YA	Holocaust
SCHILDWACH	Lea				Zmigrod			F		YA	Auschwitz
SCHILDWACH	Ester		1895	Zmigrod	Zmigrod	Benjamin		F		JG	Holocaust
SCHIPS	Wolf		1889	Zmigrod	Zmigrod	Benjamin		M		BD	Holocaust
SCHIPS	Rachla		1879	Zmigrod	Zmigrod			F		BD	
SCHLEICHER	L				Zmigrod			M		JG	
SCHLOSS	Schja				Zmigrod			M		JG	USA
SCHLOSS	Salomon		1888	Zmigrod	Zmigrod			M		JG	
SCHLOSS	Chaim F			Zmigrod	Zmigrod			M		JR	
SCHLOSS	Berl		1884	Zmigrod	Zmigrod	Chaim Fishel		M		JR	
SCHLOSS	Juda			Zmigrod	Zmigrod			M		JR	
SCHLOSS	Leib W		1887		Zmigrod	Juda		M		P	
SCHLOSS	Israel		1893		Zmigrod			M		JG	
SCHMIEL	Fraidel		1888	Zmigrod	Zmigrod			F		JG	
SCHMIER	Isaac			Zmigrod	Zmigrod			M		JG	
SCHMIER	Ryfka			Zmigrod	Zmigrod			F	Isaac	JG	

Yizkor Book of Nowy Zmigrod

Family name	First name(s)	Maiden name	Birth date	Birth place	Residence	Father	Mother	Gender	Spouse	Source	Remarks
SCHMIER	Berta			Zmigrod	Zmigrod	Isaac	Ryfka	F		JG	
SCHMIER	Moses			Zmigrod	Zmigrod	Isaac	Ryfka	M		JG	
SCHMIER	Brucha			Zmigrod	Zmigrod	Isaac	Ryfka	F		JG	
SCHMIER	Mechel		1879	Zmigrod	Zmigrod			M		JG	
SCHMIER	Mojzes			Zmigrod	Zmigrod			M		JG	
SCHMIER	Frieda			Zmigrod	Zmigrod			F	Mojzes	JSS	Plaszow
SCHMIER	Fradel		1888	Zmigrod	Zmigrod			F		JG	
SCHMIER	Abraham				Zmigrod			M		JG	
SCHMIER	Efroim				Zmigrod			M		JSS	Plaszow
SCHMIER	Chana			Zmigrod	Zmigrod			F	Efroim	JSS	Plaszow
SCHMIER	Jakub		1905	Zmigrod	Zmigrod	Efroim	Chana	M		JSS	
SCHMIER	Natan			Zmigrod	Zmigrod			M		YA	Holocaust
SCHMIER	Zlata			Zmigrod	Zmigrod			F		YA	Holocaust
SCHMIER	Berl		1881	Zmigrod	Zmigrod	Izak		M		YA	Holocaust
SCHMIRER	Dawid		1924	Zmigrod	Zmigrod	Hersh		M		YA	Holocaust
SCHON	Asher			Zmigrod	Zmigrod			M		JR	
SCHON	Hinde		1878	Zmigrod	Zmigrod	Asher		F		JR	
SCHONFELD	Asher			Zmigrod	Zmigrod			M		JR	
SCHONFELD	Breindel			Zmigrod	Zmigrod			F	Asher	JR	
SCHONFELD	Hirsch		1872	Zmigrod	Zmigrod	Asher	Breindel	M		JR	
SCHOENWETTER	Moses			Zmigrod	Zmigrod			M		JR	
SCHOENWETTER	Sara			Zmigrod	Zmigrod			F	Moses	JR	

Yizkor Book of Nowy Zmigrod

Family name	First name(s)	Maiden name	Birth date	Birth place	Residence	Father	Mother	Gender	Spouse	Source	Remarks
SCHOENWETTER	Ester		1873	Zmigrod	Zmigrod	Moses	Sara	F		JR	
SCHOENWETTER	Szyje		1876	Zmigrod	Zmigrod	Moses	Sara	M		JR	
SCHOENWETTER	Herman			Zmigrod	Zmigrod	Shulem		M		YA	Holocaust
SCHOENWETTER	Pepi		1926	Zmigrod	Zmigrod	Hersh		F		BD	
SCHOENWETTER	Esther		1877	Zmigrod	Zmigrod			F		JG	
SCHOENWETTER	Hersh			Zmigrod	Zmigrod			M		T	
SCHOENWETTER	Shulem			Zmigrod	Zmigrod			M		JG	
SCHOENWETTER	Zwi		1900	Zmigrod	Zmigrod	Shulem		M		BD	
SCHONWETTER	Abraham			Zmigrod				M		JG	
SCHOENWETTER	Golda	GALANTY	1902	Zmigrod	Zmigrod	Arieh	Matel	F	Abraham	YA	Holocaust
SCHOENWETTER	Rosa			Zmigrod		Abraham	Golda	F		JG	
SCHOENWETTER	Anna			Zmigrod	Zmigrod	Abraham	Golda	F		JSS	Plaszow
SCHOENWETTER	Yossel Daw			Zmigrod	Zmigrod			M		P	
SCHOENWETTER	Henry				Zmigrod			M		JSS	Plaszow
SCHONWETTER	Dora		1892	Zmigrod	Zmigrod			F		JSS	Plaszow

Yizkor Book of Nowy Zmigrod

Family name	First name(s)	Maiden name	Birth date	Birth place	Residence	Father	Mother	Gender	Spouse	Source	Remarks
SCHREIBER	Jakob				Zmigrod			M		T	
SCHREINER	Abraham				Zmigrod			M		JSS	Plaszow
SCHREINER	Moshe				Zmigrod			M		JSS	
SCHTRENGER	Hersz			Zmigrod	Zmigrod			M		JSS	Plaszow
SCHUMANN	Hersz				Zmigrod			M		JG	USA
SCHUMANN	Dora				Zmigrod			F		JG	USA
SCHUMANN	Schubin		1865		Zmigrod			M		JG	USA
SCHUMANN	Gittel		1900		Zmigrod			F		JG	USA
SCHUMANN	Moishe		1904		Zmigrod			M		JG	USA
SCHUMANN	Ettie		1892		Zmigrod			F		JG	USA
SCHUMANN	Schewa		1898		Zmigrod			F		JG	USA
SCHUMANN	Pincus		1902		Zmigrod			M		JG	USA
SCHUMANN	Moshe			Zmigrod	Zmigrod			M		JG	
SCHWALB	Salomon			Zmigrod	USA	Landsma nschaft in NY		M		JG	
SCHWINGER	Wolf		1886	Zmigrod	Zmigrod			M		YA	
SEEMAN	Aron Ber			Zmigrod	Zmigrod			M		JR	
SEEMAN	Beile			Zmigrod	Zmigrod	Aron Ber		F		JR	
SEGE	Rachel		1887	Zmigrod	Zmigrod			F		BD	
SEGINER	Chawa		1877	Zmigrod	Zmigrod	Shmul		F		JSS	Plaszow
SEGNER	D				Zmigrod			M		JG	
SEGNER	Josef				Zmigrod			M		JG	
SEILER	Hinda				Zmigrod			F		JG	

Yizkor Book of Nowy Zmigrod

Family name	First name(s)	Maiden name	Birth date	Birth place	Residence	Father	Mother	Gender	Spouse	Source	Remarks
SEKLER	Efraim				Zmigrod			M		P	
SHAMIR	Lea			Zmigrod	Zmigrod			F		JG	
SHAMIR	Mendel				Zmigrod			M		P	
SHAPIRO	Hersh			Zmigrod	Zmigrod			M		BD	
SHTARK	Chaim				Zmigrod			M		P	
SHTARK	Yehezkel				Zmigrod			M		P	
SHTARK	Moshe			Zmigrod	Zmigrod			M		WS	USA
SHTRENGER	Berish				Zmigrod			M		P	
SHTRENGER	Lucia			Zmigrod	Zmigrod	Yossef		F		YA	Holocaust
SHTRENGER	Marilka			Zmigrod	Zmigrod	Yossef		F		YA	Holocaust
SHTRENGER	Nina			Dukla	Zmigrod	Chanah		F		JSS	
SHTRENGER	Renia			Zmigrod	Zmigrod	Yossef		F		YA	
SHTRENGER	Josef				Zmigrod			M		JSS	
SHTRENGER	Salomon				Zmigrod			M		JSS	Plaszow
SILBER	Ruchel		1891		Zmigrod			F		JSS	Plaszow
SILBER	Markus		1905		Zmigrod			M		YA	
SILBERMAN	Salomon				Zmigrod			M		YA	
SILBERMAN	Chana		1890	Zmigrod	Germany	Pinhas		F		YA	Holocaust
SINDEL	Yulius		1887	Zmigrod	Germany	Pinhas		M		JG	Holocaust
SINDEL	Gitel		1897	Zmigrod	Germany	Itzhak		F		JG	Holocaust
SINGER	Freidel		1883	Zmigrod	Zmigrod			F		JG	died 1828
SKIDWERTS	Shmelke			Zmigrod	Zmigrod			M		JSS	
SKIDWERTS	Wolf			Zmigrod	Zmigrod			M		JSS	Plaszow

Yizkor Book of Nowy Zmigrod

Family name	First name(s)	Maiden name	Birth date	Birth place	Residence	Father	Mother	Gender	Spouse	Source	Remarks
SKIDWERTS	Nussen			Lodz	Zmigrod			M		JSS	
SMIETANA	Zlaty			Lodz	Zmigrod			F		JSS	
SMIETANA	Icek		1898	Lodz	Zmigrod			M		JSS	Plaszow
SMIETANA	L.				Zmigrod			M		JG	USA
SMIETANA	Izak		1898	Lodz	Zmigrod	Nusen		M		JG	USA
SMIETANA	Dawid			Zmigrod			Zlaty	M		JSS	
SOBOL	Rose			Zmigrod				F		JG	USA
SOBOL	Israel				Zmigrod			M		JG	USA
SOMMER	Menahem			Zmigrod	Zmigrod			M		P	Holocaust
SPATZ	Hawa			Zmigrod	Zmigrod			F	Menahem	P	Holocaust
SPATZ	Isak		1886		Zmigrod			M		JG	USA
SPEILVOGEL	Samuel		1883		Zmigrod			M		BD	
SPEILVOGEL	Sheincze		1877		Zmigrod			F		YA	
SPEILVOGEL	L				Zmigrod			M		YA	Holocaust
SPERLING	Shmuel Y			Zmigrod	Zmigrod			M		JR	
SPERLING	Lenora		1881	Zmigrod	Zmigrod	Shmuel Y		F		JR	
SPERLING	Samuel			Zmigrod	Zmigrod			M		JR	
SPERLING	Hendel			Zmigrod	Zmigrod	Samuel		F		JR	
SPERLING	Schmiel			Zmigrod	Zmigrod			M		JR	
SPERLING	Gittel			Zmigrod	Zmigrod			F	Schmiel	JR	
SPERLING	Sara		1873	Zmigrod	Zmigrod	Schmiel	Gittel	F		JR	
SPERLING	Dawid		1885	Zmigrod		Shmerl		M		JG	USA
SPERLING	Dawid		1872	Zmigrod		Shmerl		M		JG	

Yizkor Book of Nowy Zmigrod

Family name	First name(s)	Maiden name	Birth date	Birth place	Residence	Father	Mother	Gender	Spouse	Source	Remarks
SPERLING	Berish		1884	Zmigrod	Zmigrod			M		JG	
SPERLING	Chaje G		1879	Zmigrod	Zmigrod			F		JG	
SPERLING	Freudel		1885	Zmigrod	Zmigrod			F		JG	
SPERLING	Matel		1878	Zmigrod	Zmigrod			F		JG	
SPERLING	Rachel		1881	Zmigrod	Zmigrod			F		YA	
SPERLING	Samuel		1921	Zmigrod	Zmigrod			M		JG	
SPIERER	Yechiel		1889	Zmigrod		Avraham		M		JG	
SPINER	Chaim			Zmigrod	Zmigrod			M		JR	
SPINER	Hicel			Zmigrod	Zmigrod			F	Chaim	JR	
SPINER	Dawid J		1871	Zmigrod	Zmigrod	Chaim	Hicel	M		JR	
SPIRA	Schyje			Zmigrod	Zmigrod			M		JR	
SPIRA	Roze		1866	Zmigrod	Zmigrod			F	Schyje	JR	
SPIRA	Feige			Zmigrod	Zmigrod	Schyje	Roze	F		JR	
SPIRA	Avraham			Zmigrod	Zmigrod			M		JG	
SPIRA	Chiel			Zmigrod	Zmigrod			M		JG	
SPIRA	Sara	LESER		Zmigrod	Zmigrod			F	Chiel	JG	
SPIRA	Haskel		1914	Zmigrod	Zmigrod	Chiel	Sara	M		JG	
SPIRA	Feige		1866	Zmigrod	Zmigrod			F		JG	
SPIRA	Hersch			Zmigrod	Zmigrod			M		JG	
SPIRA	Chaje	RABER		Zmigrod	Zmigrod			F	Hersch	JG	
SPIRA	Race		1882	Zmigrod	Zmigrod	Hersch	Chaje	F		JG	
SPIRA	Markus L		1884	Zmigrod	Zmigrod	Hersch	Chaje	M		JG	
SPIRA	Josef			Zmigrod	Zmigrod			M		JG	

Family name	First name(s)	Maiden name	Birth date	Birth place	Residence	Father	Mother	Gender	Spouse	Source	Remarks
SPIRA	Niche	REK		Zmigrod	Zmigrod			F	Josef	JG	
SPIRA	Dwore		1881	Zmigrod	Zmigrod	Josef	Niche	F		JG	
SPIRA	Braindel		1885	Zmigrod	Zmigrod	Josef	Niche	F		JG	
SPIRA	Markus		1888	Zmigrod	Zmigrod	Josef	Niche	M		JG	
SPIRA	Itta		1889	Zmigrod	Zmigrod	Josef	Niche	F		JG	
SPIRA	Moses			Zmigrod	Zmigrod			M		JG	
SPIRA	Blume	KURZMAN		Zmigrod	Zmigrod			F	Moses	JG	
SPIRA	Leib		1883	Zmigrod	Zmigrod	Moses	Blume	M		JG	
SPIRA	Zlate		1884	Zmigrod	Zmigrod	Moses	Blume	F		JG	
SPIRA	Wolf		1884	Zmigrod	Zmigrod			M		JG	
SPIRA	Esther			Zmigrod	Zmigrod			F		JG	
SPIRA	Mendel H		1886	Zmigrod	Zmigrod			M		BD	
SPIRA	Yocheved			Zmigrod	Zmigrod			F		BD	
SPIRA	M				Zmigrod			M		JG	USA
SPRIA	Mozes				Zmigrod			M		JG	
SPRINGER	Isak		1892		Zmigrod			M		JG	
SPRINGER	Sische		1886	Zmigrod	Zmigrod			M		JSS	
SPRINGER	Wolf		1882	Zmigrod	Zmigrod			M		JSS	
SPRINGER	Markus			Osiek	Zmigrod			M		JSS	Plaszow
STADTFELD	Peril			Osiek	Zmigrod			F	Markus	JG	
STADTFELD	Pinkas		1898	Osiek	Zmigrod	Markus	Peril	M		JG	
STADTFELD	Sheindel	GETZ			Zmigrod			F		BD	
STECHER	Izrael				Zmigrod			M		JG	USA

Yizkor Book of Nowy Zmigrod

Family name	First name(s)	Maiden name	Birth date	Birth place	Residence	Father	Mother	Gender	Spouse	Source	Remarks
STECHER	L				Zmigrod			M		JG	
STECHER	Chaim				Zmigrod			M		JG	
STECHER	Chana			Zmigrod	Zmigrod			F		JG	
STECHER	Aron			Zmigrod	Zmigrod			M		JG	
STECHER	Reisel	PESSEL	1869	Zmigrod	Zmigrod			F	Aron	JG	
STECHER	Etta			Zmigrod	Zmigrod	Aron	Reisel	F		JG	
STECHER	Esriel			Zmigrod	Zmigrod			M		JG	
STECHER	Feige	OCHWAT		Zmigrod	Zmigrod	Esriel		F	Esriel	JG	
STECHER	Hersch		1904	Zmigrod	Zmigrod	Esriel	Feige	M		JG	
STECHER	Bruche	WEINBERGER	1903	Zmigrod	Zmigrod	Hersch		F	Hersch	JG	
STECHER	Leie		1929	Zmigrod	Zmigrod	Hersch	Bruche	F		JG	
STECHER	Erna		1930	Zmigrod	Zmigrod	Hersch	Bruche	F		JG	survived
STECHER	Feiga	OCHWET		Zmigrod	Zmigrod			F		JG	survived
STECHER	Hersch			Zmigrod	Zmigrod			M		JG	
STECHER	Rachel	LAKS		Zmigrod	Zmigrod			F	Hersh	JG	
STECHER	Chaje G		1871	Zmigrod	Zmigrod	Hersh	Rachel	F		JG	
STECHER	Chajem		1885	Zmigrod	Zmigrod	Hersh	Rachel	M		JG	
STECHER	Dwore S		1888	Zmigrod	Zmigrod	Hersh	Rachel	F		JG	
STECHER	Hersch			Zmigrod	Zmigrod			M		JG	
STECHER	Pesche	SCHUSS		Zmigrod	Zmigrod			F	Hersch	JG	
STECHER	Chajem		1885	Zmigrod	Zmigrod	Hersch	Pesche	M		JR	
STECHER	Samuel		1886	Zmigrod	Zmigrod	Hersch	Pesche	M		JG	survived
STECHER	Tzwi			Zmigrod	Zmigrod			M		P	Holocaust

Family name	First name(s)	Maiden name	Birth date	Birth place	Residence	Father	Mother	Gender	Spouse	Source	Remarks
STECHER	Brucha	WEINBERGER		Zmigrod	Zmigrod			F	Tzwi	P	Holocaust
STECHER	Erna		1938	Zmigrod	Zmigrod	Leib	Brucha	F		JG	
STECHER	Leje		1912	Zmigrod	Zmigrod	Leib	Brucha	F		JG	
STECHER	Leib			Zmigrod	Zmigrod			M		JG	
STECHER	Golde	TRACHMAN		Zmigrod	Zmigrod	Leib		F	Leib	JG	
STECHER	Taube		1877	Zmigrod	Zmigrod	Leib	Golde	F		JG	
STECHER	Samuel		1879	Zmigrod	Zmigrod	Leib	Golde	M		JG	
STECHER	Esther		1881	Zmigrod	Zmigrod	Leib	Golde	F		JG	USA
STECHER	Malka		1881	Zmigrod	Zmigrod	Leib	Golde	F		JG	USA
STECHER	Gittel		Jul-83	Zmigrod		Leib	Golde	F		JG	USA
STECHER	Izzie		Apr-92	Zmigrod		Leib	Golde	M		JG	
STECHER	Hersh		1896	Zmigrod	Zmigrod	Leib	Golde	M		JG	
STECHER	Selde		1884	Zmigrod	Zmigrod	Leib	Golde	F		JG	
STECHER	Eisig		1882	Zmigrod	Zmigrod	Leib	Golde	M		JG	
STECHER	Reuven		1895	Zmigrod	Zmigrod	Leib	Golde	M		JG	
STECHER	Mindel			Zmigrod	Zmigrod	Leib	Golde	F		JG	
STECHER	Naftali J			Zmigrod	Zmigrod	Leib	Golde	M		JG	
STECHER	Minnie			Zmigrod	Zmigrod	Leib	Golde	F		JG	
STECHER	Mayer			Zmigrod	Zmigrod			M		JG	
STECHER	Chaje			Zmigrod	Zmigrod		Chaje	F	Mayer	JG	
STECHER	Ester		1869	Zmigrod	Zmigrod	Mayer		F		JG	
STECHER	Moses			Zmigrod	Zmigrod			M			
STECHER	Chaye			Zmigrod	Zmigrod			F	Moses		

Yizkor Book of Nowy Zmigrod

Family name	First name(s)	Maiden name	Birth date	Birth place	Residence	Father	Mother	Gender	Spouse	Source	Remarks
STECHER	Chaim		1871	Zmigrod	Zmigrod	Moses	Chaje	M		JG	
STECHER	Nathan			Zmigrod	Zmigrod			M		JG	
STECHER	Reisel		1882	Zmigrod	Zmigrod			F		JG	
STECHER	Sch.		1867	Zmigrod	Zmigrod			M		JG	
STECHER	Seinwel			Zmigrod	Zmigrod			M		JG	
STECHER	Gittel	ALSTER		Zmigrod	Zmigrod			F	Seinwel	JG	
STECHER	Moses		1886	Zmigrod	Zmigrod	Seinwel	Gittel	M		JG	USA
STECHER	Josef M		1889	Zmigrod	Zmigrod	Seinwel	Gittel	M		JG	USA
STECHER	Emanuel			Zmigrod	Zmigrod			F		JG	
STECKLER	Gussie			Zmigrod	Zmigrod			F		JG	
STECKLER	Arje		1867	Zmigrod	Zmigrod			M		JG	
STEIN	Moses S			Zmigrod	Zmigrod			M		JR	
STEIN	Mazal			Zmigrod	Zmigrod			F	Moses S	JR	
STEIN	Chaim A		1871	Zmigrod	Zmigrod	Moses S	Mazal	M		JR	
STEIN	Chiel		1876	Zmigrod	Zmigrod	Moses S	Mazal	M		JR	
STEIN	Hersch			Zmigrod	Zmigrod			M		JR	
STEIN	Hene			Zmigrod	Zmigrod			F	Hersch	JR	
STEIN	Marjem		1876	Zmigrod	Zmigrod	Hersch	Hene	F		JR	
STEIN	David			Zmigrod	Zmigrod			M		JG	
STEIN	Gittel		1882	Zmigrod	Zmigrod			F		JG	
STEIN	Miskat		1882	Zmigrod	Zmigrod			M		YS	Holocaust
STEIN	Reisla		1915	Zmigrod	Zmigrod			F		YA	Holocaust
STEIN	Adele			Zmigrod	Zmigrod	Naphtali		F		JG	USA

Family name	First name(s)	Maiden name	Birth date	Birth place	Residence	Father	Mother	Gender	Spouse	Source	Remarks
STEIN	Michael		1882	Zmigrod	Zmigrod	Avraham		M		JSS	Holocaust
STEIN	Luis			Zmigrod	USA			M		JG	
STEIN	Sala				Zmigrod			F		JG	
STEIN	Lisa							F		BD	
STEIN	Yehuda				Zmigrod			M		P	
STEIN	Fishel			Zmigrod	Zmigrod			M		JG	
STEINBAU	Chaim			Zmigrod	Jaslo					R	
STEINHAUS					Zmigrod			M		JG	
STENGER	Samuel J.		1884	Zmigrod	Zmigrod			M		JG	
STERBRECHER	Asher			Zmigrod	Zmigrod			M		P	
STERN	Moszes			Zmigrod	Zmigrod			M		JR	
STERN	Beile		1881	Zmigrod	Zmigrod	Moszes		F		JR	
STERN	Genia			Zmigrod	Zmigrod			F		JG	USA
STERN	Perla			Zmigrod	Zmigrod			F		JG	USA
STERN	Regina		1883		Zmigrod			F		JG	USA
STERN	Golda		1903		Zmigrod			F		BD	
STERN	Henie		1893		Zmigrod			F		JG	
STERTZER	G				Zmigrod			M		JG	
STOCKER	Sheindel		1887	Zmigrod	Zmigrod			M		YA	Holocaust
STRE	Moses		1887	Zmigrod	Zmigrod			F		YA	Holocaust
STRE	Berl		1872	Zmigrod		Nathan		M		JSS	
STRENGER	Salomon N			Zmigrod	Zmigrod			M		JR	
STRENGER			1886	Zmigrod	Zmigrod			M		JR	

Yizkor Book of Nowy Zmigrod

Family name	First name(s)	Maiden name	Birth date	Birth place	Residence	Father	Mother	Gender	Spouse	Source	Remarks
STRUL	Abraham			Lodz				M		JSS	Plaszow
STRYCHARZ	Yenty	TANOMANI		Lodz				F	Abraham	JSS	Plaszow
STRYCHARZ	Eliasz		1904	Lodz	Zmigrod	Abraham	Yenty	M		JSS	Plaszow
STRYCHARZ	Moses		1904		Zmigrod			M		JSS	Plaszow
STRYCHARZ	Rosa				Zmigrod			F		YA	Holocaust
STRYCHARZ	Elias				Zmigrod			M		YA	Holocaust
STRYCHOWER	Rachel				Zmigrod			F		JG	
SUEDWERT	Shmelke							M		P	
SUEDWERT	Leje	BERGER	1877	Zmigrod				F	Shmelke	P	
SUEDWERT	Abraham		1880			Shmelke	Leje	M		P	
SUEDWERT	Zacharai H					Shmelke	Leje	M		P	
SUEDWERT	Chana		1897		Zmigrod	Nute		F		YA	Holocaust
SZAMIR	Dow		1906		Korczyna	Moshe		M		YA	Holocaust
SZAMIR	Efraim		1897		Zmigrod	Itzhak		M		YA	Holocaust
SZAMIR	Nute		1922		Zmigrod	Ephraim		M		YA	Holocaust
SZAMIR	Szalom		1908		Zmigrod	Moshe		M		JSS	Holocaust
SZAMIR	Zlata		1920		Zmigrod	Ephraim		F		YA	Holocaust
SZAMIR	Tobias				Zmigrod			M		YA	Holocaust
SZAMIR	Moshe Tz				Zmigrod			M		YA	
SZAMIR	Gittel				Zmigrod			F	Moshe T	YA	
SZAMIR	Lea				Zmigrod	Moshe Ti	Gittel	F		YA	
SZCZYGLASKI	Nachman		1910		Zmigrod	Yaakow		M		JG	
SZTERN	Rachel		1912		Zmigrod	Yaakow		F		JG	

Family name	First name(s)	Maiden name	Birth date	Birth place	Residence	Father	Mother	Gender	Spouse	Source	Remarks
SZTERN	Meir Leib				Zmigrod			M		P	
TABIZEL	Leibish			Zmigrod	Zmigrod			M		JG	
TAUB	Baruch			Zmigrod	Zmigrod			M		P	Holocaust
TEITELBAUM	Yekel			Zmigrod	Zmigrod			M		JR	
TEITELBAUM	Yosef G		1887	Zmigrod	Zmigrod			M		JR	
TELLER	Sarah			Zmigrod	Zmigrod			F	Baruch	P	Holocaust
TELLER	Rachel			Zmigrod	Zmigrod	Baruch	Sarah	F		P	Holocaust
TELLER	Yaacov			Zmigrod	Zmigrod	Baruch	Sarah	M		P	Holocaust
TELLER	Genia		1895	Zmigrod	Zmigrod			F		JG	
TENCZER	Ben Tzion			Zmigrod	Zmigrod			M		JG	
TIER	Chaja			Zmigrod	Zmigrod			F		P	
TIER	Chaim			Zmigrod	Zmigrod			M		JG	
THALER	Meilech			Zmigrod	Zmigrod			M		JR	
THALER	Hudes			Zmigrod	Zmigrod			F	Meilech	JR	
THALER	Tobe		1869	Zmigrod	Zmigrod	Meilech	Hudes	F		JR	
TRACHMAN	Chaje	LANG		Zmigrod	Zmigrod			F	Chaim		
TRACHMAN	Dewora		1878	Zmigrod	Zmigrod	Chaim	Chaje	F		JG	
TRACHMAN	Braindel		1880	Zmigrod	Zmigrod	Chaim	Chaje	F		JG	
TRACHMAN	Markus		1883	Zmigrod	Zmigrod	Chaim	Chaje	M		JG	
TRACHMAN	Sender		1888	Zmigrod	Zmigrod	Chaim	Chaje	M		JG	
TRACHMAN	Eisig			Zmigrod	Zmigrod			M		JG	
TRACHMAN	Breindel			Zmigrod	Zmigrod			F	Eisig	JG	
TRACHMAN	Chana S		1872	Zmigrod	Zmigrod	Eisig	Breindel	F		JG	

Yizkor Book of Nowy Zmigrod

Family name	First name(s)	Maiden name	Birth date	Birth place	Residence	Father	Mother	Gender	Spouse	Source	Remarks
TRACHMAN	Chaim		1886	Zmigrod	Zmigrod	Eisig	Breindel	M		JG	
TRACHMAN	Hersch			Zmigrod	Zmigrod			F	Hersch	JG	
TRACHMAN	Leie			Zmigrod	Zmigrod			F		JG	
TRACHMAN	Simche		1869	Zmigrod	Zmigrod	Hersch	Leie	M		JG	
TRACHMAN	Isaak			Zmigrod	Zmigrod			M		JG	
TRACHMAN	Ester			Zmigrod	Zmigrod			F	Isaak	JG	
TRACHMAN	Pincas		1875	Zmigrod	Zmigrod	Isaak	Ester	M		JG	
TRACHMAN	Josef			Zmigrod	Zmigrod			M		JG	
TRACHMAN	Marjem			Zmigrod	Zmigrod			F	Josef	JG	
TRACHMAN	Selde		1868	Zmigrod	Zmigrod	Josef	Marjem	F		JG	
TRACHMAN	Chaje Sara		1869	Zmigrod	Zmigrod	Josef	Marjem	F		JG	
TRACHMAN	Chiel		1872	Zmigrod	Zmigrod	Josef	Marjem	M		JG	
TRACHMAN	Leib			Zmigrod	Zmigrod			M		JG	
TRACHMAN	Moses I			Zmigrod	Zmigrod			M		JG	
TRACHMAN	Schifre	FELS		Zmigrod	Zmigrod			F	Moses I	JG	
TRACHMAN	Chane		1885	Zmigrod	Zmigrod	Moses I	Schifre	F		JG	
TRACHMAN	Peretz			Zmigrod	Zmigrod			M		JG	
TRACHMAN	Lea	BLANK		Zmigrod	Zmigrod			F	Peretz	JG	
TRACHMAN	Golde		1931	Zmigrod	Zmigrod	Peretz	Lea	F		JG	
TRACHMAN	Samuel		1936	Zmigrod	Zmigrod	Peretz	Lea	M		JG	
TRACHMAN	Chaim			Zmigrod	Zmigrod			M		JG	
TRACHMAN	Leie			Zmigrod	Zmigrod			F	Chaim	JG	
TRACHMAN	Frieda		1869	Zmigrod	Zmigrod	Chaim	Leie	F		JG	

Family name	First name(s)	Maiden name	Birth date	Birth place	Residence	Father	Mother	Gender	Spouse	Source	Remarks
TRACHMAN	Leibisch		1872	Zmigrod	Zmigrod	Chaim	Leie	M		YA	Holocaust
TRACHMAN	Ester		1876	Zmigrod	Zmigrod	Chaim	Leie	F		YA	Holocaust
TRACHMAN	Lola			Zmigrod	Zmigrod	Aaron		F		JSS	Plaszow
TRACHMAN	Eliezer			Zmigrod	Zmigrod	Chaim		M		JSS	Plaszow
TRAUB	Sender				Zmigrod			M		P	
TRAUB	Markus				Zmigrod			M		JG	USA
TRAUBE	Efroim				Zmigrod			M		YA	Auschwitz
TRAUBE	Sara		1891		Zmigrod			F		JG	USA
TROCHMAN	Chaja		1870	Zmigrod	Zmigrod	Hersh		F		JG	USA
TROM	Rosa		1888		Zmigrod			F		JG	
TUST	Sara		1895		Zmigrod			F		JG	
TUST	Eliyahu				Zmigrod			M		P	
TZANGER	Ide			Zmigrod	Zmigrod			F		JG	
TZANGER	Moshe S			Zmigrod	Zmigrod			M		JG	
TZANGER	Yaacov			Zmigrod	Zmigrod			M		JG	
TZANGER	Yudel			Zmigrod	Zmigrod			M		YA	
TZANGER	Zalman			Zmigrod	Zmigrod			M		YA	Holocaust
TZANGER	Meir		1915	Zmigrod	Zmigrod	Benjamin		M		T	
TZANGER	Sara	BUKSBAUM	1887	Zmigrod	Zmigrod	Naphtali		F		T	
TZANGER	Moshe S				Zmigrod			M		T	
TZANGER	Yudel				Zmigrod			F		T	
TZANGER	Ides				Zmigrod			F		JG	
TZANGER	Zalman				Zmigrod			M		JG	

Yizkor Book of Nowy Zmigrod

Family name	First name(s)	Maiden name	Birth date	Birth place	Residence	Father	Mother	Gender	Spouse	Source	Remarks
TZANGER	Benjamin		1890	Zmigrod	Zmigrod	Yona		M		BD	
TZANGER	Jonas				Zmigrod			M		BD	
TZANGER	M			Zmigrod	Zmigrod			M		JG	
TZANGER	S			Zmigrod	Zmigrod			M		JG	
TZANGER	m.		1883	Zmigrod	Zmigrod			M		JG	
TZANGER	Hersch		1882	Zmigrod	Zmigrod			M		JG	
TZANGER	Jonas		1882	Zmigrod	Zmigrod			M		JG	
TZANGER	Moses M.		1887	Zmigrod	Zmigrod			M		P	
TZANGER	Zywie		1879	Zmigrod	Zmigrod			F		P	
TZANGER	Aaron			Zmigrod				M		P	
TZANGER	Towa	BAUMEL		Zmigrod				F	Aaron	P	USA
TZANGER	Oscar		1925	Zmigrod		Aaron	Towa	M		P	Israel
TZANGER	Meir			Zmigrod		Aaron	Towa	M		P	USA
TZANGER	Nachum			Zmigrod		Aaron	Towa	M		JSS	Plaszow
TZANGER	Henry			Zmigrod		Aaron	Towa	M		JG	
TZANGER	Itzhak			Zmigrod	Zmigrod			M		YV	
TZIGLER	Hana			Zmigrod	Zmigrod	Itzhak		F	Itzhak	YV	
TZIGLER	Chaim			Zmigrod	Zmigrod	Itzhak	Hana	M		YV	
TZIGLER	Nachum				Zmigrod			M		P	
TZIGLER	Meir				Zmigrod			M		P	
TZIGLER	Zissel				Zmigrod			M		P	
TZIGLER	Leibish			Zmigrod	Zmigrod			M		P	
TZIGLER	Sarah			Zmigrod	Zmigrod			F	Leibish	P	

Family name	First name(s)	Maiden name	Birth date	Birth place	Residence	Father	Mother	Gender	Spouse	Source	Remarks
TZIGLER	Alter Leib			Zmigrod	Zmigrod			M		JG	
TZIMMERMAN	Shlomo			Zmigrod				M		JG	
TZINGER	Yossef			Zmigrod	Zmigrod			M		P	
TZINGER	Cirel		1921	Zmigrod	Zmigrod			F		JG	
TZION	Mayer			Zmigrod	Zmigrod			M		JR	
TZUKERMAN	Benjamin W			Zmigrod	Zmigrod			M		JR	
UNGER	Elias			Zmigrod	Zmigrod			M		JG	
UNGER	Soura	HERBACH		Zmigrod	Zmigrod			F	Elias	JG	
UNGER	Salman		1884	Zmigrod	Zmigrod	Elias		M		JG	
UNGER	Gimpel		1918	Zmigrod	Zmigrod		Soura	M		JG	
UNGER	Markus D			Zmigrod	Zmigrod			M		JG	
UNGER	Fraidel			Zmigrod	Zmigrod			F	Markus D		
UNGER	Sheindel		1867	Zmigrod	Zmigrod	Markus D	Fraidel	F		JG	USA
UNGER	Samuel		1901	Zmigrod	Zmigrod			M		JG	USA
UNGER	Chaim			Zmigrod	Zmigrod			M		P	Holocaust
UNGER	Zelda			Zmigrod	Zmigrod			F	Chaim	P	Holocaust
UNGER	Bernhard		1887	Zmigrod	Zmigrod			M		JG	
UNGERFELD	Samuel			Zmigrod	Zmigrod			M		JG	
UNGERFELD	Zywia			Zmigrod	Zmigrod			F		JG	
URIECH	Abraham		1882	Zmigrod	Zmigrod			M		YA	
WACH	Gittel		1882	Zmigrod	Zmigrod			F		YA	
WACHS	Elimelech		1907	Zmigrod	Zmigrod	Naphtali		M		BD	
WAGSCHAL	Yaakow		1910	Zmigrod	Zmigrod	Yehiel		M		JG	

Yizkor Book of Nowy Zmigrod

Family name	First name(s)	Maiden name	Birth date	Birth place	Residence	Father	Mother	Gender	Spouse	Source	Remarks
WAGSCHAL	Meir				Zmigrod			M		P	
WAGSCHAL	Ozjasz			Zmigrod	Zmigrod			M		YA	Holocaust
WAGSCHAL	Shia			Zmigrod	Zmigrod			M		JG	USA
WAGSCHAL	Rozalia		1889	Zmigrod	Zmigrod	Shmerl		F		JG	
WAHL	Ruchel		1889		Zmigrod			F		JG	
WAHL	Hersch			Zmigrod	Zmigrod			M		P	Holocaust
WAHRSAGER	Chana			Zmigrod	Zmigrod			F	Hersch	P	Holocaust
WALLACH	Chana		1883	Zmigrod	Zmigrod			F		P	Holocaust
WALTER	Israel			Zmigrod	Zmigrod			M		JR	
WALTER	Trane	TZIMET		Zmigrod	Zmigrod			F	Israel	J	
WALTER	Joel		1878	Zmigrod	Zmigrod	Israel	Trane	M		J	
WALTER	Feige R		1878	Zmigrod	Zmigrod	Israel	Trane	F		JG	
WALTER	Freide		1881	Zmigrod	Zmigrod	Israel	Trane	F		J	
WALTER	Shyje H		1882	Zmigrod	Zmigrod	Israel	Trane	F		J	
WALTER	Chaje		1885	Zmigrod	Zmigrod	Israel	Trane	F		J	
WALTER	Beile		1888	Zmigrod	Zmigrod	Israel	Trane	F		J	
WALTER	Simche B			Zmigrod	Zmigrod			M		JR	
WALTER	Sime S		1885	Zmigrod	Zmigrod	Simche B		F		JR	
WALTER	Moshe			Zmigrod	Zmigrod			M		P	Holocaust
WALTER	Sarah			Zmigrod	Zmigrod			F	Moshe	P	Holocaust
WALTER	Naftali			Zmigrod	Zmigrod			M		JG	USA
WALTER	Hersh			Zmigrod	Zmigrod			M			
WALTER	Hannah	STECHER		Zmigrod	Zmigrod			F	Hersh		

Yizkor Book of Nowy Zmigrod

Family name	First name(s)	Maiden name	Birth date	Birth place	Residence	Father	Mother	Gender	Spouse	Source	Remarks
WALTER	Feige R		1878	Zmigrod	Zmigrod	Hersh	Hannah	F			
WALTER	Friede		1880	Zmigrod	Zmigrod	Hersh	Hannah	F			
WALTER	Taube		1882	Zmigrod	Zmigrod	Hersh	Hannah	F		JG	USA
WALTER	Chaje		1883	Zmigrod	Zmigrod	Hersh	Hannah	F		JSS	
WALTER	Naftali		1885	Zmigrod	Zmigrod	Hersh	Hannah	M			
WALTER	Mozes		1887	Zmigrod	Zmigrod	Hersh	Hannah	M			
WALTER	Jakub				Zmigrod			M		JSS	Plaszow
WALTER	Noa				Zmigrod			F		YA	Plaszow
WALTER	Salomon				Zmigrod			M		YA	Holocaust
WALTER	Chaim			Zmigrod	Zmigrod			M		J	
WALTER	Dwoire	STECHER		Zmigrod	Zmigrod			F	Chaim	J	
WALTER	Chane		1886	Zmigrod	Zmigrod	Chaim	Dwoire	F		J	
WALTER	Abraham		1880		Zmigrod	Chaim	Dwoire	M		JSS	Plaszow
WALTER	Seinwel L		1885	Zmigrod	Zmigrod	Chaim	Dwoire	F		J	
WALTER	Chiel		1887	Zmigrod	Zmigrod	Chaim	Dwoire	M		J	
WALTER	Eisik		1888	Zmigrod	Zmigrod	Chaim	Dwoire	M		J	
WALTER	Chaim				Zmigrod			M		P	
WALTER	Gitla			Zmigrod	Zmigrod			F	Sz Findling		
WALTZMACHER	Feige		1904	Zmigrod	Zmigrod	Shulem		F		YA	Holocaust
WASSERLAUF	Lea		1913	Zmigrod	Zmigrod	Shulem		F		YA	Holocaust
WASSERLAUF	Nachman		1906	Zmigrod		Shulem		M		YA	Holocaust
WASSERLAUF	Lea			Zmigrod	Gorlice	Shulem		F		YA	Holocaust
WASSERMAN	Eidil			Zmigrod	Zmigrod	Shulem		M		YA	Holocaust

Yizkor Book of Nowy Zmigrod

Family name	First name(s)	Maiden name	Birth date	Birth place	Residence	Father	Mother	Gender	Spouse	Source	Remarks
WASSERMAN	Feige			Zmigrod	Gorlice	Shulem		F		YA	Holocaust
WASSERMAN	Reifka			Zmigrod	Zmigrod	Simche		F		YA	Holocaust
WASSERMAN	Henia		1886	Zmigrod	Germany	Eliezer		F		YA	Holocaust
WASSERMAN	Awraham			Zmigrod				M		P	
WASSERMAN	Zygmunt			Zmigrod	Zmigrod	Herman		M		JG	Holocaust
WASSERMAN	Philip			Zmigrod	Zmigrod	Herman		M		JG	Holocaust
WASSERSTROM	Samuel E			Zmigrod	Zmigrod			M		JG	
WEG	Rachla			Zmigrod	Zmigrod			F	Samuel E		
WEG	Chana			Zmigrod	Zmigrod	Samuel E	Rachla	F		JG	
WEG	Judes			Zmigrod	Zmigrod	Samuel E	Rachla	F		JG	
WEIN	Taube			Zmigrod	Zmigrod	Samuel E	Rachla	F		BD	
WEIN	Nuchi			Zmigrod	Zmigrod	Samuel E	Rachla	F		JG	
WEIN	Mordechai			Zmigrod				M		JG	
WEIN	Sarah	RUTENBERG						F	Mordechai	YA	
WEIN	Bluma					Mordechai	Sarah	F		YA	
WEIN	David			Zmigrod	Zmigrod			M		JG	
WEINBERG	Markus			Zmigrod	Zmigrod			M		YA	Holocaust
WEINBERG	Jente L	ASHKENASE		Zmigrod	Zmigrod			F	Markus	YA	Holocaust
WEINBERG	Yossef		1910	Zmigrod	Zmigrod	Mordechai		M		YA	Holocaust
WEINBERG	Markus				Zmigrod	Shabtai		M		JSS	
WEINBERG	Ryfka		1882	Zmigrod	Zmigrod	Reuven		F		JG	
WEINBERG	Josef			Zmigrod	Zmigrod			M		JG	

Yizkor Book of Nowy Zmigrod

Family name	First name(s)	Maiden name	Birth date	Birth place	Residence	Father	Mother	Gender	Spouse	Source	Remarks
WEINBERGER				Zmigrod	Zmigrod			M		JG	
WEINBERGER	Gittel		1880	Zmigrod	Zmigrod			F		JG	
WEINBERGER	Chaskel			Zmigrod	Zmigrod			M		JG	
WEINBERGER	Kallman			Zmigrod	Zmigrod			M		J	
WEINFELD	Chaje R		1877	Zmigrod	Zmigrod			F	Kallman	J	
WEINFELD	Leie		1877	Zmigrod	Zmigrod	Kallman	Chaje Reisel	F		J	
WEINFELD	Sara		1879	Zmigrod	Zmigrod	Kallman	Chaje Reisel			J	
WEINFELD	Mechel		1880	Zmigrod	Zmigrod	Kallman	Chaje Reisel			J	
WEINFELD	Zalel		1882	Zmigrod	Zmigrod	Kallman	Chaje Reisel			J	
WEINFELD	Markus H			Zmigrod	Zmigrod			M		JG	
WEINFELD	Feiga	RABI	1879	Zmigrod	Zmigrod			F		JG	
WEINFELD	Sara		1886	Zmigrod	Zmigrod	Markus H	Feiga	F		YS	
WEINFELD	Avraham		1874	Zmigrod	Zmigrod	Markus H	Feiga	M		JG	
WEINFELD	Munig			Zmigrod	Zmigrod	Gimpel		M		JG	
WEINFELD	Abish			Zmigrod	Zmigrod			M		JG	
WEINFELD	Emanuel			Zmigrod	Zmigrod			M		JG	
WEINFELD	Hena D			Zmigrod	Zmigrod			F	Emanuel	JG	
WEINSTAIN	Feige		1889	Zmigrod	Zmigrod	Emanuel	Hena Dache	F		JG	
WEINSTEIN	Czejwa		1900	Zmigrod	Zmigrod	Emanuel	Hena Dache	F		JG	

Yizkor Book of Nowy Zmigrod

Family name	First name(s)	Maiden name	Birth date	Birth place	Residence	Father	Mother	Gender	Spouse	Source	Remarks
WEINSTEIN	Berl			Zmigrod	Zmigrod			M		JG	
WEINSTEIN	Riwka			Zmigrod	Zmigrod			F	Berl	JG	
WEINSTEIN	Josef		1868	Zmigrod	Zmigrod	Berl	Riwka	M		JG	
WEINSTEIN	Emmanuel			Zmigrod	Zmigrod			M		JG	
WEINSTEIN	Hene	FERBER		Zmigrod	Zmigrod			F	Emmanuel	JG	
WEINSTEIN	Laja		1936	Zmigrod	Zmigrod	Emmanuel	Hene	F		JG	
WEINSTEIN	Feivel			Zmigrod	Zmigrod			M		JG	
WEINSTEIN	Chaje	NEGER		Zmigrod	Zmigrod			F	Feivel	JG	
WEINSTEIN	Menase		1877	Zmigrod	Zmigrod	Feivel	Chaje	M		JG	
WEINSTEIN	Abraham A.		1879	Zmigrod	Zmigrod	Feivel	Chaje	M		JG	
WEINSTEIN	Mordechai		1881	Zmigrod	Zmigrod	Feivel	Chaje	M		JG	
WEINSTEIN	Dwore		1883	Zmigrod	Zmigrod	Feivel	Chaje	F		JG	
WEINSTEIN	Naftali		1885	Zmigrod	Zmigrod	Feivel	Chaje	M		JG	
WEINSTEIN	Gimpel			Zmigrod	Zmigrod			M		JG	
WEINSTEIN	Estera	WILKENFELD		Zmigrod	Zmigrod			F	Gimpel	JG	
WEINSTEIN	Mechel		1887	Zmigrod	Zmigrod	Gimpel	Estera	M		JG	
WEINSTEIN	Sigmunt		1889	Zmigrod	Zmigrod	Gimpel	Estera	M		JG	
WEINSTEIN	Marja		1899	Zmigrod	Zmigrod	Gimpel	Estera	F		JG	
WEINSTEIN	Emmanuel		1904	Zmigrod	Zmigrod	Gimpel	Estera	M		JG	
WEINSTEIN	Hersch			Zmigrod	Zmigrod			M		JG	
WEINSTEIN	Malke	ROSENZWEIG		Zmigrod	Zmigrod			F	Hersch	JG	
WEINSTEIN	Jakob		1885	Zmigrod	Zmigrod	Hersch	Malke	M		JG	

Yizkor Book of Nowy Zmigrod

Family name	First name(s)	Maiden name	Birth date	Birth place	Residence	Father	Mother	Gender	Spouse	Source	Remarks
WEINSTEIN	Schachme Leib		1892	Zmigrod	Zmigrod	Hersch	Malke	F		JG	
WEINSTEIN	Rachela		1895	Zmigrod	Zmigrod	Hersch	Malke	F		JG	
WEINSTEIN	Josef			Zmigrod	Zmigrod			M		JG	
WEINSTEIN	Ija	KAUFMAN		Zmigrod	Zmigrod	Josef		F	Josef	JG	
WEINSTEIN	Helena		1906	Zmigrod	Zmigrod	Josef	Ija	F		JG	
WEINSTEIN	Laja		1936	Zmigrod	Zmigrod	Josef	Ija	F		JG	
WEINSTEIN	Markus H			Zmigrod	Zmigrod			M		JG	
WEINSTEIN	Laja			Zmigrod	Zmigrod	Markus H	Laja	F	Markus H	JG	
WEINSTEIN	Regina			Zmigrod	Zmigrod	Markus H	Laja	F		JG	
WEINSTEIN	Samuel		1904	Zmigrod	Zmigrod	Markus H	Laja	M		JG	
WEINSTEIN	Regina		1905	Zmigrod	Zmigrod	Markus H	Laja	F		JG	
WEINSTEIN	Wolf		1906	Zmigrod	Zmigrod	Markus H	Laja	M		JG	
WEINSTEIN	Osias			Zmigrod	Zmigrod			M		JG	
WEINSTEIN	Frieda	SCHMIER		Zmigrod	Zmigrod			F	Osias	JG	
WEINSTEIN	Marjem H		1919	Zmigrod	Zmigrod	Osias	Frieda	F		JG	
WEINSTEIN	Shmuel			Zmigrod	Zmigrod			M		JG	
WEINSTEIN	Helena			Zmigrod	Zmigrod			F	Shmuel	JG	
WEINSTEIN	Mendel		1930	Zmigrod	Zmigrod	Shmuel	Helena	M		JG	
WEINSTEIN	Rene		1931	Zmigrod	Zmigrod	Shmuel	Helena	F		JG	
WEINSTEIN	Szyje			Zmigrod	Zmigrod			M		JG	

Yizkor Book of Nowy Zmigrod

Family name	First name(s)	Maiden name	Birth date	Birth place	Residence	Father	Mother	Gender	Spouse	Source	Remarks
WEINSTEIN	Fradel	SCHMIER		Zmigrod	Zmigrod			F	Szyje	JG	
WEINSTEIN	Samuel E		1905	Zmigrod	Zmigrod	Szyje	Fradel	M		JG	
WEINSTEIN	Moses		1920	Zmigrod	Zmigrod	Szyje	Fradel	M		JG	
WEINSTEIN	Reisla		1927	Zmigrod	Zmigrod	Szyje	Fradel	F		YA	Holocaust
WEINSTEIN	Henoch		1905	Zmigrod	Zmigrod	Szyje	Fradel	M		YA	Holocaust
WEINSTEIN	Josef			Zmigrod	Zmigrod	Gimpel		M		YA	Holocaust
WEINSTEIN	Zishe			Zmigrod	Zmigrod	Gimpel		M		JSS	Plaszow
WEINSTEIN	Yaakow			Zmigrod	Zmigrod	Gimpel		M		JSS	
WEINSTEIN	Israel			Zmigrod	Zmigrod			M		JSS	Plaszow
WEINSTEIN	Osias			Zmigrod	Zmigrod			M		JSS	Plaszow
WEINSTEIN	Isak		1911	Zmigrod	Zmigrod	Osias		M		JSS	
WEINSTEIN	Zygmunt				Zmigrod			M		JSS	
WEINSTEIN	Mania				Zmigrod			F		BD	
WEINSTEIN	Josef				Zmigrod			M		JG	USA
WEINSTEIN	H				Zmigrod			M		JG	USA
WEINSTEIN	Abish		1865		Zmigrod			M		JG	
WEINSTEIN	Laf		1897		Zmigrod			M		JG	
WEINSTEIN	Chajem		1888	Zmigrod	Zmigrod			M		JG	
WEINSTEIN	Moses			Zmigrod	Zmigrod			M		JR	
WEINSTEIN	Beile			Zmigrod	Zmigrod			F	Moses	JR	
WEINSTEIN	Dawid		1867	Zmigrod	Zmigrod	Moses	Beile	M		JR	
WEINTRAUB	Dwora		1871	Zmigrod	Zmigrod	Moses	Beile	F		JR	
WEINTRAUB	Michael		1887	Zmigrod	Zmigrod			M		JSS	Plaszow

Yizkor Book of Nowy Zmigrod

Family name	First name(s)	Maiden name	Birth date	Birth place	Residence	Father	Mother	Gender	Spouse	Source	Remarks
WEINTRAUB	Moses		1886	Zmigrod	Zmigrod			M		JSS	Plaszow
WEINTRAUB	Berl				Zmigrod			M		JG	
WEINTRAUB	Leib			Zmigrod	Zmigrod			M		JSS	
WEINTRAUB	Ester		1905	Zmigrod	Zmigrod			F	Leib	JSS	
WEINTRAUB	Bernard			Zmigrod	Zmigrod	Leib	Ester	M		JSS	Plaszow
WEINTRAUB	Sara		1885	Zmigrod	Zmigrod			F		JG	
WEINTRAUB	Ryfka R			Zmigrod	Zmigrod			F		JG	
WEINTRAUB	Mendel			Zmigrod	Zmigrod			M		YV	
WEINTRAUB	Kalman			Zmigrod	Zmigrod			M		JR	
WEISER	Chaje R			Zmigrod	Zmigrod			F	Kalman	JR	
WEISS	Marcus		1869	Zmigrod	Zmigrod	Kalman	Chaje Reisel	M		JR	
WEISSFELD	Reizl			Zmigrod	Zmigrod			F	Mendel	YV	
WEISSFELD	Meir			Zmigrod	Zmigrod			M		P	
WEISSFELD	Wolf			Zmigrod	Zmigrod			M		JR	
WEISSMAN	Rechel		1883	Zmigrod	Zmigrod	Wolf		F		JR	
WEISSMAN	Mina			Zmigrod	Zmigrod			F		JG	
WEISSMAN	Hencie			Zmigrod	Zmigrod			F		JG	
WEISSMAN	Moses		1886	Zmigrod	Zmigrod			M		JSS	Plaszow
WELLISH	Dawid			Zmigrod	Zmigrod			M		JG	
WISTREICH	Sara		1884	Zmigrod	Zmigrod			F		JR	
WISTREICH	Berl			Zmigrod	Zmigrod			M		JR	
WISTREICH	Bashe			Zmigrod	Zmigrod			F	Berl	JR	
WISTREICH	Riwke		1869	Zmigrod	Zmigrod	Berl	Bashe	F		JR	

Yizkor Book of Nowy Zmigrod

Family name	First name(s)	Maiden name	Birth date	Birth place	Residence	Father	Mother	Gender	Spouse	Source	Remarks
WISTREICH	Hersh				Zmigrod			M		JG	
WISTREICH	Ester		1883	Zmigrod	Zmigrod			F		JG	
WISTREICH	Mechel			Zmigrod	Zmigrod			M		JR	
WISTREICH	Chana M			Zmigrod	Zmigrod	Mechel		F		JR	
WIELICZKER	Fraidel	FINDLING		Zmigrod	Zmigrod			F		YA	Holocaust
WILK	Leibish			Zmigrod	Jaslo					R	
WILK	Frida		1887	Zmigrod	Germany	Zeew		F		YA	Holocaust
WILNER	Mendel			Zmigrod	Zmigrod			M		JR	
WILNER	Feige			Zmigrod	Zmigrod			F	Mendel	JR	
WINFELD	Reisel		1869	Zmigrod	Zmigrod	Mendel	Feige	F		JR	
WINTER	Mendel			Zmigrod	Zmigrod			M		JR	
WINTER	Pessel			Zmigrod	Zmigrod			F	Mendel	JR	
WINTER	Beile R			Zmigrod	Zmigrod	Mendel	Pessel	F		JR	
WINTER	Hanna		1896	Zmigrod	Germany	Itzhak		F		YA	Holocaust
WINTER	Moses		1886	Zmigrod	Germany	Dawid		M		JG	USA
WINTER	Szaul		1884	Zmigrod	Germany	Shmuel		M		JSS	Plaszow
WINTER	Dora		1892	Zmigrod	Zmigrod			F		JSS	Plaszow
WINTER	Rachel			Zmigrod	Zmigrod			F		JG	
WINTER	Dawid			Zmigrod	Zmigrod			M		JSS	Plaszow
WINTER	Dawid			Zmigrod	Zmigrod			M		JR	
WINTER	Hersch		1888	Zmigrod	Zmigrod	Dawid		M		JR	
WINTER	Rachel			Zmigrod	Zmigrod			F		P	
WIST	Nute				Zmigrod			M		P	

Family name	First name(s)	Maiden name	Birth date	Birth place	Residence	Father	Mother	Gender	Spouse	Source	Remarks
WIST	Pinkas				Zmigrod			M		YA	Holocaust
WISTREICH	Brandel							F	Pinkas	YA	
WOHLMUTH	Jakub			Zmigrod	Zmigrod	Pinkas	Brandel	M		BD	
WOHLMUTH	Wigdor				Zmigrod	Pinkas	Brandel	M		JSS	Plaszow
WOHLMUTH	Arieh			Zmigrod	Zmigrod	Pinkas	Brandel	M		YA	
WOHLMUTH	Ester Etel			Zmigrod	Zmigrod	Pinkas	Brandel	F		YA	
WOHLMUTH	Lea			Zmigrod	Zmigrod	Pinkas	Brandel	F		YA	
WOHLMUTH	Mendel			Zmigrod	Zmigrod	Pinkas	Brandel	M		YA	
WOHLMUTH	Rachel			Zmigrod	Zmigrod	Pinkas	Brandel	F		YA	
WOHLMUTH	Frymet		1907	Zmigrod	Zmigrod	Yaakow		F		JG	
WOHLMUTH	Leib			Zmigrod	Zmigrod			M		JR	
WOHLMUTH	Natan		1888	Zmigrod	Zmigrod	Leib		M		JR	
WOHLMUTH	Nachman				Zmigrod			M		JG	
WOHLMUTH	David			Zmigrod	Zmigrod			M		JG	
WOHLMUTH	Abraham			Zmigrod	Zmigrod			M		JSS	Plaszow
WROBEL	Yaakow				Zmigrod			M		P	
WROBEL	David			Zmigrod	Zmigrod			M		JG	
WROBEL	Shprintze	FINDLING		Zmigrod	Zmigrod			F	David	JG	
WROBEL	Lea			Zmigrod	Zmigrod			F		JG	
WROBEL	Meyer			Zmigrod	Zmigrod			M		YA	
WYMISZLER	Mindel			Zmigrod	Zmigrod			F		JSS	
WYMISZLER	Chaim		1877	Zmigrod	Jaslo	Yaakow		M		JSS	Holocaust
WYMISZLER	Abraham			Lodz	Zmigrod			M		JSS	Plaszow

Yizkor Book of Nowy Zmigrod

Family name	First name(s)	Maiden name	Birth date	Birth place	Residence	Father	Mother	Gender	Spouse	Source	Remarks
WYMISZLER	Brucha			Lodz	Zmigrod			F	Abraham	JSS	
WYMISZLER	Moses		1907	Lodz	Zmigrod			M		JG	
YDUSCHER	B.			Zmigrod		Abraham	Brucha	M		YA	Holocaust
ZAKON	Aron		1887	Zmigrod	Zmigrod			M		JSS	Plaszow
ZAKON	Pinhas			Zmigrod	Zmigrod			M		P	
ZAKON	Sime			Zmigrod	Zmigrod			F	Pinhas	JR	
ZAN	Lazar		1872	Zmigrod	Zmigrod	Pinhas	Sime	M		JR	
ZANGER	Meilech			Zmigrod	Zmigrod			M		JR	
ZANGER	Chaje			Zmigrod	Zmigrod			F	Meilech	JR	
ZANGER	Awraham		1887	Zmigrod	Zmigrod	Meilech	Chaje	M		JR	
ZANGER	Tova	BAUMEL		Zmigrod	Zmigrod			F	Aron	P	
ZANGER	Meir			Zmigrod		Aron	Tova	M		P	survived
ZANGER	Nachum			Zmigrod		Aron	Tova	M		P	survived
ZANGER	Henry			Zmigrod		Aron	Tova	M		P	survived
ZANGER	Oscar		1925	Zmigrod				M		P	
ZANGER	Yaakow				Zmigrod			M		P	
ZANGER	Israel				Zmigrod			M		JG	
ZANGER	Beile R		1895	Zmigrod	Zmigrod			F		JG	
ZAND	Chaim		1889	Zmigrod	Zmigrod			M		JG	
ZARON	Sheindel		1881	Zmigrod	Zmigrod			F		JG	
ZAWISCHA				Zmigrod	Zmigrod			M		JSS	Plaszow

Family name	First name(s)	Maiden name	Birth date	Birth place	Residence	Father	Mother	Gender	Spouse	Source	Remarks
ZEFF	Hencze		1884	Zmigrod	Zmigrod			F		JSS	Plaszow
ZELL	Josef				Zmigrod			M		BD	
ZELL	Rubin				Zmigrod			M		JG	
ZELL	N				Zmigrod			M		JG	
ZELL	Mayer			Zmigrod	Zmigrod			M		JR	
ZELLER	Eidel		1887	Zmigrod	Zmigrod	Mayer		F		JR	
ZELLER	Yosef			Zmigrod	Zmigrod			M		JR	
ZIEGLER	Rachel		1888	Zmigrod	Zmigrod	Yosef		F		JR	
ZIEGLER	Naftali			Zmigrod	Zmigrod			M		JR	
ZIEGLER	Sheindel		1885	Zmigrod	Zmigrod	Naftali		F		JR	
ZIEGLER	Berl			Zmigrod	Zmigrod			M		JR	
ZIEGLER	Malka R			Zmigrod	Zmigrod			F	Berl	JR	
ZIEGLER	Hene		1872	Zmigrod	Zmigrod	Berl	Malka Reisel	F		JR	
ZIEGLER	Aron Ber			Zmigrod	Zmigrod			M		JR	
ZIEGLER	Samuel		1881	Zmigrod	Zmigrod	Aron Ber		M		JR	
ZIEGLER	Cyrel		1879	Zmigrod	Zmigrod			F		JG	
ZIEGLER	Ester R		1884	Zmigrod	Zmigrod			F		JG	
ZIEGLER	Itte		1882	Zmigrod	Zmigrod			F		JG	
ZIEGLER	Josef M		1883	Zmigrod	Zmigrod			M		JG	
ZIEGLER	Malke		1885	Zmigrod	Zmigrod			F		JG	
ZIEGLER	Markus		1889	Zmigrod	Zmigrod			M		JG	
ZIEGLER	Rachel		1887	Zmigrod	Zmigrod			F		JG	
ZIEGLER	Samuel		1882	Zmigrod	Zmigrod			M		JG	

Yizkor Book of Nowy Zmigrod

Family name	First name(s)	Maiden name	Birth date	Birth place	Residence	Father	Mother	Gender	Spouse	Source	Remarks
ZIEGLER	Shyje		1877	Zmigrod	Zmigrod			M		YA	Holocaust
ZIEGLER	Shyje		1883	Zmigrod	Zmigrod			M		P	
ZIEGLER	Yehoshua		1902	Jaslo	Zmigrod	Naphtali		M		P	Holocaust
ZIEGLER	Peril			Zmigrod	Zmigrod			F		P	
ZIEGLER	Hersh D			Zmigrod	Zmigrod			M		JSS	Plaszow
ZIEGLER	Shia			Zmigrod	Zmigrod			M		JSS	Plaszow
ZILBER	Sarah		1904	Zmigrod	Zmigrod			F		YA	
ZILBER	A			Zmigrod	Zmigrod			M		P	
ZILBER	Simha			Zmigrod	Zmigrod			M		P	
ZILBER	Rivkah	TZIMET		Zmigrod	Zmigrod			F	Simha	P	
ZILBER	Shmulke			Zmigrod	Zmigrod	Simha	Rivkah	M		JSS	Plaszow
ZIMET	Yudel			Zmigrod	Zmigrod	Alter Leib		M		JG	
ZIMET	Yente			Zmigrod	Zmigrod			F	Yudel	JG	
ZIMET	Pearl			Zmigrod	Zmigrod	Yudel	Yente	F	N Leibner	JG	
ZIMET	Fishel			Zmigrod	Zmigrod	Yudel	Yente	M		JG	
ZIMET	Feige	TZIGLER		Zmigrod	Zmigrod			F	Fishel		
ZIMET	Meyer		1872	Zmigrod	Zmigrod	Fishel	Feige	M		JR	
ZIMET	Chaje		1876	Zmigrod	Zmigrod	Fishel	Feige	F		JR	
ZIMET	Yoel		1879	Zmigrod	Zmigrod	Fishel	Feige	M		JR	
ZIMET	Roze		1882	Zmigrod	Zmigrod	Fishel	Feige	F		JR	
ZIMET	Hersh		1889	Zmigrod	Zmigrod	Fishel	Feige	M		JG	
ZIMET	Zacharia			Zmigrod	Zmigrod			M		P	

Yizkor Book of Nowy Zmigrod

Family name	First name(s)	Maiden name	Birth date	Birth place	Residence	Father	Mother	Gender	Spouse	Source	Remarks
ZIMET	Chawa	KLEIN		Zmigrod	Zmigrod			F	Zacharia	P	
ZIMET	Matel			Zmigrod	Zmigrod			M		P	
ZIMET	Yossef					Zacharia	Chawa	M			
ZIMET	Blima			Zmigrod	Zmigrod			F	Josef	JR	
ZIMET	Dawid		1869	Zmigrod	Zmigrod	Yossef	Blima	M		J	
ZIMET	Fishel			Zmigrod	Zmigrod	Yossef	Blima	M		J	
ZIMET	Sender			Zmigrod	Zmigrod	Yossef	Blima	M		JG	
ZIMET	Mirele	LANG		Zmigrod	Zmigrod			F	Sender	survived	
ZIMET	Matel		1882	Zmigrod	Zmigrod	Sender dairy store	Mirele	F		P	survived
ZIMET	Ester		1885	Zmigrod	Zmigrod	Sender dairy store	Mirele	F		JR	
ZIMET	Dawid		1897	Zmigrod	Zmigrod	Sender dairy store	Mirele	M		JR	
ZIMET	Shia			Zmigrod	Zmigrod	Sender dairy store	Mirele	M		P	survived
ZIMET	Mina	LANG		Zmigrod	Zmigrod			F	Shia	Holocaust	
ZIMET	Abraham			Zmigrod	Zmigrod	Shia	Mina	M		P	
ZIMET	Sabina			Zmigrod	Zmigrod	Shia	Mina	F		P	Holocaust
ZIMET	Israel P			Zmigrod	Zmigrod	Shia	Mina	M		P	Holocaust
ZIMET	Mechel			Zmigrod				M		P	

Yizkor Book of Nowy Zmigrod

Family name	First name(s)	Maiden name	Birth date	Birth place	Residence	Father	Mother	Gender	Spouse	Source	Remarks
ZIMET	Rose	PINSKER		Zmigrod				F	Mechel	J	
ZIMET	Lippe		1884	Zmigrod		Mechel	Rose	M		J	
ZIMET	Sara Ryfke		1885	Zmigrod		Mechel	Rose	F		J	
ZIMET	Efroim		1888	Zmigrod		Mechel	Rose	M		J	
ZIMET	Sender			Zmigrod	Zmigrod			M		J	
ZIMET	Feige C	ERREICH		Zmigrod	Zmigrod			F	Sender	J	
ZIMET	Matel		1882	Zmigrod	Zmigrod	Sender	Feige Chan	F		J	
ZIMET	Ester		1885	Zmigrod	Zmigrod	Sender	Feige Chan	F		J	
ZIMET	Dawid		1887	Zmigrod	Zmigrod	Sender	Feige Chan	M		J	
ZIMET	Abraham C			Zmigrod	Zmigrod			M		J	
ZIMET	Rysze			Zmigrod	Zmigrod			F	Abraham C		
ZIMET	Malka P		1884	Zmigrod	Zmigrod	Abraham C	Rysze	F		J	
ZIMET	Shimon			Zmigrod	Zmigrod			M		J	
ZIMET	Bayle F	RABBI		Zmigrod	Zmigrod			F	Shimon	J	
ZIMET	Yente		1876	Zmigrod	Zmigrod	Shimon	Bayle Feige	F		J	
ZIMET	Joel		1879	Zmigrod	Zmigrod	Shimon	Bayle Feige	M		J	
ZIMET	Marjem		1879	Zmigrod	Zmigrod	Shimon	Bayle Feige	F		J	
ZIMET	Leiser			Zmigrod	Zmigrod			M		J	

Family name	First name(s)	Maiden name	Birth date	Birth place	Residence	Father	Mother	Gender	Spouse	Source	Remarks
ZIMET	Ester			Zmigrod	Zmigrod			F	Leiser	J	
ZIMET	Beile C		1866	Zmigrod	Zmigrod	Leiser	Ester	F		J	
ZIMET	Chaje R			Zmigrod	Zmigrod			F	KWeifeld	J	
ZIMET	Rywke			Zmigrod	Zmigrod			F	S Findling	J	
ZIMET	Trane			Zmigrod	Zmigrod			F	I Walter	J	
ZIMET	Hersh			Zmigrod	Zmigrod			M		J	
ZIMET	Shprincze	LANG		Zmigrod	Zmigrod	Hersh		F	Hersh	JG	
ZIMET	Hiel			Zmigrod	Zmigrod	Hersh	Shprincze	M		JG	
ZIMET	Gittel			Zmigrod	Zmigrod	Hersh	Shprincze	F		JG	
ZIMET	Tzipporah			Zmigrod	Zmigrod	Hersh	Shprincze	F		JG	
ZIMET	Mindel	LANG		Zmigrod	Zmigrod		Hersh	F	Hersh	JG	2nd wife
ZIMET	Wolf D			Zmigrod	Zmigrod	Fishel	Feige	M		JG	
ZIMET	Giselle							F	Wolf Dawid		
ZIMET	Margalit					Wolf D	Giselle	F		P	
ZIMET	Fannie					Wolf D	Giselle	F		P	
ZIMET	Nahum					Wolf D	Giselle	F		P	
ZIMET	Leibish			Zmigrod	Zmigrod	Fishel	Feige	M		JG	
ZIMET	Nette					Leibish		M	Leibish		
ZIMET	Fannie					Leibish		F		P	
ZIMET	Shia			Zmigrod	Zmigrod	Sender dairy store	Mirele	M		P	survived
ZIMET	Mina	LANG		Zmigrod	Zmigrod			F	Shia	Holoc	

Yizkor Book of Nowy Zmigrod

Family name	First name(s)	Maiden name	Birth date	Birth place	Residence	Father	Mother	Gender	Spouse	Source	Remarks
										aust	
ZIMET	Chaya			Zmigrod	Zmigrod	Sender dairy store	Mirele	F	Baruch	P	
ZIMET	Dawid		1887	Zmigrod	Zmigrod	Josef	Blima	M		JR	
ZIMET	Shimshon			Zmigrod	Zmigrod			M		JR	
ZIMET	Hinde			Zmigrod	Zmigrod			M	Shimshon	JR	
ZIMET	Fishel			Zmigrod	Zmigrod	Shimshon	Hinde	M		J	
ZIMET	Hersch		1872	Zmigrod	Zmigrod	Shimshon	Hinde	M		JR	
ZIMET	Malka	BLUMENFELD		Zmigrod	Zmigrod			F	Dawid	P	survived
ZIMET	Katriel				Berlin	Dawid	Malka	M		P	survived
ZIMET	Mendel	KANNER		Zmigrod	Zmigrod			M	Matel	P	
ZIMET	Riwka			Zmigrod	Zmigrod			F		P	
ZIMET	Ester		1922	Zmigrod	Zmigrod			F		P	
ZIMET	Baruch			Zmigrod	Zmigrod			M		JR	
ZIMET	Pesel			Zmigrod	Zmigrod	Baruch	Pesel	F	Baruch	JR	
ZIMET	Hersch B		1872	Zmigrod	Zmigrod	Baruch	Pesel	M		JR	
ZIMET	Matel,			Zmigrod	Jaslo	Meir		F		JG	Holocaust
ZIMET	Hadassah			Zmigrod	Zmigrod			F	Yossef	JG	
ZIMET	Motel			Zmigrod	Zmigrod			M		YA	Holocaust
ZIMET	Sara R		1885	Zmigrod	Zmigrod			F		YA	Auschwitz
ZIMET	Chaja			Zmigrod	Zmigrod	Adi		F		YA	Holocaust
ZIMET	Leib		1895	Zmigrod	Zmigrod	Ephraim	Feige	M		YA	Holocaust

Family name	First name(s)	Maiden name	Birth date	Birth place	Residence	Father	Mother	Gender	Spouse	Source	Remarks
ZIMET	Dawid			Zmigrod	Zmigrod	Ephraim		M		YA	Holocaust
ZIMET	Yossef A			Zmigrod	Zmigrod			M		P	Holocaust
ZIMET	Tzivia							F	Yossef A		
ZIMET	Chawa		1908	Zmigrod	Zmigrod	Yossef	Tzivia	F		YA	
ZIMET	Mordechai		1912	Zmigrod	Zmigrod	Yossef	Tzivia	M		YA	
ZIMET	Chaim		1914	Zmigrod	Zmigrod	Yossef	Tzivia	M		YA	
ZIMET	Yaakow W		1918	Zmigrod	Zmigrod	Yossef	Tzivia	M		JG	
ZIMET	Rachel		1920	Zmigrod	Zmigrod	Yossef	Tzivia	F		T	
ZIMET	Ester		1922	Zmigrod	Zmigrod	Yossef	Tzivia	F		T	
ZIMET	Reisel			Zmigrod	Zmigrod	Fishel	Feige	F	Sender	JG	
ZIMET	Shmuel			Zmigrod	Zmigrod			M		P	
ZIMET	Zale Tzwi			Zmigrod	Zmigrod			M		YV	
ZIMET	Hentche			Zmigrod	Zmigrod			F	Zale Tzwi	YV	
ZIMMER	Lippa			Zmigrod	Zmigrod	Simha	Rivkah	M		JSS	Plaszow
ZINDEL	Israel			Zmigrod	Zmigrod			M		P	
ZINDEL	Baruch			Zmigrod	Zmigrod			M		JR	
ZINDEL	Pessel			Zmigrod	Zmigrod			F	Baruch	JR	
ZINDEL	Hersch B.		1876	Zmigrod	Zmigrod	Baruch	Pessel	M		JR	
ZISHIK	Israel				Zmigrod			M		JSS	Plaszow
ZISHIK	Abraham				Zmigrod			M		JSS	Plaszow
ZISHIK	Moses				Zmigrod			M		JSS	
ZOMMER	Samuel				Zmigrod			M		JSS	
ZWASS	Baruch				Zmigrod			M			

Yizkor Book of Nowy Zmigrod

Family name	First name(s)	Maiden name	Birth date	Birth place	Residence	Father	Mother	Gender	Spouse	Source	Remarks
ZWASS	Herman				Zmigrod			M			
ZWASS	Mozes				Zmigrod			M		JSS	Plaszow
ZWASS	Abraham				Zmigrod			M		JSS	Plaszow
ZWASS	Pinhas			Zmigrod	Zmigrod			M		JR	
ZWASS	Hitzel			Zmigrod	Zmigrod			F	Pinhas	JR	
ZWASS	Zishe		1872	Zmigrod	Zmigrod	Pinhas	Hitzel	M		JR	

THE

       END

            OF

               THE

                  JEWISH

                     COMMUNITY

KADDISH…

**Place in Zmigrod where the selection took place on July 7. 1942.
(Picture donated by Jean Krieser, a descendant of Zmigrod)**

The slaughter at Halbow on July 7, 1942. The brotherly graver is sourounded by a fence in the forest. Some families have erected tombstones on the site.
(Picture donated by Jean Krieser, a descendant of Zmigrod)

INDEX

A

B

C

D

E

Edelstein, 45
Edelstein, 180
Ehrlich, 179
Eichner, 94, 181, 182, 183, 189, 191, 198, 251, 252, 253, 256
Einhorn, 22, 138, 144
Einhorn, 29, 183, 184
Eisenbach, 184
Eisenberg, 24, 26, 57, 60, 63, 65, 91, 137, 138, 139, 144, 154
Eisenberg, 29, 94, 174, 184, 185, 186, 267
Eisenberger, 185
Ekiert, 185
Ellert, 185
Emer, 183, 185
Emmer, 185
Endel, 185
Endzweig, 185, 186
Engel, 10, 45, 137
Engel, 94, 186
Engelhardt, 42
Engelhardt, 183, 186, 187
Englard, 256
Erbich, 187
Erbstein, 187
Erbster, 187
Erreich, 29, 94, 95, 187, 188, 237, 301
Errenreich, 95
Erteszek, 188

F

Facher, 95, 188, 189
Fascher, 215
Fasser, 189
Feder, 29, 95, 159, 160, 189
Feferberg, 189
Feibel, 189
Feier, 29, 160, 189, 190
Feigenblum, 190
Feld, 29, 160, 190
Feldstein, 190
Feldsztajn, 190
Feller, 45
Feller, 160, 190
Fels, 190, 283
Fenner, 190
Fennig, 95, 190
Ferber, 191, 291
Feryszka, 191
Fessler, 25, 60, 65
Fessler, 191
Feuer, 176, 191
Filler, 191

Findling, Xviii, 3, 14, 18, 22, 23, 45, 47, 48, 49, 50, 83, 84, 137, 140, 142, 144, 147, 288, 302
Findling, 29, 95, 191, 192, 193, 194, 195, 196, 197, 198, 199, 200, 201, 202, 242, 245, 248, 267, 295, 296
Fink, 202
Finkelstein, 156
Fisch, 95
Fischer, 202
Fish, 160, 202
Fisher, 24
Fishler, 202
Frachman, 202
Frenkel, 67
Frenkil, 202
Freund, 60, 65
Freund, 95, 202, 203
Frichson, 203, 253
Friedman, 95, 203
Frihiling, 203
Frumet, 64, 65, 93, 169
Frumet, 204
Fusenfest, 204

G

Galanty, 204, 271
Galer, 204
Galler, 252
Garnreich, 204
Gelb, 29, 204
Geller, 95, 204
Gensterman, 204
Gentz, 26, 123, 142, 144
Gester, 96, 205
Gettenberg, 30, 205
Getz, 22
Getz, 205, 276
Getzel, 205
Getzler, 96, 205, 206, 215, 249
Getzlet, 30
Ginsberg, 56
Ginzberg, 65
Ginzberg, 96, 206
Glantz, 206
Glaser, 206
Glasser, 30
Gleich, 61
Gleich, 206
Glezer, 206
Goetz, 206
Gold, 96, 206
Goldberg, 30, 207
Goldblat, 244
Goldblatt, 207
Goldfarb, 30, 207
Goldfinger, 207

T

www.ingramcontent.com/pod-product-compliance
Lightning Source LLC
Chambersburg PA
CBHW050408110426
42812CB00006BA/1835